The World of Elizabeth Inchbald

The World of Elizabeth Inchbald

Essays on Literature, Culture, and Theatre in the Long Eighteenth Century

EDITED BY
DANIEL J. ENNIS
E. JOE JOHNSON

UNIVERSITY OF DELAWARE
UNIVERSITY OF DELAWARE PRESS

NEWARK

Library of Congress Cataloging-in-Publication Data

Names: Ennis, Daniel James, 1970- editor. | Johnson, E. Joe (Edward Joe), editor.
Title: The world of Elizabeth Inchbald : essays on literature, culture, and theatre in the long eighteenth century / edited by Daniel J. Ennis and E. Joe Johnson.
Description: Newark, Delaware : University of Delaware Press, 2022. | Includes bibliographical references and index.
Identifiers: LCCN 2021041085 | ISBN 9781644532577 (hardcover) | ISBN 9781644532560 (paperback) | ISBN 9781644532584 (epub) | ISBN 9781644532591 (pdf)
Subjects: LCSH: Inchbald, Mrs., 1753-1821—Criticism and interpretation. | Inchbald, Mrs., 1753-1821—Influence. | Jenkins, Annibel. | English literature—18th century—History and criticism. | Theater—Great Britain—History—18th century. | Great Britain—Intellectual life—18th century. | Great Britain—Civilization—18th century.
Classification: LCC PR442 .W675 2022 | DDC 820.9/005—dc23/eng/20211222
LC record available at https://lccn.loc.gov/2021041085

A British Cataloging-in-Publication record for this book is available from the British Library.

♾ The paper used in this publication meets the requirements of the American National Standard for Information Sciences—Permanence of Paper for Printed Library Materials, ANSI Z39.48-1992.

udpress.udel.edu

Distributed worldwide by Rutgers University Press

Manufactured in the United States of America

Contents

Acknowledgments

For their institutional support on this project, we would like to thank both Coastal Carolina University and Clayton State University. For his assistance with procuring a photograph of Annibel Jenkins and for a copy of her final conference presentation, we would like to thank her nephew, Robert Peacock.

The editors would like to thank the contributors for their patience, as this was a long-gestating project. Gratitude is also owed to a series of graduate assistants at Coastal Carolina University: Ben Counts, Hannah Grippo, Lindsey Holt, Andy Lesh, Madison Rahner, and Haleigh Woodlief.

Introduction

Daniel J. Ennis and E. Joe Johnson

The genesis for *The World of Elizabeth Inchbald: Essays on Literature, Culture, and Theatre in the Long Eighteenth Century* occurred at the April 2013 annual meeting of the American Society for Eighteenth-Century Studies (ASECS) in Cleveland, Ohio, where many of this volume's contributors had gathered and were fondly remembering Annibel Jenkins, who had died the previous month. As the editors and contributors to this volume can attest, Jenkins was highly reputed for encouraging her colleagues to pursue scholarship in the eighteenth-century world writ large, that is, the very scholarship on display at the multi-disciplinary meetings of eighteenth-century studies societies such as ASECS and the Southeastern American Society for Eighteenth-Century Studies. This volume's titular "world" is, therefore, a deliberate nod both to the resulting variety of essays in this volume and to Jenkins's final scholarly work on the eighteenth-century London newspaper *The World*.

Like other newspapers of its day, *The World* always included articles on a "world" of subjects: with accounts of diplomatic and government matters; reports on society matters and current events; reviews of theatrical and operatic productions, literature, and art; and much more. This essay collection should, therefore, be seen as being akin to an eighteenth-century newspaper or a modern-day multidisciplinary conference, here with a through line connecting Jenkins's major scholarly work on theatre history in Great Britain and, more lastingly and expansively, her lifework of mentorship of her colleagues in the world of eighteenth-century studies.

One of the key figures in this essay collection is Elizabeth Inchbald, or, as she was known in her own era, "Mrs. Inchbald," who enjoyed a prolific and acclaimed career as a dramatist, novelist, and critic. Inchbald—whose artistry and influence helped define late Georgian and Regency culture in Great Britain and whose lifetime saw such major historical events as Britain's loss of the

American colonies, the convulsions of the French Revolution, and ultimate victory in the Napoleonic Wars—lacked a definitive, modern biography (the only account of her life dated from 1833) until the appearance of Jenkins's *I'll Tell You What: The Life of Elizabeth Inchbald* in 2003.[1] The latter is distinguished by Jenkins's relentless attention to detail, a quality that attracted both positive and negative comments from reviewers.[2] Taking no received biographical claims on faith, Jenkins mined Inchbald's pocketbook diaries for quotidian specifics. What emerges is an emphatically economic biography in which Jenkins spins a life from the threads of Inchbald's fiscal exigencies. We are told that Inchbald was "one of the first professional writers to succeed in writing both plays and novels," who, early in her career, lived "on the edge of real poverty" and, in her later years, was the sole breadwinner for her family.[3] Inchbald's professional decisions—what to write, with whom to publish—are placed in sharp relief through Jenkins's decision to provide exhaustive economic detail.

I'll Tell You What reminds readers that Inchbald helped form and benefited from literary networks. Novelists Mary Wollstonecraft, Mary Shelley, William Godwin, and Maria Edgeworth make appearances. From the theatre world comes an army of allies and rivals, including Sarah Siddons, West Digges, the Kemble family, Tate Wilkinson, and both George Colemans. Inchbald was able to maintain friendships with Thomas Holcroft and John Burgoyne, two men of wildly different temperaments and politics. Yet for all this parade of names, it is the special connections between Inchbald and her compatriots that provide readers a comprehensive portrait of creative society in London during the late Hanoverian period.

By coining the phrase "Inchbald Woman" to describe the kind of self-reliant female characters Inchbald introduced to the stage and the page, Jenkins gives a name to an emerging character type that would become increasingly familiar to early nineteenth-century audiences. As Barbara Mackey points out, the prototype of the Inchbald Woman was Inchbald herself.[4] Tasked with surviving in two worlds—theatre and publishing—and keenly aware of professional expectations, Inchbald favored female characters who exuded independent competence. When Inchbald created the character of Lady Euston for the comedy *I'll Tell You What* (1785), the playwright did not have far to go to find a template for the Inchbald Woman's combination of resourcefulness and virtue. Inchbald herself moved from actress (in York and then in London) to playwright, to translator and adapter, to critic, to editor, at each point making professional decisions with the knowledge that her many dependents looked to her for support and that many women writers and actors saw her as an exemplar. Jenkins makes clear that Inchbald's "driving passion to become a writer" was fueled by her rejection of dependence.[5]

More than many eighteenth-century women artists, Inchbald worked in overlapping commercial and aesthetic spheres, managing her business affairs, her image as performer, and her literary reputation with a keen eye for the ways literary, economic, theatrical, and political concerns mixed to form late Georgian culture. As such, her career is a handy synecdoche for the arc of English belles lettres in the long eighteenth century. Inchbald the performer was mentored by figures firmly rooted in the age of Garrick, but her closest stage allies later in her career were the exponents of the new-fashioned Kemble-Siddons performing aesthetic. Inchbald the writer's novel *A Simple Story* (1791) earned the author a place in the pantheon of late eighteenth-century women writers,[6] yet it is Inchbald's later novel *Nature and Art* (1796) that captures the destabilizing frisson of an England in the shadow of the Terror in France.

Inchbald the translator helped to bring French theatre to Great Britain, as James Boaden noted concerning one such venture: "She undertook the translation, or adaptation; for she used her original always freely on such occasions: and, after reflecting a week, began to naturalize it in English."[7] Heretofore underappreciated is Inchbald the editor, whose taste did so much to define a dramatic canon for readers and audiences of the nineteenth and twentieth centuries. Her monumental *British Theatre* (twenty-five volumes, 1808) spanned Shakespeare to Joanna Baillie. Inchbald's subsequent editorial project, *Modern Theatre* (ten volumes, 1811), helped fix the dramatic corpus of the Regency at a time when reading was becoming an increasingly popular way to experience the plays of Richard Brinsley Sheridan, Hannah Cowley, and Inchbald herself. Indeed, the emergence of readers' theatre is the amplifying factor in Inchbald's influence, as she did not select the plays herself but instead provided the headnotes.[8]

Because it was Jenkins's pioneering work that revealed in full the enormous web of influencers, collaborators, theatrical antecedents, and literary descendants that made up Inchbald's world, it is a tribute to the scholar that this volume begins and sustains a conversation about the larger conditions that formed a London-based "creative" whose livelihood depended on tracking and shaping the public's taste. Inchbald's active period—from stage roles in the 1770s to her editorial works in the early nineteenth century—covers an extraordinary time of cultural change in Great Britain. The essays in this collection elucidate this emerging cultural space—a Britain of colonies lost and found, a nation of readers and critics, a polis where the stage was truly the mirror of the age. While not all the essays in this collection directly engage the life and works of Inchbald, the reader will, we hope, see a common thread as these essays "build out" the context and deepen the texture of Inchbald's world.

Misty G. Anderson's opening essay brings Inchbald into our century. Crediting Jenkins with helping to renew interest in Inchbald studies and to promote attention to early female playwrights, Anderson reviews recent productions of Inchbald's plays to demonstrate that these mainstays of the eighteenth-century stage continue to be relevant in the twenty-first century. In Anderson's words, Inchbald's plays embody the "relation of the personal to the political, of the local to the global, and of entertainment to ethics." Anderson's thoughtful consideration of Inchbald-as-playwright is complemented by Martha F. Bowden's original treatment of Inchbald-as-novelist. Bowden's essay "The Structure of Fable in Inchbald's *Nature and Art*" juxtaposes Inchbald's 1796 novel with the fables of Aesop, as compiled by Samuel Croxall, and John Gay's *Fifty-One Fables in Verse*. The novel *Nature and Art* has long resisted easy generic classifications, and in Bowden's analysis, Inchbald's volume occupies a generic space between novel and fable.

Stretching back to the stage tradition that formed so much of Inchbald's aesthetic as a playwright, Cynthia J. Lowenthal's "'That Unnatural Mixture': Nostalgia and Anxiety in Late Restoration Tragicomedy" juxtaposes Aphra Behn's *Widow Ranter* with John Dryden's *Don Sebastian*, finding in both an intersection between politics, economics, culture, and history as expressed through the lenses of European colonialism and British nostalgia. Behn's and Dryden's renegades slip into the margins of upper- and lower-class morality, crossing "the borders between the separate realms of the classical and the grotesque, beings who are *of* but not *from* the region." In another fresh take on Behn's dramaturgy, Randa Graves, in "'My Business Ashore': Libertine Conduct and Maritime Context in *The Rover*," juxtaposes Captain Willmore, the titular rover, with the eponymous main character of Thomas Killigrew's *Thomaso, or the Wanderer*. Willmore emerges as the more complicated character by far; while Thomaso served as adequate inspiration, Behn provides her Willmore with "a series of performative maneuvers" that highlight the contradictions of English patriotism during the Interregnum. As Inchbald edited Behn in a circuitous manner, via the inclusion of Thomas Southerne's stage adaptation of *Oroonoko* in the *British Theatre* collection, Behn stands as Inchbald's most obvious artistic ancestor: an actor-novelist-playwright-editor, a professional woman in masculine professions.

Inchbald's editorial legacy is echoed in this collection by John Vance, in "After the Great War: The Restoration and Eighteenth Century on the London Stage, 1919–1929." Vance's essay outlines a booming period of theatrical production during which theatregoers in London "came away realizing and further appreciating that their country's rich and enjoyable theatrical heritage clearly extended beyond the works of William Shakespeare," highlighting in particular productions of plays from the long eighteenth century. That "beyond Shakespeare" is the stage canon as fixed by Inchbald's anthologies. Heather McPherson's "*Speculum Mundi*: Caricature and the Stage" uses a virtual reconstruction of Jenkins's collection of artwork and theatrical prints as her source for an examination of the history of caricature. In outlining this collection, McPherson traces the historical development of caricature as an art form, including the evolution of its generic boundaries, the marketing techniques that led to the proliferation of images, and the contexts in which caricatures flourished. She observes that such works "mirror and mock contemporary society and mores much as social comedies did" in the theatre, while at the same time satirizing "the histrionics of the stage." Inchbald's own encounters with popular prints were both direct, in that theatrical prints were used to illustrate *British Theatre*, and indirect, as Jenkins argues that the structure of Inchbald's novel *Nature and Art* mirrors that of a Hogarth print sequence.

Inchbald's work as a novelist, coming at the end of the eighteenth century, benefited from the maturity of the novelistic tradition. That tradition is examined in the contributions of Mita Choudhury and W. B. Gerard. In "Narratives of Emerging Markets and Mercantilist Mappings in Defoe's London," Choudhury draws on *A General History of the Pyrates* to argue that Defoe's pirates operated using a subjective cartography shaped by sentimentalism, moralizing, and mythmaking. Gerard's essay, "'Uncle to All the World': The Virtual Afterlives of Captain Tobias Shandy, 1831–1948," examines depictions of *Tristram Shandy*'s Uncle Toby over time. Gerard recognizes in Tobias Shandy the fundamental framework within which everything from breakfast cereal mascots to abolitionist inspirations was built. Toby survives in part thanks to the elegance of Sterne's prose, a quality shared with Inchbald's work.[9]

When Elizabeth Kraft called upon scholars of eighteenth-century literature to rethink the very structure of the canon in a 2017 review of *The Cambridge Companion to Women's Writing in Britain, 1660–1789*, she reminded us of the possibility of defining a tradition (not a countertradition) that might be constructed around Behn, Anne Finch, and Delarivier Manley at one end of the century, and Inchbald at the other end.[10] Claudia Thomas Kairoff, in her essay, "Speaking through the Prophets: Anne Finch, Politics, and Religion," describes Finch as a political prophet. Through deft use of paraphrase, Finch placed biblical prophets in the service of her arguments about education, politics, and even pacifism. As Kairoff explains, Finch's affectation of a prophetic persona "is striking for its religious and political implications," in part because Finch's own background would have led her to associate female prophets with "ignorance, religious apostasy, and treason." Finch knew, as Inchbald was later to learn, that sensitivity to the publishing market was particularly important for women writers. That market is explored by Hugh Reid in his essay, "'Hazardous Purchasing Almost Anything': The Intriguing Relationship of the Wartons, Subscription Lists, and the Eighteenth-Century Book Trade." Here Reid traces the history of subscription-based publishing in early modern England through the Warton family, especially the brothers Thomas the younger and Joseph. The brothers initially approached publishing as a means of settling Thomas the Elder's outstanding debts by both printing and selling his collected poetry but also went on to become publishers in their own right.

As befits Jenkins's enduring interest in American culture, two contributors have chosen to highlight eighteenth-century colonial subjects. Calhoun Winton's

"One of Thomas Bray's Apostles of Literacy: Thomas Bacon" traces the life and career of Thomas Bacon—author, bookseller, musician, poet, and clergyman—as he moved from humble beginnings in Ireland to colonial Maryland, where he became an early legal publisher and advocate for education. As Bacon was moving from the Old World to the New, Thomas Jefferson was essaying the reverse, as the reader will learn in Robert M. Craig's "Thomas Jefferson's Sojourn in Nîmes: Revolutionary Politics and Architecture." This essay examines Jefferson's architectural discoveries while he was serving in Europe as a diplomat, discoveries that would eventually give rise to Jeffersonian architecture.

The scholarly essays conclude with Professor Jenkins herself and an Inchbald project that has been little discussed by other scholars. In 2006, Jenkins delivered a plenary address at the annual meeting of the Southeastern American Society for Eighteenth-Century Studies in Athens, Georgia. That talk, printed here under the title "The World of *The World*," features her characteristic blend of wit and erudition, as the London newspaper *The World, and Fashionable Advertiser* is contextualized though a fascinating romp through the historical and cultural context of the British capital, circa 1787–1789. Inchbald was an essential contributor to *The World*, and that newspaper was, in its brief time, the chronicler of her world. Inchbald wrote arts and culture columns for the newspaper, signed by "The Muse," and was a likely source of small items of theatrical gossip and countless observations of London society. Like most newspapers of the era, *The World* contains items about international affairs, politics, and military matters. The "fashionable advertiser" mission of the periodical was fulfilled by Inchbald and her social circle, reporting on upcoming plays, new novels, and the goings-on of the literati. Jenkins's address brings us (admittedly punningly) back to Inchbald, who as a teen declared "she would rather die than live any longer without seeing the world."[11]

This essay collection then draws to a close first with an afterword by Paula R. Backscheider, which juxtaposes Inchbald's professional trajectory with Jenkins's scholarly one to establish the lasting contributions of both to the world of letters, followed by a dedicatory poem by Jenkins's longtime friend and colleague Don Russ. The contributors to this collection, with their sensitivity to context, their ranging across genres and sources, and their unabashed fascination with the eighteenth-century cultural panorama, invoke the best of Annibel Jenkins—friend, colleague, and mentor.

NOTES

1. James Boaden, *Memoirs of Mrs. Inchbald: Including Her Familiar Correspondence with the Most Distinguished Persons of Her Time*, 2 vols. (London: Richard Bentley, 1833); Annibel Jenkins, *I'll Tell You What: The Life of Elizabeth Inchbald* (Lexington: University Press of Kentucky, 2003).

2. For examples of reviews, see Barbara Mackey, "Review of *I'll Tell You What: The Life of Elizabeth Inchbald* by Annibel Jenkins," *Theatre Journal* 56, no. 4 (2004): 715–716; Susan

Staves, "Review of *I'll Tell You What: The Life of Elizabeth Inchbald* by Annibel Jenkins," *Albion: A Quarterly Journal Concerned with British Studies* 36, no. 2 (2004): 314–316.

3. Jenkins, *I'll Tell You What*, 137.

4. Mackey, "Review of *I'll Tell You What*."

5. Jenkins, *I'll Tell You What*, 97.

6. Eleanor Ty, *Unsex'd Revolutionaries: Five Women Novelists of the 1790s* (Toronto: University of Toronto Press, 1993).

7. Boaden, *Memoirs of Mrs. Inchbald*, 2:244. Some examples of her translated adaptions discussed by Jenkins in her Inchbald biography include *The Midnight Hour* (performed 1787, published 1788), *Animal Magnetism*, (1788, 1789), and *The Child of Nature* (1788, 1788).

8. See Lisa A. Freeman, "On the Art of Dramatic Probability: Elizabeth Inchbald's Remarks for the British Theatre," *Theatre Survey* 62, no. 2 (2021): 163–181.

9. Terry Castle, *Masquerade and Civilization: The Carnivalesque in Eighteenth-Century English Culture and Fiction* (Stanford, CA: Stanford University Press, 1986), 11.

10. Elizabeth Kraft, "Reordering Perception of Literary History and Criticism from the Viewpoint of Eighteenth-Century Women Writers," supplement, *The Eighteenth Century: Theory and Interpretation* 58 (2017).

11. Boaden, *Memoirs of Mrs. Inchbald*, 1:7.

CHAPTER 1

Inchbald for Our Time

Misty G. Anderson

Like many who became aware of Elizabeth Inchbald's plays in the late twentieth century, I had the benefit of Annibel Jenkins's direct guidance and encouragement. While Anne Mellor, Patricia Sigl, and Katherine M. Rogers provided the early scholarship that would establish Inchbald's place in theatrical history, Annibel Jenkins was a one-woman Inchbald publicity venture, particularly within the Southeastern American Society for Eighteenth-Century Studies (SEASECS) community, engaging young scholars about their own work and sharing her infectious enthusiasm for Inchbald. Jenkins's role in the development of Inchbald studies mirrored the approachability and humanity of the plays themselves. While we cannot credit her entirely with the recent interest in Inchbald on the contemporary stage, Jenkins was part of a movement of attending to early female playwrights, and she thankfully had the opportunity to witness the start of an Inchbald revival on the twenty-first-century stage. The New York Juggernaut Theatre included Inchbald's *Such Things Are* (1788) in its 2003 series on eighteenth-century female playwrights, along with *Wives as They Were, Maids as They Are* (1797) and a total of twenty plays by women from Aphra Behn to Joanna Baillie. Greg Poljacik directed *The Massacre* (1792) for the Halcyon Theatre's Alcyone Festival in Chicago in 2008, and Suzy Messerole directed *The Widow's Vow* (1786) for Theatre Unbound in Minneapolis in 2005. Colin Blumenau's work at the Theatre Royal in Bury St. Edmunds, close to the Suffolk home of Inchbald, reintroduced audiences to full-scale productions of *Wives as They Were, Maids as They Are* and *Animal Magnetism*, which played in repertoire in September 2008. The next year, Blumenau directed Inchbald's only (censored) tragedy, *The Massacre*, complete with an original score that emphasized the persistence of global atrocities, genocide, and large-scale violence through world music and a multicultural cast.

In this essay, I review some of these recent productions of Inchbald's work to build an argument that Inchbald remains a linguistically available, playable, and politically vital playwright for our times. My argument that her work continues to speak to our age brings together an awareness of the dramaturgical history that shaped these plays, the political climate in which she wrote them, and the degree to which she offers us a usable past that can be animated by the struggles for justice in the twenty-first century. That so many of the concerns that troubled Inchbald—colonialism, racism, sexism, greed, and the human capacity for cruelty and inhumanity—continue to resonate with audiences is an unfortunate effect of histories of power. That her plays, with their well-honed sense of stagecraft, entertainment, and engaging characters, can still make those concerns available in meaningful and stageworthy ways is to Inchbald's credit. She wove the threads of comedy and farce into a fabric of psychological questions about human suffering, social justice, and institutional cruelty. The result was what I term *demanding entertainment*, plays that make emotional demands on audiences even as they also please and delight those audiences. This broadly Horatian proposition echoes Daniel O'Quinn's explicitly political formulation of the "entertaining crisis," or the mediation of eighteenth-century history *as* entertainment through performances that engaged and managed audience anxieties about Britain in a state of constant war.[1] The shadow of global violence falls across more immediate and often comic questions about what ethical relationships look like in the small and large communities we inhabit. The relation of the personal to the political, of the local to the global, and of entertainment to ethics keeps Inchbald's plays relevant to new audiences.

From Her Time to Ours

The spatial realities of late Georgian theatre required Inchbald to solve material problems created by the size of the main houses. In 1792, Drury Lane increased its seating capacity to 3,600; by comparison, in 1732, it had held only about a thousand spectators. Covent Garden likewise went from accommodating around a thousand in the 1730s to 2,170 in 1782, and then to 3,013 in 1792.[2] Because of this arms race for ticket sales, which made way for larger audiences and more spectacular fare, the more densely written and verbally complex plays that still held the stage in midcentury began to fall away in favor of semi-opera, spectacle, and new comedies and tragedies. Shakespeare remained, but Etherege and most of Congreve's oeuvre gave way to large-scale entertainments. For instance, Miles Peter Andrews's gothic *Mysteries of the Castle* (1795), with music and crowd-pleasing sets, and Robert Broderip's *Black-Eyed Susan*, a nautical melodrama from 1829, were unapologetically populist, with lavish sets and broad humor. In 2007, the Theatre Royal in Bury St. Edmunds used the latter to launch its Restoring the

Repertoire series to illustrate how late Georgian theatre worked in its newly restored space. Plays by Centlivre, Cibber, Farquhar, Sheridan, and Murphy continued to be popular in the late eighteenth century, along with afterpieces by Foote, Garrick, and Fielding, but the wit comedies of the Restoration had largely disappeared; the exceptions, like Sheridan's adaptation of Congreve's *Love for Love* (1695), proved the rule.

The majority of the offerings in the 1790s were oratorios (dominated by Handel), comic operas like John O'Keefe's *The Agreeable Surprise* (1783), Henry Bate's *The Flitch of Bacon* (1789), Colman the Younger's *Inkle and Yarico* (1787), or Isaac Bickerstaffe's *Love in a Village* (1763), along with musical farces such as Prince Hoare's *No Song, No Supper* (1792) or *My Grandmother* (1794).[3] Inchbald was one of a few contemporary playwrights, along with Thomas Holcroft, who managed to craft successful, new, popular nonmusical comedies and plays that worked for larger audiences and the spaces that held them. New plays had to address the sonic realities of echo and projection, as well as distant sight lines in houses triple the size of those for which Congreve, Centlivre, and Cibber had written. Inchbald's linguistic economy met the physical conditions of the late Georgian playhouse. Her more compact lines, clear blocking, and punctuating tableaux allowed actors to communicate in the almost cavernous houses of the late eighteenth century. She also perceived and responded advantageously to the shifting taste in comedies.

Since the mid-eighteenth century, British audiences had favored comedies that were more humane than those of the Restoration or even the early eighteenth century, where sexual infidelity, disposable lower-class characters, and relatively unproblematic aristocratic privilege were still rampant. The term *sentimental* has been used to describe the shift away from Restoration comedy and toward a gentler, less cynical form, though "sentimental" can obscure the complex double plots and character development that plays like *The English Merchant* (1767) or *The Discovery* (1763) achieve. Boaden, Inchbald's early biographer, does not use the term *sentimental* to describe her comedies, but he did claim more generally that she "mixes her gaiety with her pathos, and the tear is scarcely dry, when you are summoned and willing to join in the most irresistible merriment" (*Memoirs*, 1:240). The tear to which Boaden refers is the manifestation of such engagement and ethical sympathy. The affective mixture implicates the audience by engaging their sympathies as well as their sense of humor to involve them in the lives of her fictional characters.

Inchbald's spare style allowed for tableau moments and reactions in which the audience was asked to participate in moments of moral accountability by looking together with the characters at scenes of confession, recognition, and repentance. This appeal to audience response also reflects the performance theories and practices of late Georgian theatre. In her own time, Sarah Siddons's powerful performances would bring audiences to wailing and tears with pathetic roles like Isabella, "so expressive of her horror . . . that every auditor instantly becomes pervaded with a correspondent sympathy."[4] Inchbald's comedies made use of this affective immediacy to invite receptive audiences into sympathetic relationships with her characters.

Inchbald's plays also balance a political progressivism on issues of gender, human rights, and economic injustice against a morally grounded set of demands for ethical behavior. Inchbald's thematic interests in divorce, colonialism, and revolution ask the audience to register the abuses of power, both individual and institutional, as represented in the play and then reject that abuse. While the implication of the audience in Inchbald's plots does not reach the traumatic immediacy of an Artaudian theatre of cruelty, the tableaux serve to hold their collective gaze on scenes of institutionalized cruelty, failures of compassion, and the consequences of war and greed. In this way, Inchbald uses them to underscore moments of recognition, implication, and meaning for an audience at a great physical distance from the stage. To the extent that her work embodies Artaud's longing for a representation of reality and a "passionate and convulsive conception of life," it participates in a broadly modern theatrical project.[5] The palpable sense of moral failure and its consequences, particularly in "the inescapable impetus of the crowd" in *The Massacre*, anticipate aims of the grander projects of post–World War I theatre and its social function in an age of mass media.[6] But even her comedies participate in the sense of urgency for social justice and the audience's implication in the larger social project. The unspoken acts referenced in the title of *I'll Tell You What*, the blanket reply of "everyone has his fault," or the wordless, and thus meaningless, evasions of Twineall in *Such Things Are* comically iterate the potentially tragic failures of compassion and communication in Inchbald's dangerously global economies.[7] Her approach is less an assault on the audience and more an appeal to them, but they are not meant to escape the circuit of implication and responsibility.

These historical features of Inchbald's dramaturgy and the thematic and political content of her plays are doorways for twenty-first-century audiences, directors, and actors. In some sense, the very open-endedness of Inchbald's worldview is a part of what keeps her works available for interpretation. Inchbald's politics were progressive but difficult to classify as clearly as those of Godwin, Holcroft, Wollstonecraft, and others in her circle. Her complicated relationship to the Roman Catholic identity of her girlhood in Standingfield, just outside of Bury St. Edmunds, led her to question church authority, though she was never fully alienated from it. Her plays retain a strong moral commitment to the value of human life, which informs her representations of the abuses of colonialism, of the French Revolution, and of masculine authority in marriage. This seriousness of purpose, combined with her crowd-pleasing ability to navigate the physical and emotional landscape of the rapidly changing late-century playhouse, makes her a playwright for our own time.

Such Things Still Are

On May 16, 2003, I had the pleasure of seeing a staged reading of *Such Things Are*, which was part of the Juggernaut Theatre Company's series "The First 100 Years: The Professional Female Playwright," a project coordinated by Mallory Catlett and Gwynn MacDonald. The evening was a revelation: not only did a staged reading of a relatively obscure, 216-year-old play, with actors seated at music stands, fill a small theatre in the Bronx, but Inchbald's lively, thoughtful, and virtually uncut 1787 comedy moved the audience to both raucous laughter and collective sympathy without the benefit of ornament or action. The larger project of "The First 100 Years" involved a range of theatre companies from the Classical Theatre of Harlem to the Flying Fig to the New York Theatre Workshop, hosting twenty-one readings of works by Behn, Centlivre, Cowley, Inchbald, and Baillie.

That the Pregones Theatre sponsored the reading of *Such Things Are* offers a glimpse of the possibilities for politically and culturally engaged productions of Inchbald's plays. The Pregones Theatre, or Teatro Pregones, was founded in 1979 by Rosalba Rolón to create works after the style of Latin American and Caribbean *colectivos*, performing ensembles whose mission was to create theatre arts for the community. Many of its early productions toured, in Spanish, in the tristate area, before the company established a home in the Bronx. Pregones has since merged with the Puerto Rican Traveling Theater (founded in 1967) and expanded to two performances spaces, one in the Bronx and one in midtown Manhattan, both of which bring a range of Latino performers, playwrights, and theatrical traditions to audiences with the expressed purpose of developing both artists and communities.[8]

Teatro Pregones, a collective of performers who share a sense of political and cultural mission with Inchbald's prison reformer John Howard, was able to deliver this play set in colonial Indonesia. *Such Things Are* was originally performed on the eve of the trial of Warren Hastings, the governor-general of Bengal, who was impeached over allegations of crimes and misdemeanors after his resignation. The play opened at Covent Garden on February 10, 1787; Hastings's accusers, led by Philip Francis, Charles Fox, and Edmund Burke, had been attacking him steadily in the press since 1784, an effort that culminated in his arrest on May 21, 1787. Sumatra's eighteenth-century history followed the broad pattern of colonial hubris and self-congratulatory missionary zeal that Hastings's career mapped and came to represent. While the Dutch and Portuguese played leading roles in Sumatra's history, the island had been claimed in part as an English colony since an East India Company charter of 1659. Sumatra represented British hopes and idealism about governing ethically in the colonial age, hopes and ideals vexed by contradictions within the colonial project. Kathleen Wilson observes that the Baptist merchant Joseph Collett, tapped in 1711 for a gubernatorial position in British Bencoolen, established Fort Marlborough as the main British outpost of Sumatra after abandoning the cramped York Fort, which was known for corruption, inefficiency, and "intemperance."[9] Collett attempted to remedy some of the worst abuses of power as well as to impede the racial and ethnic mixing of the colony's Malagasy, Portuguese, British, Dutch, West African, and Chinese populations in a mestizo culture that had evolved from years and mixtures of colonial presence.

Sumatra was linked to St. Helena by sea route that brought cargo, most notably West African and Mauritanian slaves, Chinese laborers, planters, and felons. High hopes about its Edenic fertility and utopian governmental possibilities slowly dissolved as Fort Marlborough became "a supply station and a hedonistic oasis for homeward-bound company ships coming around the Cape of Good Hope," with foodstuffs produced by slaves and through farming techniques that led to rapid deforestation.[10] After Collett and then a people's revolt, "tyrannical" local governance followed. Locals set fires at the fort, and the British were forced to take refuge at sea from 1719 to 1723.[11] The subsequent reestablishment of the colonial presence involved complex negotiations with local competing rajas, a circumstance that is reflected in *Such Things Are*.

The underlying human rights abuses and biopolitics represented in *Such Things Are* remain relevant to modern audiences. The Pregones's staged reading of *Such Things Are* in the Bronx came less than two years after the terrorist attacks of September 11, 2001, which gave Americans a new sense of vulnerability and, with it, new vocabularies of revenge, administration, and governmentality. The Department of Homeland Security, established eleven days after the attacks, evoked a frontier sensibility through the term *homeland* and with it a sense of the possible threats to the same. Similar questions of loyalty and terror circulate through *Such Things Are* and its culture of surveillance. Lord Flint, a "very dangerous man" who "carries everything he hears to the ministers of our suspicious Sultan," makes Sir Luke especially uneasy. Lord Flint, an Englishman brought up in Sumatra, where he "imbibed all this country's cruelty" (1.4), is loyal to the Sultan rather that Britain.[12]

The relationship between colonials and cruelty echoed the abuses of the Hastings regime for its first audiences, but the references to tyranny, torture, and its normalization in a permanent state of colonial war work translate easily, for twenty-first-century viewers, to fears about "Islamic terrorists" and the abridgment of privacy in the name of "homeland security." Lord Flint is an example of what Terry Eagleton has called the institutional quality of most wickedness, which can tip over into evil in conditions where individuals (like Flint) can commit atrocities as a matter of bureaucratic boredom.[13] Lady Tremor seems to be already poisoned by his influence when she hears of people being hung by their thumbs or made to dance on a hot gridiron: "That is one of the tortures I have never heard of!" she exclaims. "O! I should like to see it of all things!" When Sir

Luke replies that "by keeping this man's company, you'll soon be as cruel as he is," he seems to have spoken too late (1.4).

The nervous laughter that these lines and others generated at the 2003 reading underscored the durability of Inchbald's three most farcical characters, Lord Tremor, Lady Tremor, and Mr. Twineall. Inchbald's main accomplishment in each case is in providing a vehicle for comic action that can carry social and cultural heft. As the play opens, Lord and Lady Tremor have been in Sumatra for some sixteen years and are dependent upon, as well as participants in, the Sultan's court. The exact length of their residence is a matter of marital disagreement, mainly because the number would set the age of Lady Tremor at a horrifyingly advanced age of thirty-two. Though the spouses quibble over the details, the story is that Lady Tremor "came over from England exactly sixteen years ago . . . the year of the great Eclipse (1764) . . . near seventeen—and without one qualification except your youth—and not being a Mullatto" (1.2). Katharine M. Rogers omits "and not being a Mullatto" in her edition of the play in *The Meridian Anthology of Restoration and Eighteenth-Century Plays by Women*, which is an interesting choice given that both the first edition, published in 1994, and the Dublin edition include it; by 1800, however, the line had been omitted.[14]

Lord Tremor's insult speaks volumes about the context of their courtship. Though Lady Tremor (clearly without title upon their meeting) has youth, beauty, and at least one suit of "fine clothes" when she arrives in Sumatra, her eligibility is tied to two other important features: her whiteness and her "letters of recommendation, from two great families in England" (1.2). The meaning of her body, dislocated from England as a colonial seeking to profit in Sumatra on the marriage market, requires a provenance to guarantee both race and class viability. She moves through a global economy like the primary colonial market in spices (as well as more recently introduced cash crops like coffee, tea, tobacco, and sugar) that brought Lord Tremor to Sumatra with the hope of vast riches.[15] Twineall, the name-dropping, people-pleasing young hopeful fresh off the ship from Britain, makes for an easy contemporary parallel in an age of social media and networking. Twineall intends to climb his way into the fragile colonial society by ingratiating himself with the Tremors and Lord Flint. However, in order to teach young Twineall a lesson, Mr. Meanwright maneuvers Twineall into tormenting these three characters with their faults, while thinking he is appealing to their vanity.

He praises Sir Luke's valor when, in reality, Sir Luke ran from battle; he flatters Lady Tremor on her noble ancestry when she, in fact, comes from common stock; and he makes insinuating remarks about the Sultan to Lord Flint, thus risking the literal loss of his head. Twineall's personal marketing strategy is to ingratiate himself by discovering how to please each of the British colonists (and to explain the meaning of his name!): "Once I become acquainted with people's dispositions, their little weaknesses, foibles, and faults, I can wind, twist, twine, and get into the corner of every one's heart, and lie so snug, they can't know I'm there till they want to pull me out, and find 'tis impossible" (2.16). But in addition to the content-free quality of his relationships, all of which are based on calculated flattery, he has also learned to speak without words, or to empty them of meaning. He explains that even the word *ridiculous* has "changed its former sense, and was [*sic*] become a mode to express satisfaction" (1.9). His signature linguistic trait, however, is his embrace of a new "fashion, in England, of speaking without any words at all" (1.9). Inchbald's eighteenth-century version of "newspeak" digs at political bluster and its circulation in an age of newspapers.[16]

Twineall's evasions have a familiar modernity about them; he sounds like a political figure, news anchor, or pundit speaking to avoid an actual commitment recorded by the media. Twineall demonstrates his technique: "really it appears to me e-e-e-e-e—(*mutters and shrugs*)—that is—mo-mo-mo-mo-mo (*mutters*)—if you see the thing—for my part—te-te-te-te—and that's all I can tell about it at *present*" (1.9). Twineall is a reminder of the modern world of media and its capacity for emptiness, which we share with Inchbald's age. When he uses the strategy a few lines later to avoid Haswell's question about whether there has been any act on behalf of the poor clergy, he makes a point that works by analogy for any number of contemporary social relief measures that receive more lip service than funding in our own time. For these reasons and others, Inchbald plays without footnotes.

The demand Inchbald places on her audience through this tendentious joking finds its clear anchor in Mr. Haswell, the stand-in figure for John Howard, the prison reformer. Haswell is remarkable to the prison guards because he seems to be moved by the misery all around him: "Who would suppose you had been used to see such places!—you look concerned. . . . I wonder you should come, when you seem to think so much about them" (2.21). Haswell replies: "O that, that is the very reason!" and so implicates the audience in a circuit of empathy and sensibility. As we "see" with him, the man who should be hardened to these sights but who feels fresh grief, we should also be moved. (These lines come from a section of the play that was also reproduced as a pocket edition and in the newspapers.) Zedan, the Indian prisoner, steals Haswell's pocketbook in desperation and rejoices both in his potential escape and in seeing Haswell's misery until Haswell's generosity touches him. Initially, he sees Haswell as simply a proxy for the colonials "who spurn me—who treat me as if, in my own island, I had no friends who loved me . . . —Taskmasters, forgetful that I am a husband—a father—nay, a man" (2.22).

The Pregones Theatre reading could not physically show Zedan's theft, the subsequent return of the wallet, or Haswell giving Zedan money and, with it, an overwhelmingly charitable feeling that "makes me love even my enemies." The scene still worked, as it seems to have in the pocket edition for readers (2.28). The structured plea for compassion, propelled by the ethical distance between the Keeper and Haswell on the one hand and Zedan's before and after experience of Haswell's charity on the other, drives the audience's identification not so much with Haswell but with the effects of his benevolence. As we watch his charitable attempts at reform, we see his world transform from the cruel space tyranny has created—visually punctuated by the prison walls—to the mild and gentle emotional space, underscored by lighting cues, as well as the female prisoner's longing description of "the sun, the air, fields, woods, and all that wondrous world" (2.26).

The more sentimental elements of the play, including Haswell's sterling goodness and the pathetic reunion of Arabella and the Sultan, continue to be playable on their own technical merits and sadly accessible amid the twenty-first-century political realities of prisoners of war, the analogy between dungeons and solitary confinement, and the persistence of torture. These grim realities make Haswell's moral heft and the politicized scene of virtuous activism that shapes his character plausible and playable. In my limited experience of producing the play as readers' theatre, both Haswell's scenes of charity and the reunion of Arabella and the Sultan prove powerful and support Haythornthwaite's conclusion in the *Dublin Review* that in *Such Things Are,* Inchbald reached her highest dramatic effort.[17] The tableau in which the Sultan, himself a stand-in for an earlier sultan killed in battle, recognizes his beloved Arabella, whom he has imprisoned for years, was written and staged to work in the cavernous Covent Garden of 1788. The Sultan, beginning to realize that he has unknowingly imprisoned his beloved wife, who now sues "to transfer the blessing you have offered, to one of those who may have friends to welcome their return from bondage," throws himself upon a sofa, the stage direction par excellence for the man of sensibility (and a move already being parodied by Frances Burney in her then-unpublished *Love and Fashion*) (5.68). He then reveals himself, causing Arabella to faint, then to exclaim: "Is this the light you promised?—(*To Haswell.*)—Dear precious light! Is this my freedom? To which I bind myself a slave forever—(*Embracing the Sultan*)—What I *your* captive?—Sweet captivity! More precious than an age of liberty!" (5.68).

While the use of slavery by analogy discomfits modern audiences, Inchbald's underlying point, that choice is the true liberty, and that liberty is only meaningful in community, carries the moment, even in a much smaller venue than the one Inchbald first used.[18] The modulation of the Sultan's severity, exposed now as a performance of tyranny, into a lover's authentic affection has melting potential that the present political turmoil in Darfur, Iraq, Syria, and other places only amplifies. The threat of torture, scenic references to the dungeon, and the real effects of the Sultan's performance of tyranny provide a moving contrast to Arabella's vulnerability, blending elements of a mythic fairy tale with a politically urgent message about forgiveness and the disruption of cycles of violence. The expression of romantic love between Arabella and the Sultan becomes fully social and even revolutionary as the Sultan hands over his signet ring to Haswell, "with power to redress the wrongs of all who suffer" (5.68). To the degree that the play uses sentimental tropes and themes, it actively deploys them to make larger points about human rights and civil liberties.

Both the Classic Theatre Company of New York 2008 production and the Theatre Royal 2009 production of *The Massacre* grappled similarly with the urgency of Inchbald's work for our times through her only extant tragedy. Like *Such Things Are* and its message about colonial abuses of power, *The Massacre* taps a vein that continues to be close to home in a global economy: revolutionary violence and its effects on human lives. Inchbald sets her play, ostensibly about the Paris riots of 1792, in 1572 at the St. Bartholomew's Day massacre of Protestants in Paris, during the French Wars of Religion. These paralleled histories allow contemporary audiences, who get to see the play that eighteenth-century audiences did not, through a roughly proximate historical distance that only highlights the ongoing humanitarian crisis of violence to noncombatants in sites of revolutionary and counterinsurgency chaos.

The overwhelming and embodied reality of death and violence pours forth in *The Massacre*'s lines and implied setting. Eusèbe Tricastin, returning to his family from the chaos, explains, "I fought with the assassins, and fell amongst my brethren—at that moment my senses left me.—When they returned, and I put out my arms to embrace my fellow sufferers, I found I clasped nothing but dead bodies.—I rose from the horrid pile, and by a lamp discerned (all gashed with wounds) faces, . . . poor helpless victims of ferocious vengeance, pale, convulsed with terror, and writhing under the ruffian's knife. . . . I saw infants encouraged by the fury of their tutors, stab other infants sleeping in their cradles."[19] Inchbald, quoting Horace Walpole in her "Advertisement" contained in the published version of *The Massacre*, announced her play's subject and the events described as "the essential spring of *terror* and *pity*," key words that Burke used in his analysis of the sublime and, later, in his own more royalist account of revolutionary terror.[20] The elements of sublime terror build a politics out of the record of human suffering. At the heart of the play is the Tricastin family, trapped in their house by a mob. They are eventually separated, tried, and vindicated, but not before their accuser Dugas can murder the family during the trial. The theme of what Jenkins called "the gloss of judicial respectability" implicates the mob over the judicial system per se while also highlighting the ineffectuality of governmental complicity and the horrifying farce of sham trials.[21]

Inchbald's politics, once again, are not so much ambiguous as they are complicated. Her sympathy for republican thought and her friendships with Godwin (who may have borrowed the main title *Things as They Are* for his novel now commonly known as *Caleb Williams*[22] from Inchbald herself) and with Thomas Holcroft speak to her ongoing conversation with the radicals of her day. But her positions, even in the novels, are nuanced rather than doctrinaire.

Figure 1.1. Playbill, *The Massacre*, dir. Colin Blumenau, 2009, Theatre Royal, used by permission of the Theatre Royal, Bury St. Edmunds.

Personal suffering, individual injustice created by larger structural arrangements of power, and physical peril center her politics. As *Guardian* reviewer Chris Arnot put it, "Inchbald supported the ideals of the French Revolution, but not what you might call its execution."[23] Blumenau's production of *The Massacre* called on a multicultural cast, with actors from Somalia, India, Pakistan, and Northern Ireland, and modern dress with an indistinct set that is somewhere hot but otherwise unspecified. The stark playbill cover brings a stunningly modern aesthetic to the audience's attention with a stylized and bloodied M on a flat black background, as can be seen in figure 1.1. Blumenau's use of Eammon O'Dwyer's haunting and varied original score, which bounced between modern and world music tones, and a recitation in Arabic in an interlude were part of his deliberately Brechtian strategy to provide "alienation effects" that would give audiences pause and implicate them in the action.[24] As the *East*

Anglia Daily Times review put it, the ambiguity allows the production to reference events from "the English Civil War, which set brother against brother, to the French Terror, the persecution of Jews in 1930s Germany and the Rwandan genocide of the 1990s."[25] Ambiguity here becomes a virtue by generalizing the human rights abuses attendant on modern war and asking the audience to make broad connections between them.

Theatre Royal and Restoring the Repertoire

The Massacre was one of the later productions in the Restoring the Repertoire project, which in all mounted seven productions either written in or popular during the late Georgian period. The project began in 2007 at the Theatre Royal in Bury St. Edmunds, Suffolk, the oldest extant, functioning Georgian theatre. Restoring the Repertoire was an ambitious, multiyear commitment to reviving Georgian and Regency plays for a general audience, spearheaded by Colin Blumenau. The projected coincided with the reopening of the 1819 theatre after a careful restoration of the building, its friezes, and elaborate decorations, all according to architect William Wilkins's original plans.

The first production was of Douglas Jerrold's nautical melodrama *Black-Eyed Susan*. Blumenau's stated aim, to present "a play that audiences could understand and enjoy, that wouldn't feel like something culled from the ivory tower of Academe, but that was also well crafted and carefully written," speaks both to the historicism and the populism of the project.[26] The restored Theatre Royal, shown in figure 1.2, reduced the number of available seats from the original plan (as artistic director Colin Blumenau noted, contemporary audiences would not tolerate the crush of the crowd as readily as their Georgian and Regency counterparts did), but it made room for historical set design, including a perspective set, re-created machinery for manipulating wooden racks of waves, and the use of the forestage to encourage forms of interaction now largely lost to modern audiences.

In the fall of 2008, Blumenau directed a double bill of Inchbald, with *Wives as They Were, Maids as They Are* and *Animal Magnetism*. The Theatre Royal chose the plays out of its ongoing rehearsed readings series. In the case of *Wives as They Were*, Blumenau and his team set out to "discover the radicalism" of the play in "a way that resonated for us in the twenty-first century."[27] The production team was aware that they were facing the double-edged sword of popular historical interest in the period. During a tour of the Theatre Royal, one can dress up in Georgian costume bits from the shop and have a silhouette drawn in the style of the period. The nearby Ickworth House, ancestral home of the Hervey family, infamous in the eighteenth century thanks to Pope's poison pen and, to later generations, thanks to a rich family history of debauchery, is an important eighteenth-century landmark estate and National Trust property.

Figure 1.2. Interior of the Theatre Royal, Bury St. Edmunds.

Concurrently with the opening of *Wives as They Were*, Ickworth hosted a weekend of Georgian military history, with historical reenactors staging an encampment, quadrille, and country dancing. The rotunda of the house was itself built as a gallery for objects and paintings from the Earl of Bristol's grand tour, a reminder that the culture of self-conscious display and performance is part of Georgian history. The house now also features, as do many British country houses turned museums, *Downton Abbey*—styled tours of the servant's quarters and kitchens. Playing off of the historical interests of visiting crowds has become a survival strategy for many museums and homes; for the Restoring the Repertoire series, period fascination thus presented both an opportunity and a potential danger. How can a director, cast, and crew make a play like *Wives as They Were, Maids as They Are* generate interest and audience and yet avoid the trap of becoming another Georgian curiosity, a costume drama museum piece?

Designer Kit Surrey tackled the problem directly by making it a visual trope of the set; each character emerges from a museum vitrine, a glass display box, as can be seen in figure 1.3. The vitrines were meant to illustrate the escape of the characters from the "mausoleum of history" which "preserves them in aspic," as Blumenau put it.[28] If history can trap a play and rob it of its potential radicalism, however, then thoughtful historicism might be the way out. Reviewers seemed to agree: Timothy Ramsden approved of the metaphor, "with its combined sense of

Figure 1.3. Production still from *Wives as They Were, Maids as They Are*, Theatre Royal, 2008, photography courtesy of Mike Kwasniak.

showing-off and confinement within their public facades by characters in period costume, who pose in their cages like museum exhibits before entering."[29]

The Oregon Shakespeare Festival's 2005 production of Cowley's *The Belle's Stratagem* (1780) took a similar approach to the play's history and found a visual device that would provide a context for critical reflection. Set designer William Bloodgood's miniature versions of Georgian buildings designed by Sir John Soane became furniture and props, thus unsettling perspective with a scale that makes human beings both monstrous and strangely vulnerable to buildings that now move (figure 1.4). The design encouraged active visual reflection on historical artifacts as well as contemporary parallels in the commodification of human relationships, the function of luxury goods, and the speed at which material wealth can change hands in a globally monetized economy.

While Inchbald's mainpieces are close to modern playable length, particularly in comparison with earlier Restoration and eighteenth-century repertoire, Blumenau (under the pen name Daniel O'Brien) edited transitions, consolidated servant parts into distinct characters, and made modest adaptations to *Wives*. One of the more curious changes he made to the script was the omission of the stage directions that appear in the first editions of the play. Entrances and exits remain as marked, but directions such as the instructions that Maria Dorrillon begins a speech "recovering," or that she breaks in the midst of it "stifling her tears," are gone. The omissions point up the difficulties of editing dramatic text

Figure 1.4. Production still from *The Belle's Stratagem*, Oregon Shakespeare Festival, 2005. Photo courtesy of William Bloodgood, scenic designer.

and the complex interactions of manuscripts (the primary evidence for a working script), production history, and the collaboration between booksellers and printers "as partners in the creative process."[30] To the extent that booksellers hoped the printed play would be a profitable substitute for the experience of the theatre for those who could not get to the play (or, a re-creation of the experience for those who could), the early editions provide a useful, if imperfect, archive of performance as well, a "means of recapturing the stage experience."[31] But for a contemporary production, those same directions, notes, and didascalies can present a problem, a filter of action, motion, and response, a filter that at best hinders a director from his or her own vision and at worst becomes an alienating addendum of historical behavior that no longer seems relevant.

Inchbald's *Wives* underscores the function of patriarchal authority in the lives of its female characters. The comedy's heroine, Maria Dorrillon, awaits her father's return from the Indies and in the meantime has become a fashionable, witty young woman enmeshed in gambling debts and implicit, romantic obligations. To either side of her are Lady Priory, who is subject to her husband's archaic patriarchalism and absolute control, and Lady Raffle, Maria's friend who represents the temptation of falling further into the fashionable gambling game. A letter to the editor of the *Monthly Mirror* from May 1797 observed the tricky business of the play's comic situation: "If Lady Priory be intended as an amiable pattern of conjugal submissiveness, and Miss Dorrillon and Lady Mary as foils to make her character appear still more exemplary and worthy of imitation, I think it will be difficult to prove that there is sufficient authority to bear out the design, since the attentions of Lady Priory to her husband are the offspring of fear and not of affection."[32]

Joannah Tincey, the actor who played Lady Priory in Blumenau's 2008 production, had to address this central issue of Lady Priory's motives in order to make the play readable for a twenty-first-century audience. Blumenau explains that their discovery process led them to a usable interpretation of Lady Priory's agency in her given circumstances: Lady Priory acts out of neither fear nor affection but more out of an innate sense of conservative spousal duty. For a modern actor the trick is to try to imbue such conservatism with a sense of realism. This is not as hard as it sounds since her pragmatism gives her an empowered strength that resonates with a contemporary performer. Ultimately it is she who makes the decision to reject the advances of Mr. Bronzley and return to her husband. This again places the power in her hands and turns her into an appealing challenge for a modern actor—a challenge that Tincey embraced with real skill and enthusiasm.[33]

By placing the source of Lady Priory's agency in her pragmatic apprehension of the status quo patriarchalism that is writ large in her marriage and in her subsequent recognition that, by accepting Lord Priory's tyranny, "she can live a life that is not entirely unacceptable," Blumenau and Tincey solved the problem of audience sympathy, or what a 1797 reviewer called "sufficient authority" for her character. A victimized Lady Priory would sabotage the comic spirit, but a performance that establishes both her strength and her vulnerability in the face of a set of social gender relations, manifest in her husband's extremes, makes the abuses of patriarchalism the object of laughter. Reviews of the 2008 production declare Blumenau successful in delivering both "belly laughs" and "the dilemma faced by eighteenth-century women dramatists: they could satirize male brutality but were expected to endorse marriage."[34] Lord Priory and Sir William Dorrillon (masquerading as the aptly named "Mr. Mandred") are the most egregious cases of patriarchal cruelty, illustrating both paternal and marital domination in the name of ideal femininity.

In one of the most disturbing lines of the play, Sir William says, What I see so near perfection as woman, I want to see perfect. We, Mr. Norberry, can never be perfect, but surely women, women, might easily be made angels!" (1.3). Sir William commences "angel-making" upon his return from the Indies by first observing his long-lost daughter, who gambles, spends, and flirts, and then refusing to help her with her debts, for which she is eventually imprisoned. His demanding, disciplinarian role torments him more than Maria, who responds with overwhelming affection and duty as soon as he reveals himself. The Priorys potentially present more of a challenge for a modern director, cast, and audience because Lord Priory's methods are patently abusive by modern standards. He keeps Lady Priory locked up by day, uses sleep deprivation tactics to control her, and exploits his bad temper to his advantage: "It causes me to be obeyed without hesitation, no liberty for contention, tears, or repining" (1.7).

Blumenau reflects that Lord Priory is, again, a product of his time and environment:

> He is extreme in his views certainly, but Inchbald is painting a satirical portrait of her male-dominated society's paradigm of self-satisfied and self-appointed seniority. As the object of such satire the character is played in the same way that any actor would approach such a challenge. John [Webb] worked at finding the central truths of the character and then explored how to exaggerate both the characteristics that suited those truths and how to deliver them in a way that was provocative in its extremity. Never tipping into caricature, John managed to create a totally monstrous yet utterly believable Lord Priory. The moments of extremity are thus comfortably contained within the satirical whole. It was an object lesson in the actor's craft.[35]

Lord Priory's totalitarian hubris sanctions a kidnapping, during which Mr. Bronzley tests his wife's virtue. The success of Blumenau's approach to Lord Priory, making him the object of satire without descending to caricature, was born out in reviews noting the hilarity of "Lord Priory's recipe for 'conjugal sunshine'" and declaring the scene in which "Lady Priory undoes her tumescent wooer by producing her knitting" to be the funniest of the production.[36] The enthusiastic audience response illustrates both the critical edge to Inchbald's gender politics and its enduring appeal for audiences. Sir William's severity and Lord Priory's abusive totalitarianism are both exposed and trumped by Maria's filial affection and Lady Priory's canny understanding of gender relations as a matter not of romantic love but of realistic management. Delivering this complex reality to a contemporary audience requires both careful historical work and the discovery of these characters in the present.

Ultimately, Maria's reformation in the fifth act is suspect across generations of audiences: earlier reviewers opined that it was not enough of a reformation, while twenty-first-century reviewers noted that the ending as written seems too much of a compromise of Maria's agency. Blumenau chose to play the problem in its ambiguity rather than resolve it for the audience. After discussions with the cast, which revealed a wide range of beliefs and prejudices about feminism and about Inchbald's intention, Blumenau consolidated the message around the textual ambivalence of Maria's "seeming resolution" to marry, which is actually more her father's agreement with Sir George. Maria has "owned her readiness to become the subject of a milder government" (5.94) after her father's severity and her own gambling debts. As Blumenau recalled, "We ultimately decided that we wanted to reflect this ambivalence in the conclusion, leaving the audience to make their own decision about what happened at the end. . . . Given this ambition it became a question of the actors being careful not to make decisions on the audience's behalf to the point that the actor playing Miss Dorrillon ended the final scene with a shrug of her shoulders accompanied by an interrogative look at the audience. Should she? Or shouldn't she?"[37] In his director's note about the play's ending, he encouraged audiences not to "be fooled by its seeming patness" and to look for the critical voice beyond the scripted dialogue. Reviewer Joanne Mace agreed that "the final poses and facial expressions . . . hint at the deeper story" of emerging gender roles and the radical edge of Inchbald's gender politics.[38]

The Theatre Royal's production of *Animal Magnetism*, Inchbald's adaptation of Antoine-Jean-Bourlin Dumaniant's *Le médecin malgré tout le monde* (1786), was equally successful and played in repertoire with *Wives as They Were*, allowing audiences on select days to have the experience of an Inchbald mainpiece and an Inchbald afterpiece. The Inchbald plays marked a return to language and delivery in Georgian comedy (after the more visual extravaganza of *Black-Eyed Susan*), and her sturdy farce proved an excellent and popular vehicle. While *Animal Magnetism* avoids the heavy topicality of colonialism, revolution, and tyrannical patriarchalism, it does embrace the still-resonant topic of medical quackery, as familiar to contemporary audiences through their browser's pop-up ads as it was to Londoners of yore encountering Franz Anton Mesmer and local quacks James Graham and Gustavus Katterfelto. Reviews praised the clever content and the accessible production, which picks up on the theme of female confinement, but with a farcical victory for the women and their lovers. Ivan Howlett wrote appreciatively of its "slapstick and stage-farce techniques," which lead to "hilarious shenanigans."[39] The accessibility of the production and the evangelizing effect of her farce, which was among her most performed works in her own time, bring more theatregoers into the experience of discovering Inchbald's vitality for our era.

The SEASECS Players is a minor but popular tradition of the annual meeting of the Southeastern American Society for Eighteenth-Century Studies. Theatre has been an important part of many of these meetings, including Coastal Carolina University's traveling production of *The Tragedy of Tragedies* (1731), directed by Sandi Shackelford and produced for the 2003 meeting by Daniel J. Ennis. Ennis and company followed up in 2004 with Inchbald's *The Mogul Tale* (1788), directed by Stephen Fawcett. That production, presented at the SEASECS meeting in Savannah, Georgia, appears to have been the first American production of *The Mogul Tale* since 1797. The SEASECS Players presented scenes from *The Suspicious Husband* (1747) in 2008 at Auburn, as well as other events, readings, and traditional papers over the years. The Players assembled to read Frances Burney's *The Witlings* (written in 1779) in 2011 at Wake Forest and have presented a staged reading most years since, including Garrick's *The Bon Ton* (1775) and *The Male Coquette* (1757), and scenes from Sheridan's *The Rivals* (1775),

Figure 1.5. *Animal Magnetism*, SEASECS, Gainesville, Florida, 2015. Pictured: Misty Anderson, Hugh Reid, Daniel J. Ennis. Photo courtesy of Lauren Holt.

Goldsmith's *She Stoops to Conquer* (1773), and other small entertainments. Our latest attempt at Inchbald came in 2015, alas, too late for Annibel Jenkins to be in the audience, but we trust that she would approve our choice of *Animal Magnetism*, an afterpiece she herself deemed "hilarious" (figure 1.5). We think she would be glad to know that we are still spreading the word about Inchbald's achievements, her relevance, and her playability in our own time.

NOTES

1. Daniel O'Quinn, *Entertaining Crisis in the Atlantic Imperium, 1770–1790* (Baltimore: Johns Hopkins University Press, 2011), 2–5.

2. Harry William Pedicord, *The Theatrical Public in the Time of Garrick* (Carbondale: Southern Illinois University Press, 1966), 6; James Melton, *The Rise of the Public in Enlightenment Europe* (London: Cambridge University Press, 2001), 160.

3. Production records taken from Charles Beecher Hogan, ed., *The London Stage, 1600–1800, Part 5: 1776–1800*, vol. 2–3 (Carbondale: Southern Illinois University Press, 1968), 1217–2238, https://catalog.hathitrust.org/Record/000200105.

4. Thomas Gilliland, *The Dramatic Mirror*, vol. 2 (London: C. Chapple, 1808), 974.

5. Antonin Artaud, "The Theatre of Cruelty," in *The Theory of the Modern Stage*, ed. Eric Bentley (New York: Penguin Books, 1968), 66.

6. Kimberly Jannarone, *Artaud and His Doubles* (Ann Arbor: University of Michigan Press, 2012), 118.

7. See Robert Vork, "The Things No One Can Say: The Unspeakable Act in Artaud's *Les Cenci*," *Modern Drama* 56, no. 3 (2013): 306–326.

8. For more information concerning the Pregones/Puerto Rican Traveling Theater, or Pregones/PRTT, see https://pregonesprtt.org.

9. Kathleen Wilson, "Rethinking the Colonial State: Family, Gender, and Governmentality in Eighteenth-Century British Frontiers," *American Historical Review* 116, no. 5 (2011): 1301.

10. Wilson, 1307. See also Clement Hawes, *Poor Relations: The Making of a Eurasian Community in British India, 1773–1833* (London: Routledge, 1996).

11. Capt. Alexander Hamilton, *A New Account of the East Indies*, vol. 2 (Edinburgh: John Mosman, 1727), 116, https://wellcomecollection.org/works/yskbgy5u/items?canvas=130. Also quoted in Wilson, "Rethinking the Colonial State," 1306n44.

12. All references to the first edition of *Such Things Are* (London, 1788) are made parenthetically by act and page unless otherwise noted.

13. Terry Eagleton, *On Evil* (New Haven, CT: Yale University Press, 2010), 143.

14. Katharine M. Rogers, ed., *The Meridian Anthology of Restoration and Eighteenth-Century Plays by Women* (New York: Meridian, 1994).

15. Adrian Vickers, *A History of Modern Indonesia* (Cambridge: Cambridge University Press, 2005), 11.

16. For a thoughtful reading of this play in its colonial context, see Daniel O'Quinn, *Staging Governance: Theatrical Imperialism in London, 1770–1800* (Baltimore: Johns Hopkins University Press, 2005), 144–163.

17. Peter Haythornthwaite, "Mrs. Inchbald," *Dublin Review* 13, no. 2 (April 1885): 282.

18. My thanks to Julian Olds and Shelby Johnson for making this point abundantly clear as the Sultan and Arabella in a readers' theatre production of *Such Things Are* in Knoxville, Tennessee, on April 12, 2012.

19. Elizabeth Inchbald, *The Massacre: Taken from the French. A Tragedy, of Three Acts in Prose* (London: Printed for C.G.J. and J. Robinson, Pater-Noster Row, 1792), 8.

20. Inchbald, v.

21. Annibel Jenkins, *I'll Tell You What: The Life of Elizabeth Inchbald* (Lexington: University Press of Kentucky, 2003), 321.

22. William Godwin, *Things as They Are; or, The Adventures of Caleb Williams* (London: Printed for S. Crosby, Stationers-Court, Ludgate Street, 1794).

23. Chris Arnot, "Playwright Elizabeth Inchbald: A Clear Voice amid the Mob," *The Guardian*, June 15, 2009, http://www.theguardian.com/stage/theatreblog/2009/jun/15/playwright-elizabeth-inchbald-bury-theatre-royal.

24. "Director's Interview," Theatre Royal website, http://www.theatreroyal.org/theatre-information/history/restoring-the-repertoire/massacre/.

25. Mark Crossley, "Play Premieres after 250 Years," *East Anglia Daily Times*, June 24, 2009, http://www.eadt.co.uk/what-s-on/play_premieres_after_250_years_1_194890.

26. "Restoring a Georgian Playhouse: An Interview with Colin Blumenau," in *The Oxford Handbook of the Georgian Theatre*, ed. Julia Swindells and David Taylor (Oxford: Oxford University Press, 2014), 339.

27. Colin Blumenau, preface to *Wives as They Were, Maids as They Are* (Bury St. Edmunds: Stagescripts, 2008), 4.

28. Blumenau, 4.

29. Timothy Ramsden, "Love, Money and Morals in an Invigorating Amalgam," *ReviewsGate*, May 21, 2003,http://www.reviewsgate.com/index.php?name=News&file=article&sid=4152.

30. Shirley Strum Kenny, "Editing Restoration and Eighteenth-Century Plays," *Modern Philology* 85, no. 4 (1988): 409.

31. Kenny, 412.

32. "Wives as They Were, Maids as They Are," *Monthly Mirror*, April 1797, 249.

33. Interview with Colin Blumenau, email, January 9, 2014. I gratefully acknowledge Colin Blumenau's generosity in providing answers to my interview questions via email.

34. Hugh Homan, "Review of *Wives as They Were and Maids as They Are*," *The Stage* 11 (September 2008), http://www.thestage.co.uk/reviews/review.php/21735/wives-as-they-were-and-maids-as-they-are; Michael Billington, "Review of *Wives as They Were and Maids as They Are*," *The Guardian*, September 12, 2008, http://www.theguardian.com/stage/2008/sep/13/theatre.

35. Blumenau, interview, 2.

36. Joanne Mace, "Review of *Wives as They Were*," *Gazette*, September 13, 2008, http://www.basingstokegazette.co.uk/news/2452412.m5ec/?from=ec&to=2452412&l=review_wives_as_they_were_at_the_haymarket_until_october_4; Billington, "Review of *Wives as They Were and Maids as They Are*."

37. Blumenau, interview, 2.

38. Mace, "Review of *Wives as They Were*."

39. Ivan Howlett, "Forgotten Play Is a Real Gem," *East Anglian Daily Times*, April 23, 2008, http://www.eadt.co.uk/what-s-on/forgotten_play_is_a_real_gem_1_200007.

CHAPTER 2

The Structure of Fable in Inchbald's *Nature and Art*

Martha F. Bowden

In "Masculinity and Morality in Elizabeth Inchbald's *Nature and Art*," Shawn Lisa Maurer points to the 1796 novel's "failure to fit solidly within any generic category" as the explanation for the relative obscurity of *Nature and Art* compared with Inchbald's earlier novel *A Simple Story* (1791).[1] Is the work a story of women's oppression, of the inequities of social structure, of pure goodness versus studied opportunism, of false and true education? Maurer describes its opening as a "fairy tale" but also discusses the text as an illustration of the truly moral man. This distinction points directly at the fable, which traditionally has been seen as a means of conveying moral instruction, particularly for youth. Indeed, collections of fables were very popular and widely published in the period in which Inchbald was writing. Considering *Nature and Art* as a fable allows us to incorporate all the descriptors I have listed here in a single discussion of moral education and its relationship to power.[2]

The analyses of Annabel Patterson, Mark Loveridge, and Jayne Elizabeth Lewis, all of whom identify Aesop's fables as discourses of power from the point of view of the oppressed, support the premise of this essay, that a fabular structure underlies Inchbald's small but rich text, and that it provides a means of drawing gender and class issues into a more general emphasis on pedagogy and power.[3] While applying the motifs of the fable as a moral commentary on these issues, however, Inchbald does not cite or retell any recognizable fables from the classical and modern traditions. Instead, she uses the fable as an organizational strategy. The text is a series of scenes and vignettes that exemplify moral problems in the Aesopian manner; they often conclude with the moral sentiment they are meant to illustrate. This substructural form explains a number of features of the text that have been perceived as detrimental in the past and provides a locus for the overtly didactic strains of its commentary. As Patterson, Loveridge, and Lewis make clear, the fable collection was a standard of eighteenth-century publication. Well-known poets like John Dryden, John Gay, and Aphra Behn produced collections, and many other authors published translations, collections, and adaptations of individual fables. Lewis notes that from the 1740s to the 1770s, fables were used as part of a young woman's education. The texts were also read by young men; according to Loveridge, Aesop had been a school text in England since the sixteenth century.[4] Because Aesop was thought to be a contemporary of Homer, his fables, like Homer's epics, were considered the foundations on which all future genres were built. Thus, the fable would have been a familiar genre to Inchbald's audience, both men and women.

Patterson argues that the primary purpose of Aesop's fables is to allow the powerless to speak out against the inequities of their society, and that they were never meant to provide pleasant moral stories for children. She does not include Gay's fables in her analysis because she believes they are too transparently pedagogical.[5] For this essay, I am drawing on Gay's two series of fables (1727 and 1738), and Samuel Croxall's collection of Aesop's fables (1722).[6] Both collections were reprinted repeatedly throughout the eighteenth century and into the nineteenth, and were therefore available to Inchbald and her audience as a common frame of reference. Her readers would recognize that *Nature and Art* is both pedagogical itself and a reflection of the pedagogy of a popular form of narrative.

Gay's and Croxall's fables are useful in teasing out the resonances of the term *nature*, which Gay uses two senses: in the first place, nature is Mother Nature, the nurturing, authentic force without art or artifice, neither deceitful nor hiding menace. For example, as can be seen in figure 2.1, when the Dog in Gay's Fable XVII, "The Shepherd's Dog and the Wolf" (1727 series), tries to persuade the Wolf to stop preying on the Sheep, the Wolf replies that he is only behaving naturally:

> Nature design'd us beasts of prey
> As such when hunger finds a treat
> 'Tis necessary Wolves should eat. (23–25)

Henry Norwynne Junior is usually connected with nature in this sense, although he is more lamb than wolf. In the second place, nature is the essential self that lies beneath artifice and cannot be finally expunged; it wells up through the carapace of polish and education. Thus, in Fable XV, "The Philosopher and the Pheasants" (1727 series), the philosopher wonders what it is about human beings that makes animals run away: "Fly they our figure or our nature?" (14). The mother pheasant's warning to her children to be especially wary of men answers his question: "In him ingratitude you find, / A vice peculiar to the kind" (27–28). It is not the philosopher's appearance but his essential self that they fear.

The only fable in Croxall specifically identified with nature in the index, under the heading, "Nature: The force of it," also reflects this meaning. In "The Young

Figure 2.1. Uncredited 1757 illustration based on earlier versions, "The Shepherd's Dog and the Wolf," in *Fables by the Late Mr. Gay* (London, 1757). Image courtesy of E. Joe Johnson.

Man and his Cat," the young man, in love with his pet, prays to Venus to change her into a woman so that he can marry her. On the wedding night, however, the cat-bride reverts to her feline nature and jumps from the marriage bed to pursue a mouse. The goddess is "offended to see her sacred Rites profaned by such an indecent Behaviour" (274). But she also realizes that "her new Convert, though a Woman in outward Appearance, was a Cat in her Heart." As illustrated in figure 2.2, she restores the cat to her original state, "that her Manners and Person might be agreeable to each other" (274). Croxall's "application" or moral uses the story to illustrate the limits of education in overcoming nature: "Her Laws are so strong that it is in vain for us to oppose them; we may refine and improve, but can never totally alter her works" (275). Art can only do so much.

Maurer describes Henry Junior as a static character.[7] He is in fact a type rather than an individual, as Gay claims all his characters are, although many of them have been identified as references to Walpole: ". . . and I draw from general nature / Is't I or you then fix the satire?" (1738 series, 1:37–38). Henry's invariable goodness may be attributed to the transparency of his nature; nothing is hidden in it. In the same way, the depiction of William Norwynne Senior is not a specific indictment of the Church of England, nor of any particular cleric, any more than William Junior's character is intended to be a direct criticism of the law. Together they represent the power structures that serve to control and suppress the already powerless, here represented by Hannah Primrose, who is attacked and becomes pregnant by the younger William. The latter eventually sentences her to death without recognizing her. Annibel Jenkins, who links the satire in the novel with the subject matter of the prints being sold in London at the time, describes the text as "Inchbald's ironic view of everything in her world."[8]

The good-natured characters, including old and young Henry Norwynne, Rebecca Rymer, and Hannah Primrose, are helpless in the face of merciless power. On the other hand, William Junior, whom Maurer describes accurately as more interesting because more complex than Henry, is the character in whom nature, in the second sense used in the Aesopian fable, erupts on occasion through the art that disguises it, causing him to feel guilt, longing, and self-disgust. Maurer makes the same point when she contends that "nature" and "art" form not a dichotomy but a continuum, and that each of the four main characters requires interactions with one of the others to highlight the tension between the two forces.[9] Employing the two definitions of nature that I have identified earlier, Jenkins points out that any rigid schema that places each character definitively in the category of either nature or art is doomed to failure. She notes that while Henry Senior is normally connected with nature, the violin playing by which he saves William and himself from penury and pays for William's education is in fact an art. She argues that nature itself, the domain of Mother Nature, "Offered very little pleasure and no profit, however tempting the idea of escaping the evils of civilization." Henry Senior's retreat into the pure nature of

FABLE CLXII. *The* Young Man *and his* Cat.

A Certain young Man uſed to play with a Cat; of which he grew ſo fond, that at laſt he fell in Love with it, and to ſuch a Degree, that he could reſt neither Night nor Day for the Exceſs of his Paſſion. At laſt he prayed to *Venus*, the Goddeſs of Beauty, to pity him, and relieve his Pain. The good-natured Goddeſs was propitious, and heard his Prayers; before he aroſe up from kneeling, the Cat, which he held in his Arms, was transformed into a beautiful Girl. The Youth was tranſported with Joy, and married her that very Day. At night they went to Bed, and as the new Bride lay encircled in the Embraces of her amorous Huſband, ſhe unfortunately heard a Mouſe behind the Hangings, and ſprung from his Arms to purſue it. *Venus*, offended to ſee her ſacred Rites profaned by ſuch an indecent Behaviour; and perceiving that her new Convert, though a Woman in outward Appearance, was a Cat in her Heart, ſhe made her return to her old Form again, that her Manners and Perſon might be agreeable to each other.

The

Figure 2.2. Fable CLXII, "The Young Man and his Cat," in Samuel Croxall, *Fables of Aesop and Others: Translated into English with Instructive Applications and a Print before each Fable*, 14th ed. (London, 1789), 274. Image courtesy of the author.

the African continent nearly results in his death and that of his son. Hannah's fate and her child's "offer the most dramatic example of the real tragedy of relying on Nature—pure innocence without the constraint of the 'art' of reason."[10]

The Pedagogical Context of Inchbald's Fable

Emile, Jean-Jacques Rousseau's 1762 treatise on "natural" pedagogy, which Maurer identifies as a significant background text for *Nature and Art*, might be seen as an obstacle in considering *Nature and Art* as a form of modern fable, because Rousseau completely disapproved of letting young people read both Aesop and his seventeenth-century French adaptor Jean de La Fontaine. In context, however, Rousseau is objecting to teaching children to read at all: "Emile will never learn anything by heart, not even fables, not even those of La Fontaine," because they are "only words," and Rousseau argues that children do not learn from words but only images; what appears to be book learning is, in reality, parroting. For this reason, Emile will not read a book until he is twelve. What is more, fable morality is useless to children: no child understands the morals but, in fact, it "would be still worse if they did, for the morals in them are so mixed and disproportionate to their age that it would lead them more to vice than virtue." Rousseau maintains that children inevitably learn the wrong moral: they "make fun of the crow but they all take a fancy to the fox." In dismissing fables for children, however, he claims, "Fables instruct men, but the naked truth has to be told to children."[11] And that is the point: Inchbald is not writing *Nature and Art* for children but about them; the adults who read it will be able to locate the correct morals, and to admire those characters who deserve admiration. Patterson explains that Locke, whose *Some Thoughts Concerning Education* (1693) was highly influential in the period, especially for Rousseau when he came to write *Emile*,[12] owned at least six collections of fables, and that Locke believed that children should read Aesop so that they could reflect upon the fables as adults. He published a Latin version of Aesop for children, with English translations interleaved. Such a volume would fulfill the two purposes for placing Aesop in the hands of children: to teach them lessons in morality while at the same time giving them a straightforward Latin text in preparation for eventually tackling Virgil and Horace.[13]

Loveridge links fables with the eighteenth-century novel as a prose form that, in the right hands, provides moral instruction to readers. He sees a change in the use of the fable through the period: "moral and political" readings in the early part of the century give way to "moral and sentimental" explication by the 1770s.[14] After Gay's deliberate yoking of fable and political critique, especially in the 1738 series, authors began to back off from overt political interpretation and to retreat into a neutral zone with their collections.[15] *Nature and Art* employs both approaches to moral fable, the political, in the careers of the two Williams, and the sentimental, in the fortunes and misfortunes of the Henrys and the two women. Hannah Primrose's story engages both the sentimental and the political because her fate and that of her child invoke strong sympathy while also acting as an illustration of the power of class and gender. According to Maurer, readers frequently have difficulty with a perceived disjunction between the two volumes: "They find a problematic dissonance between the largely satiric first volume . . . and the tragic, sentimental, indeed even at times melodramatic second volume."[16] Examining the novel's fabular strategies resolves the dilemma, since the fable can be presented both satirically and sentimentally.

Both Croxall and Gay present their collections as pedagogical texts whose assumed audience is young people in need of guidance. Like most fable collections of the period, both Gay's and Croxall's books are illustrated. Because each fable has its own separate illustration, engravings in Gay and woodcuts in Croxall, the tale is doubly inscribed in word and image, an ancient pedagogical technique. Both Croxall's *Fables of Aesop and Others* (1722) and Gay's *Fables* (1727) are dedicated to children of the aristocracy. Croxall dedicates his book to George, Viscount Sunbury, Baron Halifax, son of the first Earl of Halifax, claiming that he did so because the young viscount's precocity inspired the work:

> You must not be surprised at my begging Your Protection for this little Book, when I assure You it was principally intended for Your Perusal. I had often wished to see something of this Kind published by an able Hand: And, for want of that, have sometimes had an Inclination to do it myself: But never came to any Resolution in that Point, till very lately; when, at *Horton*, I had the pleasure to find your Lordship, though but in your fifth Year, capable of reading any Thing in the *English* Tongue without the least hesitation. ("Dedication," n.p.)

The fables he sets before this precocious child, who would have been seven years old when the book was first published,[17] are "Lectures of Morality" that will instruct him in the virtues required for him to live up to his admirable and illustrious father, whom Croxall praises later in the dedication. The stories "abound in a Variety of Instruction, Moral and Political . . . and demonstrate to us, by a Kind of Example, every Virtue which claims our best Regards, and every Vice which we are most concerned to avoid" ("Dedication").

Gay's first series is dedicated to William Augustus, Duke of Cumberland and the son of George II. Prince William, who would have been six when the volume was published, appears not to have imbibed much moral instruction from the book, or perhaps he reversed the utility Croxall applauds, by following vice and avoiding virtue. He is known to history as the Butcher of Culloden for his ferocious treatment of the Stuart supporters in the Jacobite Rebellion of 1745 (Gay, 2.621). The dedication appears in the first fable, "The Lyon, the Tyger, and the Traveller," which concerns itself with the correct behavior of a monarch. The preliminary to the tale, which is nearly as long as the fable itself, urges Prince William to

> Accept . . . the moral lay,
> And in these tales mankind survey;
> With early virtues plant your breast,
> The specious arts of vice detest. (1–4)

His second, more seriously political, series, from 1738, has no single dedicatee. Instead, each fable opens with a prologue addressed to a different entity, generally a type and not a specific historical individual, for example, "To a Lawyer," "To a Friend in the Country."

Croxall's introduction takes the traditional form of a life of Aesop; Gay, however, introduces the 1727 collection with a dialogue between a philosopher and a shepherd about the origins of wisdom. The Shepherd claims that study and travel are insufficient for learning about human beings, "For man is practis'd in disguise" (29). Instead, "The little knowledge I have gain'd / Was all from simple nature drain'd" (33–34). In addition to learning from nature and the animal kingdom how to live a good life and to despise vice, he also learns how to eschew affectation and cruelty:

> From nature too I take my rule
> To shun contempt and ridicule.
> I never with important air
> In conversation overbear;
> Can grave and formal pass for wise,
> When men the solemn owl despise? (51–56)

The artifice of vice that hides true nature under a pleasant surface causes many misunderstandings in the Inchbald novel: young Henry is constantly being misled by surfaces and gets himself into trouble by seeing people and their actions with the clear literalness of nature. Hannah Primrose, in the unguarded state of her artless mind and heart, cannot fathom that young William would not contemplate marrying her under any circumstances.

Croxall's table of contents and index provide further indications of his pedagogical intent. The table of contents is an alphabetical index of titles rather than a list that follows the order of the volume; the index itself is an alphabetized guide to the principles and characteristics elucidated in the fables. These paratextual features suggest that the book is not designed to be read straight through from start to finish but selectively as particular qualities or virtues need to be emphasized. The alphabetized table of contents suggests familiarity with the fables in the book since it assists the knowledgeable teacher or student in finding specific stories quickly, as if looking up a recipe in a cookery book or a cure in a manual of medicine.

Gay's second set of fables, which is darker and more overtly political than the first, allows us to consider power more specifically, although there are some references to essential gifts and personality. For example, educating a young dunce in the arts or sciences merely spoils a good tradesman:

> Whether he blunders at the bar,
> Or owes his infamy to war,
> Or if by license or degree
> The sexton shares the doctors fee,
> Or from the pulpit by the hour
> His weekly floods of nonsense pour,
> We find (th'intent of nature foil'd)
> A taylor or a butler spoil'd.[18]

But in this series, he is more directly, and less cheerily, concerned with power and politics; this fable also refers to incapable people being promoted to important positions because they are friends of the minister and not because they have any ability. The long prologues that preface each tale and the extended morals at the end cause the tales themselves to appear almost secondary; they are there to illustrate the argument of the prologues and provide an example for the morals to reflect upon, rather than the prologue serving to introduce the tale and the application to underline the moral lesson. These particular fables therefore provide a useful bridge to a novel like *Nature and Art*, which both appropriates and transforms the fable structure. When fable is appropriated by the novel, the narrative omits the tale and its articulate animals altogether and presents instead only the prologue and its application, with their direct references to human nature.

The Fabular Characteristics of *Nature and Art*

Maurer's introduction to the novel describes it as "both treatise and tragedy," that "speaks in the timeless voice of the fairy tale, yet its incidents depend upon a historically specific engagement with contemporary concerns."[19] The specificity of the historical reference, however, suggests the fable rather than the fairy tale; fables are much more connected to reality, on occasion introducing historical characters and always avoiding magical resolutions to the conflicts they describe. Thus, the tale itself begins in the manner of fable, rather than the fairy tale: "At a time when the nobility of Britain were said by the Poet Laureate, to admire and protect the arts, and were known by the whole nation to be patrons of music—William and Henry, youths under twenty years of age, brothers, and the sons of a country shopkeeper who had lately died insolvent, set out on foot for London, in the hope of procuring by their industry a scanty subsistence."[20] Not "once upon a time, far, far away," but in Britain, with two recently orphaned brothers traveling to London to seek their fortunes. The hint at a kind of golden age is undermined by the ironic tone of the comments about the poet laureate and the generosity of the nobility toward the arts. The chronology is vague, however, as in a fiction rather than a history, and the brothers' last name is not revealed until chapter 23 (89). By setting up the polarities of the pairs of attributes and characters—nature and art; Henry and William in two generations; Hannah and Rebecca, the two heroines—Inchbald further invokes the moral structure of the fable. Fairy tales more often have three characters, with a pattern of repetition followed by the exception of the third character: two ugly sisters and a beautiful one, for example. Jenkins points toward fable when she links Inchbald's texts with Hogarth's print series,[21] which include *Industry and Idleness* (1747), contrasting two apprentices, Francis Goodchild and Tom Idle, one of his "modern moral series."[22]

As an example of the vagueness of reference, William Senior's ecclesiastical career and especially his titles show a disjunction between the titles he assumes and the actual functioning of the Church of England. When William becomes a dean, he does not appear to be attached to any particular region or diocese; he winters in London and spends the summers in the country. Even in an age of pluralism and neglect, deans, whether diocesan or rural, had duties and obligations that he does not even attempt to fulfill; Maurer's footnote to the term conflates the two different titles, not surprisingly given that Inchbald does not engage him in any of the activities we would expect from either position (47n1). Rural deans had the oversight of specific nonurban portions of the diocese; diocesan deans had the oversight of the cathedral and official diocesan duties, besides writing the bishop's pamphlets for him, which appears to be William's main occupation. The diocesan dean, not the rural dean, was third in the church hierarchy, below archbishops and bishops. Should Inchbald have had any interest in portraying him realistically in his various duties, there would be references to diocesan politics and the cathedral clos. Further, when he is in the country, where there is a curate in place, he appears to exert clerical authority when, in fact, he would have no authority at all unless the curate were attending to one of William's livings or the summer home were in a rural dean's jurisdiction. William as dean and bishop represents not the church but social authority, as the curate's response makes clear: "For his own part, he had no will, judgment, or faculties; but that he submitted in all things to the superior clergy" (120). William as clergyman, therefore, is not an indictment of the church alone but a representative of the hierarchical structures of power, a representation that is reinforced when he acts as magistrate, in which position his chief role seems to be making Henry's, Rebecca's, and Hannah's lives as miserable as possible.

The episodic nature of the plot emphasizes the text's relationship to a collection of fables. An example is the story of Lady Clementina, William Senior's wife, and the libel, an episode that is a type of fable in structure and purpose. There is really no need for this incident from a plot perspective, nor does it seem to be necessary in order to develop her character. Lady Clementina, like Henry, is not a rounded character but a type—a wealthy, worldly, upper-class woman with a strong sense of entitlement. Instead, like most fables, the episode's chief purpose is to provide an occasion for the moral.[23] Inchbald describes Lady Clementina as a "fine lady," where the term *fine* is a synonym for *idle* (66). One day she returns from her visits in tears because someone has published a libel against her: "A public print has accused me of playing deep at my own house, and winning all the money" (67).[24] Her vanity is perfectly illustrated in the little detail that, in the midst of all her woes, she casts "her eye into a looking-glass to see how rage became her" (66). William, still a dean, and the bishop, who have been working on a pamphlet together, immediately go on the attack and decide that the author, the printer, and the publisher should be punished. But when the author of the libel arrives, he explains that not she but Lady Catherine Newland, who shares her initials, is the target. When Lady Clementina protests that Lady Catherine was never known to gamble, a vice to which she herself has admitted, he responds that he only chooses the innocent as his target: "We apprehend nothing from them—their own characters support them—but the guilty are very tenacious, and what they cannot secure by fair means, they will employ force to accomplish" (68). He concludes by assuring her, "I have too much regard for a wife and seven small children, who are maintained by my industry alone, to have written any thing in the nature of a libel upon your ladyship" (69). The author's defense becomes the application or moral on the nature of hypocrisy. The role of the author, who despite his subservient position nonetheless gets the last word, is an example of Loveridge's doubled fable: the dean and his wife appear to have won the contest, because they are assured that they are not the targets of his satire, but the author speaks the truth, accusing Lady Clementina of precisely the vice that the libel contains. Gay makes a similar point about self-conviction in the prologue, "To a Lawyer," to Fable I, 1738 series:

> If I lash vice in gen'ral fiction,
> Is't I apply or self-conviction?
> Brutes are my theme. Am I to blame,
> If men in morals are the same?
> . . .
> Who claims the fable, knows his right. (49–52, 56)

The general abuses of power and the specific nature of power exerted on women are exemplified in the lives of Inchbald's two heroines, Hannah Primrose and Rebecca Rymer. It is Hannah's natural goodness that causes her to be seduced by the naturally selfish William, and the power of reputation wielded by church and state, in the persons of William Senior, as magistrate, and the curate, Mr. Rymer, makes the sad ending of her story inevitable. Her punishment is mitigated to some extent when the dean discovers that the father of the child is his own son. The exposure of the latter's identity, as would be customary in cases where both man and woman are of Hannah's class, would denigrate the dean's own status. But nothing can ultimately protect her because of the ways in which women's virtue is defined. According to Katherine S. Green, Inchbald's "casual linking of 'evil institutions' to 'private life' would have been unmistakable references to the theory of necessity," popularized in England by John Thelwall, a radical thinker and spokesperson for the London Corresponding Society, to which a close friend of Inchbald's, William Godwin, belonged.[25] Necessitarianism, a theory that appears to negate the possibility of free will, would make Hannah's fate unavoidable: "Such women become criminals as a result of their victimization by systems associated with patronage and patriarchy: organized religion, institutions of the law, society, and even family."[26] These are precisely the institutions that fable addresses, in its indirect and sometimes doubled way, and thus the fable is a logical vehicle for a woman to adopt when arguing against a power structure.

Rebecca also demonstrates her true nature, first in accepting the child and caring for him and then, when all is revealed and she gives him up, agreeing to wait to be married to Henry Junior while he seeks his long-lost father. In between, however, her false confession to being the mother of the child is precisely what the abuses of power lead us to expect. The confession is wrung out of her by her father and the dean; coercion gets the bully the desired result, but not necessarily the truth. That in itself is a moral fable, as Inchbald's summative comments suggest. When Rebecca first faces her father, "his crimsoned face, knit brow, and thundering voice, struck with terror her very soul." Inchbald reflects, "Innocence is not always a protection against fear—sometimes less bold than guilt" (101–102). Rebecca, under the pressure of her family's interrogation, is "beguiled by solicitations, and terrified by threats, like women formerly accused of witchcraft, and other wretches put to the torture," and therefore "thought her present sufferings worse than any that could possibly succeed, and felt inclined to confess a falsehood . . . to obtain a momentary respite from reproach" (103). This direct parallel between Rebecca's story and historical incidents—witch trials and torture—resembles the kind of explication in Croxall, in which the exploits of the animal figures are read as parables of human behavior.

Both Hannah and Rebecca are true to their natures, as Aesop would predict; they cannot be otherwise, like the cat turned into the beautiful lady. Their very different endings are related not to their loving different people but to their own knowledge of the world. Hannah is unable to see William's true nature and therefore loves his external, artificial self. Her lack of perception is symbolized in her difficulty in reading William's letter, which takes her "two weeks, day and night, to find out the exact words" (87). Rebecca, whose innate good sense is enriched by the education that her class provides her, is able to see past William to Henry and therefore to love a man who will not try her virtue, although he certainly tries her patience. Confident in her fidelity—rightly so—he returns after nearly twenty years to an aged Rebecca who, in his eyes, is still the beautiful young woman he loves. But then, her beauty was always in his eyes anyway. The two women together form a fable about nature, education, and the arbitrary and unjust workings of social prejudice.

Jenkins points out that, despite the fairy-tale nature of the opening, the novel is quite realistic in its portrayal of Henry: even with the very good income he makes as a musician, he cannot be considered a gentleman because of his profession. He thus uses his income to send William to the university, where he will be prepared for a more socially acceptable occupation. Describing the novel's neglect as "unfortunate," she points out that it "is a direct commentary on some of the major characteristics of the 1790s . . . as that world was revealed in the newspapers, prints, plays, and most of all, in the hundreds of conversations that floated about London."[27] Nowhere is the realism so evident as in the ending, which is certainly no fairy tale. It would take the magic of fairy tale or the loose attachment to realism of the early romance to bring about a happily-ever-after scenario at the end of this story. Rebecca and the two Henrys are united after years of separation, but although Rebecca continues to be beautiful in Henry's eyes, even he has to admit that they are no longer young and have missed out on parentage. They are certainly brave in the face of the many blows that fate issues because nature has given them the character to recognize the virtues of their situation: "By forming an humble scheme for their remaining life, a scheme depending upon their *own* exertions alone, on no light promises of pretended friends, and on no sanguine hopes of certain success; but with prudent apprehension, with fortitude against disappointment, Henry, his son, and Rebecca, (now his daughter) found themselves, at the end of one year in the enjoyment of every comfort which such distinguished minds knew how to taste" (152–153). Repeating the dichotomy in her title, Inchbald claims that they are "alive to every fruition with which nature blesses the world; dead to all out of their power to attain, the works of art." Their resources allow them "a small house, or hut, placed on the borders of the sea," and a garden that produces enough food to feed them and have something left over to take to market (153). Maurer points out that even this ending is in fact unrealistic, despite its lack of creature comfort: "We are never told how Henry and his son, who have spent nearly two decades in an attempt to return to England, or the impoverished Rebecca, who has passed the years waiting for Henry's return by eking out a simple living with sewing and spinning, managed to purchase, or even lease, their hut."[28]

This ending, however, is not as stark as the original one, which Inchbald revised after some criticism. The first edition ends with the younger Henry's ironic statement in response to his father's announcement that the poor enjoy a pleasure unknown to the rich, "one token of esteem from the person whom we consider as our superior." Rebecca adds that the rarity of the gift makes it even more valuable, to which Henry replies, "Certainly . . . and yet those in poverty, ungrateful as they are, murmur against that government from which they receive the blessing" (154). In the second edition, Inchbald continues the conversation, with Henry Senior claiming that the poor are subservient as a result of "early education, of early prejudice," an impression so deep that it is retained into adulthood. Henry Junior calls for a new world in which "the idol" of material possessions and desire for wealth "will be broken," so that the poor will "no more be their own persecutors" (154). In the first edition, Henry's statement about the ungrateful poor is followed by a more extended commentary on the state of the world, which suggests that the only way to cope is to leave running the country to the politicians, just as society leaves other aspects of life to the professions—physicians, lawyers and soldiers. He ends rather fatalistically: "That it is not upon earth that we are to look for a state of perfection—it is only in heaven—and there, we may rest assured, that no practitioner in the professions I have named, will ever be admitted to disturb our eternal felicity" (156–157).

Maurer, who includes the original conclusion in the Broadview edition, calls it "strangely ironic," citing the *Moral and Political Magazine*, which dismissed it as "a piece of irony so ill placed, that it is painful, and even with some readers is liable to be misunderstood for the serious expression of the writer's sentiment" (156).[29] But in its very irony, it resembles fable more closely than does the hopeful statement of the second or the *Candide*-like garden cultivation in both books. Fables never end with a deus ex machina rescue for the characters; the endings of fables are consonant with life in our own world, in which human nature experiences no magical transformation. Gay's fable "The Butterfly and the Snail" exemplifies the unavoidable constancy of nature:

I own my humble life, good friend;
Snail was I born, and snail shall end.
And what's a butterfly? At best,
He's but a caterpillar drest:
And all thy race (a num'rous seed)
Shall prove of caterpillar breed.[30]

Likewise, all Aesop's animals have to be true to their natures and cannot avoid their fates. Thus in Croxall's "The Stag in the Ox-Stall," while the Stag is able to hide for a time in the barn, because neither the servant nor the bailiff looks very carefully around the place, when the Master arrives, the Stag cannot avoid his "hundred eyes." Croxall's moral is "That nobody looks after a man's affairs so well as himself," but the Stag's end is equally about the impossibility of avoiding the inevitable (33–35). In Croxall's Aesop, predators prey on the weak: "When a cruel ill-natured Man has a mind to abuse one inferior to himself, either in Power or Courage, though he has not given the least Occasion for it, how does he resemble the Wolf... whenever ill People are in Power, Innocence and Integrity are sure to be persecuted" ("The Wolf and the Lamb," 3–4).

In Henry's contention that there will be no lawyers, soldiers, or physicians in heaven to disturb the hard-won peace of the poor, we see in miniature the critique of power with which the text has been concerned. Like all fables, it takes a dim view of the high and mighty but does not unseat them. Gay's "The Council of Horses" (Fable XLIII, 1727 series) is a mordant tale whose final message is to accept subjugation for a time in order to enjoy an eventual retirement: "Appease your discontented mind, / And act the part by Heav'n assign'd" (61–62). The colt has argued that horses are not by their natures designed to be enslaved by human beings, but, having heard the wise old steed's advice, "The colt submitted, / And, like his ancestors, was bitted" (63–64). Yet the doubled meaning that Loveridge locates in the fables is here as well; arguing for the "energy of paradox," he claims that parables and fables work "for and against structures of power, inside and outside them."[31] The two Henrys and Rebecca appear overwhelmed by social factors they are unable to withstand, while their tormentors rest secure in their comfort, even in the grave, but it is clear that the family has triumphed in that their lives are filled with love, fidelity, and peace. When the two Henrys finally return from Africa and are on their way to Anfield to retrieve Rebecca, they meet William Senior's funeral procession, which they join "at a little distance"; they are "the only real mourners in the train... in rags, but in tears" (146).

The rest of the Williams' story is filled in by an Aesop-like figure, a poor laborer who comments on the fate of his social superiors. Lady Clementina has been dead for four years, killed by her own vanity: "she caught cold by wearing a new-fashioned dress that did not half cover her," a description that is "concluded with a hearty laugh" (146–147). The laborer's eulogy on the bishop is even worse: he speculates that the bishop is in hell, claims he had no use for the poor, and announces, "I should be sorry that my master's sheep... should have no better pastor—the fox would soon get them all" (147). This statement reverses the application back into the animal world of fable at the same time as it twists ironically the standard image of the bishop as the shepherd of his flock. William Junior, meanwhile, is alive and in his father's house, "as proud as Lucifer," but without his wife: "She made a mistake, and went to another man's bed—and so her husband and she were parted—and she has married the other man." With unconscious irony, in his ignorance of the two Williams' behavior toward Hannah Primrose, he notes that any other person, "my wife or yours," would have been made to fulfill the prescribed penalty for adultery, "do her penance in a white sheet—but as it was a lady, why, it was all very well." Henry Senior provides the moral to these episodes, which demonstrate "want of charity and Christian deportment.... He almost wished himself back on his savage island, where brotherly love could not be less than it appeared to be in this civilized country" (148).

By contrast, Henry, his father, and Rebecca are living blameless, even happy, lives and are spared the contempt of their neighbors, which his uncle and cousin have earned. They are in neither the ordered community of a utopia nor the easeful bounty of a golden age pastoral, but they do have both community and subsistence and are "exempt from patronage and from controul" (153). Since the story of their relatives has indicated just how little peace or joy the works of art bring, their fable has a propitious ending, fixed within the natural world and bounded by its realities. That is the closest fable comes to a happy ending: that the necessities and natural laws that bound our lives will at some point work in our favor. Inchbald's muted ending, more realistic than triumphant, indicates the rewards that the world truly grants to virtue. Its very realism confirms the employment of the structure of fable.

NOTES

1. Shawn Lisa Maurer, "Masculinity and Morality in Elizabeth Inchbald's *Nature and Art*," in *Women, Revolution, and the Novels of the 1790s*, ed. Linda Lang-Peralta (East Lansing: Michigan State University Press, 1999), 155. Maurer also thinks the critical neglect can be attributed to the novel's focus on successive generations of men, not women, like *A Simple Story*. Some of the few existing critical analyses do focus on the women of the text, however, especially Hannah Primrose.

2. This essay fulfills a charge I was given many years ago. When she was writing *I'll Tell You What*, Annibel Jenkins insisted on more than one occasion that I should write about *Nature and Art*. At the time, I was working on a project on the Church of England, and she believed that the Inchbald work would be very interesting to me for that reason. It is indeed interesting to me, although I do not think it is really a book about the church. Investigating this novel, however, has given me an opportunity to pursue a different line of inquiry, one that has interested me for some years now. Annibel continues to direct our work, even beyond the grave.

3. Annabel Patterson, *Fables of Power: Aesopian Writing and Political History* (Durham, NC: Duke University Press, 1991); Mark Loveridge, *A History of Augustan Fable* (Cambridge: Cambridge University Press, 1999); Jayne Elizabeth Lewis, *The English Fable: Aesop and Literary Culture, 1651–1740* (Cambridge: Cambridge University Press, 1996).

4. Lewis, *English Fable*, 12, 48; Loveridge, *History of Augustan Fable*, 55.

5. Patterson, *Fables of Power*, 149. Loveridge describes Lewis's argument as a "riposte" to Patterson's argument against Aesop as a text for children (*History of Augustan Fable*, 4).

6. John Gay, *Poetry and Prose*, ed. Vinton A. Dearing and Charles E. Beckwith, 2 vols. (Oxford: Clarendon Press, 1974); Samuel Croxall, *Fables of Aesop and Others: Translated into English with Instructive Applications and a Print before each Fable*, 14th ed. (London, 1789). I am using the fourteenth edition rather than an earlier one because it is so close in date to the publication of *Nature and Art* (1796). All references to Gay and Croxall will be from these editions and will be cited parenthetically in the body of the essay. Gay's fables are cited by line number and Croxall's by page number.

7. Maurer, "Masculinity and Morality," 159.

8. Annibel Jenkins, *I'll Tell You What: The Life of Elizabeth Inchbald* (Lexington: University Press of Kentucky, 2003), 385.

9. Maurer, "Masculinity and Morality," 158.

10. Jenkins, *I'll Tell You What*, 383.

11. Jean-Jacques Rousseau, *Emile, or On Education*, intro., trans., and notes by Allen Bloom (New York: Basic Books, 1979), 112–117.

12. "This book is of capital importance for Rousseau's project, not only because he adopts much of it, but especially because it represents the other great modern alternative" (Patterson, *Fables of Power*, 481n4). Locke and Rousseau differ markedly, however, in their opinions on the utility of fable.

13. Patterson, *Fables of Power*, 137.

14. Loveridge, *History of Augustan Fable*, 43, 73.

15. Loveridge, 55.

16. Shawn Lisa Maurer, "Introduction," Elizabeth Inchbald, *Nature and Art*, ed. Shawn Lisa Maurer (Peterborough, ON: Broadview Press, 2005), 21.

17. W. A. Speck, "Dunk, George Montagu, Second Earl of Halifax (1716–1771)," *Oxford Dictionary of National Biography* (Oxford: Oxford University Press, 2004; online ed., May 2006), accessed July 30, 2014, https://doi.org/10.1093/ref:odnb/8266.

18. Fable XIV, 1738 series, "The Owl, the Swan, the Cock, the Spider, the Ass, and the Farmer," 39–46.

19. Maurer, 20.

20. Elizabeth Inchbald, *Nature and Art*, ed. Shawn Lisa Maurer (Peterborough: Broadview Press, 2005), 41. All references to *Nature and Art* will be from this edition and will be incorporated into the essay parenthetically by page number.

21. Jenkins, *I'll Tell You What*, 385.

22. "Hogarth: Hogarth's Modern Moral Series," *Hogarth*, exhibition, Tate Britain, February 7 to April 29, 2007, Tate Museum, http://www.tate.org.uk/whats-on/tate-britain/exhibition/hogarth, accessed August 1, 2014.

23. Gay's letter to Swift of May 16, 1732, suggests that he started with the moral and then wrote a fable to illustrate it: "Though this is a kind of writing that appears very easy, I find it the most difficult of any that I ever undertook; after I have invented one Fable, and finish'd it, I despair of finding out another; But I have a moral or two more which I wish to write upon" (Gay, *Poetry and Prose*, 2:631).

24. By "print," she means not an image but a paragraph, which is obvious when her husband reads it.

25. Katherine S. Green, "'The Idol Will Be Broken': Necessitarianism, Class, and Gender in Inchbald's *Nature and Art*," *New Perspectives on the Eighteenth Century* 8, no. 1 (Spring 2011): 3–4.

26. Green, 9.

27. Jenkins, *I'll Tell You What*, 373–374.

28. Maurer, "Masculinity and Morality," 172.

29. "Nature and Art. By Mrs. Inchbald. 2 vols, small octavo, 6s. Robinsons. [Concluded.]," *The Moral and Political Magazine of the London Corresponding Society*, September 1796, 177–180. The review of Inchbald's volume can be found in the "Review of Books" section in the magazine.

30. Fable XXIV, 1727 series, 39–44.

31. Loveridge, *History of Augustan Fable*, 30.

CHAPTER 3

Narratives of Emerging Markets and Mercantilist Mappings in Defoe's London

Mita Choudhury

"She was a wonder, a legend," notes Bernard Porter in an online review—"the writer Alexander Kinglake said that when he was a child in the 1820s Lady Hester Stanhope's name was as well known to him as Robinson Crusoe's, though he thought Crusoe was more believable."[1] Lady Hester Stanhope represents, one might argue, a destabilizing force in British culture because she was not only a woman fascinated by the Middle East but also one who frequently assumed the garb of a Middle Eastern man. To Alexander Kinglake (author of *Eothen: Traces of Travel Brought Home from the East* [1844]) and other producers and consumers of travel narratives, Stanhope's legendary status was thus linked to images of her masquerading as a Syrian soldier, a Bedouin Arab, or an Albanian chief. Her flamboyant performances were not on the London stage but on location, in Syria, from where Stanhope emerged as—to use Joseph Roach's term—"a mass-circulation image." Of little interest to the British consumer was the archaeological significance of Tadmor or the glories of the Mesopotamian civilization. Instead, British consumer culture was decidedly modern and fully invested in what Roach has described as the It-Effect, a "personality-driven mass attraction," which in this case capitalized on Stanhope's delightfully deviant self-fashioning, her self-imposed exile (in Barbary), her cross-dressing, her horsemanship, her messianic fantasies, and her serial lovers.[2]

In Kinglake's nostalgic retrospection, Robinson Crusoe appears, in contrast to Stanhope, as a sober and reflective voyager whose pilgrimage also evokes awe but for radically different reasons—or so one would assume if Kinglake was thinking only of Defoe's *Crusoe*. Later in the century, thanks to Richard Brinsley Sheridan and (composer) Thomas Linley Sr., Defoe's classic was revived with an innovative twist: *Robinson Crusoe; or Harlequin Friday*, an afterpiece first performed at Drury Lane on January 29, 1781, which went on to have a modest run.[3] Of significance to the discussion here is this artistic maneuver from Crusoe to Friday, from formal narrative to playful pantomime, from substance to entertainment, and from the didactic to the realm of pure pleasure. In individual and collective memory, the real and the imagined are often indistinguishable and can be equally powerful, especially in retrospect, and easily substituted, one for the other. Thus, both theories of the narrative and the methodologies employed, say, in biographies show that the real and the imagined coexist despite the disciplining strictures of genre distinctions that fail to regulate the porous borders between fiction and fact.[4] Therefore, the materiality of Defoe's *Robinson Crusoe* and the corporeality of the legendary Hester Stanhope evoke—in equal measure and through heightened images of distance and difference—intense reactions that do not have to acknowledge the divide between that which is realistic or "believable" and that which is real.[5]

New geographic knowledge led to the refinement of existing cartographic skills and to the proliferation of mercantilist ventures that bolstered the economic might of the various competing European maritime powers, including Britain, France, Holland, Portugal, and Spain. Crusoe and Stanhope catered to this collective Pan-European desire for the fusion of geography, cartography, and commerce packaged as fantasy or mythology. I launch this discussion of British mercantilism in the eighteenth century as a narrative trope with reference to Crusoe and Stanhope to underscore the point that neither posed a threat to the establishment, particularly to the imperatives for discovery (sexual, material, or spiritual) and the more strategic game plan for trade, commerce, and the pursuit of empire. In what form, then, does the threat to nation or civilization, such as it was, emerge?

Pursuing a provisional response to this question, I turn to a "maritime history," which is important neither because it is a reliable documentation of eighteenth-century mercantilist ventures, nor because it represents a sophisticated narrative style or creative substance, but because it raises important issues about the mechanisms that legitimized mercantilist ventures—mechanisms that, in retrospect, reveal the frenetic efforts to protect and preserve the ambitious scope of Enlightenment (in this case, British) geography:[6] *A General History of the Pyrates* (1724).[7] This voluminous compendium of the lives of pirates has suffered because of its contested status in the Defoe canon. It has been relegated to the margins of critical discourse about early eighteenth-century culture, refused admission to the hall of maritime or travel historiographies, and denied literary status due, at least in part, to its identification as a "minor work of literature" by none other than Manuel Schonhorn, the scholar who has argued most vociferously for its inclusion in the Defoe canon.[8] Whether authored by the mysterious Captain Charles Johnson or by the prolific Daniel Defoe, this "history" presents, in a remarkable blend of fact and fiction, prosaic accounts of high-stakes games in the perilous seas, thick descriptions of catastrophic encounters with various Others, and unpredictable reversals of fortune. Moreover, the vast scale of this *History*, spanning the Eastern, Western, Northern, and Southern Hemispheres, exposes the potency and efficacy of maritime schemes launched and executed in the *absence* of state sponsorship and almost exclusively beyond the borders of what was regarded as civil society. Charting a parallel territorial expansionism and drawing a radically different map from the one that anchors state-sponsored naval enterprise as well as bona fide trade and commerce, this *History* challenges all the assumptions of legitimacy and law that came to be associated with the Enlightenment not just in Britain but in Europe in general.

I argue here that this bastard *History* thus provides the ideal occasion for a discussion of what I see as several related issues, including the pathology of maritime criminality; the scientific foundations of eighteenth-century maps versus the subversive potential of pirates' rough-hewn charts; and the function of (what might be considered in retrospect as) grotesque portraits of disenfranchised imperialists. I argue in conclusion that the economic viability of empire was dependent upon the identification and systematic elimination of rogues (or rogue states in today's parlance), at a time when Defoe and his contemporaries were laying the foundation for a London that would be the preeminent imperial capital.[9]

The Pathology of Maritime Criminality

Maritime criminality was seldom perceived or described as such. The mythmaking projects that Captain Cook and his exploits spawned were cast in the Crusoesque mold with the added value of the discovery of "real" prospects on the vast Pacific. Beginning with the work of Marshall Sahlins and of Gananath Obeyesekere, and continuing on to the recent revisionist perspectives on these exploits, the story of Cook and others of his ilk has been stripped of the romantic aura that Victorian imperialism used as a suitable crutch for the times.[10] Obeyesekere was the first to establish decisively the connection between Cook and Kurtz, while Sahlins discussed why Cook's acts of going native could no longer be whitewashed and packaged as innocuous divergences from stated goals. On the Hawaiian island, the imported god of plenty was, in fact, in search of greener pastures that would replenish the resources of the British Isles, which had to maintain a competitive edge among the competing European maritime powers. But the yarns woven by, for instance, Cook's biographer J. C. Beaglehole and the evaluative criteria laid out in Ian Watt's influential "rise of the realist novel" demonstrated the lingering power of Enlightenment mythmaking projects and the unshakable foundations of "great works"—illustrating for our purposes here and now the extent to which modernity had yet to throw off the yokes of early modernity.[11] In fact, the scholarship of the post-World War II period remained committed to the recuperation and systematic studies of tradition (rational objective), with nostalgia providing the main impetus for such projects (underlying sentiment). Narratives of maritime criminality—such as those contained in *A General History of the Pyrates*—were thus marginalized because they were neither literary nor historical (commissioned by the state). To the contrary, they were anomalous and aberrant; therefore, to sustain the "order of things" they had to be appropriately tagged in the print culture as "other."[12]

Throughout the eighteenth century, the systematic legitimization of voyages of discovery came to have a reciprocal relationship with (or dependency on) the print industry that capitalized on the exuberant demand for (real or imagined) discovery. *Robinson Crusoe* was first published in 1719. James Cook embarked upon his first voyage in 1768. And these are, of course, the tip of the proverbial iceberg. Realism—a vital element driving the demand and supply in the booming print industry—necessitated the accommodation of the threats to these uplifting endeavors. And the threats to the kind of civilized order or disciplined culture that Defoe visualized, for instance, came in many different forms: the massive depopulation that a plague could bring about; the primitive instincts of natives in distant lands who could defeat the spiritual instincts of the civilized; the human propensity to succumb to the calls of the flesh or the wild. It is in this sense that criminality and aberrant behaviors in general enjoyed a special (albeit not new) social status.[13]

Criminality extended from land to sea and back again to land, where the full measure of the legislative process could be enacted; but juridical authority could not be exercised in equal measure on land and sea because the links between the two realms were fragile and thus difficult to sustain. Shylock put it best when he summarized for the Renaissance spectator the dual sources of threats to commercial ventures thus: "But ships are but boards, sailors but men; there be *land* rats, and *water* rats, water thieves and land thieves—I mean pirates" (emphasis added). In this astute assessment of risks in the business of commerce, Shylock argued that the vulnerabilities are about equal on land and at sea; additionally, these threats are compounded by the fragility of both "boards" and (Christian) morals, neither of which, according to Shylock, should be taken for granted. "And then there is the peril of waters, winds and rocks."[14] This perception of the dual threat resonates through the early modern period, and certainly in the eighteenth century, which is when we find printed and bound in the same volume as *A General History of the Lives and Adventures of the Most Famous Highwaymen, Murderers, Street-Robbers etc.*, a companion piece with the following title: *A Genuine Account of the Voyages and Plunders of the most Notorious Pyrates*. Published in 1734, six years after the publication of *A Plan of the English Commerce* (1728), this sizable dissertation, consisting of 525 pages, is attributed to Captain Charles Johnson, a pseudonym that, according to some scholars, Defoe might have used. This volume represents a more comprehensive treatment of the subject of criminality than the one published ten years earlier, which focused only on the following: *A General History of the Robberies and Murders of the Most Notorious Pyrates, and their Policies, Discipline, and Government* (1724).[15]

The introduction to the 1734 edition reveals a subversive stance that makes a mockery of state-sponsored or establishment historiographies with delectable irony thus:

> What was Nimrod but a successful Free-booter? and what were all the founders of Monarchies, but Encroachers on the Properties of their Brethern and Neighbours? *Alexander* was a Plunderer of the first Magnitude, and all his extraordinary Exploits, with which we have so long been amused, and which we have been taught to speak of with so much Admiration, were only Robberies committed upon Men every Way better than himself. *Caesar*, that other prodigious Name, was a Plunderer of his native Country, or (as the great *Cowley* has warmly and nobly express'd it) *a Ravisher of his own Mother*. What better can we call any of his Successors who have sacrific'd the Lives and Liberties of Thousands of their Fellow-Creatures to an extravagant Passion? Whether we name it Tyranny, Ambition, or only Greatness of Soul, 'tis much the same, while the Effects of it are so very terrible. Happy are we that we can produce, at least, no modern instances of Robbers of this kind from our own Histories! (*Lives and Adventures*, 1)

Notice that this mockery is directed at legends created and sustained elsewhere by populist mythologies that, according to the author, should not be allowed to make truth claims. If the effects of action are "terrible," in other words, then, irrespective of social or cultural status, the action must be regarded in retrospect as being tainted. Perhaps unsurprisingly, the opening paragraph of this introduction ends with an invocation to nationalist sentiment thus: "Our own Histories" are distinctive and different.[16] Additionally, the treatment of the issue of criminality is not as simplistic as one might expect, for in the paragraph immediately following the one just quoted, the author identifies the then collective source of anxiety thus: "But even in *Great-Britain*, where Property is better secur'd than anywhere else in the Universe, and where the Hands of the Prince (were he inclin'd to make a Prey of the People) are restrain'd, even here, I say, it is impossible to prevent Men of the lower Class from plundering their Fellow-Subjects" (*Lives and Adventures*, 4). The threat to civil society emanates from a specific and identifiable source: the lower class. "The Life of Sir John Falstaff" is the first item in this ambitious roster of criminals because, by implication, it was Falstaff who tempted Prince Hal to join the ranks of thieves and robbers. The encyclopedic scope of this history is thus framed by its opening narrative, which is almost entirely indebted to Shakespeare's treatment of the Falstaff legend and which hinges upon the idea that resistance to criminality should be innate in princely authority. Despite and also due to his serious moral lapses, Falstaff provides the ideal prelude to instruction. And in the reformation of the prince lies the most stringent imperative for an ideal society divided by class and ordered by monarchical authority—a good example of how eighteenth-century writers continue to borrow from the Renaissance whenever necessary.

The imperial reach of monarchical authority is codified and articulated with particular force toward the beginning of the eighteenth century when the need for ensuring the viability of the mercantilist infrastructure is clearly understood as urgent.[17] Thus the 1724 edition focusing exclusively on *A General History of the Robberies and Murders of the Most Notorious Pyrates* includes the following proclamation: "By his Majesty's Lieutenant Governor, and Commander in chief, of the Colony and Dominion of Virginia, A PROCLAMATION, Publishing the Rewards given for apprehending, or killing, Pyrates." Following this item is "An ABSTRACT of the Civil Law and Statute Law now in Force, in Relation to Pyracy." The "proclamation," issued during the reign of George I (ca. 1719), locates its jurisdiction "between the Degrees of thirty four, and thirty nine, of Northern Latitude, and within one hundred Leagues of the Continent of Virginia, or North Carolina" and outlines the rewards for presenting "proof" of either "taking" or, "in case of resistance . . . killing of all or every such Pyrate." At the top of the list of the most wanted appears "Edward Thatch, commonly call'd, Captain Thatch, or Black-beard," for the capture of whom the reward was £100.00.[18] "For every other Commander of a Pyrate Ship, Sloop, or Vessel, forty Pounds," and the list goes on to include "every Lieutenant, Master, or Quarter-Master, Boatswain," and so on. The "abstract" points to the philosophical and practical distinctions between pirates and common enemies and between lawless entities and states that sponsor lawlessness in order to harm the interests of another state or nation thus: "A Pyrate is Hostis humanis generis, a common Enemy, with whom neither Faith nor Oath is to be kept, according to Tully. . . . Though Pyrates are called common Enemies, yet they are properly not to be term'd so. He is only to be honoured with that Name, says Cicero, who hath a Commonwealth, a Court, a Treasury, Consent and Concord of Citizens, and some Way . . . of Peace and League." The histories of piracy are not only positioned in sharp contrast to the Crusoe-Stanhope model of global engagement, but they are also deeply invested in the potential for imperial aggrandizement in a world plagued by a variety of risks emanating from both internal and external sources. The collections of rogue narratives are thus instructive instruments disguised as history and designed to provide a historiography of readily identifiable threats to empire.

The antiheroes in *A General History* are more than just that. Take, for instance, Edward Teach, who had "a very good Understanding" with the governor of North Carolina. The governor performed Teach's wedding ceremony—the fourteenth one, with a native girl of sixteen. The narrative then goes on to record that Teach's "Behaviour in this State was something extraordinary; for while his sloop lay in Okerecock (Ocracoke) Inlet, and he ashore at a Plantation, where his wife lived, with whom after he had lain all Night, it was his custom to invite five or six of his brutal Companions to come ashore, and he would force her to prostitute herself to them all, one after another, before his face" (76). A calm and detached anthropological stance characterizes this narrator for whom the monstrosity of piracy is more than the monstrous acts and moral depravity of specific pirates. The marriage contract that, in the Teach case, received the blessings of the lawful representative of the Crown was, in fact, a contract to torture and torment the natives.[19] For the narrator of the *History*, the pathology of this criminal act is linked to the physical attributes of Teach, alias Blackbeard, who sported a beard of "extravagant Length" and whose eyes were "fierce and wild." The purpose of presenting these physical attributes, these "Extravagancies," he points out, is to highlight "to what a Pitch of Wickedness, human Nature may arrive, if its Passions are not checked" (84–85). Mercantilist imperatives coincided with the imperatives of the Enlightenment even as juridical and moral proclamations captured some of the rallying cry for strict enforcement of disciplined interactions with trading and colonial outposts.[20] The grotesqueness of Sir John Falstaff and his transgressions were of vital importance to the sustenance of monarchy; the exploits of Captain Teach were not just grotesque but also macabre and devoid of any value—commercial or moral—to the specifically mercantile and more generally financial establishment such as it was toward the beginning of the eighteenth century.

Charlotte Sussman has argued that in *A Journal of the Plague Year* (1722), Daniel Defoe is not telling a story about individuals or cultures but about "collective stories" or "fictions of population" in which "the face of London dissolves into every face."[21] Elsewhere, I have added that in "Defoe's *Journal*, the paralyzing fears of imminent doom, the paranoid fantasies of self-effacement and mutilation—images embedded in his graphic and dense narrative premised upon the plague—are not markers of a particular individual's pathology but have to be read as the pathology of a nation that dares to imagine a grotesque end even as it lays the foundations of an imperial future."[22] The same thick description and imagery pervade *A General History of the Pyrates*, which is a mythology of the threat to the mercantilist foundations of empire—home-grown threats that have the potential to subvert the liberal social contract theories empowering trade, commerce, colony, and the pursuit of wealth. On the distant coasts of Brazil, Madagascar, or Guinea, lawless extranational entities identify and occupy new territories if not new modus operandi for governing colonial settlements.[23] Their newfound lands could expand the scope of state-sanctioned trade and commercial practices that would further the global reach of Britain's power and influence. The logic of this counterhegemonic means toward creating virtual territories ripe for real expansion—the principle that sustains *A General History*—was not stuff that necessarily reinforced for the middle class the pleasures of reading. Form thus colluded with content.[24] In fact, the "characters" in this pseudohistory operate in distant waters as the savages that Crusoe encounters or as the "natives" that Cook and Kurtz were to become. The narratives that describe the pirates' exploits overlap, intersect, and chart with clinical detachment the passage of British pirates who rape and pillage American, Carib, Asian, and African coasts. The fact is, as Susan Ronald has pointed out, from the time of Elizabeth I, "legitimate trade became a precarious way to earn a living," and thus state sponsorship of piracy was considered to be sound trade principle.[25] The Enlightenment social contracts, on the other hand, endowed upon trade an aura of Crusoesque legitimacy, which Asia is still fighting to undermine.

The Rationality of Maps

What I describe in the previous section as the Crusoe-Stanhope model of global engagement could not be sustained by appeals to fantasy alone; in fact, histories and narratives of discovery relied in equal measure upon the probability, if not certainty, guaranteed by maps. The purpose of this section is to examine the real as well as the symbolic function of maps, since both functions contribute toward advancing knowledge and expanding the options for trade and commerce. "Real" maps developed by cartographers, company officials, or naval entities and sponsored by the state embed (within the grid of latitude and longitude) scale, dimension, and distance. This material culture of maps was complemented by "cognitive" maps that, in a more abstract sense, create the consciousness that emerges as a result of sustained or even peripheral contact with "real" maps or with the activities that these maps facilitate: travel, discovery, adventure. The scientific basis and systematic methods of authentication of "real" maps, then, have a reciprocal, albeit tangled, relationship with the maps of cognition. So, for instance, the reader in London who happened to be a consumer of Barbary captivity narratives had a certain (cognitive) map of Marrakech in mind if she read Elizabeth Marsh's *The Female Captive* (1769).[26] In this biographical narrative, Morocco is mapped from a specific perspective in real time-space while the cartographic-cum-colonial agendas of Britain's Mediterranean empire are repressed by the tantalizing story of a British female held captive in an Islamic culture.[27]

What kinds of maps do pirates produce and employ? The story of Bartholomew Roberts and his crew, like so many narrative segments in *A General History of the Pyrates*, follows a predictably random and haphazard organizational pattern. We are told that, when he set sail from London, Roberts was "in an honest Employ," for he was in the business of "taking in Slaves for the *West-Indies*." Thereafter, as the elected successor of Captain Davis—a notorious pirate and thus a worthy predecessor—Roberts assumes the title of commander and is asked to head to Brazil. The author observes that this switching of roles, from a legitimate purveyor of slave labor to the illegitimate privateering and patrolling of the high seas for pillage and profit, was not easy for Roberts: "In the Beginning he was very averse to this Sort of Life, and would certainly have escaped from them, had a fair Opportunity presented it self; yet afterwards he changed his Principles, as many besides him have done upon another Element, and perhaps for the same Reason too, viz. Preferment,—and what he did not like as a private Man he could reconcile to his Conscience as a Commander" (194). In other words, for Roberts the discomfort associated with trading in slaves disappears when there is a direct and palpable correlation between questionable trade practices and personal profit. After presenting in the chapter on Roberts a brief history of the struggles between the Dutch and Portuguese to secure their colonial interests in Brazil, a contest in which Portugal emerges with an advantage, the author adds a "description of Brazil."[28] This lesson in geography functions as more than mere context for the narrative. If Bartholomew Roberts is the principal "character," then why digress into detailed discussions of maps of distant and unfamiliar terrain? Who is the target audience for this long-winded narrative? The three principal trading towns along the Brazilian coast are St. Salvadore, St. Sebastian, and Pernambuca. It is the harbor of the last that seems to be of strategic significance to the author:

> The Harbour of Pernambuca is, perhaps, singular, it is made of a Ledge of Rocks, half a Cable's length from the Main, and but a little above the Surface of the Water, running at that equal Distance and Height several Leagues, towards Cape Augustine, a Harbour running between them capable of receiving Ships of the greatest Burthen: The Northernmost End of this Wall of Rock, is higher than any Part of the contiguous Line, on which a little Fort is built, commanding the Passage either of Boat or Ship, as they come over the Bar into the Harbour: On the Star-board Side . . . after you have enter'd a little Way, stands another Fort (a Pentagon) that would prove of small account, I imagine, against a few disciplin'd Men; and yet in these consists all their Strength and Security, either for the Harbour or the Town.[29]

The passage can be read as a summary of the topographical, physical, and tactical challenges of piracy. But notice that the map of the harbor is not just a map that can be (or has been) useful to pirates but one that is "capable of receiving Ships of the greatest Burthen," ones that advance the interests of bona fide trade. Additionally, the fort that exists would have a "commanding" view of the passage of ships (or sloops for that matter) and be ideal for surveillance of the sort necessary for colonial enterprises. The authorial gaze—if one characterizes it as such—is the gaze of a competing colonial power, gauging and assessing the profits of the Portuguese.[30]

On occasion, the author also presents a combined account of the geography and the natural history of a region, as, for instance, in the chapter on Captain Edward England, which focuses in part on Madagascar:

> *Madagascar* is an island larger than *Great Britain*, most of it within the Tropick of Capricorn, and lyes East from the Eastern Side of Africa: It abounds with Provisions of all Sorts, Oxen, Goats, Sheep, Poultry, Fish, Citrons, Oranges, Tamarinds, Dates, Coco-Nuts, Bananas, Wax, Honey, Rice; or, in short, Cotton, Indigo, or any other Thing they will take Pains to plant, and have understanding to manage: They have likewise Ebony, a hard wood like Brazil, of which they make their lances. . . . What is most incommodious, are the numerous swarms of locusts on the Land, and Crocodiles or Alligators in the Rivers. Here, in St. Augustine's Bay, the ships sometimes touch for Water, when they take the inner passage for India, and do not design to stop at Johanna. . . . [T]his inner Passage or Channel, has its Northern and Southern Currents strongest where the Channel is narrowest, and is less, and varies on different Points of the Compass, as the Sea comes to spread again, in the Passage cross the Line. (131)

In this segment, the author acknowledges tacitly the importance of location, location, location, but more immediately he wants the reader to see that the difficulties of distance are mitigated by the resources, resources, resources on this island. Once again, Captain England provides the occasion for a discussion of the pros and cons associated with navigating the waters around Madagascar. The historian points out that this "passage to India"—via St. Augustine's Bay—is paved with crocodiles and alligators, which, he implies, both company and pirate ships have to contend with and navigate with equal skill. For the most part, the narratives of lands and shores infested by British pirates are not judgmental but clinical, dispassionate, based upon information mined from various sources,[31] and compiled with an eye toward presenting the most comprehensive picture of the environments within which British subjects—disenfranchised and disillusioned mariners and sailors—carried on their business alongside various state-sponsored trading companies. But a dispassionate stance should not be mistaken for a disinterested one. This *History*, appearing as it did in an opportune moment, is neither neutral nor innocuous. However, to its credit, it plays havoc with the Enlightenment divide between legitimate and illegitimate maritime enterprises.

In a recent discussion of the "presumed rationality of maps," Matthew Edney has underscored the importance of geography in the context of eighteenth-century "polite learning." Educated Europeans had extensive exposure to maps of all sorts, he argues, whether through geography texts widely disseminated in schools or, in later life, in their capacity as bureaucrats, politicians, or mercantilists. Of specific interest to my discussion here is the distinction Edney makes between geographic maps, which were widely circulated in the public sphere, and sea charts, harbor maps, and surveys, which "had a restricted circulation among mariners and company officials and did not circulate in the public." Edney goes on to say that "it was the geographical map's power to organize space in a truthful manner that underlay the eighteenth-century use of 'mapping' as a metaphor for classification and categorization."[32] Needless to say, "the organization of space in a truthful manner" was not valued for its own sake, as the desired outcome of scientific rigor, but rather as a means to expansionist ends (whether in India, which is Edney's focus, or elsewhere). Most scholars agree that there were at least two types of cartographic instincts at play in contemporary material culture, representing two parallel but distinctly different trajectories and patterns of consumerism. The geographic map—legitimized and authenticated by those who claimed to have authority, such as Herman Moll, James Rennell, and the Foster brothers—was designed for the purpose of extending the knowledge base of the educated class and furthering the interests of state-sponsored trade and commerce. The charts and harbor maps generated by buccaneers, privateers, and pirates that relied on all sorts of local knowledge were entirely functional, contingent, and designed for the purpose of extending the interests of illegitimate and unsanctioned maritime activities. While the former is always privileged, the latter is inevitably vilified, even when the result of (what might broadly be described as) cartographic desire in both instances is self-aggrandizement.

How rational were the maps that were officially sanctioned? Throughout the eighteenth century, and well after Robinson Crusoe embarked upon his mythological voyage, the logbooks based upon observations of captains and crew of "legitimate" enterprises were notoriously unstable and thus the source of contentious debate. Consider, in this context, the case of Alexander Dalrymple, who published *An Account of the Discoveries Made in the South Pacifick Ocean* (1767), and John Hawkesworth, who published *An Account of the Voyages Undertaken by the Order of his Present Majesty* (1773). The former was an East India Company official, while the latter had been commissioned, during the reign of George III, to write an official "account." Both might be regarded as members of the establishment and legitimate entities who were commissioned or qualified to write on the subject of one of the most chimerical projects of the eighteenth century: the search for a continent in the South Pacific. Their heated exchanges began when, in his "account," Hawkesworth raised questions about Dalrymple's hypotheses and conclusions. In response to this appeared *A Letter from Mr. Dalrymple to Dr. Hawkesworth* (1773), in which the author attempted to correct a variety of misconceptions and errors in judgment and fact. Almost immediately, in his "preface" to the 1773 second edition of his "account," Hawkesworth—virtually on his deathbed at this point—attacked once again the man who had become by then his most formidable rival in the business of choreographing the accounts of British voyages of discovery.[33] The big difference between the two men was, of course, the fact that Dalrymple himself undertook many of these voyages on behalf of his employer (1759–1764), while Hawkesworth was a writer for hire. And even with his East India

Company credentials, Dalrymple was not an insider because he "had not been bred up in the Royal Navy."[34]

In the preface to his "account," Dalrymple demonstrates the fundamental fluidity of maps and the contested nature of cartographic claims and counter-claims decades after the dust from the South Sea Bubble had settled. Challenging the premise of Hawkesworth's observations about the voyages of Captain Cook, Dalrymple lashes out thus: "Dr. Hawkesworth *supposes* that in the beginning of September, 1769, Captain Cook was in the Latitude 40°. S, that from this Situation he stood to the NW into 30°. S, and then SW again towards 40°. S, and thence Westward to New Zeland:—But *I think this is highly improbable*, because Captain Cook could not be *so absurd* to *make choice* of the Equinox for attempting discoveries in a *high* South Latitude." In the context of the *Endeavour*'s logbook, Hawkesworth observed that the charts and the narratives (that are presented in tandem) "coincide." However, if there are any differences, Hawkesworth contends that the charts be used because they are of "unquestionable authority." If "the nautical events are related too minutely," asked Dalrymple, why should there be any discrepancies? He then goes on to "mention a few instances where the Charts and Narratives essentially differ."[35] If the official charts and maps are unstable, they have, in fact, much in common with those narratives and charts that are used for piracy, and a philosophical as well as practical distinction between the two realms—official and unofficial—is thus harder to make than is generally assumed. The science and business of mapping was only slightly improved in the late century when compared with the earlier endeavors in Defoe's London.

Whether we incorporate Bruno Latour's inscriptions created by visual representations—as Matthew Edney has skillfully done—or we turn to Jonathan Lamb's conceptualization of the "vision of territory as truth," early modern visual culture has to be read as an active agent of change. That which is witnessed is that which always already has the potential for ownership by an external/alien or powerful/patriarchal agent. However, instead of a straightforward evolution we find a haphazard progression from visualization or acts of cognition to the "real" business of trade, commerce, and acquisition of colony.[36] Buccaneering in this sense is no different from trading, commerce, settlement, and colonization, for all these enterprises create and sustain scientific maps or "acts of cognition" that provide the foundations for empire.[37] Natural history and ethnography are often combined to produce a systematic map that is legitimized by state or company sponsorship. The map is then automatically incorporated into a systemic register that creates a demand for more histories and for more "savagified narrators"—to use Jonathan Lamb's term—who supplied the insatiable demand for what I am characterizing here as the Crusoe-Stanhope model of global engagement.[38] Dalrymple, Hawkesworth, and other purveyors of discovery narratives had well-scripted but often competing agendas. Defined by the imperatives of questionable trade practices and contingent motivations, and victimized by their status as prostitutes of commerce, the pirates, on the other hand, were disinterested in sustaining any profound or influential myths of social, political, and geographic mapping.

The Disenfranchised Imperialist

A discussion of the spatial and geographic dimensions of maps must inevitably turn to a consideration of the early and illegitimate architects of mapping. The argument in this section underscores the need to purloin the notion of the "reluctant pilgrim" and reinscribe it in the category of what I am describing as the "disenfranchised imperialist" or the pirate. Pirates were not reluctant in any sense of the term when it came to turning a quick profit. However, albeit lacking the authority derived from state-sponsored trade and commercial ventures, they were unconscious and unthinking proponents of the early capitalism that engendered imperialism—having a more indirect relationship to territorial aggrandizement than the colonial enterprises of the East India Company or the Royal African Company. The pirates' missionary zeal is thus channelized toward amassing wealth at the expense of distant subjects of foreign nation-states. In their ruthless pursuit of wealth, they provided subversive alternatives to the notion of anthropological voyages or religious pilgrimages; therefore, the types of narratives that these pirates inspired were ones that can now be recuperated to study not just their global exploits and unmitigated savagery but also their unthinking contributions to a cause about which they were indifferent.

In "Captain Misson's Failed Utopia, Crusoe's Failed Colony," Lincoln Faller cites Marcus Rediker and Peter Linebaugh, but points out ways in which his reading of *A General History* differs from theirs:

> By the 1720s . . . "thousands of pirates . . . had . . . self-consciously built an autonomous, democratic, egalitarian social order of their own, a subversive alternative to the prevailing ways of the merchant, naval, and privateering ship and a counterculture to the civilization of Atlantic capitalism with its expropriation and exploitation, terror and slavery." Though [Rediker and Linebaugh] frequently cite Johnson's *History of the Pirates* as a historical source, they have nothing at all to say about Misson and Libertalia, not even as a fantastical projection of, inevitably, forlorn hopes. . . . Better probably to see this text as a kind of "sport," an instance of free-wheeling, utopian and dystopian imagining from a single powerful premise. Like *Robinson Crusoe* and *Gulliver's Travels*, it breaks Europeans away from Europe to see what might happen.[39]

Neither the utopian-dystopian dichotomy nor the impulse to see what might happen elsewhere when freed from the bonds of European Enlightenment can capture the full force and meaning of what I am characterizing here as the disenfranchised imperialists—particularly if their exploits are examined through the lens of the author of *A General History*.

If the pirates are positioned as members of a Defoesque counterculture who either consciously or unwittingly set themselves up in opposition to Atlantic capitalism, the critique of their mission and the overlapping interests of state-sponsored versus piratical enterprises must be addressed as I have attempted to do briefly here. I do not see the spirit of "sport" in any aspect of this history, which presents, I would argue, anything but a freewheeling attitude on the part of the narrator toward maritime contingencies of all sorts that he describes in depth in this history. In other words, we need to make distinctions between the action that is accidental, that which is contingent, and that which is premeditated or rehearsed: the actions of the pirates might have been freewheeling in the sense that they were not governed by any laws established by and in civil society. However, the narrative order and discipline that the author imposed upon the freewheeling and lawless actions of these agents were deliberate, considered, and crafted into a "history" that would address very specific anxieties of the South Sea Bubble era.

Any countercultural stance is inevitably associated with the benevolent (and "liberal") impulse of resistance to oppressive authority (particularly, I would argue, when any movement or group is characterized as such in the post-1960s Anglo-American academy). If there are countercultural elements in *A General History*, these appear in the messages from the authorial pulpit that are interspersed throughout. Pointing to the moral implications of piracy, consider how the narrator delivers an uncompromising punch with delightful precision in this passage that appears at the end of the chapter on Captain Edward England:

> Here they sate down to spend the Fruits of their dishonest Industry, dividing the Spoil and Plunder of Nations among themselves, without the least Remorse or Compunction, satisfying their Conscience with this Salvo, that other People would have done as much, had they had the like Opportunities. I can't say, but if they had known what was doing in England, at the same Time, by the *South-Sea* Directors, and their Directors, they would certainly have had this Reflection for their Consolation, viz. that whatever Robberies they had committed, they might be pretty sure they were not the greatest Villains then living in the World. (134)[40]

The analytic stance of the narrator of *A General History* is straightforward and uncompromising. Consider also, for instance, this observation in the chapter on Captain Roberts:

> The Royal African Company has a Fort on a small Island call'd Bence Island, but 'tis of little Use, besides keeping their Slaves; the Distance making it incapable of giving any Molestation to their Starboard Shore. Here lives at this

> Place an old Fellow, who goes by the Name of *Crackers*, who was formerly a noted Buccannear, and while he followed the Calling, robb'd and plundered many a Man; he keeps the best House in the Place; has two or three Guns before his Door, with which he Salutes his Friends, the Pyrates, when they put in, and lives a jovial Life with them, all the while they are there. (226)

The divide between the officers of the Royal African Company (originally the Company of Royal Adventurers Trading to Africa)—legitimate representatives of the Crown—and the privateers of questionable provenance is utterly and completely diluted, if not destroyed, when the contingencies of these distant outposts are held up to the sort of scrutiny which the narrator of *A General History* does not shy away from. But, eventually, the interests of state must supersede all other peripheral and illegitimate interests, and the narrator is clear on this point:

> Here follows a List, of the rest of those lawless Merchants, and their Servants, who carry on a private Trade with the Interlopers, to the great Prejudice of the Royal African Company, who with extraordinary Industry and Expense, have made, and maintain, Settlements without any Consideration from those, who, without such Settlements and Forts, would soon be under an Incapacity of pursuing any such private Trade. Wherefore, 'tis to be hop'd, proper Means will be taken, to root out a pernicious Set of People, who have all their Lives, supported themselves by the Labours of other Men. (226)

Donning a distinctly nationalist cap, the author complains, in other words, that the trading outposts and infrastructure—"Settlements and Forts"—supplied by the Royal African Company provide the necessary infrastructure for facilitating the operations of private trade. But from the British perspective, the interests of private trade can never be allowed to jeopardize or threaten the interests of the Royal African Company, whose members have displayed "extraordinary industry and expense" toward establishing legitimate trade practices. On the one hand, the narrative outlines a fluidity and interchangeability of personnel, including captains, commanders, and crew; on the other hand, the interests of state—erected upon sound theoretical and ideological principles of trade and commerce—come first even though there is little difference between the impact of either category of trade and commerce on settlements elsewhere.

In his discussion of racial liberalism and the problems inherent in Lockean and Kantian notions of equality, Charles Mills has argued that "the moral equality of people in the state of nature demands an equality of treatment (juridical, political, and economic) in the liberal polity they create. The state is not alien or antagonistic to us but the protector of our rights. . . . The good polity is the just polity, and the just polity is founded on safeguarding our interests as individuals."[41] The author of *A General History* is, I would argue, consistently Lockean in his liberal stance even when he acknowledges—unwittingly—some of those fundamental problems in the theories of liberalism in the Enlightenment that we in the philosophical, historical, and literary circles are now examining more closely. Appearing as it did in the immediate aftermath of the South Sea Bubble, *A General History of Pyrates* is more than a catalog of the monstrous propensity of some "true-born" Englishmen and women to chart a parallel global trajectory.

Robinson Crusoe receives the accolades it richly deserves only so long as it is immunized against the mercantilist and colonialist germs that it harbors—an immunity derived from the separation of politics from literature, of the real from the imagined, and the contingent from the strategic. As pantomime, *Crusoe* is jolly good fun, and no one could combine horseplay with high-stakes state affairs with greater panache than Richard Brinsley Sheridan. At a time when the loss of America loomed large and the Warren Hastings rumblings could be heard loud and clear, Sheridan and Linley relegate Friday to a hilarious harlequinade, immunizing further a fiction of forced labor (among other issues). If stripped of this immunity, the fruits of Defoe's passionate labor, his search for spiritual enlightenment, and his masterful manipulation of language take on new meaning and new power. This shift in perspective, facilitated by postcolonial revisionism, is best represented in J. M. Coetzee's interpretation of *Robinson Crusoe* as "unabashed propaganda for the extension of British mercantile power in the New World and the establishment of new British colonies."[42] The discipline that spirituality demands, the order that the grotto represents, the single-mindedness that a pilgrimage teaches, and the endurance that a risky voyage necessitates contribute variously to the creation of a (Christian) character who can defuse the malevolent face of imperialism. Like Falstaff or Fagin, Macheath or Jonathan Wild, the rogues in *A General History of the Pyrates* serve a different purpose. Their otherness, their subversive actions, their blatant criminality, and their uncouth accoutrements serve—through systemic mechanisms of contrast and containment—to legitimize and sanitize mercantilist mappings and narratives of emerging markets in the eighteenth century.

When framed as narrative and thus fiction, maritime criminality masks the pervasive cultural inclination for expansion in eighteenth-century Britain. In this sense, empire and colony were not only state-sponsored ambition; in retrospect, we find that British maritime might was fictionalized and recorded in collective memory such that digression, or entertainment such as Defoe's *History*, blended with the historiographical record to produce a mythos of adventure on the high seas. This mythos was premised upon a delightful amalgam, much like the real exploits of Hester Stanhope (historiography) and the romantic functionality of stories (narrative)—about her foreign transgressions. Meanwhile, the commercialization of leisure and the increasing sophistication of diversion created a ready market for sanctimonious stories of nation and what we now call identity politics.[43] Codified as homegrown but foreign-bred and unsanctioned, piracy thus entered the historical register as negative mythos so as to legitimize, among other institutions, the British navy and various corporate entities.[44]

NOTES

1. Bernard Porter, "It Just Sounded Good," review of Kirsten Ellis, *Star of the Morning: The Extraordinary Life of Hester Stanhope*, *London Review of Books* 30, no. 20 (October 23, 2008), https://www.lrb.co.uk/the-paper/v30/n20/bernard-porter/it-just-sounded-good. See also Alexander William Kinglake, *Eothen: Traces of Travel Brought Home from the East*, rev. ed. (New York: George Putnam, 1849).

2. See Joseph Roach, *It* (Ann Arbor: University of Michigan Press, 2007), specifically 1 and 3. Significantly, Hester Stanhope was called Queen Zenobia when she was in Palmyra (see Porter, "It Just Sounded Good"). On the London stage, Zenobia was both the lead female character in Handel's opera *Radamistus* (which was first performed at the King's Theatre on April 27, 1720) and also the eponymous heroine of G. Cocchi's opera *Zenobia* (which was first performed at the King's Theatre on January 10, 1758).

3. Information about performances and their dates is from Emmett L. Avery, *The London Stage, 1660–1800: A Calendar of Plays, Entertainments & Afterpieces* (Carbondale: Southern Illinois University Press, 1960).

4. About Maximillian E. Novak's *Daniel Defoe: Master of Fictions: His Life and Ideas* (2001), John Richetti says the following: "Defoe has been immensely attractive to biographers because his voluminous writings allow them to speculate about the personality that must have been behind the various and distinct voices that he projects in that astonishing river of writing, especially the fiction. Novak has succumbed . . . to this temptation to summon this particular ghost. Novak's exhaustive book is often enough a species of biographical fiction in which a mysterious and elusive authorial presence is transformed into a familiar human subject." See John Richetti, "Writing about Defoe: What Is a Critical Biography?," *Literary Compass* 3, no. 2 (2006): 74.

5. For the vastness of the eighteenth-century map and the varieties of documentation related to early modern travel, see Felicity A. Nussbaum, *The Global Eighteenth Century* (Baltimore: Johns Hopkins University Press, 2003).

6. In "Defoe, Commerce, and Empire," Srinivas Aravamudan describes in the context of Defoe's well-known fictions the author's "global perspective on trade." See Aravamudan's chapter in *A Cambridge Companion to Daniel Defoe*, ed. John Richetti (Cambridge: Cambridge University Press, 2008), 45–63.

7. Daniel Defoe, *A General History of the Pyrates*, ed. Manuel Schonhorn, rev. ed. (New York: Dover, 1999). Hereafter cited parenthetically in the text.

8. In his introduction to *A General History of the Pyrates*, Manuel Schonhorn observes the following: "Ordered, arranged, detailed, and well researched, Volume I of Defoe's pirate history is nevertheless of minor literary importance. . . . Also, confronted with an abundance of factual material, Defoe perhaps felt no need to expand the volume with dramatic or imaginative sequences. In this case, ships' names, armaments, locations, booty and the many other incidentals of voyaging which he had gathered were organized in coherent and readable structure, with a minimum of invention" (xxxiv). I argue that this history has major cultural significance, with or without the imprimatur of Daniel Defoe.

9. In this context, see, for instance, Mita Choudhury, *Nation-Space in Enlightenment Britain: An Archaeology of Empire* (New York: Routledge, 2019), specifically "The Spatial Dimension of Enlightenment Time," 15–49.

10. See, respectively, Marshall Sahlins, *Islands of History* (Chicago: University of Chicago Press, 1985), and Gananath Obeyesekere, *The Apotheosis of Captain Cook: European Mythmaking in the Pacific* (Princeton, NJ: Princeton University Press, 1992).

11. See, respectively, James Cook, *The Journals of Captain James Cook on His Voyages of Discovery*, ed. J. C. Beaglehole (London: Hakluyt Society, 1955), and Ian Watt, *The Rise of the Novel: Studies in Defoe, Richardson and Fielding* (Berkeley: University of California Press, 1957).

12. I use the expression "order of things" in the Foucauldian sense. Perhaps the most useful commentary on the Crusoesque propensity for order is by Novak, who has described in compelling detail Crusoe's cave, which is "the scene of a contented, ordered life." The order is thus associated with Crusoe's "Christian life," and chaos with his fears of the supernatural or "his terror at experiencing the falling rocks and earth from the earthquake." See Maximillian E. Novak, "The Cave and the Grotto: Realist Form and Robinson Crusoe's Imagined Interiors," *Eighteenth-Century Fiction* 20, no. 3 (Spring 2008), specifically 449 and 453.

13. By this I simply mean the following: the full implications of the Falstaffian threat to monarchy, for instance, was much more than what Shakespeare's (supremely memorable) character could possibly embody, or the Renaissance spectator could possibly understand. However, this subversive threat to monarchy and the idea of Britain was, of course, very real not just during the reign of Elizabeth but throughout early modernity.

14. See M. M. Mahood, ed., *The Merchant of Venice* (Cambridge: Cambridge University Press, 2003), 83–84.

15. Since this discussion is not concerned with issues of attribution, I have not delved into the arguments and counterarguments presented by any of the following: P. N. Furbank and W. R. Owens, Henry C. Hutchins, John Robert Moore, and Maximillian E. Novak. See Charles Johnson, *A general history of the robberies and murders of the most notorious pyrates, and also their policies, discipline and government, from their first rise and settlement in the island of Providence, . . . With the remarkable actions and adventures of the two female pyrates, Mary Read and Anne Bonny. To which is prefix'd an account of the famous Captain Avery* (London: Ch. Rivington, J. Lacy, and J. Stone, 1724). See also Charles Johnson, *A General History of the Lives and Adventures of the Most Famous Highwaymen, Murderers, Street Robbers, etc. To which is added, A Genuine Account of the Voyages and Plunders of the most Notorious Pyrates* (London: J. Janeway, 1734). Henceforth cited parenthetically as *Lives and Adventures.*

16. There is a strong undercurrent of nationalism that simmers right below the surface of *A General History* and emerges randomly as in this example. However, scholars who write about issues of race and nation in Defoe focus on his major works—those that have been attributed to him. See, for instance, Aparna Dharwadker, "Nation, Race, and the Ideology of Commerce in Defoe," *The Eighteenth Century: Theory and Interpretation* 39, no. 1 (1998): 63–84. Anna Neill has described the contradictions in Crusoe's perceptions of nationhood thus: "Apparently forgetting already how recently he himself was marked as a nationless outlaw, Crusoe identifies entirely with his merchant fellow travelers in his fear of this lawless wild over which no nation clearly has dominion." Anna Neill, "Crusoe's Farther Adventures: Discovery, Trade, and the Law of Nations," *The Eighteenth Century: Theory and Interpretation* 38, no. 3 (1997): 227.

17. Of importance here is the passing of the Act of Parliament on Privateering (1708). Manuel Schonhorn reminds us that this act "is directly attributable to the failure of the British fleets to inflict any appreciable damage on the shipping of the Crown's enemies. In this Act an effort was made to restore to privateering all the old spirit of adventure which permeated our sea story in the reign of Elizabeth." Following the passage of this act, privateering became reinvigorated because privateers were no longer required to turn over a fifth of their acquisitions to the Crown. See Schonhorn, introduction, xx–xxi. Presumably written during the years leading up to 1724, *A General History of Pyrates* is also enriched by the "experience of defeat" (to borrow Christopher Hill's expression) after the South Sea Bubble burst and the phony foundation of that chapter in the history of speculation was revealed for what it was.

18. Thatch is a variant of Teach. See *Robberies and Murders*, 91–92, 317–320. In the Schonhorn edition the proclamation appears, as it does here, in the chapter "Of Captain Teach, alias Black-Beard.," 78–79. For a discussion of the difficulties of ascertaining what this amount, £100.00, meant in the early eighteenth century, see Robert D. Hume, "The Economics of Culture in London, 1660–1740," *Huntington Library Quarterly* 69, no. 4 (2006): 487–533.

19. Referring specifically to *Robinson Crusoe*, *Farther Adventures*, and *Captain Singleton*, Aravamudan has described the "excessive and unmotivated violence in Defoe's fiction" as "shocking and explosive." Aravamudan, "Defoe, Commerce, and Empire," 81. This shock value, of course, is mostly a retrospective value that has been added (in postmodernity) to a variety of eighteenth-century imperial encroachments, which were at the time sanctioned and sustained not just by Protestant Christianity but by the institutions that collectively supported mercantilist projects, anthropological expeditions of all sorts, and "adventure" in general.

20. For a discussion of Edmund Burke's opposition to a trading company acting as a state, see Nicholas B. Dirks, *The Scandal of Empire: India and the Creation of Imperial Britain* (Cambridge, MA: Belknap Press, 2006), "Sovereignty," 167–207. Of late there has been considerable interest in the issue of "criminals and colonies," which is the title of a special session of the Modern Language Association in 2011, for instance, the description for which ran as follows: "On the cultural interchange between criminal punishment and colonialism."

21. Charlotte Sussman, "Memory and Mobility: Fictions of Population in Defoe, Goldsmith, and Scott," in *A Companion to the Eighteenth-Century English Novel and Culture*, ed. Paula R. Backscheider and Catherine Ingrassia (Oxford: Blackwell, 2005), 192.

22. Choudhury, *Nation-Space in Enlightenment Britain*, 18–19.

23. The trial documents that appear in several narratives in *A General History* list the pirates' city of origin and/or place of birth. See, for instance, the list of arraigned pirates at the trial held on July 18, 1718, in Defoe, *A General History of the Pyrates*, 103. The pirates' places of domicile are listed in the court documents. So, for instance, a pirate could be "late of London" or "late of Dublin" or "late of Charles-Town." See *General History*, 104. The place of domicile is of course different from the place of origin or birth. Providing the former information to the exclusion of the latter can often obfuscate the identity of British subjects and the identification of their exploits.

24. In his discussion of the lives of the two pirates that appear in *A General History*—Captain Misson and Captain Tew—Lincoln Faller observes that "both tell stories of failed colonies in ways . . . that also fail as stories." Tew was a real person, Faller rightly reminds us, while Misson was fictional. I would add that a retrospective view—fueled by full knowledge of what happened throughout the later eighteenth and nineteenth centuries—allows us to see the enormity of British anxieties related to naval and mercantilist enterprises. Defoe and his contemporaries understood that "failure" in the race for colonies was not an option, which is why narratives of failure would resonate with a sizable readership not only in London but also in Dublin and in all the trading towns in eighteenth-century Britain. It is helpful in this context to review N.A.M. Rodger, *The Command of the Ocean: A Naval History of Britain, 1649–1815* (New York: Norton, 2005). See Lincoln Faller, "Captain Misson's Failed Utopia, Crusoe's Failed Colony: Race and Identity in New, Not Quite Imaginable Worlds," *The Eighteenth Century: Theory and Interpretation* 43, no. 1 (Spring 2002): 1–17, specifically 2.

25. Susan Ronald, *The Pirate Queen* (New York: HarperCollins, 2007), specifically "The Politics of Piracy, Trade, and Religion," 55–66 and specifically 60.

26. "Marsh was born in Hampshire in 1735, the daughter of a ship's carpenter and dockyard official employed by the Royal Navy first at Minorca, then at Gibraltar, and finally at Chatham. Through her father, then, Marsh was connected both to the British state and to

the business of empire." See Linda Colley, "The Narrative of Elizabeth Marsh: Barbary, Sex, and Power," in *The Global Eighteenth Century*, ed. Felicity A. Nussbaum, (Baltimore: Johns Hopkins University Press, 2003), 138–150 and specifically 139.

27. See Colley's comments on this issue at 149–150.

28. About *Robinson Crusoe*, Novak says the following: "A historian of Brazil's economic development was able to point to Defoe's novel as embodying an exact description of the methods necessary to succeed as a sugar planter in Brazil during the seventeenth century." See Novak, "The Cave and the Grotto," 466. Novak is referring here to Stuart Schwartz, *Sugar Plantations in the Formation of Brazilian Society: Bahia, 1550–1835* (Cambridge: Cambridge University Press, 1985), 211–212.

29. *History of the Pyrates*, chapter IX: "Of Captain Bartholomew Roberts," 194–287 and specifically 197 and 201.

30. The author consistently weighs the pros of cons of colonial acquisitions thus: "The Portuguese here are darker than those of *Europe*, not only from a warmer Climate, but their many Intermarriages with the Negroes. . . . The Women (not unlike the Mulatto Generation every where else) are fond of Strangers; . . . but the unhappiness of pursuing Amours is, that the Generality of both Sexes are touched with venereal Taints, without so much as one Surgeon among them, or any Body skill'd in Physick" (*General History*, 100).

31. See, for instance, Manuel Schonhorn's discussion of the strong possibility that Defoe had access to the documents related to the trial of Bartholomew Roberts and his crew (introduction, xxxi–xl).

32. Matthew H. Edney, "Bringing India to Hand: Mapping an Empire, Denying Space," in Nussbaum, *The Global Eighteenth Century*, 65–78 and specifically 72–73. See also Matthew H. Edney, *Mapping an Empire: The Geographical Construction of British India, 1765–1843* (Chicago: University of Chicago Press, 1999).

33. Alexander Dalrymple, *An Account of the Discoveries made in the South Pacific, previous to 1764* (London, 1767); John Hawkesworth, *An Account of the Voyages Undertaken by the Order of his Present Majesty for making discoveries in the Southern Hemisphere*, 3 vols. (London, 1773); Alexander Dalrymple, *A Letter from Mr. Dalrymple to Dr. Hawkesworth* (London: J. Nourse, T. Payne, Brotherton and Sewell and others, 1773); John Hawkesworth, *A Preface* to the second edition (of *An Account of the Voyages*) (London, 1773).

34. Moreover, Dalrymple believed there should be full disclosure in matters related to these official voyages whereas Hawkesworth was interested in promoting the interests of Britain and making sure that historiographies such as Dalrymple's would not provide a public register of the successes of similar voyages undertaken by the Spanish and Dutch. Dalrymple's position on explorations may also be regarded as more strategic—since he wanted to present the contemporary endeavors in terms of the ones in the past whereas Hawkesworth's approach was tactical because all that mattered to him was the here and now. See Dalrymple, *A Letter from Mr. Dalrymple*, 1–2 and passim.

35. Dalrymple, 21, 23–24.

36. In his study of eyewitness accounts of the South Pacific, Jonathan Lamb points to an "improvement in knowledge" from what he describes as "the uncertain anthropology of the early explorers" and the "haphazard cartography of privateers" to the "superb drawings of Parkinson, limned precisely to illustrate the Linnaean method of Joseph Banks's observations." The reason for this improvement, Lamb argues, can be found in the "contingent desires motivating the privateers," as well as in "the more disciplined satisfactions of scientific inquiry." See Jonathan Lamb, "Eye-Witnessing in the South Seas," *The Eighteenth Century: Theory and Interpretation* 38, no. 3 (1997): 201.

37. Most important for my purposes here is Lamb's useful summary (in "Eye-Witnessing") of first-person testimonials that, instead of contributing to an overall "improvement in knowledge"—or despite this efficacious end—create among metropolitan readers an ever

lustful demand for what Lamb calls "savagified narrators" that represent "the inescapable barbarism of uncontrolled eye witnessing" See Lamb, 206–207.

38. The account of this trial appears in the narrative about Major Stede Bonnet and his crew. "The King's Commission to Judge Trot was read, and a Grand Jury sworn, for finding of the several Bills, and a learned Charge given them by the said Judge, wherein he first shewed, that the Sea was given by God, for the use of Men, and is subject to Dominion and Property, as well as the Land. 2ndly, He particularly remark'd to them, the Sovereignty of the King of *England* over the *British Seas*. 3rdly, He observed, that as Commerce and Navigation could not be carry'd on without Laws; so there have been always particular Laws, for the better ordering and regulating maritime Affairs; with an historical Account of those Laws, and Origin." See Schonhorn, 103.

39. See Faller, "Captain Misson's Failed Utopia," 4.

40. "Privateering" was in the national interest when there was a need for privateers; but the seamless borders between privateering and piracy presented a problem as the pirates pushed and tested the boundaries of decency to such extreme levels that their actions could not be condoned.

41. See Charles W. Mills, "Racial Liberalism," *PMLA* 123, no. 5 (October 2008): 1381.

42. See J. M. Coetzee, "Daniel Defoe, Robinson Crusoe," in *Stranger Shores: Literary Essays, 1986–1999* (New York: Penguin, 2001), 21.

43. See Darryl P. Domingo, *The Rhetoric of Diversion in English Literature and Culture, 1690–1760* (Cambridge: Cambridge University Press, 2016).

44. See, for instance, William Dalrymple's discussion of Walter Raleigh, Francis Drake, and other adventurers in *The Anarchy: The Relentless Rise of the East India Company* (London: Bloomsbury, 2019), specifically "1599," 1–57.

CHAPTER 4

Thomas Jefferson's Sojourn in Nîmes

REVOLUTIONARY POLITICS AND ARCHITECTURE

Robert M. Craig

When John F. Kennedy hosted a group of Nobel Prize winners at a gala dinner party at the White House in 1962, he is reported to have commented as follows about the distinguished individuals gathered together for the occasion: "I think this is the most extraordinary collection of talent, of human knowledge, that has ever been gathered together at the White House, with the possible exception of when Thomas Jefferson dined alone."[1] No one among the Nobel laureates took his remarks as a slight, but rather as an acknowledgment of the multisided character of one of the most creative intellects and accomplished individuals in American history.

Thomas Jefferson named three contributions for which he hoped he would be remembered that he instructed be listed on his tombstone: his authorship of the Declaration of Independence, his role in establishing Virginia's Statute for Religious Freedom, and his founding of the University of Virginia.[2] It is significant, in the spirit of such memorials, that millions have benefited from this immortal Jefferson legacy, but it is also noteworthy that Jefferson did not mention his role as third president of the United States. Hundreds of schoolchildren learn of Jefferson the revolutionary, diplomat, president, and statesman, far sooner than they know, for instance, about Jefferson the architect, a role in many ways equally revolutionary as that of Jefferson the political theorist and leader of America's struggle for independence.

As founder of the University of Virginia, Jefferson was also its campus designer and architect of "the academical village." He not only approached architectural design as a scholar, but also subscribed to the notion that architecture itself had a didactic purpose. Fundamental to this dual role of revolutionary and scholar/architect was Jefferson's belief that architecture offered evidence of the advancement, or stagnation, of a civilization, and that architecture could also mold the sensibilities of a people. A society's ability to build nobly, to erect an architecture appropriately expressive of a national character, depended on the models of excellence to which that nation's peoples were exposed. In closing the chapter on colonial America, Jefferson was a revolutionary as much in architecture as in politics.

Recognizing early in life his own limitations on such matters as an informed taste in building styles, the result of his upbringing in the western part of Virginia and his limited travel beyond those almost frontier environs, Jefferson turned to books, amassing one of the most important libraries of his day, a collection that made up the formative catalog of the Library of Congress. Among his American contemporaries, Jefferson was one of the most curious, most learned individuals of his day and an avid reader. Moreover, the whole world could be an open book, and travel became an opportunity for self-education. When his other roles as politician and statesman took him beyond his agrarian setting in Albemarle County to the colonial capital of Williamsburg, or to Philadelphia and eventually to Europe, he repeatedly took the opportunity to travel farther afield in order to educate himself in a wide range of subjects and cultural pursuits, including his investigation of preferred models for an appropriate architecture both for his personal residences and for the new nation at large.

Travel was a lifelong interest, and Jefferson believed exposure to other cultures and societies informed one's personal sensibilities and a people's collective public taste, as well as contributing to the improvement of civilization. His travel was always investigatory, providing opportunities for keen observation and scientific documentation of anything and everything that stimulated his curious mind. Official duties that took him away from his beloved Monticello at least offered the desirable opportunity to learn, and his schoolroom, whenever possible, was outside the legislative hall or ministerial chamber. When his wife's ill health prompted him on two occasions to refuse appointment as a diplomatic envoy abroad, Jefferson told Lafayette, "I lose an opportunity . . . of combining public service with private gratification, of seeing countries whose improvements in science, in arts, in civilization, it has been my fortune to admire at a distance, but never to see."[3]

The potential effect of this provincialism on one of Jefferson's keen interests, architecture, is telling. Jefferson hoped that the new nation that he had helped form would develop a fine architecture, worthy of the democratic experiment, but in his view, almost no architecture at home offered evidence of elegance or even competence. In his *Notes on the State of Virginia*, Jefferson wrote, circa 1781, "The private houses are very rarely constructed of stone or brick, much the greater portion being of scantling and boards, plaster with lime. It is impossible to devise things more ugly, uncomfortable, and happily more perishable. There are two or three plans, on one of which according to its size, most of the houses in the State are built."[4] The consequence of such ordinary building was clear. "A country whose buildings are of wood," Jefferson concluded, "can never increase in its improvements to any considerable degree. Their duration is highly estimated at 50 years. Every half century then our country becomes a tabula rasa, whereon we have to set out anew, as in the first moment of seating it. Whereas when buildings are of durable materials, every new edifice is an actual and permanent acquisition to the state, adding to its value as well as to its ornament."[5]

Whenever and wherever Jefferson traveled (especially later, when he finally did voyage to Europe), he looked at architecture, but he also displayed a breadth of interests as a tourist, always inquisitive and observant and a diligent recorder of useful data on many subjects. In France, his inclinations to record empirical evidence and practical information focused frequently on wine, the weather, and commercial and agricultural issues, demonstrating the objective side of his character as a gentleman scientist of the Age of Enlightenment. On the other hand, his observations of and response to architecture could at times be emotional, as evidenced by his famous admission of gazing for hours at a single, landmark building. In architecture, too, his thinking was revolutionary, standing above that of his contemporaries. His observations in the field had a purpose springing from his desire to discover a better stylistic model that could improve public taste in America at a critical and formative period of societal and cultural development of the new nation.

In his pursuit of models for the new American democracy, Jefferson found English architecture generally lacking in the level of design excellence that his books on architecture promised. He admired English gardens, but England's architecture, he recorded, displayed some of the most wretched design he had ever seen. In disparaging English architecture, Jefferson wrote to John Page that his comments on unworthy building design did not mean "to except America, where it is bad, nor even Virginia, where it is worse than any other part of America."[6] In the face of unacceptable colonial architecture, Jefferson looked to travel as a means to discover a revolutionary architecture to match the revolutionary politics and recent events in which he had taken a leading role. When an architectural site became an object of interest during his travels, this eighteenth-century gentleman became a student, intent on educating himself so as to better educate American citizens back home on matters of taste.

In contrast to provincial architecture in Virginia and "wretched" architecture in England, France was another matter, although Jefferson asserted that London's architecture was better than that of Paris (this was pre-Haussmann Paris, of course), and Philadelphia's better than London's![7] Jefferson liked the French, and concerning French culture, he recorded this conclusion: "Were I to proceed to tell you how much I enjoy their architecture, sculpture, painting, music, I should want words. It is in these arts they shine."[8] Whatever his thoughts about Philadelphia, his assessment of the state of architectural taste in America remained low. "The genius of architecture," he lamented, "seems to have shed its maledictions over this land. Buildings are often erected, by individuals, of considerable expense. To give these symmetry and taste would not increase their cost." But in America, "the first principles of the art are unknown, and there exists scarcely a model among us sufficiently chaste to give an idea of them."[9] America was ready for an aesthetic revolution, and Jefferson was just the revolutionary to spark it.

Like any traveler's architectural views, Jefferson's were informed by the sites he saw, however limited they may be. To a large degree, the aesthetic opinions of his youth were shaped by the architecture of the colonial capital of Williamsburg, Virginia. In 1760, Jefferson went to Williamsburg to study at the College of William and Mary; nine years later, and until the Revolution, Jefferson represented Albemarle County in the House of Burgesses there. He returned to Williamsburg as governor of Virginia in 1779. Throughout this period, he became familiar with the colonial capital but concluded that in architectural terms there was nothing there worthy of emulation. However beloved it may be for subsequent visitors, the now-restored prerevolutionary architecture of colonial Williamsburg did not please Jefferson. He considered the so-called Wren Building at William and Mary, together with the Public Hospital there (not extant), to be "rude, mis-shapen piles, which but that they have roofs, would be taken for brick-kilns."[10]

What was missing was an explicit classicism, which Jefferson considered fundamental to meritorious architecture. He wanted columns. Although he found that the Governor's Palace in Williamsburg was spacious, was "prettily situated," and had some level of commodity within, it "was not handsome without," although it was "capable of being made an elegant seat."[11] Since it lacked columns, one of Jefferson's early suggestions as a learned gentleman with an interest in architecture was to propose a temple front for the residence. A portico would ennoble the brick kiln, and books Jefferson had collected provided models for use of columns, for adaptation of temple fronts, and for other borrowed elements of classicism.[12] In late Georgian America, such explicit classicism was revolutionary.

Jefferson's personal library, amassed throughout his life, made clear the benefits of the classical language of architecture. Notably, he owned a copy of Palladio's *I quattro libri dell'architettura* (*Four Books of Architecture*, 1570) in which the ancient Roman temple front was repeatedly adapted to loggias, porches, and monumental facades of villas and country estates on the Veneto.[13] These sophisticated farm buildings, which Palladio had designed for a new generation of Italian agricultural elite, offered what Jefferson later called chaste models for America. Indeed, Jefferson was the very embodiment of the enlightened

American farmer, both architect and client for classicism in an environment not unlike Palladio's. A major development of the early years of the republic has been characterized as the Hamilton-Jefferson debate in America, setting the worlds of commerce, money, and business at odds with the pastoral ideal of the western, rural farmer.[14] A parallel can be found in the changing world of the Veneto in northern Italy to which Palladio had earlier responded in the sixteenth century: the death of Venetian mercantile supremacy and the rise of the Vicenza farmer class. Palladian models for an architecture to house this rising farmer class could fit right into the Jeffersonian agrarian ideal in the new American republic.

Jefferson's first scheme for Monticello (ca. 1777), therefore, adopted the form of the double-portico elevation of Palladio and in turn established a classical model for American houses constructed by Jefferson's generation and by subsequent pioneers who spread Jeffersonian Palladianism westward. Prior to the first Monticello, there were earlier, although rare, Palladian double porticos in America, most notably Drayton Hall (ca. 1730), near Charleston, and the Miles Brewton House (ca. 1769) in the same town, houses influenced by Anglo-Palladian models from England or known from books, rather than being spawned by Jefferson. Ann Byrne, however, has studied the dissemination of the first Monticello scheme, at a vernacular level, and has found examples of Jefferson-inspired double porticoed houses erected throughout the Old and New South, spreading into the trans-Appalachian middle states. That such a feature is evidenced as far distant as New Echota, Georgia, in a house built for Joseph Vann, a Cherokee Indian chieftain, is almost certainly not a product of book models so much as a populist migration of Jeffersonian influence.[15]

Public taste, Jefferson thought, would be *most* effectively improved by the example of public architecture. In addition to his homes, Monticello and Poplar Forest, Jefferson's best-known built works were in the public realm: the Virginia State Capitol and the buildings of the University of Virginia. They are the alpha and omega of his career as a confirmed classicist architect and are the embodiments of the benefits to Jefferson of both travel and books. In addition, they personify Jefferson's role as teacher-architect, as each was conceived as an embodiment of the ideal, as didactic architecture promoting classicism as a model for an improving public taste. The form of the Virginia State Capitol derived directly from Jefferson's knowledge of books as well as his experiences as a traveler in search of roots.

Both books and travel opened the door to the lost (in America at least) heritage of classicism. Jefferson sought to reestablish connections with a classical Western civilization that for eighteenth-century America had been linked to England, but which barely manifested itself in American Georgian architecture and was not typical of the colonial architecture Jefferson found wretched. With the umbilical attachment to the mother country now cut, an architectural isolation threatened even more. The infant American republic was a nation without a history. Historic roots and republican values, for Jefferson as a traveler in Europe, were to be rediscovered: they would be found in classical republics, in ancient Rome whose virtues were embodied in the very stone of its preserved classical architecture. If Jefferson's knowledge of the Western traditions in architecture had been limited, prior to 1784, to books, for the five years between 1784 and 1789, his travel experiences were able to expand his thoughts and aesthetic sensibilities.

Jefferson Abroad: Confirming the Architect's Classical Taste

In 1784, Jefferson was appointed minister to France, a post he accepted eagerly, recognizing that it opened new opportunities for travel. His wife had died in 1782, and Jefferson now felt free to accept the commission. As mentioned earlier, he had expressed to Lafayette his belief that travel abroad would allow him "to [combine] public service with private gratification." Jefferson looked forward to observing improvements in science and the arts in civilized countries abroad, following itineraries as prescribed by public duty as well as by personal interests and amusement. He left New York in July; landed in Portsmouth, England, twenty-one days later; almost immediately crossed the channel; and was on his way to his post at the Court of Versailles. By the time he returned to Virginia in 1789, he had traveled to six European countries.

There were diplomatic duties, of course, but Jefferson's secondary agenda was as a tourist. Sometimes his activities as a tourist were typical of the sightseeing procedures of many newcomers to foreign countries: "In great cities, I go to see what travelers think alone worthy of being seen; but I make a job of it, and generally gulp it all down in a day." But he was a Jefferson, not a Hamiltonian, and preferred the countryside and small towns. "On the other hand," Jefferson continued, "I am never satiated with rambling through the fields, examining the culture and the cultivators, with a degree of curiosity which makes some take me to be a fool, and others to be much wiser than I am." In summary, Jefferson wrote Lafayette from Nice, "I am constantly roving about, to see what I have never seen before and shall never see again."[16]

At times Jefferson the wine connoisseur dominated, and the American routed his travels to noted vineyards, sampling local wines and describing in his notebook their characteristics and prices and his numerous purchases.[17] On other occasions, he studied canals; farming practices; the economic hardships, housing, and way of life of the working poor; or implements for harvesting rice in northwestern Italy. In this latter pursuit of information about the Piedmont rice culture, Jefferson even arranged for a muleteer "who passes every week between Vercelli and Genoa" to "smuggle a sack of rough rice for me to Genoa; it being death to export it in that form."[18] Jefferson's interest in his side trip to northern Italy was to compare the Piedmont rice with that of the Carolinas and to study

Piedmont husking machines to determine how the Italians cleaned their rice. Finally, whether in Paris or while traveling, Jefferson embraced architecture: his search for "chaste and perfect" European models of taste for the arts of his new country.[19]

Jefferson wrote to Madison in September 1785, stating clearly his intentions first to observe art and architecture, and then to provide models for the benefit of improving American public taste. "How is a taste in this beautiful art to be formed in our countrymen," Jefferson asked Madison rhetorically, "unless we avail ourselves of every occasion when public buildings are to be erected, of presenting to them models for their study and imitation?" He wrote of architecture's imprint on the mind for good or bad: "The comfort of laying out the public money for something honourable, the satisfaction of seeing an object and proof of national good taste, and the regret and mortification of erecting a monument of our barbarism which will be loaded with execrations, as long as it shall endure . . . you see I am an enthusiast on the subject of the arts. But it is an enthusiasm of which I am not ashamed, as its object is to improve the taste of my countrymen, to increase their reputation, to reconcile them to the rest of the world, and procure them its praise."[20]

These comments to Madison had been prompted by a request Jefferson received during the summer of 1785 from the Virginia Assembly regarding plans for the new state capitol building. Jefferson was in France, and yet his colleagues in Virginia knew well that he was, among all Virginians, the best for advice in architectural matters. Jefferson consulted Charles Louis Clérisseau, a prominent French neoclassical architect. Clérisseau had won the Prix de Rome in 1751.[21] He had accompanied Robert Adam on his grand tour (and also executed drawings for Adam's 1764 publication, *Ruins of the Emperor Diocletian's Palace at Spalatro in Dalmatia* [now Croatia]) and, significantly for Jefferson, was the author of *The Antiquities of France: Monuments de Nîmes* (1778, 42 plates). Clérisseau was the ideal collaborator to draw on classicism as a model for the Virginia capitol project and to work with Jefferson on preliminary plans.

Jefferson had not yet visited Nîmes, the subject of Clérisseau's portfolio of "antiquities" renderings, and so Jefferson was familiar with the Maison Carrée there only through drawings. The design relationship between the Maison Carrée in Nîmes and the Virginia State Capitol is evidenced by Clérisseau's model, now displayed at the capitol. As Jefferson explained in his *Autobiography* (written in 1821):

> I was written to in 1785 (being then in Paris) by Directors appointed to superintend the building of the Capitol in Richmond, to advise them as to a plan. . . . Thinking it a favorable opportunity of introducing into the state an example of architecture in the classic style of antiquity, and the Maison quarrée of Nismes [Maison Carrée of Nîmes], an antient Roman temple, being considered as the most perfect model existing . . . I applied to M. Clerissault, who

> had published drawings of the Antiquities of Nismes, to have me a model of the building made in stucco, only changing the order from Corinthian to Ionic, on account of the difficulty of the Corinthian capitals.[22]

It was a revolutionary architecture; nothing like it yet existed in the colonies or the early republic.

Jefferson understood that American craftsmanship and familiarity with classical design were still undeveloped, and the inability of native carvers to execute, for instance, an ornate Corinthian capital encouraged the simplification of the order. Jefferson continued, "To adapt the exterior to our use, I drew a plan for the interior, with the apartments necessary for legislative, executive, and judiciary purposes, and accommodated in their size and distribution to the form and dimensions of the building. These were forwarded to the Directors in 1786, and were carried into execution, with some variation not for the better, the most important of which however admit of future correction."[23]

Jefferson described his designs as "not the brat of a whimsical conception" but "simple and sublime . . . copied from the most precious, the most perfect model of antient architecture remaining on earth; one which has received the approbation of near 2000 years, and which is sufficiently remarkable to have been visited by all travelers," including one day himself, he hoped.[24] So the model and drawings were sent to Richmond well before Jefferson had traveled to Nîmes to see the Roman temple on site. Like many students of architecture since, Jefferson first knew the building from books and by means of drawings before he experienced it as a tourist. But he remained eager to study ancient Roman classical architecture firsthand and, in 1787 he finally had the opportunity to go to Nîmes. What brought him to southern France?

Jefferson's travels in Europe during his diplomatic mission as minister to the court at Versailles have been well documented.[25] After arriving in Paris on August 6, 1784, he soon began to think of France as his second home; he liked the French, saw the sights in Paris, visited the gardens and court at Versailles, went "almost daily" to the Tuileries, and was "violently smitten" by the architecture of the Hôtel de Salm along the Seine. The cylindrical riverfront bay of the Hôtel de Salm, for instance, influenced his later designs for Monticello. A similar seed may have been planted by the Comte d'Artois's Château de Bagatelle and its park, which Jefferson visited with Maria Cosway.

But Jefferson's new world was to extend beyond Paris. In the spring of 1786, he traveled for six weeks in England; the following spring, he toured southern France and northern Italy (February 28–June 10, his most extensive trip outside of Paris); and in the spring of 1788 he traveled to Holland, Belgium, and parts of Germany. Although in his quest for classicism he never got to Rome, it was during his travel through Provence and Languedoc that he saw some of the best-preserved ruins of ancient Roman architecture in Europe. For his work as an architect, this trip was significant. Jefferson wrote William Short that, in architecture, his focus everywhere was "the remains of antiquity. These are more in number and less injured by time, than I expected, and have been to me a great treat. Those in Nismes, both in dignity and preservation, stand first."[26]

Conspiracy among the Roman Columns: Vendek and Jefferson's Other Agenda

What did Jefferson do in Nîmes? We know he visited the Pont du Gard, compared the arena at Nîmes with that at Arles, and toured other Roman ruins much as countless tourists before and since have done. Arriving finally at the pseudo-peripteral Corinthian temple, which for centuries has been known as the Maison Carrée and had served as the model for his Virginia capitol, Jefferson recorded his now-familiar emotional reaction to classical architecture. In a letter of March 20, 1787, to Madame de Tessé, Lafayette's aunt and a frequent correspondent, and almost in awe before the ancient monument, Jefferson wrote that he sat before the Roman temple "gazing whole hours . . . like a lover at his mistress."[27] Jefferson continued, "The stocking weavers and silk spinners around it consider me as an hypochondriac Englishman, about to write with a pistol the last chapter of his history." How maudlin! He went on to describe to Madame de Tessé: "This is the second time I've been in love since I left Paris. The first was with a Diana at the Chateau de Laye Epinaye in the Beaujolois, a delicious morsel of sculpture by Michael Angelo Slodtz. This, you will say, was in rule, to fall in love with a fine woman: but, with a house! It is out of all precedent! No, madam, it is not without a precedent in my own history."[28] Jefferson confessed that, as a tourist, he was not a casual observer of architecture or landscape, and he might well have described his trip to southern France as his formative "grand tour": "From Lyon to Nismes I have been nourished with the remains of Roman grandeur."[29]

However, Nîmes was both an architectural destination and a side trip that was potentially conspiratorial, for the American revolutionary leader was no ordinary traveler, and Roman ruins were not his only reason for going there. Jefferson indicated to his daughter Patsy that "other considerations also concurred—instruction, amusement, and abstraction from business, of which I had too much in Paris."[30] But in a double twist of diplomatic intrigue, there were alleged reasons, and real reasons, for Jefferson's renowned sojourn in Nîmes. His rendezvous there with "Vendek" concerned another revolution and is a remarkable episode in Jefferson's life, which has remained a mere footnote in Jefferson studies.

Six months earlier, on September 4, 1786, in Paris, Jefferson fell and broke his right wrist. It was more than a sprain and appears never to have been properly set. At the time, he had been planning a trip to southern France for the following month. The court was to sojourn to Fontainebleau on October 10, and Jefferson planned to spend the first week at Fontainebleau but then to absent himself for the remainder of the court's continuance there. He wrote to Colonel William S. Smith nine days after his accident that his plan was to tour as far as the canal at Languedoc, where he hoped to obtain information helpful to "such of our states as are engaged in works of that kind."[31] His wrist was slow to heal, however, and likely discouraged travel, although Jefferson told Maria Cosway it was the "lateness of the season" that "obliges me to decline my journey to the South of France."[32]

To any writer and prolific correspondent, a dislocated wrist is no minor irritant, and Jefferson's wrist was still troublesome the following spring. His letters during this period are less abundant and many had to be written with his left hand. While recuperating in Paris, for instance, he wrote several short letters to excuse his delays in proper correspondence, indicating writing was slow and still painful.[33] A month after his accident, however, he also received his first letter from Vendek, a young revolutionary studying at the University of Montpellier in southern France and seeking a private audience with Jefferson. The wrist continued to bother him, and winter was approaching, so Jefferson remained in Paris but responded to Vendek two weeks later by letter. As it happened, Jefferson was advised to visit mineral springs to restore his hand, and he told John Adams that, among the several recommended locations of healing waters, he elected to visit the medicinal spa at Aix-en-Provence because it was closest to the seaports he wanted to tour: Marseilles, Bordeaux, Nantes, and Lorient.[34] It was also near Montpellier.

Travel was never of singular purpose for Jefferson. When he finally left Paris for southern France on February 28, 1787, despite his still-painful wrist, it took him a month to arrive at Aix, as he was always stopping to indulge some scientific, artistic, or agrarian interest. He wrote to William Short, "Architecture, painting, sculpture, antiquities, agriculture, the condition of the laboring poor fill all my moments."[35] But once he arrived at Aix, he stayed for four days, took forty showers although "without sensible benefit," so he finally concluded that it was "useless to continue them." He wrote Short again, this time from Toulon, reporting, "My wrist strengthens slowly; [but] it is time that I took as the surest remedy, & that I believe will restore it at length."[36]

In the meantime, Jefferson had arranged a rendezvous in Nîmes with his correspondent Vendek, an appointment initially instigated by letters written to Jefferson the previous October and November, when Jefferson had first planned his trip to southern France, but which his injury had forced him to postpone. The letters that had been signed Vendek were penned in an idiosyncratic French by a young Brazilian revolutionary named José da Maia (or Maya) and sent to Jefferson in Paris from Montpellier. "J'ai une chose de tres grande consequence à Vous communiquer," wrote da Maia, "mais comme l'etat de ma santé ne me permet pas de pouvoir avoir l'honeur d'aller Vous trouver à Paris, je Vous prie de vouloir bien avoir la bonté de me dire, si je puis avec sureté Vous la communiquer par lettre; puisque je suis etranger, et par consequent peu instruit des usages du pays. Je Vous demande bien pardon de la liberté, que prends, et je Vous prie aussi d'en addresser la reponse à Mr. Vigarons Conseiller du Roy, et Professeur en medicine a l'Université de Montpellier."[37]

Jefferson's response of October 16 has been lost, but da Maia's subsequent letter of November 21 explains why this young Brazilian revolutionary wanted to confer with Jefferson "safely." Jefferson was already a figure of renown as author of the Declaration of Independence and was considered by the Brazilian to be the leading statesman of the successfully established United States of America. Revolutionaries in Brazil were contemplating a revolt against the Portuguese there, a revolution that was modeled in the spirit of the American Revolution against Mother England. Jefferson, now minister to France, charged with securing formal recognition from and establishing good relations with European powers, including Portugal, now found himself in correspondence with a Brazilian revolutionary seeking advice from the noted American revolutionary, concerning the overthrow of Portugal in Brazil. Both Jefferson, at the Court of Versailles, and John Adams, at the Court of St. James, were aware of the need not to jeopardize relations between the new United States and Portugal. Indeed, a central role of both Adams in London and Jefferson in Paris was to consolidate, not undermine, the establishment of the United States within diplomatic circles of late eighteenth-century Europe.

Thus, while still recuperating from his accident in Paris, Jefferson received a second letter from Vendek dated November 21, 1786. "Je suis Bresilien," da Maia writes, and he gets right to the point in describing the plight of Brazilians under Portuguese rule and his hope that Brazil, with America's help, can follow its example in rebelling against the mother country: "Vous savez, que ma malheureuse patrie gémit dans un affreux esclavage, qui devient chaque [jour] plus insupportable depuis l'epoque de Votre glorieuse independence, puisque les barbares Portugais n'epargnent rien pour nous rendre malheureux de crainte que nous suivions Vos pas."[38] Da Maia then cites the Brazilians' circumstances in Jeffersonian terms as being counter to natural law: "Et comme nous connoîçons, que ces usurpateurs contre la loi de la nature, et de l'humanité ne songent, que à nous accabler, nous nous sommes decidés à suivre le frappant exemple, que Vous venez de nous donner, et par consequence à briser nos chaines, et à faire revivre notre liberté, qui est toutàfait morte, et accablée par la force, qui est le seul droit, qu'ont les Européens sur l'Amerique."[39]

The Brazilians needed help in gaining their own independence, and da Maia tells Jefferson that help should come from the United States. Moreover, the Brazilian revolutionaries were prepared to pay for America's assistance:

> Mais il s'agit d'avoir une puissance, qui donne la main aux Bresiliens, attendu que l'Hispanie ne manquera pas de se joindre à Portugal; et malgré

> les avantages, que nous avons pour nous defendre, nous ne pourrons pas le faire, ou du moins il ne seroit pas prudent de nous hazarder sans etre surs d'y reussir. Cel[à] posé, Monsegneur, c'e[s]t Votre nation, que nous croyons plus propre pour donner du secours non seulement parce que c'est elle, qui nous a donné l'exemple, mais aussi parce que la nature nous a fait habitants du meme continent, et par consequence en quelque façon compatriotes; de notre part nous sommes pre[ts] à donner tout l'argent, qui sera necessaire, et à temoigner en tout temps notre reconnoissence envers nos bienfaisants.[40]

That is the gist of it, da Maia tells Jefferson, and the very reason he came to France, inasmuch as going to America to consult with American revolutionaries would have raised suspicions: "It's for you now to judge whether it can take place." If Jefferson needed to consult his country, da Maia was in a position to provide him with whatever further information was necessary.[41]

We know what then transpired thanks to a letter Jefferson wrote to John Jay in May 1787 after he had returned to Paris from southern France. Jefferson certainly felt compelled to tell Congress of his communications with da Maia. He sent Jay a copy in the original French of da Maia's November 22, 1786, letter ("omitting only the former parts"), and Jefferson detailed how he came to meet the Brazilian clandestinely in Nîmes: "As by this time I had been advised to try the waters of Aix, I wrote to the gentleman my design, and that I would go off my road as far as Nisme, under the pretext of seeing the antiquities of that place, if he would meet me there."[42] The reference to "pretext," of course, was itself specious. Jefferson *wanted* to see the Roman sites in Nîmes, and as his letter to Madame de Tessé shows, his interest in Nîmes was not casual. But it was also a means to meet with the Brazilian revolutionary without the suspicion da Maia feared from a more formal meeting in Paris or America. "He met me," Jefferson related to John Jay, "& the following is the sum of the information I received from him." I quote Jefferson's letter at length, for it shows his thoroughness in recording what appears to be lengthy consultation(s?) between the revolutionaries.

Da Maia first described the makeup of the population of Brazil and its potential involvement in any revolution. As Jefferson relays the information to Jay:

> Brazil contains as many inhabitants as Portugal. They are 1. Portuguese. 2. Native whites. 3. Black & mulatto slaves. 4. Indians civilized and savage. 1. The Portuguese are few in number, mostly married there, have lost sight of their native country as well as the prospect of returning to it & are disposed to become independent. 2. The native whites form the body of their nation. 3. The slaves are as numerous as the free. 4. The civilized Indians have no energy & the savage would not meddle. There are 20,000 regular troops. Originally these were Portuguese, but as they died off they were replaced by natives, so that these compose at present the mass of the troops and may be counted on by their native country. The officers are partly Portuguese partly Brazilian.

> Their bravery is not doubted, & they understand the parade but not the science of their profession. They have no bias for Portugal but no energy either for anything. The priests are partly Portuguese, partly Brazilian, and will not interest themselves much. The Noblesse are scarcely known as such. They will in no manner be distinguished from the people. The men of letters are those most desirous of a revolution. The people are not much under the influence of their priests, most of them read & write, possess arms, & are in the habit of using them for hunting. The slaves will take the side of their masters. In short, as to the question of revolution, there is but one mind in that country.[43]

Jefferson then conveyed to Jay the problem of a lack of leadership in Brazil and commented on the availability of funds to pay for outside help:

> But there appears no person capable of conducting a revolution or willing to venture himself at its head, without the aid of some powerful nation, as the people of their own might fail them. There is no printing press in Brazil. They consider the North American revolution as a precedent for theirs. They look to the United States as most likely to give them honest support & from a variety of considerations have the strongest prejudice in our favor. This informant is a native and inhabitant of Rio [de] Janeiro the present metropolis which contains 30,000 inhabitants, knows well St. Salvador the former one, and the mines d'or which are in the center of the country. These are all for a revolution, &, constituting a body of the nation, the other parts will follow them. The King's fifth of the mines yields annually 13 millions of crusadoes or half dollars. He has the sole right of searching for diamonds & other precious stones which yields him about half as much. His income alone then from these two sources is about 10 millions of dollars annually: but the remaining part of the produce of the mines, being 26 millions, might be counted on for effecting a revolution. Besides the arms in the hands of the people, there are public magazines. They have abundance of horses, but only a part of their country would admit the service of horses.[44]

And then da Maia's conversation with Jefferson outlined how the United States could help. As Jefferson reported to Jay, "They would want cannon, ammunition, ships, sailors, soldiers, & officers for which they are disposed to look to the U.S., always understood that every service & furniture will be well paid."[45]

What followed, with typical Jeffersonian thoroughness, was an assessment of resources available to support a revolution from within Brazil as well as information Jefferson shared with Jay regarding the political effectiveness of Portugal's (or Spain's) assistance in quelling a revolution.

> Corn costs about 20 livres a 100 lb. They have flesh in the greatest abundance, insomuch as in some parts they kill beeves for the skin only. The whale fishery is carried on by Brazilians altogether, & not by Portuguese; but in very

> small vessels, so that the fishermen know nothing of managing a large ship. They would want of us at all times shipping, corn & salt fish. The latter is a great article, & they are at present supplied with it from Portugal. Portugal being without either army or navy, could not attempt an invasion under a twelvemonth. Considering of what it would be composed, it would not be much to be feared, and if it failed, they would probably never attempt a second. Indeed, this source of their wealth, being intercepted, they are scarcely capable of a first effort. The thinking part of the nation are so sensible of this, that they consider an early separation inevitable. There is an implacable hatred between the Brazilians & Portuguese; to reconcile which a former minister adopted the policy of letting the Brazilians into a participation of public offices; but subsequent administrations have reverted to the ancient policy of keeping the administration in the hands of the native Portuguese. There is a mixture of natives of the old appointments still remaining in office. If Spain should invade them on their southern extremities, these are so distant from the body of their settlements that they could not penetrate thence, and Spanish enterprise is not formidable. The mines d'or are among mountains, inaccessible to any army, and Rio [de] Janeiro is considered as the strongest port in the world after Gibraltar. In case of a successful revolution, a republican government in a single body, would probably be established.[46]

All of this was essentially da Maia's information and argument in support of his solicitation of American help in a Brazilian revolution.

Jefferson was in an awkward position. However sympathetic he may have been in a revolutionary effort (not unlike his own recent experiences in removing the oppressive mantle from American colonial shoulders), he was, after all, no longer the American revolutionary and model and savior for all subsequent revolutions. So Jefferson, as he repeated to Jay, "took care to impress on [da Maia] thro' the whole of our conversation that I had neither instruction nor authority to say a word to anybody on this subject, and that I could only give him my own ideas as a single individual." That, of course, was not what da Maia had hoped to hear. Jefferson told the Brazilian that "we were not in a position to meddle nationally in any war; that we wished particularly to cultivate the friendship of Portugal, with whom we have an advantageous commerce." On the other hand, Jefferson *was* sympathetic. He admitted "that yet a successful revolution in Brazil could not be uninteresting to us," and that help from mercenaries might be possible: "that prospects of lucre might possibly draw numbers of individuals to their aid, and purer motives our officers, among whom are many excellent." Finally, Jefferson noted "that our citizens, being free to leave their own country individually without the consent of their governments, are equally free to go to any other."[47]

Thus Jefferson, on his sojourn in Nîmes, was more than an American tourist, more even than a traveling devotee of architecture. Da Maia was conducting a potentially treasonable exercise in espionage and asking Jefferson to be an accomplice by arranging for American help in an imminent Brazilian revolution. Da Maia did not receive the support from America that he had hoped for, and Jefferson's trip to Nîmes is far better known for confirming a revolution in architecture than for clandestine revolutionary plotting linked to Brazil. Nonetheless, it is interesting to note that only two years after Jefferson's meeting with da Maia, the first attempt to establish a republic in Brazil, the so-called Minas Conspiracy (Inconfidência Mineira) of 1789, was exposed, and ended on April 21, 1792, with the execution in Rio de Janeiro of "Tiradentes" (the "tooth puller"), the conspiracy's leader. Six years later, a second "Bahian" conspiracy against Portugal was exposed.[48] Brazilian independence was finally achieved in the fall of 1822, still within Jefferson's lifetime; two years before Jefferson's death, the United States, under President James Monroe, recognized Brazil in 1824. Jefferson declared in his final days his assessment that "we have no right to intermeddle with the form of government of other nations, yet it is lawful to wish to see no emperors or kings in our hemisphere, and that Brazil, as well as Mexico, will homologize with us."[49]

That principle had prevented Jefferson from conspiring with José da Maia in Nîmes thirty-five years earlier. Jefferson's influence on the Brazilian revolution would remain indirect. The only revolution that Nîmes inspired for Jefferson was an architectural one. The town, still known for its Roman antiquities, was Mecca for Jefferson and his fountainhead of classicism. In the end, the reason for going to Nîmes that he suggested as a "pretext" to the young Brazilian revolutionary was, indeed, Jefferson's real reason for visiting the town in southern France. His intention as a tourist in Provence was ultimately to improve the public taste of American citizens by exporting Roman ideals and aesthetics to the frontier. That became Jefferson's second revolution, an architectural revolution that followed his political one and that succeeded: from the days of his return to the United States in 1790, an American neoclassicism emerged in both public and private architecture in the form of what historians have labeled Jeffersonian classicism, including temple-fronted houses, a Clérisseau- and Adam-influenced American Federal style, and ultimately a national Greek Revival style of architecture.[50]

Almost immediately upon Jefferson's return to America, the subject of a new national capital in Washington, DC, offered Jefferson a major opportunity to exercise his influence on architecture. An architectural competition was held in 1792; indeed, there were three competitions for three designs that would secure classicism as the very foundation for our early national architecture. The competitions called for designs for the President's House, for the capitol building, and for the city's layout of streets and public buildings as a whole. The competitions offer evidence that the concerns of the founding fathers—George Washington, Thomas Jefferson, and others—extended beyond politics, diplomacy, European affairs, or national finance (issues of governance) to embrace aesthetics; for in this arena as well, Washington and Jefferson accepted responsibility as stewards of the new nation's welfare. For Jefferson, putting colonial buildings behind him, the aesthetic revolution prompted the spearheading of a new national architecture.

Jefferson feared that, left to its own devices, the District of Columbia might, like Williamsburg, be built up of "brick kilns" instead of embracing more propitious models of public architecture. Indeed, Jefferson, as an architect, did more than encourage a new architecture; he also submitted his own competition entry for the President's House, the residence later named the White House, and whose design was ultimately awarded to the Irish architect James Hoban. Hoban's White House had a Palladian portico, with which Jefferson would have been adequately pleased. But Jefferson's own competition entry was even more Palladian. He proposed a domed and porticoed residence based on the Villa Capra in Vicenza, perhaps Palladio's most famous house and a villa known as the Rotunda.

Jefferson's President's House would have joined a small group of landmarks—"near replicas" in the English-speaking world—that had copied Palladio's famous Rotunda during the eighteenth century. In 1725, Lord Burlington built a reduced-scale version of the Villa Capra at Chiswick, and in 1723, Colen Campbell enlarged the model into a country house southeast of London called Mereworth Castle. Jefferson's Villa Capra replica was not to be, and no doubt would today be so altered as to be little recognized, even if it had been built, inasmuch as such an ideal geometric form as Palladio's Villa Capra would be difficult to expand. To be sure, every president after Jefferson would have attempted to do so, most likely by retaining the Rotunda as a centerpiece of an ever-enlarging or unfolding of extended wings in a lateral Palladian composition of hyphens and temple end pavilions. So Jefferson, as architect, did not prevail at the President's House. Ironically, by this date, Palladianism was already old-fashioned; indeed, Jefferson's Virginia Capitol marks the transition to neoclassicism.

Jefferson's continued call for a more explicit Roman neoclassicism undoubtedly influenced the direction established for Washington in its civic monuments. The city plan by Charles L'Enfant was classically baroque, a translation, as is well known, of the garden layout at Versailles (as, indeed, Francis Nicholson's plan for Williamsburg also was, arguably, but at a less sophisticated level). But the city of Washington's great domed Capitol, so influential in the design of most subsequent state capitols, became the landmark of the new aesthetic. Thus, the third competition of 1792, that for the U.S. Capitol building, began a long period of construction, additions, and enlargements for the new nation's legislative landmark, envisioning a dome from the start, and culminating in Thomas U. Walters's huge, cast-iron dome completed during the Civil War. From the very start, Jefferson insisted the capitol building be classical. He wrote to L'Enfant on April 10, 1791, "Whenever it is proposed to prepare plans for the Capitol, I should prefer the adoption of some one of the models of antiquity which have had the approbation of thousands of years."[51] The history of construction is too long to summarize here, but we can at least note that it was Benjamin Latrobe, an English émigré architect whom Jefferson may be said to have mentored, whose rotunda established the core of the building and whose tobacco and corncob capitals went so far as to translate classical column styles into a new, American classical order.[52]

Jefferson wrote Latrobe in October 1809 congratulating him "on the successful completion of . . . the Senate chamber as well as . . . the Hall of Justice," rooms Jefferson considered to be worthy counterparts of that of the representatives. "It would give me pleasure," Jefferson continued, "to learn that Congress will consent to proceed on the middle building," the great rotunda. Jefferson's assessment of the Capitol project? "I have no doubt," he told Latrobe, "that the work when finished will be a durable and honorable monument of our infant republic, and will bear favorable comparison with the remains of the same kind of the ancient republics of Greece and Rome."[53] Latrobe's neoclassicism ultimately spread from Washington and Baltimore to New Orleans, and through his followers such as William Strickland, from Philadelphia to Nashville.

Later in life, Thomas Jefferson, the scholar architect, mentor, and educator, played a final role in promoting an improved public taste when he established the University of Virginia. He built his academic village as a model of classicism with facade elevations taken directly from the pages of books in his library. It was a contribution Jefferson named as one of the most important of his lifetime. The library was the noblest neo-Roman rotunda of the era, based on the Pantheon in Rome, the grandest domed temple of its day. Flanking each side of the collegiate green was a colonnade joining five pavilions, each modeled on a page from a prominent architectural treatise, so that students of the University of Virginia could observe, in actual built form, examples of classicism as interpreted by the great architects of antiquity and the Renaissance. Temple fronts utilized the Doric, Ionic, and Corinthian orders according to Serlio or Perrault, or other chaste and perfect models from ancient to modern (i.e., eighteenth-century) times. It was Jefferson's final great work as an architect and shaper of public taste. Jefferson's designs embodied those virtues on which education and governance and public taste were to be grounded.

Thomas Jefferson, the traveler and tastemaker, had reconnected the architecture of a new nation to the ancients. It had been his goal from the start, and it reflected Jefferson's revolutionary character, the result of his intellectual, emotional, and highly personal contemplation of an old classicism available for new uses. As we now take our own pilgrimages to Jefferson's classical expressions of a new national architecture for America, we may recall a brief episode that day in Nîmes, when the American revolutionary gazed "whole hours" like a lover at the Maison Carrée.

NOTES

1. John F. Kennedy, "Remarks at a Dinner Honoring Nobel Prize Winners of the Western Hemisphere," April 29, 1962, American Presidency Project, http://www.presidency.ucsb.edu/ws/?pid=8623.

2. "Here was buried Thomas Jefferson, author of the Declaration of American Independence, of the Statute of Virginia for Religious Freedom, and Father of the University of Virginia, born April 2D 1743 O.S. Died [July 4] [1826]."

3. Thomas Jefferson to Marquis de Lafayette, Monticello, August 4, 1781, in *Papers of Thomas Jefferson*, ed. Julian P. Boyd, assoc. ed. Mina R. Bryan and Elizabeth L. Butter, vol. 6 (Princeton, NJ: Princeton University Press, 1952), 112. Thomas Jefferson had been asked to go to France in 1776 as a minister and in 1781 as a peace commissioner. He refused both times due to family obligations. See also Thomas Jefferson to the President of the Continental Congress [John Hancock], Williamsburg, October 11, 1776, in *The Writings of Thomas Jefferson*, ed. Paul Leicester Ford, vol. 2 (New York: G. P. Putnam, 1892–1899), 91–92.

4. Thomas Jefferson, *Notes on the State of Virginia*, ed. William Peden (Chapel Hill: University of North Carolina Press, 1955), 152.

5. Jefferson, 154.

6. Jefferson to John Page, Paris, May 4, 1786, in *Papers of Thomas Jefferson*, ed. Julian P. Boyd, assoc. ed. Mina R. Bryan and Elizabeth L. Butter, vol. 9 (Princeton, NJ: Princeton University Press, 1954), 445.

7. Jefferson to Page, 445. Much of our appreciation of the urban design, uniformity of streetscape, and architectural excellence of Paris results from the later transformation of the city by Baron Georges-Eugène Haussmann during the third quarter of the nineteenth century.

8. Thomas Jefferson to Charles Bellini, Paris, September 30, 1785, in *Papers of Thomas Jefferson*, ed. Julian P. Boyd, assoc. ed. Mina R. Bryan and Elizabeth L. Butter, vol. 8 (Princeton, NJ: Princeton University Press, 1953), 569.

9. Jefferson, *Notes on the State of Virginia*, 153.

10. Jefferson, 153. See also Marcus Whiffen, *The Public Buildings of Williamsburg, Colonial Capital of Virginia: An Architectural History* (Williamsburg, VA: Colonial Williamsburg, 1958), 14.

11. Jefferson, *Notes on the State of Virginia*, 152–153.

12. For a discussion of Jefferson's proposal for remodeling the Governor's Palace and illustrations of his drawings, see Whiffen, *Public Buildings of Williamsburg*, 177–181.

13. Jefferson once wrote James Oldham (a joiner who worked at Monticello in 1801–1804), "There never was a Palladio here, even in private hands, 'til I brought one." Thomas Jefferson to James Oldham, December 24, 1804, Library of Congress, The Thomas Jefferson Papers Series 1, General Correspondence. 1651–1827, http://hdl.loc.gov/loc.mss/mtj.mtjbib014139.

14. See Morton White and Lucia White, *The Intellectual versus the City: From Thomas Jefferson to Frank Lloyd Wright* (Cambridge, MA: Harvard University Press and MIT Press, 1962).

15. See Anne DeRosa Byrne, "The American Palladian Farmhouse: The Superimposed Portico House as an Indicator of Jefferson's Presence in American Vernacular Architecture" (master's thesis, Georgia Institute of Technology, 1982).

16. Thomas Jefferson to Lafayette, Nice, April 11, 1787, in *Papers of Thomas Jefferson*, ed. Julian P. Boyd, assoc. ed. Mina R. Bryan and Frederick Aandahl, vol. 11 (Princeton, NJ: Princeton University Press, 1955), 283.

17. For Jefferson's own account of his journeys through the countryside and wine regions of the Continent in 1787 and 1788, see James McGrath Morris and Persephone

Weene, eds., *Thomas Jefferson's European Travel Diaries* (Ithaca, NY: Isidore Stephanus Sons Publishing, 1987). As biographer Dumas Malone has summarized, "He began with a map of the country, and plans of all towns where they were procurable. Because of this trip he acquired large-scale plans of Lyons, Montpellier, Marseilles, Turin, Milan, Bordeaux, and Orléans. He made it a policy to walk around the ramparts of a town when he first got there, or to go to the top of a steeple for a bird's-eye view. As a sight-seer he was diligent but discriminating, trying not to miss anything good since he was unlikely to come that way again, but not wanting to waste his time or clutter and fatigue his mind with the valueless details rattled off by guides." Dumas Malone, *Jefferson and His Time, II: Jefferson and the Rights of Man* (Boston: Little, Brown, 1951), 115.

18. Anthony Brandt, ed., *Thomas Jefferson's Travels: Selected Writings, 1784–1789* (Washington, DC: National Geographic Society, 2006), 207.

19. For a detailed account by Jefferson of his recorded observations during his 1787 trip to southern France and northern Italy, see "Notes of a Tour into the Southern parts of France, &c. "Memorandums taken on a journey from Paris into the southern parts of France and Northern Italy, in the year 1787," Brandt, 186–230.

20. Thomas Jefferson to James Madison, Paris, September 20, 1785, in *Papers of Thomas Jefferson*, 8:535.

21. The Prix de Rome is the premier competition at the French Ecole des Beaux-Arts, selecting one architectural student each year (based on elaborate drawings from an assigned project). The winner spends the year in Rome producing additional drawings and is guaranteed the top architectural jobs in France. See Donald Egbert, *The Beaux-Arts Tradition in French Architecture Illustrated by the Grands Prix de Rome* (Princeton, NJ: Princeton University Press, 1980).

22. Thomas Jefferson, *Autobiography*, in *Writings of Thomas Jefferson*, 1:63–64.

23. Jefferson, 64.

24. Jefferson to James Currie, Paris, January 28, 1786, in *Papers of Thomas Jefferson*, 9:240.

25. See Edward Dumbauld, *Thomas Jefferson, American Tourist* (Norman: University of Oklahoma Press, 1946); Wendell D. Garret, *The Worlds of Thomas Jefferson* (New York: Weathervane Books, 1972); "Traveling with a Purpose, 1787," the seventh chapter of Dumas Malone, *Jefferson and His Time*, 2:112–130; Roy Moore and Alma Moore, *Thomas Jefferson's Journal to the South of France* (New York: Stewart, Tabori and Chang, 1999); Howard C. Rice Jr., *Thomas Jefferson's Paris* (Princeton, NJ: Princeton University Press, 1976); George Green Shackelford, *Thomas Jefferson's Travels in Europe, 1784–1789* (Baltimore: Johns Hopkins University Press 1995); Douglas L. Wilson and Lucia Stanton, *Jefferson Abroad* (New York: Modern Library 1999); Brandt, *Thomas Jefferson's Travels*; Morris and Weene, *Thomas Jefferson's European Travel Diaries*.

26. Jefferson to William Short, Aix, March 29, 1787, in *Papers of Thomas Jefferson*, 11:254.

27. Thomas Jefferson to Madame de Tessé, Nisme, March 20, 1787, in *Papers of Thomas Jefferson*, 11:226.

28. Jefferson to Madame de Tessé, 226.

29. Jefferson to Madame de Tessé, 226.

30. Thomas Jefferson to Martha [Patsy] Jefferson, Aix-en-Provence, March 28, 1787, in *Papers of Thomas Jefferson*, 11:250.

31. Thomas Jefferson to Col. William Stephens Smith, Paris, September 13, 1786, in *Papers of Thomas Jefferson*, ed. Julian P. Boyd, assoc. ed. Mina R. Bryan, vol. 10 (Princeton, NJ: Princeton University Press, 1954), 362. The canal was originally named Canal royal en Languedoc (Royal Canal in Languedoc) and in 1789 was renamed the Canal du Midi; it was considered at the time to be one of the greatest engineering works of the seventeenth century.

32. Jefferson to Maria Cosway, Paris, October 12, 1786, in *Papers of Thomas Jefferson*, 10:453.

33. Thomas Jefferson to Zachariah Loreilhe, October 30 (in William Short's hand), and November 19; to Maria Cosway, November 19; and to John Trumbull, November 20, 1786, in *Papers of Thomas Jefferson*, 10:497, 543, 542–543, 546.

34. Thomas Jefferson to John Adams, Paris, July 1, 1787, in *Papers of Thomas Jefferson*, 11:515–516.

35. Thomas Jefferson to William Short, Lyons, March 15, 1787, in *Papers of Thomas Jefferson*, 11:215.

36. Thomas Jefferson to William Short, Toulon, April 7, 1787, in *Papers of Thomas Jefferson*, 11:280.

37. "I have a thing of very great consequence to communicate to you; but as the state of my health does not permit me to be able to have the honor of finding you in Paris, I implore you to be kind enough to tell me, whether I can with safety communicate by letter; since I am a foreigner, and by consequence little instructed in the customs of the country. I beg your pardon for the liberty taken, and I beg you also to address the response to Mr. Vigarons, Adviser to the King and Professor of medicine at the University of Montpellier." José da Maia to Thomas Jefferson, Montpellier, October 2, 1786, in *Papers of Thomas Jefferson*, 10:427.

38. "You know that my unhappy country groans in an awful slavery that becomes each day more unbearable since the time of your glorious independence, since the Portuguese barbarians spare nothing to make us unhappy for fear that we may follow in your footsteps." José da Maia to Thomas Jefferson, Montpellier, November 21, 1786, in *Papers of Thomas Jefferson*, 10:546.

39. "And as we may know that these usurpers against the law of nature and humanity think only of afflicting us, we have decided to follow the striking example you have just given us and consequently to break our chains, and to revive our liberty, that is entirely dead, and overwhelmed by force, which is the sole right, that Europeans have over America." da Maia to Jefferson, 546.

40. "But it is a matter of having a power, that gives the hand to the Brazilians, considering that Hispania [Spain] will not fail to join with Portugal; and in spite of the advantages, that we have to defend ourselves, we are unable to do it, or at least it may not be prudent for us to hazard without being sure to succeed in it. That posed, Monsegneur, it is your nation that we believe most proper to give help not only because it is she that has given us the example, but also because nature has made us habitants of the same continent, and by consequence in some ways compatriots; for our part we are ready to give all the money that will be necessary, and to testify in due course our recognition regarding our benefactors." da Maia to Jefferson, 546–547.

41. "Monseigneur, voila à peu près le precis de mes intentions, et c'et pour m'acquiter de cette commition, que je suis venu en France; puisque je ne pouvois pas en Amerique sans donner des soupçons à ceux qui en sçussent, c'est à Vous maintenant à juger s'elles peuvent avoir lieu, et dans le cas, que Voulussiez en consulter Votre nation, je suis en etat de Vous donner toutes les informations, que Vous trouverez necessaires." da Maia to Jefferson, 547.

42. Thomas Jefferson to the Secretary for Foreign Affairs [John Jay], Marseilles, May 4, 1787, in *Papers of Thomas Jefferson*, 11:339.

43. Jefferson to the Secretary for Foreign Affairs, 339–340.

44. Jefferson to the Secretary for Foreign Affairs, 340.

45. Jefferson to the Secretary for Foreign Affairs, 340.

46. Jefferson to the Secretary for Foreign Affairs, 340–341.

47. Jefferson to the Secretary for Foreign Affairs, 341.

48. Donald Ramos, "Social Revolution Frustrated: The Conspiracy of the Tailors in Bahia, 1798," Emanuela P. Leaf, "Brazilian Independence, Minas Gerais, and the Thomas

Jefferson Connection," *Luso-Brazilian Review* 13:1 (Summer 1976): 74–90, https://www.jstor.org/stable/3512717?seq=1#metadata_info_tab_contents.

49. Thomas Jefferson to James Monroe, December 1, 1822, in *The Works of Thomas Jefferson in Twelve Volumes, the Federal Edition*, ed. Paul Leicester Ford, vol. 12 (New York: G. P. Putnam, 1905), 273–274.

50. See Marcus Whiffen, *American Architecture since 1780: A Guide to the Styles* (Cambridge, MA: MIT Press, 1976), and the classic study of America's "national" style during Jefferson's later life: Talbot Hamlin, *Greek Revival Architecture in America* (New York: Oxford University Press, 1944).

51. Thomas Jefferson to Charles L'Enfant, Philadelphia, April 10, 1791, in *Papers of Thomas Jefferson*, ed. Julian P. Boyd, assoc. ed. Ruth W. Lester, vol. 20 (Princeton, NJ: Princeton University Press, 1982), 86.

52. See Glenn Brown, *History of the United States Capitol* (Washington, DC: United States Congress, 2007); Ihna Thayer Frary, *They Built the Capitol* (Richmond, VA: Garrett and Massie, 1940); Pamela Scott and Antoinette J. Lee, *Buildings of the District of Columbia* (New York: Oxford University Press, 1993). For views of the capitol during various stages of its history, see John Reps, *Washington on View: The Nation's Capital since 1790* (Chapel Hill: University of North Carolina Press, 1991).

53. Thomas Jefferson to Benjamin Latrobe, Monticello, October 10, 1809, in *The Papers of Thomas Jefferson: Retirement Sources*, ed. J. Jefferson Looney, vol. 1 (Princeton, NJ: Princeton University Press, 2004), 595.

CHAPTER 5

"Uncle to All the World"

THE VIRTUAL AFTERLIVES OF CAPTAIN TOBIAS SHANDY, 1831–1948

W. B. Gerard

The character of Captain Tobias Shandy has been a central part of the ongoing popularity of Laurence Sterne's novel *The Life and Opinions of Tristram Shandy, Gentleman*, and crucial in shaping perception of the text since the publication of its first two volumes in 1759. The particular affection for the character is evident, for instance, in numerous references to Uncle Toby's kindly release of the fly, which appear in such diverse sources as *The Life and Public Services of John Quincy Adams* (1849),[1] *The Poetical Works of Oliver Wendell Holmes* (1852),[2] and the work of Jules Verne,[3] as well as the more predictable venue of the popular *Beauties of Sterne* in the late eighteenth century.[4] Even among those quick to condemn the body of Sterne's work, Uncle Toby garners broad critical praise. For instance, Samuel Taylor Coleridge uses "the beautiful passage, so well known," of Toby and the fly as an example of one of "the excellencies of Sterne."[5] Sir Walter Scott calls Toby and Trim "the most delightful characters in the work, or perhaps in any other."[6] William Makepeace Thackeray points to Sterne's "recollections of the military life" as "the most picturesque and delightful parts" of his writings, citing Toby as a particularly positive attribute of an author about whom he elsewhere states, "There is not a page in Sterne's writing but has . . . a latent corruption—a hint, as of an impure presence."[7] And, early in the twentieth century, George Saintsbury trumpeted, "There is a consensus of all sound opinion to the effect that my Uncle Toby is an absolute triumph."[8]

Editions of *Tristram Shandy* published between 1831 and 1948 often featured illustrations of Uncle Toby,[9] apparently exploiting the positive impression of the character to encourage sales, and Toby-based excerpts were included in anthologies such as *Gleanings from Popular Authors, Grave and Gay* (ca. 1851) and *Famous Prose Idylls* (1899).[10] As often occurs with popular literary characters,[11] such seeds of praise, and the cultural admiration reflected in them, fostered numerous textual and visual reinventions. The aim of this discussion will be to examine a series of variant multimedia Uncle Tobys that appeared between 1831 and 1948 in the interest of establishing the "distance" of each from Sterne's original by means of the addition, subtraction, or retention of attributes; I will then venture to contextualize these modified Tobys within a broader cultural matrix.

Considering the propriety of such reinventions, Catherine Gallagher uses the prism of David Hume's *Treatise of Human Nature* to view them as "conjectural, suppositional entities *belonging* to no one, [but which] could be universally appropriated."[12] This conceptual flexibility allowed Uncle Toby to became part of the cultural "commons," a process David Brewer identifies as "imaginative expansion" and "by which the characters in broadly successful texts are treated as if they were both fundamentally incomplete and the common property of all."[13]

In addition, as part of a kind of readerly covenant, Sterne's work itself offered a unique opportunity for engagement. This has been the subject of extensive commentary, with M-C. Newbould observing that "in accepting Tristram's invitation to imagine, [readers] are tacitly accepting his authority to at least broadly direct their attention, and so are implicitly surrendering a bit of their own autonomy in return for what he has to offer."[14] The multiple renditions of Captain Tobias Shandy discussed here suggest that the open-endedness in Sterne's work might have fostered a sense of reciprocity, with some of Sterne's readers appropriating a sense of creative authority through the re-creation of his characters. By their very nature, fictional characters exhibit a malleability and pliancy that enables their adaption; they may be reimagined in any number of ways, with varying degrees of success, as long as valued original attributes linger. As Newbould points out, "Recent adaptation studies have . . . increasingly moved away from outmoded debates about 'fidelity' which value judgments involve,"[15] yet this study will necessarily consider the primacy of Sterne's Toby in comparison to derivative visions of the character. As stated earlier, the distance between these visions acts as a cultural barometer of sorts by privileging certain aspects of the character as well as adding new ones.[16]

Images of Gallantry

Two versions of Captain Tobias Shandy flowed from this "imaginative expansion" of character, manifesting themselves in nineteenth-century culture. They can be identified broadly as the amorous and the humanitarian, products of a cultural sifting process in which the various attributes of Sterne's character are emphasized or de-emphasized, making Uncle Toby into a fluid entity responsive to societal interests. Interestingly, the amorous Toby—represented repeatedly in versions of Charles Robert Leslie's oil painting *My Uncle Toby and the Widow Wadman* (1831; the popular Lumb Stocks engraving is pictured in figure 5.1)—is

Figure 5.1. Lumb Stocks's popular steel engraving (1853), 25.7 × 17.4 cm. (10.1 × 6.8 in.), after Charles Robert Leslie's oil painting (1831). Private collection.

almost entirely a visual construction, while the Toby associated with didactic benevolence is represented primarily through text.

Leslie renders the widow Wadman's "attack" on Toby in his sentry box, originally described in part by Sterne:

> —I am half distracted, captain Shandy, said Mrs. Wadman, holding up her cambrick handkerchief to her left eye, as she approach'd the door of my uncle Toby's sentry-box—a mote—or sand—or something—I know not what, has got into this eye of mine—do look into it—it is not in the white—
>
> In saying which, Mrs. Wadman edged herself close in beside my uncle Toby, and squeezing herself down upon the corner of his bench, she gave him an opportunity of doing it without rising up—Do look into it—said she.
>
> Honest soul! thou didst look into it with as much innocency of heart, as ever child look'd into a raree-shew-box. . . .
>
> I see him yonder with his pipe pendulous in his hand, and the ashes falling out of it—looking—and looking—then rubbing his eyes—and looking again, with twice the good nature that ever Galileo look'd for a spot in the sun. . . .
>
> —If thou lookest, uncle Toby, in search of this mote one moment longer—thou art undone. (*TS*, 8.24.705–707)[17]

Toby's infatuation with the widow—later confirmed by the bursting of a blister on his hindquarters—is portrayed by Tristram as a meeting of a savvy woman and a less-than-savvy man. Readers may recall Toby's innocence about women, indicated earlier by his staring at a crevice in the chimney after being challenged by his brother for not knowing "the right end of a woman from the wrong," which here is tested by the wily widow. There is irony, of course, in the site of the attack: the sentry box, symbol of Toby's military stratagems, his headquarters, and generically a checkpoint against approaching enemies. Beyond that, though, is the ironic presentation of a kind and modest battle-scarred war veteran hopelessly pitted against a cunning and aggressive woman.

Leslie's iconic painting features much of the dynamic inherent in Sterne's text. Toby intently and helplessly searches for the mote, with one of his hands on his leg and the other casually holding his pipe; his expression and body language reveal an obliviousness to the widow's attack. Innocently yet also somewhat provocatively, the widow uses the fingers of both hands to hold open her eye wide open, while she also wedges her elbow atop his, a focus of the painting emphasized by increased central illumination. She manages simultaneously to be receptive and assertive, while Toby, as Tristram describes him, is drawn into the eye's "gentle salutations." Leslie also significantly frames the moment when Tristram cites his own visual interaction—"I see him yonder with his pipe pendulous in his hand" (*TS*, 8.24.706)—offering the painting, as it were, as a projection of the narrator's perspective.

Initially displayed at the Royal Academy exhibition of 1831, the painting was an instant success. Critics raved. In 1834, *Arnold's Magazine of the Fine Arts* gushed about its "exquisite drawing, fine perception of female beauty, and quaint and quiet humour. . . . It is altogether a faultless work, a real gem of Art, and for the excellencies pointed out, cannot be equalled by any of the old masters."[18] Leslie would go on to paint at least five additional versions, according to W. G. Day, a clear indication of interest in the image.[19]

The popular thirst for reproductions wed to emergent technology meant that additional versions of *My Uncle Toby and the Widow Wadman* also proliferated in other media. Most prominent was Lumb Stocks's steel engraving of circa 1853, produced shortly after the painting's debut and continuing in print for more than fifty years; its content is very similar to that of the original, but with the widow's handkerchief and Toby's map slightly larger and the lighting more evenly distributed. As Day points out, one indication of the image's ubiquity can be found in an illustration by Phiz (aka Hablôt K. Browne) for an 1847 edition of Dickens's *Dombey and Son*, where it resides, framed, in Major Bagstock's dining room.[20] As the century marched on, the image would appear on Prattware dinner plates, pot lids, and pin dishes beginning in the 1840s,[21] as the basis of *Vanity Fair*[22] and *Punch*[23] cartoon parodies, on bookmarks offered by the Scottish Widows Fund,[24] and as postcards published by the National Gallery of British Art.[25]

Leslie's design also assumed literally another dimension in the form of a larger-than-life statue by the English sculptor Robert Ball Hughes in 1834. The work, probably made of plaster, was displayed for a time at the American Academy of Fine Arts in New York, and though lost or destroyed, it evidently made an impression.[26] A reviewer in an 1858 issue of the *Atlantic* lists it among significant works of art, which also include the horses of San Marco and Donatello's *San Giorgio*,[27] and fifty years after the initial exhibition, the sculpture was lauded in a poem about Hughes in the *Boston Evening Transcript*.[28] Though no image exists of Ball's work, it was the apparent basis for a multitude of smaller statues that followed, starting with what appears to be a clay model exhibited in the Hall of Sculpture during the Great London Exposition of 1862 and reproduced as a stereo card, part of a series entitled "Gems of Statuary."[29] Afterward, mass-produced bisque and polychrome porcelain versions appeared, as well as larger plaster models painted in different colors (figure 5.2), ranging from 22 to 29 centimeters (8.6 to 11.4 in.) in height.[30]

Leslie's version of Toby and the widow also was appropriated for the label of "My Uncle Toby's Tobacco," ca. 1859.[31] The label's depiction simplifies the original, minimizing the background (in particular the map) while retaining much of the figures' detail. Toby's pipe remains prominent, and the title "My Uncle . . ." situates the consumer as a Shandean himself, employing a usage not uncommon in the nineteenth century.[32] (An intriguing counterpoint is the clergyman George Trask's use of "Uncle Toby" for an 1860 anti-tobacco book aimed at young men.)[33]

Figure 5.2. A late-century plaster statue, 29 cm. (11.4 in.), adapted from Robert Ball's 1834 larger-than-life grouping. Private collection.

Clearly the image of Uncle Toby and the widow Wadman proliferated in the nineteenth century for a reason. In his introduction to Leslie's *Autobiographical Recollections* (1860), Tom Taylor states, "There is more prurience in Sterne's pen than in Leslie's pencil. In his hands, the widow becomes so loveable a person, that we overlook the fierceness of the amorous siege she is laying to Uncle Toby's heart; while Uncle Toby himself is so thoroughly the gentleman,—so unmistakeably innocent and unsuspecting, and single-hearted,—that the humour of the situation seems filtered of all its grossness."[34] Taylor's assessment, in emphasizing the "humour" of the scene and erasing its sexuality, suggests the value contemporaneous audiences found in the image. Toby becomes mildly aggressive and the widow almost passive, to connect with and project Victorian gender expectations.

The perceived interplay of characters is crucial to the success of this tableau, and the roles they assume as described by Taylor are of particular interest. Most centrally, Leslie's rendition strips Sterne's scene of much of its sly realism about the widow's motives as well as of its emphasis on her crafty machinations, both of which paint Toby as the unsuspecting and somewhat helpless victim of her scheming. Contrasted with the assertiveness of the widow's pose in the painting, however, is a hint of softness in the gentleness of her expression and the flowing lines of her prominent handkerchief. Toby, in turn, retains his aura of innocence, but his positioning implies a forceful latency that goes beyond Sterne's description of an impotent invalid; instead, his firmly planted feet, spread knees, and resolved curiosity present a more able and centered character, complemented by an expression of determination rather than helpless entanglement. Unlike Sterne's Toby, Leslie's seems able to take control, to guide rather than be guided. He also appears to be healthier—no crutch is in evidence—and is focused on the widow. Thus, rather than depicting a man's entrapment, Leslie's image hints at his willingness to allow a woman to entrap him (and perhaps even a willingness for mutual entrapment.)

The vast popularity of this Toby, in a profusion of forms, affirms the cultural interest in and approval of a gentle, innocent character, even after having suffered in war and among his martial trappings. Red-coated and buff-vested (a visual iconography reproduced elsewhere during the century), he may have served as a positive, assimilative model for British soldiers returning home after serving the empire. Toby's gentle civility is to be noted, as well, following a century known for its libertines, both real and fictitious. A man guided by genuine feeling and sympathy (as his humanitarian reinventions will emphasize), Leslie's Toby—at a close remove from Sterne's own—is masculine but an anti-rake, a telling example of an age that prided itself on manners, propriety, and community.

Another representation of Toby Shandy and the widow created in the late nineteenth century became the symbol of a well-known commercial brand. The iconic logo of the Australian company Uncle Tobys was designed by Nellie Love—described as "a keen artist and a student of literature"—in 1893. On its website, Uncle Tobys, which produces breakfast cereals and other grain products, describes Toby as "a gentle, uncomplicated lover of his fellow man," following a predominant interpretation of the character throughout the nineteenth century as a model of benevolence.[35]

The image, usually not larger than four centimeters in height on the products' packaging, depicts Toby in profile, facing the widow Wadman. Dressed in a scarlet hunter's jacket, top hat, and riding boots, he appears to be in the process of raising his hat politely to the widow; his costume suggests a shift to more socially acceptable gentlemanly pursuits rather than his obsession with military fortifications. His physical well-being is again reflected by the lack of his trademark crutch, and he stands unstooped and uninjured. The widow Wadman also is less restrained here, leaning toward Toby while he makes his courtly gesture and wrapping her hand around the back of his neck, as if to pull him closer.

Like Leslie's painting, the image stresses a dynamic relationship. Toby is depicted as hale and hearty, a practical symbol for a food company; the image admits no indulgence, either comic or tragic, for his injury. The widow's tactics have become more visibly aggressive: instead of trying to overcome Toby's reticence with an invitation to gaze into the depths of her eye, here she actively draws him into her embrace. This change might be seen as reflecting the historical empowerment of women in a period that saw an increased momentum in the woman's suffrage movement and a parallel shift in social norms allowing for a more aggressive femininity. While preserving the appeal of a naive Toby, this image also recasts the pair in what might be seen as a more realistic emblem of a society less vested in the sentiment apparent in Leslie's depiction and more interested in practical and active engagement. Robust and outgoing, both seem better suited for the challenges of the Australian frontier—certainly a very different environment than eighteenth-century Yorkshire—than do Sterne's originals.

Overall the primacy of visual representation of the Uncle Toby–widow Wadman scene, in contrast to the other adaptations of Uncle Toby in this period, may point to a simultaneously multivalent and subjectivized popular appreciation of the subject matter, since each illustration allows the projection of many possible interpretations of a primary text. Is Toby's innocence or the widow's cleverness the focus of appreciation? Does the image depict a composite idea of Uncle Toby, a cumulative idea of the character's history in the text, represented by his injury (shown by the crutch and map), his fortificational obsession (the map again, and the sentry box), or as an aggregate, do we see an honorable depiction of a military veteran? Over and above such questions, these images of Toby and the widow demonstrate the universal ability of visual interpretation simultaneously to suggest a multitude of equally valid perspectives.

Images of Benevolence

Another distinct Toby emerges in the nineteenth century, one with roots in the character as a paragon of benevolence in Sterne's text, where he repeatedly evinces a generous and gentle spirit. Three particular episodes often appear in anthologies, school readers, and newspapers that illuminate the basis of the humanitarian Toby. In the episode of the fly, Tristram relates "that where just occasions presented, or called it forth,—I know no man under whose arm I would sooner have taken shelter." He goes on to tell the story of

> an over-grown [fly] which had buzz'd about his nose, and tormented him cruelly all dinner-time . . . and which, after infinite attempts, he had caught at last, as it flew by him;—I'll not hurt thee, says my uncle *Toby*, rising from his chair, and going a-cross the room, with the fly in his hand,—I'll not hurt a hair of thy head:—Go, says he, lifting up the sash, and opening his hand as he spoke, to let it escape;—go, poor Devil, get thee gone, why should I hurt thee?—This world surely is wide enough to hold both thee and me. (*TS*, 2.12.130–131)

Significantly, Tristram notes "the lesson of universal good-will then taught and imprinted by my uncle Toby, which has never since been worn out of my mind," and emphasizes its didactic value, stating, "This is to serve for parents and governors instead of a whole volume upon the subject" (*TS*, 2.12.131). Here Toby, a soldier by trade, anthropomorphizes perhaps the least significant (and, in this case, most annoying) of living creatures, expressing extraordinary kindness and tolerance, and the narrator presents the episode as a general lesson to readers, along with a not-so-facetious recommendation that it be part of children's education, a recommendation that will prove strangely prescient.

The episode of Le Fever demonstrates another aspect of Toby's benevolence. Trim hears of a fellow officer languishing nearby who, not having eaten for days, "has a fancy for a glass of sack and a thin toast" (*TS*, 6.6.500). He is accompanied by his young son, who has "tasted almost as little as his father" and who "does nothing but mourn and lament for him night and day" (*TS*, 6.6.501). Toby quickly responds with a visit, during which he hears of the tragic death of Le Fever's wife and offers his house for the recuperation of the ailing fellow officer, whom he and Trim would personally attend. As with the previous passage, Tristram pauses for a general observation about his uncle: "There was something in his looks, and voice, and manner . . . which eternally beckoned to the unfortunate to come and take shelter under him; so that before my uncle *Toby* had half finished the kind offers he was making to the father, had the son insensibly pressed up close to his knees, and had taken hold of the breast of his coat, and was pulling it towards him" (*TS*, 6.10.512). Tristram describes his uncle as appealing to all "unfortunates" who instinctively gravitate to his "looks, and voice, and manner" for protection. Young Le Fever, who "insensibly" finds solace and shelter within his close proximity, senses this quality. While concern for physically and financially distressed individuals is evident in the afterlife of the character, his benevolent relationship with children in particular will become a significant aspect of Uncle Toby variations through the nineteenth and early twentieth centuries.

Last, as part of the story of his brother Tom's misfortunes in Portugal, Trim's tale of the "poor Negro girl" rather unexpectedly provides Sterne with an opportunity to express through Toby his humanitarian opinions about slavery. She works in the sausage shop owned by the Jew's widow, the target of Tom's advances, and Trim describes her "flapping away flies" "with a bunch of white feathers slightly tied to the end of a long cane," "not killing them." Toby responds: "'Tis a pretty picture! . . . she had suffered persecution, Trim, and had learnt mercy" (*TS*, 9.6.747). In the ensuing conversation with Trim (who initially is positioned as an unthinking defender of the status quo), Toby assaults the idea of slavery in practical and humane terms. When Trim asks "doubtingly" whether "a Negro has a soul," Toby answers, "I am not much versed . . . in things of that kind; but I suppose, God would not leave him without one, any more than thee or me." Trim, catching on like a good pupil, continues:

> Why then, an' please your honour, is a black wench to be used worse than a white one?
>
> I can give no reason, said my uncle Toby—
>
> —Only, cried the Corporal, shaking his head, because she has no one to stand up for her—
>
> —'Tis that very thing, Trim, quoth my uncle Toby,—which recommends her to protection—and her brethren with her; 'tis the fortune of war which has put the whip into our hands *now*—where it may be hereafter, heaven knows! (*TS*, 9.6.747–748)

Simply and spontaneously, Toby raises a humanitarian argument against slavery from a detail in Trim's story about his brother (another instance of unjust persecution). By citing the essential equivalence of human life and invoking a Christian and gentlemanly duty to protect the downtrodden, Toby's points are difficult to refute and, appearing toward the end of *Tristram Shandy*, are reinforced by the moral rectitude the character had previously displayed. He also demonstrates a long view of history—something we would expect more from Walter than Toby—in recognizing the randomness of fate in determining who is to be enslaved.

Not surprisingly, the first didactic adaptation of Uncle Toby casts the character as an advocate for the major political and moral issue of the period, the abolition of slavery. This Toby originates before 1831 and most often is represented through excerpts from Sterne, in particular, the passage on slavery cited earlier, which appeared frequently in English and American periodicals (particularly in newspaper notes and editorials) in the late eighteenth and early nineteenth centuries, sometimes accompanied with arguments for abolition. Along with the apostrophe to Liberty and description of the captive in *A Sentimental Journey* (1768), these excerpts appeared at times when the issue of slavery rose to wide debate, such as before the Missouri Compromise in 1820. One widely reprinted example from an imitation of Sterne went a step further, casting Dr. Slop as a splenetic proponent of slavery and with Toby elaborating on his opposition.

When Slop suggests scripture as justification for slavery, Toby responds, "I would more willingly become one of these children of affliction . . . than even speak to justify such dealing."[36]

This association was to persist: a revised excerpt beginning, "A negro has a *soul*, an' please your honor," would appear as an introduction to a chapter entitled "Prejudices against People of Color, and Our Duties in Relation to this Subject," in *An Appeal in Favor of That Class of Americans Called Africans* (1833) by Lydia Maria Child, who was at the time "probably the best-known woman writer in America." Her book expounds on the history of slavery and refutes claims about the intellectual or moral inferiority of Africans, in a sense further developing Uncle Toby's conversation with Trim in formal terms.[37]

Another outgrowth of Sterne's ability to promote a shared sentimental value in his readers was the Dicky Bird Society, one of several social activist organizations that emerged in the late nineteenth century dedicated to fostering in children a benevolent perspective toward birds and animals. William Adams, editor of the *Newcastle Weekly Chronicle*, established the society in 1876 using the pseudonym Uncle Toby; Toby's behavior in the fly episode, "so considerate and so inspiring, so completely in keeping with the everlasting doctrine of kindness," led him to adopt the name, the character having shown him "how tenderly and lovingly to treat even the creatures that sometimes torment and annoy us."[38] The proximity of Newcastle to Sterne's North Yorkshire may have been influential, as well.

This "Uncle Toby" held court in the *Chronicle*'s weekly "Children's Corner" column, dispensing his philosophy of kindness by encouraging its membership (particularly young boys) to feed wild birds and not tamper with eggs or nestlings. Frederick S. Milton notes the society's increasing popularity through the eve of World War I, when it had grown to more than 350,000 members worldwide, counting among them Alfred Tennyson, Robert Baden-Powell, and Robert Louis Stevenson, as well as many "local dignitaries."[39] Chapters were founded throughout the empire, Europe, and the United States as early as 1877, and as the society grew, so did its scope, campaigning against the use of feathers for lady's hats and the use of live pigeons and sparrows for target shooting. Eventually the Dicky Bird Society broadened its focus, in Adams's words, to "inculcate a charitable awareness among middle class children," including assisting the impoverished.[40]

The emblem of the organization depicts a wizened Uncle Toby seated and wearing a vintage coat and tricornered hat—one wonders whether he is supposed to be a survivor of the previous century. Surrounding children eagerly lean against him, and he beams at them in return. A bird, doubtless a reminder of the society's purpose, perches on the back of his chair, but the focus is on the receptive children, to whom Toby radiates his trademark kindness, the first step in the evangelism of his benevolence.

Similar humanitarian Uncle Tobys, seemingly descended from Sterne's original, would assume instructive roles in children's books in this period. Interestingly, they are featured in these texts at a remove from the primary story lines, appearing either as storyteller or mysterious relative, so lessons could be imparted without imposition on the young characters' vigorous adventures. New England Methodist minister Daniel Wise, for instance, writing under the name Francis Forrester, authored the twelve books published as the Uncle Toby's Library series, as well as Toby-themed columns in such venues as the *Sunday School Advocate*.[41] The common frontispiece of the apparently well-received book series (figure 5.3)[42] features an elderly "Uncle Toby" in knee breeches, a long coat, stock, and tricornered hat. Leaning on a walking stick—another symbol of his infirmity—he sits surrounded by assorted chubby-cheeked children who listen intently. While there is no direct reference to Uncle Toby in a sampling of the series, in *Aunt Amy; or, How Minnie Brown Learned to Be a Sunbeam* (1853), his trademark benevolence is evident in learning "how to be a sunbeam," that is, brightening the dark lives of the underprivileged.[43] A beneficiary in *Aunt Amy*, however, is the aged, one-legged "Corporal Jim," suggesting not only Toby's right-hand man but also hearkening back to Sterne's persistent consideration of needy and deserving former soldiers. Another, a poor cottager, Mrs. Button, is transformed from an unkempt and unruly condition into a polite and gracious one due to the charitable interest shown to her.[44]

Other children's texts feature faintly familiar, humanitarian Uncle Tobys through the next century. The prolific juvenile writer (and creator of Uncle Wiggily Longears) Howard Garis published *The Curlytops and Their Pets or Uncle Toby's Strange Collection* in 1921; it features an Uncle Toby, a "well off" distant relative who asks the title characters to take care of his collection of animals in his old mansion while he is away.[45] The children put on a show with them for charity, and Uncle Toby, appearing at the end of the book, offers to give them "a hundred dollars for the orphans" so they could have "a fine vacation time in the country."[46] The original character's trademark charitable quality (assuming a lineage between the two) becomes broadened and thus depersonalized from Sterne's example, losing a sense of intimacy with the victim and perhaps didactic effectiveness.

In Evelyn Davey-Collins's *Strawberry Dene* (1948), Uncle Toby retains only a slight physical resemblance to the original (figure 5.4): his gentlemanly attire had made the leap to the twentieth century, but he still smokes a pipe, albeit a modern one. Aside from his name and his kindness to animals and children, his Shandean ancestry seems uncertain; at one point, he appears, "chattering and laughing, and cracking jokes."[47] He offers the child heroes of the book a place to live but is also a distant figure, remaining in the background during the children's adventures, which include a ride in a dragonfly-plane and attending the rainbow fairies' party.[48]

Figure 5.3. Series title page signed Baker-Smith-Andrew (illustrator[s]/engraver[s]) from Francis Forrester (Daniel Wise), *Aunt Amy; or How Minnie Brown Learned to Be a Sunbeam* (Boston: Geo. C. Rand and Avery, 1856). Private collection.

The twins sitting one on each side of her, she began her story.

Figure 5.4. Illustration by M. W. Whittington from Evelyn Davey Collins, *Strawberry Dene, A Children's Story* (Ilfracombe: Arthur H. Stockwell, 1948), 53. Private collection.

The Uncle Toby of *Tristram Shandy* may be barely discernible by this time, but suggestions of a lineage from the original persist in the characters' traits of benevolence, as well as the attributes of costume, age, and pipe smoking. An interesting trajectory might be seen as this benevolence veers away from the pragmatic to the eccentric, albeit with a consistent sense of didacticism aimed at a juvenile audience.

These amorous and didactic Tobys also have been projected widely through three collections of Sterne's original text: the previously mentioned *Beauties of Sterne*, Percy Fitzgerald's *The Story of My Uncle Toby* (1871), and the lavishly illustrated *My Uncle Toby* (1908), edited by Thomas Cartwright. The earliest of these compilations, *Beauties*, first appeared in 1782, with a fourth edition the same year, and a fourteenth edition by 1799; still more editions would appear from various publishers. Obviously popular, the volumes included brief (one- to four-page) excerpts from Sterne's long fictions, sermons, and letters. The tenth edition, for instance, contains 148 items, among them "The Story of Le Fevre [*sic*]," "Mercy" (the anecdote of the fly), and "Remainder of the Story of Trim's Brother," which includes the discussion of slavery.

More of an abridgment of *Tristram Shandy, The Story of My Uncle Toby* focuses on the single character in twelve chapters, each varying in length from ten to twenty-five pages. In his introduction, Fitzgerald rebukes Thackeray's criticism and downplays Sterne's transgressions, stating, "All the passages by which [Sterne's] reputation has been made may be read by 'boys and virgins'; the coarse portions are for the most part digressions."[49] Thus the volume's contents reflect the polite idiosyncrasies of the Shandy family and their household as well as Toby's relief of Le Fever and his amour with the widow Wadman, presenting overall a balance between the comic and the sentimental.

My Uncle Toby (figure 5.5), part of the Every Child's Library series, centers even more intently on the character, and of nine chapters (perhaps an echo of *Tristram*'s nine volumes), three tell the story of "My Uncle Toby and Le Fever," one describes his amour with the widow, and one includes the brief story of the fly.[50] In his note at the beginning of the book, the editor, Thomas Cartwright, is instructional when addressing his juvenile audience: "Laurence Sterne wrote much that nobody wishes to read, but the world will always be grateful to him for having created Uncle Toby and Corporal Trim. The tale is supposed to be told by Tristram Shandy, Uncle Toby's nephew, but Toby is now uncle to all the world, and I expect you will call him your Uncle Toby before you have read a dozen pages of this little book." Eight color plates (the first polychrome book illustrations of subject matter from *Tristram Shandy*) depict what appears to be an older-looking Toby in regimental scarlet with his attributes of pipe and crutch. This Toby is more distant from the humorous than Sterne's original, and the emphasis on the military, from Toby's recovery to his fortifications, as well as the tale of Le Fever, might be seen to ennoble the British veterans and the empire after a century of European and colonial wars.[51]

Variations on Uncle Toby in this period also extended beyond the amorous and humanitarian; the 1909 Royal Doulton porcelain series entitled "Diversions of Uncle Toby," designed by Walter Nunn, suggest a broader, comic interest in the character (figure 5.6). In contrast with his preoccupations with fortifications in *Tristram Shandy*, on these plates, jugs, vases, and teapots, Toby is engaged in a variety of gentlemanly "Old English Games" (the subtitle of the series):[52] he bowls, plays cricket, and practices archery, all with an athletic form that belies his origin in Sterne, and despite the challenges his "authentic" physique might pose. The intensity of his focus on sport might be seen as an imaginative parallel to his interest in fortifications, though both share competitive and nationalistic undertones. (Toby, of course, never seems to have used the bowling green for bowling.) The series, which would run for more than twenty years, suggests a transformation of the original Toby's eccentricities to more acceptable social activities. Like the amorous Tobys examined earlier in this essay, it also promotes a more virile and active Toby, one miraculously recovered from his groin wound at Namur, and ultimately more useful to society. Other incarnations of Uncle Toby appear in the nineteenth and early twentieth centuries. For example, the famously secretive Skull and Bones Society at Yale University has its members "alternate assuming the role of Uncle Toby, who leads the sessions, moderates

Figure 5.5. The Every Child's Library representation of Uncle Toby. Private collection.

Figure 5.6. "Uncle Toby as Toxophilite" plate, 26 cm. (10.2 in.), designed by Walter Nunn, part of the Diversions of Uncle Toby series. Private collection.

debates, and takes notes"; the link to Sterne here is reinforced by other "permanent Bones names," including Yorick, Corporal Trim, and Dr. Slop.[53] As records of secret rituals are scarce, however, the degree of this Toby's fidelity to Sterne's text is difficult to discern.

But after this parade of Uncle Tobys recounted previously, how much of Sterne's is left in the recipe for "Uncle Toby's Pudding" in the 1902 recipe book *Tasty Dishes*?[54] Aside from the name—which could, of course, belong to another Toby—there is no indication of an eighteenth-century origin, although the traditional Englishness of the dish itself could be a clue.

Undoubtedly, other variations of Sterne's Uncle Toby existed between 1831 and 1948—there is too much evidence of the character's general appeal to justify a claim of comprehensiveness—yet a pattern might be observed in the examples provided earlier. In a broad sense, English-speaking culture in this period appears to have found him the most attractive figure in Sterne's work, specifically emphasizing his modest and humanitarian qualities, his authority and appeal likely augmented by his honorable military background. These qualities can be seen as a reflection of persistent ideas in Victorian culture, with the character's continuation in the early twentieth century perhaps in part the result of a continued reflexive fondness after its ubiquity the century before.

Toby's recurrent reinvention might be related to what Brewer describes as a "feedback loop or bandwagon effect" when characters appear "more socially canonical and desirable as they came to seem more common and used by all, which in turn enhanced their value and publicity that much more."[55] The Victorians' obvious fondness for the visually projected, amorous, and modest Toby may have been instrumental in prompting the numerous textual, humanitarian, and didactic versions of the character, as if piggybacking on (and adding dimensionality to) his established pictorial self. It might be noted that the amorous Toby's pictorial representations might have been best suited for their comic digestion, the eye quickly assimilating and prompting the memory of the scene for humorous effect; the textual representations of the noble, exemplary Toby, on the other hand, lend themselves to didactic purpose, for reading aloud and repetition in order to better absorb his desirable characteristics. A direct relation between these two Tobys is elusive, however, and in addition, his broad employment as a voice for the abolition of slavery predates Leslie's painting, suggesting that his moral authority—and the general affection for the character—is rooted deeply in Sterne's original text.

As a recurrent element within English-speaking culture in the nineteenth and early twentieth centuries, Captain Tobias Shandy assumed different guises, emphasizing the comic amours and humanitarian tendencies endowed by his creator. In a larger sense, though, he also represented a persistent cultural interest in Sterne's work and perhaps in Sterne himself. Remembering Tristram's (and Sterne's) complicated relationship with mortality—perhaps best illustrated in the painting by Thomas Patch—the continuous rebirth of Uncle Toby seems like one way the author delayed, or possibly defeated, death itself.[56]

NOTES

An earlier version of this chapter appeared in *XVIII New Perspectives on the Eighteenth Century* 18, no. 1 (2021): 18–41.

1. In a letter to his wife dated August 2, 1822, Adams notes of a former friend, "I now bear him no more ill will than Uncle Toby did to the fly that annoyed him with his buzzing." John Quincy Adams, *The Writings of John Quincy Adams*, ed. Worthington Chaucey Ford, vol. 7 (New York: Macmillan, 1917), 286.

2. Holmes concludes his poem entitled "Opening the Window" with "Go, my winged verse, and try,—/ Go, like Uncle Toby's fly!" *The Poetical Works of Oliver Wendell Holmes* (New York: Houghton Mifflin, 1910), 241.

3. In Verne's *Dick Sands: A Captain at Fifteen* (from the *Works of Jules Verne*, ed. Charles F. Horne, vol. 10 [New York: F. Tyler Daniels, 1911], 28), one character observes the

provenance of a story about the kindly release of a mosquito, correcting the speaker that "it was told, in nearly the same words, about Uncle Toby, in Sterne's 'Tristram Shandy'; only there it was not a mosquito, it was a common fly."

4. Beginning publication in the early 1780s, the popular *Beauties of Sterne* consistently included the stories of Le Fever and of the fly, suggesting interest in these aspects of the character.

5. Samuel Taylor Coleridge, *The Literary Remains of Samuel Taylor Coleridge*, ed. Harry Nelson Coleridge, Lecture IX (London: Pickering, 1836), 1:143, 142.

6. Walter Scott, *The Prose Works of Sir Walter Scott* (Paris: A. and W. Galignani, 1827), 5:450.

7. William Makepeace Thackeray, "Sterne and Goldsmith," in *The English Humorists, Life and Works of William Makepeace Thackeray* (New York: Pollard and Moss, 1881), 149, 156.

8. George Saintsbury, *The English Novel* (London: Dent, 1913), 130.

9. Uncle Toby appears in forty-five book illustrations (from editions of *Tristram Shandy* alone) and ten paintings in the period from 1831 to 1948. See W. B. Gerard and Brigitte Friant-Kessler, "Towards a Catalogue of Illustrated Laurence Sterne," *The Shandean* 16 (2005): 26–32, and "Towards a Catalogue of Illustrated Laurence Sterne: Paintings and Prints," *The Shandean* 18 (2007): 74–79.

10. Numerous general anthologies in the period include Uncle Toby excerpts, and the choice of selections, the volumes' themes, and accompanying illustrations are themselves in need of focused examination.

11. The most prominent examples would be Defoe's Robinson Crusoe or Swift's Gulliver, both of which appeared in many textual and visual variations of the originals; see David Blewett, *The Illustration of Robinson Crusoe, 1719–1920* (Oxford: Oxford University Press, 1996), and Jeanne K. Welcher, *Gulliveriana: Visual Imitations of Gulliver's Travels 1726–1830* (New York: Scholars' Facsimiles and Reprints, 2000). Sterne's own "Poor Maria" also endured frequent reinventions, though of a more focused and singular nature than those described earlier; see W. B. Gerard, "Icon of the Heart: Maria as Sentimental Emblem, 1773–1888," chapter 5 in *Laurence Sterne and the Visual Imagination* (Aldershot: Ashgate, 2006), 135–173. Perhaps the most relevant parallel to Uncle Toby in content and cultural persistence would be Don Quixote, as suggested by Stuart M. Tave in *The Amiable Humorist* (Chicago: University of Chicago Press, 1960).

12. Catherine Gallagher, *Nobody's Story: The Vanishing Acts of Women Writers in the Marketplace, 1670–1820* (Berkeley: University of California Press, 1994), 168.

13. David Brewer, *The Afterlife of Character, 1726–1825* (Philadelphia: University of Pennsylvania Press, 2005), 2. Liberty is taken here by broadly applying Brewer's notion of "imaginative expansion," through focusing "upon what characters allowed readers and viewers to do, rather than what those character mean in and of themselves" (15). Brewer also usefully observes the distortions that appear in similarly focused scholarship due to "the desire to hang on to the Habermasian schema" (21).

14. M-C. Newbould, *Adaptations of Laurence Sterne's Fiction: Sterneana, 1760–1840* (Farnham: Ashgate, 2013), 161.

15. Newbould, 5.

16. The concept of "adaptation" fluctuates within critical discussion, particularly in light of its broad integration in film theory. Every depiction of Toby Shandy outside of Sterne's text is in a sense an adaptation, retaining at least some physical and behavioral aspects of the original. Thus, the question of the primacy of the original, contentious within adaptation theory (see, for example, Linda Hutcheon, *A Theory of Adaptation* [Abingdon: Routledge, 2006]), is finessed here with the recognition that all of the depictions following *Tristram Shandy* are in fact derivative of the original text and none seems to aspire to supplant or seriously reinterpret the entirety of the work itself; rather, they are interested in revisiting the character with certain intents, and it is these intents that are of

particular interest to this study. Discussion of various adaptation theories could easily fill up an essay—or a book—on its own. In "Twelve Fallacies in Contemporary Adaptation Theory" (*Criticism* 45, no. 2 [2003]: 149–171), Thomas M. Leitch develops the notion of adaptation as it pertains strictly to text-to-cinema migration; in fact, literary illustration is not mentioned. Hutcheon works with a similar understanding, especially in her second edition, which is particularly expanded to embrace diverse "new media" such as video games.

17. References to *The Life and Opinions of Tristram Shandy, Gentleman*, are to the Florida edition, ed. Melvyn New and Joan New (Gainesville: University Press of Florida, 1978); cited parenthetically in the text as *TS*, followed by volume, book, and page numbers.

18. *Arnold's Magazine of the Fine Arts and Journal of Literature and Science* (London: M. Arnold, 1834), 3:546.

19. See pages 83–84 of W. G. Day, "Charles Robert Leslie's 'My Uncle Toby and the Widow Wadman': The Nineteenth-Century Icon of Sterne's Work," *The Shandean* 9 (1997): 83–208. Numerous copies of the painting were made by other artists; for instance, F. May after Charles Robert Leslie, *Uncle Toby and Widow Wadman*, oil on canvas (listed in *Furniture and Works of Art Monday 04 August 2014 11:00*, Mallams Fine Art Auctioneers [UKAuctioneers.com]), 29. In addition, the image apparently was the basis for a medallion on the base of a bronze statue of Sterne crafted midcentury by his biographer Percy Fitzgerald, now in the York Minster Library.

20. Day, "Charles Robert Leslie's," 98–102. Day observes that Dickens, who often provided specific instructions regarding his illustrations, also may have done so here (101). See also Melvyn New's perceptive article "Taking Care: A Slightly Levinasian Reading of Dombey & Son," *Philological Quarterly* 84, no. 1 (2005): 77–104.

21. For more complete information on the Prattware items, see Day, "Charles Robert Leslie's," 91 and 101–102. The pin dish was unknown to Day at the time of his writing.

22. H. L. Stephens, engr. Robert T. Hooper, "Uncle Toby and the Widow Wadman. The Characters by John Bull and Wm. H. Seward. Widow.—Do look into it—it is not in the white; tell me, do you think you see anything Green.," *Vanity Fair*, October 26, 1861, n.p.

23. [Joseph] Swain sc, engr. "Uncle Toby and Widow Wadman. (Modern Ulster version. After C. R. Leslie, R.A.'s celebrated picture.) Mrs. Ulster. 'Now, Mr. Bull, do you see any 'green' in my eye?,'" *Punch, or the London Charivari*, April 22, 1893, n.p.

24. The bookmark, produced in the early twentieth century, is printed in color and measures 17.5 by 6.5 centimeters (6.8 × 2.5 in.); concurrent variations feature other paintings in lieu of Uncle Toby and the widow. An updated version produced by the Scottish Widows Fund in the early in the twenty-first century includes Leslie's image as well as the corresponding quote from Sterne's text.

25. "Uncle Toby and Widow Wadman by C. R. Leslie," 14 × 9 centimeters (5.5 × 2.7 in.) postcard, the Wrench Series No. 90, National Gallery of British Art, ca. 1900.

26. According to Mabel M. Swan in *The Athenaeum Gallery, 1827–1873* (Boston: Boston Athenaeum, 1940), the original model of Uncle Toby and the widow Wadman "was sold to a Mr. Dorr of New York and deposited in the Boston Athenaeum as early as 1835 where it was seen in May 1835" (152). Eliza Ball Hughes, in the unpublished "Sketch of the Life of Robert Ball Hughes," notes that the sculpture "was destin'd for the Duke of Sussex who had given him the order to make it at his leisure. The group was most beautifully finished, but owing to its having occupied so much time, to the neglect of more profitable work. Owing to money troubles it never cross'd the ocean, and was finally purchased by Mr. Edwards of Boston. All honor to his name! who having purchased it for a small sum, and hearing of the regret expressed by the family that it should have been so sacrificed, at once wrote to them saying, that he would give it back if they desired it. The offer was declined but his kindness is well, and gratefully remember'd. and Boston has it" (13–14). Both of these references courtesy of the Robert Ball Hughes website, https://sites.google.com/site

/robertballhughes/. The site misidentifies stereocards (discussed later) as depicting Hughes's statue rather than the smaller model based on his original. As an example of the scale Hughes practiced, one might note his *Little Nell* in the Boston Athenaeum is 125.3 centimeters (nearly 50 in.) in height, seated (www.bostonathenaeum.org).

27. "Crawford and Sculpture," *Atlantic Monthly* 2, no. 8 (1858): n.p., Project Gutenberg.

28. From "Art and Artists," *Boston Evening Transcript*, December 30, 1885, 6:

Then Widow Wadman, note the expression there!
And Uncle Toby—can aught with them compare?

29. In addition to the yellow-backgrounded 17.3 × 8.4 centimeters (6.8 × 3.3 in.) "Gems of Statuary by Eminent Sculptors" stereocard, at least one other version was produced, similar but including the six-line passage beginning, "I am half distracted, Captain Shandy." The stereoscope, popular from the 1850s to beyond the end of the century, was a portable device that created a three-dimensional experience of an image. Other images in the "Gems of Statuary" series are credited "W. England, Photo.," apparently the photographer for the series.

30. Parian ware (a type of bisque porcelain) by the manufacturer Copeland apparently based on this model followed, measuring about 22 centimeters (8.6 in.) high. It was probably produced through the 1890s in two variations, featuring Toby with either a metal or a ceramic pipe. A polychrome group also was produced by Samson in Paris. See Day, "Charles Robert Leslie's," 102–104.

31. "My Uncle Toby's Tobacco, Richmond, Va.," ca. 1859, color lithograph printed by Everdell and Sons, New York. Information sourced from the Library of Congress website: https://www.loc.gov/item/2001697760/.

32. The "adoption" of the character implied by the free use of the term, "*My* Uncle Toby" (italics added) was a curious commonplace in this period, a testimony to the affection the character inspired.

33. George Trask, *Letters on Tobacco, for American Lads; or Uncle Toby's Anti-Tobacco Advice to His Nephew Billy Bruce* (Fitchburg, MA: George Trask, 1860).

34. *Autobiographical Recollections. By the Late Charles Robert Leslie, R.A.*, ed. and intro. Tom Taylor (Boston: Ticknor and Fields, 1860), xli.

35. This background courtesy of the Uncle Tobys website, under "Community and News" and "Brand History" (www.uncletobys.com.au/news-info/history). Befitting the character's humanitarian tendencies, the company raises funds for charities, including the goal of teaching children how to swim. See also "Uncle Toby Down Under," *The Shandean* 12 (2001): 125–126.

36. See W. B. Gerard, "Laurence Sterne, the Apostrophe, and American Abolitionism," in *Swiftly Sterneward*, ed. W. B. Gerard, E. Derek Taylor, and Robert G. Walker (Newark: University of Delaware Press, 2011), 189–190, 197–198.

37. Mrs. [Lydia Maria] Child, *An Appeal in Favor of That Class of Americans Called Africans* (Boston: Allen and Ticknor, 1833), n.p. Commentary on Child and primary text access via the University of Virginia webpage, "Abolitionism 1830–1850," http://utc.iath.virginia.edu/abolitn/childhp.html.

38. William Edwin Adams, *The History of the Dicky Bird Society by Uncle Toby* (Newcastle: for the proprietor of the *Newcastle Weekly Chronicle*, 1887), 2.

39. Frederick S. Milton, "Newspaper Rivalry in Newcastle upon Tyne, 1876–1919: 'Dicky Birds' and 'Golden Circles,'" *Northern History* 46, no. 2 (2009): 286, 289.

40. Milton, 285.

41. The strong sense of didacticism in the My Uncle Toby's Library series is suggested by titles such as *The Runaway; or, The Punishment of Pride* and *Arthur's Triumph, or, Goodness Rewarded.* One volume, *Redbrook; or Who'll Buy My Water Cresses*, echoes the tale of the watercress girl, a popular pathetic subject during the first half of the nineteenth century.

42. A contemporaneous commentator describes the *Sunday School Advocate* as "a beautifully illustrated child's paper, edited by the distinguished friend of chil[dren] Francis Forrester, and is issued semi-monthly. The nineteenth volume will commence in October, 1859. The circulation is over 200,000 copies" (www.forgottenbooks.com).

43. Francis Forrester [Daniel Wise], *Aunt Amy; or, How Minnie Brown Learned to Be a Sunbeam* (Boston: Geo. C. Rand and Avery, 1853). The end-page advertisement in *Aunt Amy* includes a statement from the *New Bedford Standard* "that no better books can be found in the whole range of juvenile literature."

44. Forrester, 50–53, 56–59.

45. Howard Garis, *The Curlytops and Their Pets or Uncle Toby's Strange Collection*, illus. Julia Greene (New York: Cupple and Leon, 1921). Fourteen titles make up "The Curlytops" series; Garis penned another seventeen series under his own name and contributed to the Tom Swift and Bobbsey Twins series pseudonymously.

46. Garis, 245–246.

47. Evelyn Davey Collins, *Strawberry Dene, A Children's Story*, illus. M. W. Whittington (Ilfracombe: Arthur H. Stockwell, 1948), 52.

48. And so on. The law of diminishing returns eventually comes into play, as with the adventurous character in C. E. Bowen's *Among the Brigands* (London: Griffith and Farran, 1875), described as "a tall, merry-looking gentleman, who was always called Uncle Toby by the young ones" (52). In *Uncle Toby's Christmas Book* (New York, 1936), a familiar identity is hinted at with a section titled "Because He Has a Particular Affection for Children, Uncle Toby Made a Special Selection of Unusual Tales for Boys and Girls" (n.p.).

49. Laurence Sterne, *The Story of My Uncle Toby*, ed. Percy Fitzgerald (Philadelphia: Porter and Coates, 1889), xxi.

50. Laurence Sterne, *My Uncle Toby*, ed. Thomas Cartwright, Every Childs Library (London: W. Heinemann, 1908). Hereafter cited parenthetically in the text.

51. The absence of the passage about the African servant girl from Fitzgerald's 1871 and Cartwright's 1908 editions may in itself be significant, possibly indicative of the historical success in the outlawing of slavery, an ebbing of interest in sentimental themes, or simply a reflection of an intense fascination with Toby's idiosyncratic but noble character, which increasingly comprises these volumes.

52. See W. B. Gerard and Brigitte Friant, "Towards a Catalogue of Illustrated Laurence Sterne: Decorative Arts," *The Shandean* 19 (2008): 105. It is worthwhile to note that the nineteenth-century depictions of Toby apparently did not take such liberties with his physical portrayal.

53. Alexandra Robbins, *Secrets of the Tomb: Skull and Bones, the Ivy League, and the Hidden Paths of Power* (New York: Little, Brown, 2002), 92. It is perhaps coincidental that the legendary Wilbur L. Cross, the first modern editor of Sterne's works (12 vols., 1904), who taught at Yale (later to become dean of the Graduate School and governor of Connecticut), was known to his students as Uncle Toby.

54. "Uncle Toby's Pudding": "*Ingredients:* One-half pint of milk, four laurel leaves, three ounces breadcrumbs, three ounces butter, three ounces white sugar, a little grated nutmeg and lemon peel, two eggs (well beaten), a glass of white wine. *Directions:* Boil the laurel leaves in the milk, and pour it boiling on to the breadcrumbs, butter, sugar, lemon peel, and nutmeg. Beat until quite cold; then add the eggs and wine. Continue to beat until ready for the oven, and bake for half-an-hour." *Tasty Dishes* (1897; New York: R. F. Fenno and Company, 1902), 123.

55. Brewer, *Afterlife of Character*, 14.

56. In a sense, the persistent lives of characters like Uncle Toby parallel the fond projection of a remarkable colleague in a collection of essays that was first envisioned as a Festschrift.

CHAPTER 6

"My Business Ashore"

LIBERTINE CONDUCT AND MARITIME CONTEXT IN *THE ROVER*

Randa Graves

When *The Rover* opened on the evening of March 24, 1677,[1] the Stuart monarchy no longer enjoyed the popularity that had been its happy lot when Charles II regained the English throne in 1660. As an ambitious, young dramatist with Royalist leanings, Aphra Behn would have understood that the tide was turning against the Crown. The revisions that Behn made to her source play for *The Rover* suggest that she navigated the political current in ways that contributed to her Restoration audience's enthusiastic reception of her most enduringly popular play. Behn's source text was Thomas Killigrew's eponymous, never-staged *Thomaso, or the Wanderer.* Written during Killigrew's continental exile and published in 1664 after he returned to England with the Stuart court, *Thomaso* languished in obscurity after its publication, whereas *The Rover* was enthusiastically received on the Restoration stage. In this essay, I will explore the possibility that the popularity of *The Rover* was due, in large measure, to strategic details in Behn's revision whose political significance have escaped critical attention.[2]

Behn shrewdly revised Killigrew's protagonist to give *The Rover* a measure of topical appeal that was absent in her source. While both Killigrew's and Behn's protagonists are banished Cavaliers and libertines, Killigrew's wandering Thomaso is also an exiled army colonel whose term of banishment plots a desultory land-based course. In contrast, Behn's roving Willmore is a naval captain, a freebooting privateer whose banishment transpires on the high seas. Situating her impecunious libertine in a financially difficult but heroic interval of Interregnum naval history, Behn drew upon the resources of Restoration dramaturgy to capitalize on her audience's nostalgic connection to the past. However, *The Rover*'s production history suggests that she also revised Killigrew's protagonist in ways that would give her play contemporary relevance, as well as historical significance. While Behn was readying *The Rover* for production, a heated controversy over funding for the Restoration fleet was transfixing the nation's attention and exacerbating tensions between Charles and his Cavalier Parliament. As I will argue, Behn's introduction of a maritime context into her revision of Killigrew's play attests to her ability to connect with her audience through a dramatic lens that looked to their present political situation as well as to their collective historical past.

Professionally and politically, Behn's decision to feature privateering in her revision of Killigrew's *Thomaso* was a canny move. In his overview of critical response to *The Rover*, J. P. Vander Motten claims that two factors enhanced the popularity of Behn's play: its author capitalized on the current vogue for witty sex comedies, and she presented her audience with a nostalgic representation of Stuart exile during the Interregnum.[3] Vander Motten's study provides a useful point of departure for understanding why Behn's play outstripped Killigrew's in popularity. However, his assessment overlooks the crucial alteration that Behn made in her protagonist's professional status. The shift, which Behn signals in her title—from Killigrew's wandering army colonel to her own roving privateer—provides a context for changes in her performative strategy and historical window, which endow Willmore with a level of audience appeal missing from Killigrew's characterization of Thomaso.

Recasting a Play

As even the most cursory reading attests, distinctions between *The Rover* and *Thomaso* are easily discernible. Jones DeRitter has cataloged several evident points of contrast: Behn combined Killigrew's two-part drama into a single production, changed its setting from Madrid to Naples, introduced a subplot, lowered the level of violence, added another female principal, and devoted more attention to the viewpoint of female characters.[4] In contrast to such an array of distinctions, a comparison of the two plays' protagonists would, at first glance, seem to yield little more than a rather tedious checklist of similarities: Thomaso and Willmore are both libertines; both belong to a band of amorous Cavaliers who remain loyal to Charles II through penurious exile; and both have a brief affair with an exceptionally beautiful courtesan. A closer reading reveals that, although Behn followed Killigrew's lead in making her protagonist a libertine, she notably altered Killigrew's model by depicting Willmore as a more aggressively combative libertine than Thomaso. This distinction is evident both in the degree to which Thomaso and Willmore engage in combat and in the types of combat in which they participate.

As their plays attest, both Killigrew and Behn understood that libertinism is not exclusively about sexual conquest. Maximillian Novak, who credits the former with introducing the libertine persona onto the Restoration stage, observes that Killigrew and other members of the exiled Stuart court would have been "attracted to libertine ideals" because "their sense of superiority as soldiers had been shattered by the victories of the parliamentary forces."[5] Both Killigrew and Behn feature libertine protagonists who had done military service for the Stuart cause prior to its defeat by Parliament, and both authors situate their protagonists in destitute exile in the aftermath of crushing Stuart losses. The connection that Novak posits between libertinism, combat, and loss is thus explicit in both *The Wanderer* and *The Rover.* However, that connection is painted with much darker hues in *The Wanderer.*

Killigrew consistently characterizes his exiled Cavalier officers as men bent on sexual conquest after having suffered devastating defeat in military combat. The point is especially germane with respect to his protagonist Thomaso. Directly or indirectly, Killigrew inscribes an edge of violence into scenes that track Thomaso's encounters with women. In his opening scene with the courtesans Paulina and Saretta, Thomaso lays hands on Paulina, eying her insolently until one of his comrades interposes to prevent Thomaso's rudeness. In an overtly violent tableau that overgoes the symbolic aggression of his assault on Paulina, Thomaso is subsequently wounded in a violent brawl with Spanish dons in the street that fronts the courtesan Angelica's house.[6] In fact, however, Thomaso's encounters with women are relatively restrained. Other than ogling Paulina and accosting her in his opening scene, he offers no actual roughness to any woman in the play. Killigrew even endows his libertine protagonist's character with a modicum of chivalry, with Thomaso saving the virtuous Serulina from dishonor and possible death during the siege of Pamplona.

A close reading of Thomaso's sexual reactions and reflections reveals that they are defensive, as well as aggressive. Professing a libertine's scorn for fidelity, Thomaso underscores his aversion to commitment by declaring to his friend Harrigo that he will "not be tied to one woman . . . for all that the sword has won or lost" (1.2.321). While Thomaso's libertine discourse in this passage is fired by bellicose rhetoric, his defensive allusion to being tied—that is, married—to one woman as a result of military defeat is telling. Having served in the Stuart army before its defeat by parliamentary forces, Thomaso and his little company are eking out a meager existence as soldiers of fortune. Officers and gentlemen of rank and title, they are also impoverished expatriates whose military losses have deprived them of the economic resources and social connections that formerly would have facilitated their access to women of their own class in England. Yet even though Killigrew imbues Thomaso's libertinism with considerable qualifications and complexity, Thomaso's behavior serves as a frame for egregiously reprehensible sexual conduct elsewhere in the play.

If the violence that Killigrew's libertine protagonist inflicts upon women is largely symbolic, the same cannot be said for his comrade Edwardo. A recent recruit from England, Edwardo is the scion of Stuart sympathizers who have contrived to retain their Essex estate by refraining from active opposition to the Puritans during the Civil War and Interregnum. Sent abroad with an ample supply of ready cash, Edwardo is currently using part of it to bankroll Thomaso and his companions. While Edwardo functions as a satiric object for Killigrew, his character also provides Killigrew with an opportunity to make an important historical point. Exiled Royalists did, in fact, depend on surreptitious support sent to them by Royalists in England.[7] However, Killigrew's depiction of Edwardo's relationship to Thomaso's company depicts the potential awkwardness of such fiscal dependence. Edwardo is a strikingly callow miscreant who mistakes courtesans and prostitutes for high-born ladies and assaults the truly virtuous and aristocratic Serulina because he misidentifies her as a woman of the streets. Since Edwardo is subsidizing Thomaso and his companions, they tolerate his untoward conduct even though his imprudent lust repels them and puts their entire company at risk.

Although sex and war may be the main themes of Killigrew's play, his depiction of Edwardo's libertinism reveals that the subtext is martial humiliation coupled with acute financial distress. While the feckless but financially secure Edwardo is offering a diamond to a woman he is attempting to seduce, Thomaso and his company are prowling for food. Ravenous, the Cavaliers attempt to cadge victuals and cash as they can: from their friend Harrigo, a low-ranking but well-fed diplomat; from strolling courtesans; or from Edwardo himself, whom they secretly despise but who may be their only recourse against slow starvation. A conversation between two of the Spanish dons attests to the Cavaliers' abysmal financial situation. As Don Carlo observes to his friend Don Pedro, the Cavaliers "eat so seldom, and dung so small, you may as soon step on a custard as on a T—in the Court; they that do S—save it for their own Pig" (3.1.343). Having thus graphically assessed the Englishmen's dismal daily routine, Carlo attributes their bleak situation to political circumstances that are unlikely to improve.

Cavaliers Adrift

Alluding to a key event in Stuart history, Carlo observes that the condition of Cavalier officers like Thomaso and his company will probably deteriorate still further due to recent developments at sea. In a sequence of linked topical allusions, he notes that "the young Prince is from the Indies come" to be "no more Admiral, but *Palatine Polyxander*, great Master of the Mares" (3.1.344). Sardonically, Carlo adds that the appointment is hardly illustrious: Cavalier horses are starving, and if one should die, its famished groom might fall on it and devour it. Alert to the chronological significance of this passage, Alfred Harbage accurately links Carlo's reference to the return of Prince Rupert of the Rhine from the Indies and his appointment as Master of the Horse. Therefore, he situates Killigrew's dramatic action between April and May 1654.[8] Harbage's reading of this passage instructively positions Killigrew's play at a specific point along the historical timeline of Stuart exile. However, in addition to chronologically positioning Killigrew's action, Carlo's mention of Prince Rupert's return from the Indies identifies a decisive turning point in Stuart resistance to parliamentary insurgency whose implications Harbage overlooks.

Along with establishing the temporal window for Killigrew's action that Harbage identifies, Carlo's evocation of the Cavaliers's deteriorating situation implicitly alludes to a crucial devolution in the Crown's opposition to parliamentary ascendancy. Rupert was a key figure in naval opposition to parliamentary insurgency. As Ronald Hutton documents, prior to Rupert's return from the Indies and his appointment as Master of the Horse, the prince served as the commander of a small fleet of privateers whose raids figured prominently in Royalist opposition to Parliament. Prince Rupert began his privateering activities when his cousin the younger Charles fled to France in 1649 to avoid being imprisoned along with his father the king. After Charles put Rupert in command of seven Royalist ships that had remained loyal to the Stuart cause, Rupert began his privateering raids on behalf of the Crown.[9] He continued to command his little fleet of privateers until 1653, when he abandoned privateering and returned, dispirited and deeply in debt, to rejoin the Stuart court at Nantes.[10] As Carlo's allusion attests, the period of Rupert's return coincided with the cessation of Royalist naval resistance and the initiation of the most desperate and despondent period in the Stuart exile.

Explicitly alluding to this dark historical moment, Killigrew's play provides a bitterly sardonic representation of the bleakest segment of Cavalier exile. With land and sea opposition extinguished and the Commonwealth firmly established on English shores, Killigrew's banished Cavaliers forage for sustenance while the budding libertine Edwardo, sent abroad by his Royalist family with money for the Stuart cause, lavishes treasure on the tawdry objects of his desire. Superficially, Killigrew's depiction of his libertine protagonist's exiled condition is bawdy and boisterous. However, beneath this rowdy tale of lean dons, elegant courtesans, and libertine Cavaliers lies a bleak historical narrative of humiliating military loss, political exile, and near starvation.

A close intertextual reading of Behn's and Killigrew's plays reveals that Behn's protagonist is more complex than Killigrew's even as Behn's Willmore faces circumstances less bleak. While Willmore is more sexually aggressive than Thomaso, Behn's staging of Willmore's sexual aggression is accompanied by visual and verbal cues designed to underscore his complexity and render him more appealing to the audience. Written by a political exile with no professional access to a stage, *Thomaso* is, in effect, a closet drama. Although he represents his protagonist as a libertine Cavalier who actively engages in sex and swordplay, Killigrew perforce relied on reading rather than performance to represent his protagonist's actions. In her adaptation of *Thomaso*, Behn transforms Killigrew's play in two important ways. Altering Killigrew's mode of presentation, she marshals the resources of Restoration stagecraft to engage her protagonist Willmore in a series of strategically staged scenes that highlight his valor while simultaneously painting him as a crass and even violent sensualist. In addition to altering Killigrew's representational strategy to enhance her protagonist's complexity and audience appeal, Behn reconfigures Willmore's historical time frame. Strategically, she situates him in a historical window where heroic Royalist privateers still sailed the seas rather than positioning him, as Killigrew does Thomaso, in the desperately despondent period that followed Rupert's return. With mercurial shifts of Killigrew's dramatic strategy and temporal window, Behn thus resituates her protagonist in her own narrative of heroic resistance rather than in Killigrew's depiction of the death throes of political hope.

When Behn adapted Killigrew's play for the Restoration stage, she endowed her libertine protagonist with enhanced dramatic heft by presenting him through stratagems that render him paradoxically at once less subtle but also in some ways more attractively exuberant than Thomaso. Whereas Thomaso vacillates between rakish impulse, Senecan reflection, and grinding penury, Willmore appears at first glance to be less complex. He makes none of Thomaso's ironically self-aware set speeches, and he is more likely to try to attempt to seduce a damsel than to rescue her from dishonor. Yet if Behn reduces the complexity of Killigrew's libertine protagonist in some aspects of his behavior, she intensifies it in others. Capable of sexual aggression that can devolve instantaneously into brutal violence, Willmore also displays striking valor and vulnerability. To signal her protagonist's complexity, Behn employs a series of performative strategies and historical allusions.

As a libertine, Willmore is, in some respects, a stereotypically comic character. His naive approach to the intricacies of sexual conquest is immediately evident in his reaction to the sexually charged atmosphere of Catholic Naples's culturally alien Carnival scene. Baffled by the subtle semiotics of Carnival conveyed in the revelers' costumes, Willmore is equally unable to parse the crude demographics of urban real estate, which position highly paid courtesans beyond the reach of lowly constables. As Nancy Copeland notes, Spanish comedies could have provided Behn with examples of maladroit libertines whose characterization mixes "attractiveness and ineptness."[11] Willmore's opening scenes depict him in both modes. When Belville asks what has brought him to Naples, Willmore responds forthrightly: "My business ashore was only to enjoy myself a little in this Carnival."[12] Rather more specifically, he adds, "Love and Mirth! Are my bus'ness in Naples, and if I mistake not the place, here's an excellent market for Chapmen of my humour" (1.2.460). Yet if Willmore is initially too unsophisticated to comprehend the supernumerary costs of lighthearted Neapolitan liaisons, he quickly grasps the reality of his situation. As a cash-strapped stranger in town, Willmore soon realizes he must have recourse either to seduction or assault, if he is to succeed in his pursuit of a sexual partner. With that realization, his initially comic presence darkens appreciably.

During the street scene that affords Behn's audience its first view of her libertine protagonist, his persona rapidly shifts. At first blush, Willmore's libertine tendencies appear little more than a heterosexual male's desire for female companionship after a long dry spell at sea. Suddenly, however, the mood of the scene turns sinister. Rose baskets in hand and breasts emblazoned with their monthly rates, a group of passing courtesans bring Willmore's latent capacity for sexual violence to the surface. Taking a scatological turn, his dialogue metaphorically conflates the courtesans' genitalia with the bush that has produced the roses they carry. As Willmore moves to arrest one of the courtesans forcibly, Belville sharply admonishes him to "use no violence here" (1.2.461). Precipitously, Behn transforms a street scene that opens in fresh air and friendship into a spectacle dominated by masked prostitutes threatened with sexual violence from a dangerous itinerant who, only seconds before, had presented himself as a man with respectable connections to the Cavalier cause.

The sinister edge that is apparent in Willmore's libertine impulses during his contact with the strolling courtesans becomes increasingly evident in successive scenes. The suggestion of violence that is apparent in his rudeness to the courtesans intensifies with his theft of Angellica's[13] portrait, itself a symbolic rape. What is only figured in his theft of the picture degenerates into ugly reality in two successive scenes during which he attempts to rape Florinda in her garden and later with four other men in Blunt's quarters. Since Behn puts the transgressive aspects of Willmore's sexuality on full display—and indeed darkens them systematically in successive scenes—it is hardly surprising that some critics have read her depiction of the latent or overt violence of Willmore's sexual encounters as an indictment of libertine conduct, especially as libertinism was connected with the restored Stuart court.[14] However, as Jeremy Webster has argued, a strong connection exists between libertinism and performance in Restoration literature.[15] Webster's point is particularly telling with respect to Behn's representation of Willmore's libertine conduct. Although she depicts the reprehensible aspects of Willmore's behavior in a carefully patterned series of scenes, Behn simultaneously utilizes the performative resources of her Restoration stage to temper her audience's potential censure of her protagonist.

Although much of Willmore's conduct attests to his coarse and even brutal libertine sensibility, Behn strategically manages her scenic resources in ways that endow her protagonist with a conflicted and evolving persona. In constructing Willmore's character, Behn makes specific use of her theatrical milieu. Affording striking new forms of visual appeal, the Restoration stage titillated audiences with multilevel sets, elaborate costumes, and painted backdrops to suggest both enclosed and outdoor environments. Restoration stagecraft also afforded scenic innovations whose significance was conceptual as well as material. As Peter

Holland observes, notable shifts occurred during this period in the way that scenes were introduced into dramatic action. No longer merely designations of place, scenes in the new Restoration dramaturgy were deployed to reinforce existing systems of values.[16] Utilizing the dramatic strategy that Holland describes, Behn moves Willmore through a succession of scenic streets, gardens, and interiors that puts the viciously transgressive aspects of his sexual conduct on full display while simultaneously situating him in a countermanding value system of valor and vulnerability.

Evident from his initial onstage appearance, Willmore's conflicted libertinism is apparent throughout his encounters with various women in three successive scenes. The intricately patterned scenarios that follow Willmore's initial appearance continue to reveal strong performative connections between the scenery of the play and escalating difficulties that provide increasingly problematic examples of his libertine conduct. As Kate Aughterson notes, Behn's plays typically include stage directions that are "complex and explicit, delineating careful blocking."[17] Such detailed patterning is clearly apparent in scenes that depict Willmore's libertine conduct. However, while Behn systematically implicates her protagonist in increasingly vicious and violent encounters with women, she attempts to blunt the opprobrium that would attach to Willmore's conduct by means of a series of performative maneuvers that simultaneously direct the audience's attention to both Willmore's bravery and his susceptibility to injury, pain, and death.

Just as Behn affords her audience shifting perspectives on Willmore's physical presence as she moves him through a succession of scenic venues, she also uses his movements through scenic space to signal the complexity of his persona. Behn sets her protagonist in motion at the conclusion of her opening street scene, during which Willmore, Belville, and the costumed courtesans have, for the most part, been stationary. In the scene that follows Willmore's encounter with the courtesans, his movements and speeches in the play are initially consistent with his stated purpose of coming to Naples during Carnival to enjoy himself. Having encountered the elegant courtesans in his opening scene, he wishes to know where they live. In particular, he and Belville are curious to see the residence of the dead general's erstwhile mistress, and they set off to discover it. However, a scene that begins with a leisurely stroll soon gathers momentum as Willmore and Belville find themselves at odds with a group of Spanish dons who are Angellica Bianca's admirers. The scene before Angellica's house presents the audience with rapid visual transitions. After brawling violently in the streets with Angelica's suitors, he subsequently treats her in her apartment with a paradoxical measure of contempt and admiration.

Willmore's initial meeting with Angellica occurs in a panoramic, multilevel setting that focuses the audience's gaze on street and buildings, on characters positioned indoors and outdoors, and on shifting points of ocular reference within a vertical and horizontal field. Rapidly reconfiguring Willmore's position in physical space, the shifting visual perspectives in the fight with the dons prefigure complex shifts that will occur in his persona during his meeting with Angellica. Once within her apartment, he reveals not only contempt for her willingness to sell herself but also admiration for her beauty and refined discourse. Just as the visual and verbal cues that Behn embeds in Willmore's first scene with Angellica encourage her audience to contemplate the complexity of his character, Behn challenges them to reconfigure their perception of his libertine character's successive scenes with Florinda. While Behn puts the reprehensible aspects of Willmore's libertine conduct on full display in the carefully plotted sequence of his two assaults on Belville's beloved mistress, she deliberately stages his libertine conduct in ways that invite her audience to hold their full censure of him in abeyance.

Most obviously, Behn underscores Willmore's valor by throwing him into three pitched battles in one night, in each of which he fights as a wounded man. The point is particularly germane, since Behn's stage directions specify that Willmore makes Angellica's acquaintance in a shirt that has been bloodied during a confrontation with her suitors (2.1.473). Willmore's bloody shirt functions as a piece of visual rhetoric whose pathos potentially works to soften the audience's opprobrium by reminding them of his bravery and susceptibility even as Behn's plot sequence implicates him in successively darker acts of libertine violence. Just as Behn uses visual rhetoric to make an appeal to pathos through the image of Willmore's blood-stained shirt, she uses other elements of his costume in subsequent scenes to signal his integrity even as his words and conduct bespeak hypocrisy. Although Willmore eventually sheds his buff for a fine suit of clothes purchased with Angellica's purse, his face is unchanged: he carries his vizard rather than wearing it. Willmore's fully visible face is another visual cue that would not have been lost on Behn's audience. Appealing to their admiration for Willmore's valor through successive instances of swordplay and then eliciting their sympathy for him through the spectacle of his bloody shirt, Behn stages a tacit appeal to her audience's trust by contrasting the captain's open face with the masked countenances of the revelers.

Behn reinforces the implicit import of visual cues that signal Willmore's valor and integrity through explicit allusions to his profession. Willmore's initial appearance identifies his professional status: he is a naval captain on shore leave, and his ship and crew await him at a bare league's distance. As Behn's title announces, Willmore is a specific kind of naval captain: he is a rover—a Royalist privateer. Prominently identifying Willmore as a rover in her title and at the beginning, middle, and end of her play, Behn repeatedly directs her audience's attention to her protagonist's professional identity. Belville uses the term respectfully and affectionately when he greets Willmore in his friend's first onstage appearance. However, like Willmore himself, the term that denotes his profession is a conflicted signifier.

While Willmore's profession occasions Belville's respect and admiration, it arouses the instant opprobrium of Angellica's maid Moretta. In contrast to Belville's warm greeting, Moretta peremptorily orders Willmore off the premises, contemptuously denouncing him as a "Pyrate Beggar" and "English Picaroon" (2.1.476). Reinforcing Belville's and Moretta's references to his professional identity, Willmore explicitly identifies himself as a rover. When Pedro opposes Willmore's marriage to his sister Hellena in the concluding scene, Willmore threatens to hold him prisoner, take him on board his ship, and show him "a damn'd *Tramontana* Rovers trick" (5.1.366–367). In characterizing Willmore as a rover, Behn insistently distinguishes him from Killigrew's protagonist. Killigrew's title identifies Thomaso as a wanderer, a term that refers generically to his status as an exiled Cavalier. In contrast, Behn's title assigns Willmore more explicitly and narrowly to a naval context that would have struck a powerful chord in her audience's collective memory.

In sharp distinction to Killigrew's depiction of Thomaso as a soldier whose best battles are behind him, Behn thus situates Willmore in a dramatic and historical time frame when freebooting Royalist privateers were still engaged in active combat on behalf of the Cavalier cause. If, as Harbage argues, it is possible to mine Killigrew's allusions for dates that situate his dramatic action chronologically, it is equally possible to detect topical allusions in Behn's play, which position it along a recognizable historical timeline that connects Willmore to specific historical dates and people. While Willmore is the captain of his own vessel, we learn he sails in the company of a prince (1.2.460). As Timothy Raylor notes, Behn's reference here is clearly to Prince Rupert of the Rhine, the only member of Stuart royalty to command the fleet of Royalist privateers.[18] We also learn from Moretta's reference to Willmore's breeches that he is arriving in Naples at a point in time that postdates the Battle of Worcester (2.2.473). It is thus possible to position Behn's action at a point between September 1651, when the Battle of Worcester was fought, and the spring of 1653, when Rupert left off privateering and returned to France to join the Stuart court at Nantes.[19] As Behn's audience would have understood, Behn is positioning her protagonist in a period when privateers would have been performing their most dangerous and committed service on behalf of the Crown. By correlating Behn's dramatic allusions to Willmore as a rover who is sailing with a prince after the Battle of Worcester with the historical timeline of Prince Rupert and his post-Worcester privateering raids, it becomes evident that Willmore's Neapolitan excursion is not simply a quest for lighthearted amorous dalliance. Instead, it is a brief carnivalesque respite from mortally dangerous duty as a Royalist privateer. Given the specificity of Behn's chronology, those members of her audience who were familiar with the details of their recent national history would most certainly have caught her drift: her libertine captain has been performing grueling, life-threatening service on behalf of his king. For playgoers who shared firsthand memories of

Interregnum rovers, Behn's embedded allusions in the opening exchange between her libertine protagonist and his friends would thus have carried a distinct shock of recognition whose charge of positive memories might arguably be expected to temper any potential censure of Willmore's egregiously transgressive sexuality. Just as she marshals the resources currently available to her on the Restoration stage to elicit a measure of sympathy and admiration for her libertine captain, Behn filters her audience's perception of Willmore through their collective memories of privateering as a historic component of heroic Cavalier exile during the Interregnum.

By comparing the dates of Killigrew's dramatic action with the dates of the dramatic action in Behn's play, it is possible to conclude that their different historical windows would have suggested very different frames of reference to Restoration audience. On the one hand, Killigrew's play would have recalled a period of defeat in which the Royalist cause was not only vanquished but mired in despondent inactivity. In contrast, Behn's action would have evoked historical memories of defeat tempered by hope and active, heroic opposition. In and of itself, the difference between Behn's and Killigrew's historical windows might account for the greater popularity of her play—after all, her revision was staged, while her model remained a published but unperformed text. However, in her reconfiguration of Killigrew's land-based wanderer-cum-privateering captain, Behn recalled not only the past struggles of Cavalier rovers on behalf of the exiled monarchy but also more recent controversies associated with English naval operations.

A Product of Its Times

When the curtain rose in the Duke's Theatre on the evening of March 24, 1677, the national political scene was marked by ongoing confrontations that were fueled, directly or indirectly, by conflicts involving naval operations and funding for the fleet. Derek Hughes observes that Behn's play nostalgically addresses an ethos of shared Cavalier values that had united Charles and his supporters during the vanished days of the Interregnum. Such comity was severely tested in the years between the Stuart Restoration and the time that the curtain rose on *The Rover.* As Hughes notes, Charles and Parliament were deeply at odds on two key points: relations with France and the Duke of York's openly Catholic religious sensibility.[20] In fact, the navy provided a link between these two problems. By factoring Behn's maritime context into a reading of her play, it is apparent that she may have had something beyond nostalgia in her sights.

On first view, Behn's evocation of the fleet in her transformation of Killigrew's land-based Thomaso into her high seas rover Willmore might appear to have been a risky move. While the heroic opposition of Royalist privateers in the Interregnum was an important component of the Cavalier legacy, a succession of recent events in Behn's own era had cast a pall on the fleet's public image. From the beginning of the Restoration, the fleet had figured prominently in escalating tensions between Charles and Parliament. The fleet was inauspiciously thrust to the forefront of public attention when Charles consented to the Test Act as a means of gaining parliamentary support for the naval operations in the ongoing Third Dutch War, only to have his brother openly resign his position as high admiral rather than subscribe to the act's anti-Catholic provisions. Compounding these problematic domestic associations with James's Catholicism, the fleet figured prominently in conflicts between Charles and his Cavalier Parliament, which erupted in the realm of international relations. As Rebecca W. Wolsk has observed, Behn's play opened at a time when the English public feared French co-option more than Dutch aggression and "resented what they viewed as French exploitation of the English fleet."[21] Behn's transformation of Killigrew's land-based protagonist into a member of the fleet touches upon yet another fraught political issue: financial support for the navy. The expense of maintaining the fleet was prohibitive, and funding for the navy was a perennial sticking point in Charles' budgetary wrangles with Parliament. Just as *The Rover* dramatically evokes financial pressures that were the common lot of Stuart seamen during the Interregnum, such pressures historically carried over into the Restoration.

During the early years of Behn's career, the fleet's financial embarrassments continued as a constant factor in the escalating tensions between Charles and his Cavalier Parliament. As the Restoration wore on, the problem of securing funds for the fleet became especially acute as relations between Charles and Parliament grew more toxic. Defiantly, Charles called and arbitrarily dismissed Parliament three times between November 1675 and February 1677. In each case, the pattern was the same: Parliament convened, Charles asked for money—always to include funding for the fleet—and recalcitrant parliamentarians demurred. Charles reacted to each of these successive rebuffs by dismissing the obstinate assembly. The last of these dismissals dragged on for an unprecedented fifteen months, a hiatus that earned it the sobriquet of the "Long Prorogation." When Charles finally reconvened Parliament on February 15, 1677, circumstances veered unexpectedly and sharply in favor of the Crown. Tracking the details of this turn, David Ogg notes that parliamentary opposition to the king's financial requests swiftly collapsed after four members of the House of Lords were consigned to the Tower in retribution for their resistance to the Crown's request to fund the fleet. Apparently intimidated by the Lords' fate, the Commons acquiesced with surprisingly little resistance to Charles's financial requests on behalf of the fleet. On February 21, Parliament agreed to Charles's request for £600,000 to fund the navy.[22] This vote was a striking success for both the Crown and the fleet, and several pieces of evidence strongly suggest that Behn capitalized upon this dual success to the distinct advantage of her dramatic career.

While Behn's reworking of *Thomaso* is obviously nostalgic, it also carries topical relevance that may be seen by connecting Behn's text to the volatile political circumstances that were in play when she was revising her source. Such a connection may not be immediately apparent. Indeed, Jane Spencer concludes that, unlike *The City Heiress* and *The Roundheads*, two plays that Behn produced early in the next decade, *The Rover* was not "tied to a particular Tory moment and message."[23] While Behn may not have been pushing a specific political agenda in *The Rover*, it seems clear she had her authorial eye on the power of the fleet to attract an audience for both historical and contemporary reasons. Several clues in *The Rover*'s production history support this conclusion.

These clues are both external and internal. A detail from the production history of Behn's play provides external evidence that she had in mind ongoing parliamentary debates concerning the fleet while she was preparing *The Rover* for production. Reviewing the production history of *The Town Fop*, a Behn comedy staged in the autumn of 1676, Janet Todd notes that rehearsals "took a month."[24] If *The Rover* also required a month for rehearsals, then it would have clearly gone into rehearsal almost immediately after funding for the fleet was secured: the crucial parliamentary approval of funds occurred on February 21, 1677, and Behn's play opened almost exactly one month later on March 24. Behn would have been perforce constrained to revise Killigrew's play very rapidly if she aimed to capitalize on public interest in the monarchy's victory over Parliament, which secured funds for the fleet. Hence her decision to transform Killigrew's land-based army protagonist into a seagoing rover would have been a shrewd move on several counts. By shifting the protagonist's professional identity and historical context from Killigrew's defeated army officers to heroically resistant privateers, she could quickly make internal changes in her play to fashion her libertine into a character who is both reprehensible and sympathetic. Glancing at popular disapproval of the libertine behavior of the Restoration court by staging instances of her protagonist's less than admirable sexual conduct, she could also present him as a complex and ultimately sympathetic figure.

By situating Willmore and his banished rovers within a matrix of conflicting values, Behn presents him—and, arguably, by extension the libertine Stuart court—as men whose shared experience bound them to a common national history in which excessive and undisciplined sexual appetites coexisted with valor, vulnerability, and ongoing national service. The possibility that Behn intended her revision of Killigrew's play to capitalize on recent political events in a way that would present the monarchy in a qualified but ultimately positive light is especially interesting if, as Todd speculates, Behn may have asked Killigrew's permission to adapt his play.[25] Given the contemporary focus on the fleet, it is unlikely Killigrew would have failed to notice a major detail such as Behn's transformation of his protagonist's professional identity or to grasp its complex range of historical and current implications.

Whether or not Behn asked Killigrew for his approval, it is clear that he tacitly gave his official sanction to her revision: as Master of the Revels, a word from him could have barred *The Rover* from the stage. With no dissent from Killigrew, Behn was clear for production. Behn's reputation as a playwright had been steadily increasing, but she needed a popular success. With *The Rover*, she had her hit. Absent an awareness of the intense national focus upon the fleet that prevailed while Behn was preparing her play for production, the change that she made in the professional identity of Killigrew's protagonist might be read as a superficial alteration—a self-serving strategy to support her insistent claim in her postscript to *The Rover* that her play was of her own devising and not merely "Thomaso *alter'd*" (521). Defending her authorial practice against potential charges of plagiarism, Behn energetically denies she has committed intellectual property theft. Although she acknowledges Killigrew as the "Proprietor" of her source and confesses she may have lifted some things from it, she insists her play's "Plot and Bus'ness" are nevertheless her own (521). Considering the obvious and extensive similarities between the two plays, Behn's claim is, of course, highly debatable. However, since her play differs strikingly from Killigrew's in its stagecraft, its historical context, and its contemporary associations, her claim to have put her own distinctive mark on *The Rover* is deliciously apt and worthy of serious consideration.

Raising questions about authorship, originality, and intellectual property, Behn's wittily oblique reference to literary piracy in her *Postscript* is an apt conclusion to a play about high seas privateering. In her day, as in our own, questions of textual ownership and authority were strenuously debated, and Behn's *Postscript* attests to her understanding that this debate could affect her reputation and her play's reception in various and complex ways. In her revision of Killigrew's text—especially her transformation of his protagonist in the immediate aftermath of the Long Prorogation—Behn shrewdly assessed the shifting winds of literary and political change. Transforming the character and context of Killigrew's protagonist, she capitalized on her audience's investment in the historic myth of cash-strapped, heroically oppositional Interregnum Cavaliers just as she astutely measured the contemporary topical appeal of funding for the Restoration fleet. Like the intrepid Cavalier rovers in her most enduringly popular play, Aphra Behn seized her moment, fixed her eye on the prize, and boldly made her way into literary history.

NOTES

1. The play was also published the same year. Aphra Behn, *The Rover. Or, The Banisht Cavaliers. As it is acted at His Royal Highness the Duke's Theatre. Licensed July 2d. 1677. Roger Lestrange* (London: Printed for John Amery, at the Peacock, against St. Dunstan's Church in Fleet-street, 1677), https://www.bl.uk/restoration-18th-century-literature/articles/the-rover-an-introduction#.

2. Critics interested in mining Behn's works for their political implications have usually begun their investigations with works that she wrote during the Popish Plot and the Exclusion Crisis, as Judy Hayden notes in *Of Love and War: The Political Voice in the Early*

Plays of Aphra Behn (Amsterdam: Rodopi Press, 2010), 2. In her study of the political content in Behn's early works, Hayden writes at length about *The Forced Marriage*, *The Amorous Prince*, *The Dutch Lover*, and *Abdelazar*, but not about *The Rover*.

3. J. P. Vander Motten, "Recycling the Exile: *Thomaso*, *The Rover*, and the Critics," in *Thomas Killigrew and the Seventeenth-Century English Stage: New Perspectives*, ed. Philip Major (Burlington, VT: Ashgate, 2013), 135.

4. Jones DeRitter, "The Gypsy, *The Rover*, and *The Wanderer*: Aphra Behn's Revision of Thomas Killigrew," *Restoration* 10, no. 2 (1986): 82–92.

5. Maximillian Novak, "Libertinism and Sexuality," in *The Cambridge Companion to Restoration Drama*, ed. Susan J. Owen (Oxford: Blackwell, 2001), 56.

6. Thomas Killigrew, *Thomaso, or the Wanderer*, in *Comedies and Tragedies* (New York: B. Blom, 1967), 2.3.336. All text references are to this edition and hereafter will be cited parenthetically.

7. Stephen Coote, *Royal Survivor: A Life of Charles II* (New York: St. Martin's Press, 2000), 130.

8. Alfred Harbage, *Thomas Killigrew: Cavalier Dramatist, 1612–83* (New York: B. Blom, 1930), 218–219.

9. Ronald Hutton, *Charles the Second: King of England, Scotland and Ireland* (Oxford: Clarendon Press, 1989), 32.

10. Hutton, 74.

11. Nancy Copeland, *Staging Gender in Behn and Centlivre: Women's Comedy and the Theater* (Burlington, VT: Ashgate, 2004), 22.

12. Aphra Behn, *The Rover. Or, The Banish't Cavaliers*. In *Plays 1671–1677: The Works of Aphra Behn*, ed. Janet Todd, vol. 5 (Columbus: Ohio State University Press, 1992), 1.2.460. All text references are to this edition and hereafter will be cited parenthetically.

13. While Killigrew spells this character's name as "Angelica," Behn spells it "Angellica."

14. For example, in *Royalist Women Writers 1650–1689* (Oxford: Clarendon Press, 2004), Hero Chalmers detects a criticism of libertinism in Behn's works that predates the Popish Plot and Exclusion Crisis (164–165). Helen Burke claims that the "Cavalier myth takes a . . . beating" in the sexually transgressive acts that Behn attributes to Willmore. ("The Cavalier Myth in *The Rover*," in *The Cambridge Companion to Aphra Behn*, ed. Derek Hughes and Janet Todd [Cambridge: Cambridge University Press, 2004], 124).

15. Jeremy Webster, *Performing Libertinism in Charles II's Court: Politics, Drama, Sexuality* (New York: Palgrave, 2005), 1.

16. See for example Peter Holland's fine analysis of the complex function of scenery in Etherege's 1668 drama *She Wou'd If She Cou'd* in *The Ornament of Action: Text and Performance in Restoration Comedy* (Cambridge: Cambridge University Press, 1979), 48–53.

17. Kate Aughterson, *Aphra Behn: The Comedies* (New York: Palgrave Macmillan, 2003), 7.

18. Timothy Raylor. "Willmore's 'Prince': A Note on Behn's *The Rover* 1.ii," *Notes and Queries* 52, no. 3 (2005): 327–329.

19. See Hutton, *Charles the Second*, 74.

20. Derek Hughes, *The Theatre of Aphra Behn* (New York: Palgrave, 2001), 83.

21. Rebecca Wolsk, "Muddy Allegiance and Shiny Booty: Aphra Behn's Anglo-Dutch Politics," *Eighteenth-Century Fiction* 17, no. 1 (2004): 6.

22. David Ogg, *England in the Reign of Charles II*, 2nd ed. (Oxford: Clarendon Press, 1956), 2:542.

23. Jane Spencer, *Aphra Behn's Afterlife* (Oxford: Oxford University Press, 2000), 188.

24. Janet Todd, *The Secret Life of Aphra Behn* (New Brunswick, NJ: Rutgers University Press, 1997), 191.

25. Todd, 214.

CHAPTER 7

Speaking through the Prophets

ANNE FINCH, POLITICS, AND RELIGION

Claudia Thomas Kairoff

In an overview of Anne Finch's writings, Jane Spencer observed Finch's reference, in her widely anthologized poem "The Introduction," to the prophet and judge Deborah as an example of ancient women's authority.[1] Spencer notes the political significance of Finch's choice: Finch's lament that no contemporary woman prophet-judge can rise to inspire her languishing country is also a Jacobite protest against the oppressive Williamite party. Spencer observes the poem's accurate description of Finch's strategic claim of withdrawing her verse from public dissemination: as a woman writer, as a defeated supporter of James II, and as a person who suffered from depression, Finch sought retreat rather than exposure.[2] Spencer's analysis of "The Introduction" is compelling, and in this essay, I will examine Finch's religious poetry, particularly some of the many poems in which Finch assumed the narrative voice of a biblical prophet, to further illuminate her choice of Deborah to exemplify women's former power.

Prophesying, in the sense of speaking as a person divinely inspired to interpret or reveal God's will, was problematic for a woman of Finch's period and status. Yet she felt compelled to witness England's departure from divinely appointed order in repudiating James, and to predict or interpret the consequences of the Revolution of 1688. While avoiding the radical claims of earlier female prophets to personal visionary experiences, she shared with predecessors the choice not to adopt the persona of "the courageous Queen Esther, the heroic Jael, the praise-singer Miriam, or the militant judge Deborah; instead, they spoke as virtual incarnations of angry male biblical prophets."[3] Finch's religious poems have a strong political, and often prophetic, dimension that has not been sufficiently acknowledged. The "shades" that Finch seeks at the end of "The Introduction" (64) represent concealment, but they also intimate the methods by which she intends to address current misrule and its potential consequences in her writings.[4]

Finch's choice to speak through, and in a mediated way as, a prophet is striking for its religious and political implications. The generation before Finch's had witnessed numerous women who attempted, through prophetic writings, to inspire their compatriots during the tumultuous Civil Wars and Interregnum. As studies by Phyllis Mack, Elaine Hobby, and others attest, prophetic texts by women of dissenting religious sects circulated throughout the mid-seventeenth century, with each work asserting these authors' right to share in religious and political expression.[5] Like the biblical prophets, such women and their male counterparts urged contemporaries, especially religious and political leaders, to hasten their efforts to cleanse England of its moral failings. Finch's omission of any mention of this group of women in "The Introduction" is significant.

As Hilary Hinds has observed, post-Restoration England was inimical to prophetic writings.[6] In "Absalom and Achitophel" (Part 1, 1681), poet laureate John Dryden counts "A numerous Host of dreaming Saints . . . / Of the true old Enthusiastick breed" (529–530) among Charles II's worst enemies.[7] In *Mac Flecknoe* (1682), Dryden portrays his adversary Thomas Shadwell as a parodic prophet Elijah, tumbling into a trapdoor instead of being assumed into a heavenly chariot (214–217). Growing up in a Royalist family and serving among the Duchess of York's maids of honor, Finch would have associated female prophets with ignorance, religious apostasy, and treason. (When, in 1742, Pope published his four-book *Dunciad*, he imagined the Dunce-king ushered into Dulness's realm by "A slip-shod Sibyl . . . / In lofty madness meditating song," in book 3, lines 15–16, glossed by William Warburton as a condemnation of religious enthusiasm.)[8]

As a comparatively well-educated woman, a conservative Anglican, and an adherent of the traditional political order, Finch was unlikely to attempt the role of prophet-judge even if her personality and circumstances had permitted her to do so. Yet for a writer in an era when politics and religion were entwined, prophetic discourse was among the most powerful modes of persuasive expression. Throughout her postrevolutionary career, Finch therefore adapted the popular technique of paraphrase to assume the authority of the biblical prophets and, thus shaded or disguised, intimated her opinion of the prevailing regimes and her belief in their eventual doom. She would have found a precedent for such verse in Katherine Philips, whose "prophetic self-fashioning position[ed] her to speak authoritatively on the vicissitudes of the state as reflections of divine will" in a Royalist contrast to contemporary millenarian prophecies.[9] "The Introduction," the first poem transcribed into both of Finch's early manuscript collections, announces her higher purpose as well as her earthly intention to confine her prophecies to a sympathetic audience.

In Finch's manuscripts, she adheres to her advice to herself, in "The Introduction": "To some few friends, and to thy sorrows sing" (62). Her poems often express bitterness over James's rejection and her struggle to cope with the personal consequences of his flight. After the arrest of her husband, Heneage, in

April 1690 while he was trying to join James, and the subsequent dismissal of his case in late November, the Finches found themselves without financial resources or the opportunity to advance themselves. When Finch says her muse will have to content herself with "dark . . . shades" (64), she is not simply presenting herself as a manuscript writer but as a poet disappointed in her culture for discouraging women's participation in public discourse and governance, in herself for being fearful of addressing "th'opposing faction," and in her fate, as the victim of political maneuvers that deprived Heneage and herself of material prospects. Confined to rural obscurity, they had to console themselves with the fact that Heneage's life had been spared although his career was ruined.

For the rest of their lives, the Finches understood themselves to be under surveillance even though, after James's death in 1701, they evidently felt free to reside again in London. Finch's later poems, such as the fables she wrote for her *Miscellany Poems* (1713), are often straightforward in their implications, and Finch seized the publishing opportunity provided by political turmoil between 1710 and 1714. A Tory campaign, first to unseat the Whig establishment, then to end the War of Spanish Succession (and, as Jacobites hoped, to reinstate James Francis Edward as heir to the British throne), emboldened Finch to join Swift, Pope, and Delarivier Manley (and, on the opposing side, Defoe) to print opinions more explicit than any she had published previously. But Finch's religious poems throughout her career, whether destined for manuscript or print, are consistent in their prophetic intimations that the kind of punishment leveled at Deborah's contemporaries might be directed toward the English for deserting their king.

Poetry as Prophecy

In the only monograph to date on Anne Finch's poetry, Charles Hinnant remarked that assessing her work is difficult because "Finch's oeuvre is one of the most diverse of any English poet."[10] One of the consequences is that those who write about Finch tend to select one poetic form or one theme in her writing and generalize from that sample. Following Wordsworth's praise of her attentive nature imagery, for example, Finch was for decades considered a "pre-Romantic" poet. Subsequent scholars have considered the protofeminist and, most recently, political aspects of her writings.[11] Political allusions are so ubiquitous in her verse that Gillian Wright concludes, "From her Jacobitism, Finch derived not just one but many of her most productive poetic subjects. It helped to give her not only a rationale for writing but also a tenable claim to insight and authority."[12]

Finch's religious poetry is beginning to receive more attention. In their book *The Anne Finch Wellesley Manuscript Poems*, Barbara McGovern and Charles Hinnant noted the persistent apocalyptic references in Finch's devotional poems: not millenarian cries for the establishment of God's kingdom on earth but wishes for divine recompense in heaven for Jacobites' sufferings. McGovern and Hinnant define Finch's verse as apocalyptic but inherently pacifist in its "forswearing of revengeful spleen and her adoption of a contemplative perspective that places faith in Christ's power to redress all earthly wrongs."[13] Wright essentially agrees with McGovern and Hinnant's reading, adding that in "A Contemplation," the final poem transcribed into the Wellesley manuscript, "Finch, so often exercised about the false judgements and undeserved censures suffered by the worthy while on earth, seems to see the redress of such wrongs as the chief joy that heaven will afford."[14] Deborah Kennedy has set Finch within the context of actively pious contemporary women, ranging from Whig supporters like Lady Mary Chudleigh and Elizabeth Burnet to Tory affiliates like Anne Somerset, Lady Coventry, and Mary Astell, all of whom produced poetry related to their Anglican beliefs.[15] Kennedy notes the joy and peace characteristic of Finch's religious poems. Kennedy's study resembles McGovern's, Hinnant's, and Wright's in concluding that Finch's repeated invocations of divine providence in poems such as "Reflections . . . upon the late Hurrycane" convey her belief that "the real wreckage of one's life would be to value 'Glorious Titles' more than 'Heaven.'"[16] As Wright finds Jacobitism inspiring a variety of poems, Kennedy believes Finch's faith, deepened in the Revolution's aftermath, motivated some of her strongest verse.

While valuing McGovern's, Hinnant's, Kennedy's, and Wright's analyses, I believe close attention to Finch's religious imagery modifies conclusions about the degree of joy, peace, and resignation expressed in her religious verse. Finch's extensive knowledge of the Bible, read analogically as was typical in her time, led to incorporation of numerous allusions and near quotations from the Book of Common Prayer, the Hebrew Bible, and the New Testament. In addition to these references, Finch also composed a number of paraphrases, updated versions of lengthy chapters and even whole biblical books. In her poems, the Hebrew Bible foreshadows the New Testament, which in turn parallels contemporary history. Finch chose her references purposefully, many from Psalms, the book of Ecclesiastes, the book of Revelation, and other sources that promise both consolation for the unjustly suffering and retribution against their enemies. Her poetic speakers often adopt a prophetic stance toward contemporary events.

While Finch was not a millenarian—an epithet associated with some of the religious groups opposed to the Stuarts in the Civil War—her poems repeatedly invoke the promise of the Second Coming, with its distribution of justice and succeeding period of bliss for the righteous. As McGovern, Hinnant, Kennedy, and Wright all observe, these allusions assign both punishment and reward not to human but to divine agency. But their insistent repetition conveys a prophetic intention in addition to being the private meditations of a devout but aggrieved Christian. Finch's paraphrases of the Psalms, Wisdom, and Ecclesiastes, and her many references to Revelation, became a vehicle for political expression when, following Heneage's arrest and release, she believed straightforward expression of her political opinions to be dangerous. As "The Introduction" declares, she felt constrained to shade herself from the consequences of outright speech even while attempting (to paraphrase "The Introduction") to rescue the nation with her laws.

Prophetic and Poetic Traditions

While care must be taken to distinguish between Finch's Jacobite denunciations of her country's rulers and women's prophetic writings of the previous generation, their writings were part of recent cultural tradition if not models for emulation. Indeed, as Hinds notes, Finch's poems share with those predecessors' writings a "forceful predication on and commitment to an imagined future," motivated by "a vision of, and a longing for, a different kind of world . . . whether that desire be for a different kind of social organization, for retribution against unjust oppressors, or for ecstatic union with the returned Christ."[17] Although her commitment to the previous regime and established church dictated a less iconoclastic approach, and the notoriety of writers such as Mary Cary, Anna Trapnel, and Anne Wentworth would have dissuaded her from publishing similarly adamant discourse, Finch nevertheless shared their desire for a future cleansed of present sins against divine order.

In her various prophetic paraphrases, Finch sometimes assumed the prophet's role of predicting imminent ruin for James's betrayers. Her allusions are sometimes oblique. "To my Sister Ogle Decbr-31-1688-," for example, is a poem about her wished-for reunion with her sister, currently a maid of honor serving Princess Anne, in the intermediate aftermath of the Revolution, when Ogle was among Anne's retinue left in London while Anne joined her husband in William's camp. Metaphorically speaking about how the sisters will eventually make up for lost time, Finch claims that

> The sun, that stood to look on War,
> And lengthened out that fatal day,
> For Kindnesse, more engaging far,
> Will longer sure, his fall delay. (13–16)

Finch refers to a battle in which Joshua, assisted by God, commanded the sun to shine until his troops had destroyed their enemies (Joshua 10:12–14). In Finch's poem, her request that time stand still for the sisters' loving reunion outweighs Joshua's demand for time to achieve vengeance. But the allusion surely reflects Finch's preoccupation at that time with pertinent books of the Bible, and particularly her hope that God will intervene and permit James to defeat his opponents. Her allusion to Joshua therefore suggests her personal wish for vengeance as well as for sisterly reunion. Finch's prophetic allusions were not always so nuanced: as we will see in more detail later, in "Reflections . . . upon the late Hurrycane," Finch interpreted a recent natural disaster as God's punishment of the English for deserting their Stuart rulers.

Finch's prophetic discourse, subtle or forthright, is pervasive. While occasionally speaking directly to her readers in prophetic mode, Finch most often chose biblical intermediaries. In her paraphrases of the Psalms, Finch adopted the voice of David; in her paraphrases of Wisdom and Ecclesiastes, she assumed the guise of David's son Solomon. Both were among the most powerful kings of Israel and communicated directly with God. Finch's assumptions of the role of prophetic speaker, as in "To the Revd. Mr. Bedford," are instances that convey urgency by their comparative rarity, as if only dire circumstances compelled her to assume a Deborah-like role. In "To the Revd. Mr. Bedford," she promises to intercede with authorities on behalf of her friend, a nonjuring clergyman unjustly imprisoned from 1714 to 1718.

In her poem, Finch represents herself fruitlessly attempting to gain the attention of a self-interested courtier, declaring: "Yet still I will your cause persue / Th'unrighteous Judge the harden'd Jew / As soon might be at rest as I / Will leave them till they all comply" (55–58). Her poem denounces contemporary Whig lawmakers and their mercantile supporters, whom she held responsible for "The Land depraved where I was born" (52). Her speech resembles the prophets' addresses to ancient Jewish rulers and priests who refused to heed their warnings.[18] Finch's prophetic denunciation of those in power in "To the Revd. Mr. Bedford" returns us to her portrait of Deborah in "The Introduction." There, she recalls biblical accounts of ancient women rulers:

> A Woman here, leads fainting Israel on;
> She fights, she wins, she tryumphs with a Song,
> Devout, Majestick, for the subject fitt,
> And far above her arms, exalts her witt.
> Then, to the peacefull, shady Palm withdraws,
> And rules the rescu'd Nation, with her Laws. (45–50)

In her Bible, Finch would have read that "Deborah a prophetesse, the wife of Lapidoth . . . judged Israel" (Judges 4:4) during a time when God had punished the Israelites' "evil" by selling them "into the hand of Jabin king of Canaan" (Judges 4:1–2). Deborah's song thanked God after she correctly prophesied that Jael, and not Israel's military commander Barak, would assassinate Sisera, leader of Jabin's army, after a battle leading to Jabin's defeat. Finch's reference to Deborah, as Spencer suggested, is therefore not just a general example of how women were once powerful public figures. Deborah specifically led Israel while it was subject to a foreign ruler as a punishment for "evil" behavior.

Finch's example seems to ask why no such woman has stepped forward at the time the poet is writing, when another "Israel" has rejected its divinely sanctioned king and become subjected to a militaristic, foreign ruler. Her anguished rhetorical question, "How are we faln, faln by mistaken rules?" (51) answers itself: modern women are incapable of fulfilling Deborah's role because they are "Education's, more than Nature's fools" (52). Centuries of poor education have robbed women such as Finch of the confidence to speak their minds to "th'opposing faction" (57), both men in general and the political faction that had unseated James II. Those who, like the radical mid-seventeenth-century prophets, promoted their visions were misguided and doomed by ignorance. The disabling "fears" that dissuade Finch from seeking figurative laurels—either for poetry or for a Deborah-like victory over her political enemies—are both lack of confidence due to flawed education and more practical fears associated with speaking truth to power in the manner of an ancient prophet. Finch's adamant tone in "To the Rev. Mr. Bedford" most likely portrayed accurately her quest for his release, prompted by the trials of an innocent clergyman suffering in "the Land depraved where I was born." Significantly, however, the poem remained in manuscript during her lifetime.

Politics, Paraphrase, and Prophecy

More typical of Finch's verse were numerous paraphrases of psalms and other biblical texts written to predict the consolation of innocent sufferers and the punishment of their oppressors. Hannibal Hamlin has discussed psalm paraphrases throughout the early modern period. Poets and hymn writers might compose such adaptations to answer the need for Protestant translations of the Bible or simply to replace the awkward versification of the official Sternhold and Hopkins psalm settings.[19] Besides emulating David, thought to be the Psalms' composer and the prototypical inspired poet, poets could express contemporary sentiments both private and public through biblical analogues. Among the most popular, Hamlin observes, was Psalm 137 ("By the rivers of Babylon, there we sate downe, yea we wept"),[20] the response of the exiled Israelites when called upon to sing by their Babylonian masters.[21] Hamlin notes that Psalm 137 was paraphrased by various poets throughout the period, representing both sides during the Protestant Reformation and the Civil Wars.[22] Hamlin notes the appropriateness of this psalm for poets, many of whom were literally exiled due to their beliefs and allegiance.[23] Finch's decision to paraphrase Psalm 137, possibly soon after the Revolution of 1688, is therefore unsurprising.

At a time when some Jacobites were exiled with their king, others, like the Finches, were exiled from the centers of power where they had expected to spend their lives. James II himself referred to London as "Jerusalem," the captured city to be reconquered by his followers, the "Israelites."[24] Hamlin observed that translators of Psalm 137 were inspired by "lament for exile, anxiety over loss, tension between the need to express grief and the inability to do so, and the desire for revenge."[25] The reader of the King James Version indeed found the psalm glossed as representing "The constancie of the Jewes in captivity. The Prophet curseth Edom and Babel." Finch, unlike most translators, stopped short of the psalm's seventh through ninth verses, with their plea for God's destruction of their captors' cities and inhabitants: "Happy shall he be that taketh and dasheth thy little ones against the stones" (Psalm 137:9). She focuses instead on the plight of the singer. In place of the psalmist's question, "How shall we sing the Lord's song: in a strange land?" (v. 4), she imagines the captives' lyres refusing to insult their owners by producing joyful music ("But cheerful sounds, the strings refuse, / Nor will their Masters greifs, abuse," 11–12). She elaborates on the captives' grief, adding details such as the mourners' "rent garments" (17). She defines the biblical psalmist's pledge, "If I doe not remember thee, let my tongue cleave to the roofe of my mouth," as the loss of poetic ability: "My tongue, her vocal gift [will] resign, / And Sacred verse, no more be mine" (23–24). These lines confirm both Kennedy's and Wright's assertions that religion and Jacobitism, respectively, inspired Finch's verse, as Finch attests that political commitment inspires her "Sacred verse."

Finch's version of Psalm 137 supports the claim that her political views were quiescent, as she omits its graphic hope for vengeance. On the other hand, as Hamlin noted, the psalm attracted sufferers due to its endorsement of revenge. Lingering behind Finch's paraphrase is the threat left unexpressed, but which all Christians knew concluded the psalm. Finch apparently struggled to overcome her wish for temporal divine retribution in the early years following the Revolution. In "Some Reflections in a Dialogue Between Teresa, and Ardelia. On the 2d. and 3d. Verse, of the 73d: Psalm," she described her frustration in an imaginary conversation with her younger half sister, Dorothy Ogle. Elaborating on the biblical verses, she complains that her political enemies, characterized as "The Proud" (21), nevertheless "posses the mighty Store . . . Whilst I, in fears to loose, and cares to keep, / Obtain but daily bread, with interrupted sleep" (26, 29–30). Teresa/Ogle dissuades her from such thoughts, reminding her—as in the psalm—that the apparently prosperous will ultimately suffer for their "mighty sums of Vice" (39). Chastened, Ardelia/Finch admits she had failed to recall "the end of Glorious men, / Nor thought how lost they were, nor how abandon'd then" (74–75). Although poor and suffering, she acknowledges God's support in trials that will lead her to heaven while her opponents are destined for hell. Finch's rendering transforms the King James Version's gloss on Psalm 73—that faith yields "knowledge of Gods purpose, in destroying of the wicked and sustaining the righteous"—from an intimation of her enemies' impending defeat ("How are they brought into desolation as in a moment?," v. 19) into a promise of their eternal damnation.

Finch's psalm paraphrases extend Hamlin's observation regarding Psalm 137: through them she consoled herself for her and Heneage's losses, exhorting herself to maintain faith in God and trust that she and her fellow sufferers would be vindicated in heaven, if not on earth. She chose her psalms with care: "The 146th Psalm Paraphras'd," for example, reiterates Psalm 73's promise of reward for those who trust God. "Put not your trust in Princes" (v. 3), admonished the psalmist. Finch's version asks, "In man, in Princes, who the Sceptres sway, / Can there be faith repos'd, can there be trust?" (5–6), an appropriate question given her dilemma under the new King William. Psalm 146 promises relief for the suffering: "The Lord preserveth the strangers, he relieveth the fatherlesse and widow: but the way of the wicked he turneth upside downe" (v. 9). Finch adds another verse, promising

> Those, that are fallen, he again erects,
> The wicked, that persue ungodly ways,
> He searches out, he frustrates, and detects,
> He ruines their designs, and on them, builds his praise. (29–32)

Her stanza reverses the biblical promise that the wicked will be upended, promising instead that the just will be turned right side up. Here Finch comes close to forecasting temporal doom for James's opponents. She represents the voice of Sion, of King James's "Israelites" who are secure in their righteous course.

We have no way of knowing the order in which she composed most of her paraphrases, or even their dates, but taken together they illustrate a psychological struggle to accept the Revolution's consequences and find comfort in maintaining her faith, and her loyalty to James, even as the psalmist maintained his faith in God throughout the Israelites' vicissitudes. One example suggests that her decision to accept the inevitable was almost physically sickening. In Psalm 119, part 10, the poet asks God to rescue him from undeserved suffering. "Let the proud be ashamed, for they dealt perversely with me without a cause: but I will meditate in thy precepts" (v. 78). Finch omits this verse; her paraphrase implies that her suffering has been an illness rather than the political punishment suggested in the Bible. God's mercy will be a "just proportion'd Cordial," or medicine, in future trials (20). While the psalmist asked, "Let my heart be sound in thy statutes; that I be not ashamed" (v. 80), Finch concludes with a heartfelt plea:

> That I may live,
> thy mercy send,
> From thence, my vital breath I draw,
> My life, does on thy love, depend,
> And all my love, is on thy Law. (21–24)

While the psalmist asserts his relief will justify God, demonstrating his care for one "sound in [his] statutes," Finch simply asserts her love for divine law and hope that God will reciprocate by maintaining her life. There is no sense that her recovery will serve a public function or affront her enemies, but her pointed declaration of trust in divine law conveys Finch's contempt for temporal justice. The Finches, particularly after the husband Heneage's arrest in April 1690, while trying to join James in France, no doubt felt themselves barred from further overt political activity on James's behalf.[26] Although the charges against Heneage were dropped for lack of evidence, the Finches' sojourn in Kent, to which Heneage cryptically referred as "my confinement to a country life" until after James's death, implies the cost of his release.[27] Finch's psalm adaptations reflect genuine struggle even if they attempt resignation.

A final example of psalm paraphrase, rare because it can be dated, suggests that Finch was gratified at least once by a catastrophe inflicted on England for deserting the Stuarts. Finch concluded her "Reflections upon part of the 8 th. verse of the 148. Psalm. Winds and storms fulfilling his Word. In a Pindarick Poem upon the late Hurrycane" with a "Hymn Composed of the 148 th. Psalm Paraphras'd." The ode, dated February 9, 1704, in manuscript, commemorated a disastrous storm that lashed England, especially Kent, on November 26, 1703. Numerous sermons, pamphlets, and poems interpreted the storm as divine vengeance for human crimes depending on the commentator's political perspective. Daniel Defoe, for example, was moved to write two responses, a poem and a book, both called "The Storm."[28] Defoe's poem blamed opponents of Queen Anne's peace negotiations, Scottish Jacobites, and nonjurors (lords, including bishops, who refused to swear allegiance to William or Anne as heads of the Church of England instead of James or his son) for the hurricane. His prose account provided meteorologic data as well as accounts of the damage to England's crops, fleet, and infrastructure for those concerned about the human and economic costs of the disaster.

Finch's response was, unsurprisingly, quite different. Her ode, an elaborate meditation on the biblical reference to "stormie wind fulfilling his word" (v. 8), acknowledges, "You have obey'd you Winds that must fulfill / The Great Disposer's righteous Will" (1–2). Her poem opens with a description of the storm's purposeful obliteration of the forests supplying British shipbuilders with vessels and masts (15–31). The ode concludes dramatically with an account of the destruction of the merchant fleet (258–280) and Royal Navy (283–297), instruments of the usurping government and its mercantile supporters. In between, she observes the collapse of country seats ("Pallaces," 65–82) and misers' homes (163–175), crushing those complicit in post-Revolution rule. Most famously, she attributes the deaths of Bishop Richard Kidder and his wife, crushed when a chimney stack collapsed the roof of their palace, to insufficient piety. Kidder had succeeded Thomas Ken as bishop of Bath and Wells when the former became a nonjuror after the Revolution.[29] Finch remarks, "Oh Wells thy Bishops Mantion we lament, / So Tragical the Fall so dire th'Event" (97–98), refusing to assign a divine cause for the disaster. "Yet strictly pious KEN hadst thou been there / This fate we think had not become thy share" (101–102).

These lines, reversing the belief of those like Defoe who considered the nonjurors traitors, caused Finch some anxiety before she circulated them in manuscript. In a letter to her brother-in-law and trusted adviser, Thomas Thynne, Lord Weymouth, she protested, "I hope I doe not make any unfit reflections nor can be thought Injurious to the dead by giving in point of piety some preference to the Living."[30] She says she will not show the poem to anyone until Thynne sends "A line of Advice." Although not a nonjuror, Thynne, who housed Ken at his Longleat estate, evidently signified his opinion that the poem was not seditious, because Finch later included it in her *Miscellany Poems* of 1713, complete with her reference to Ken and his successor. In Finch's view, God was lenient in refraining from England's "total Wreck" (299). She calls Britons to join in thanking God, leading their praise in an appended psalm paraphrase:

> lett the Poet after God's own Heart
> Direct our Skill in that sublime part
> And our weak Numbers mend. (302–304)

David was thought to have written the Psalms partly to atone for his sins, making him the ideal figure to invoke for a hymn expressing national repentance. But perhaps more significantly, ever since John Dryden had portrayed Charles II, in the guise of David, as "Israel's Monarch, after Heaven's own Heart," in "Absalom and Achitophel" (7), paraphrasing 2 Samuel 13:14 (where David is "a man after [God's] owne heart"), the epithet was associated with the Stuart king.

It is as if Finch takes on the voice of not only of David but also James in exhorting all of England—its sky and earth, birds and animals, young and old, men and women—to praise God for the cleansing storm. King, Lords, and Commons ("The Hymne," 41–50; see Psalm 148:11) are also invited not only to thank God but to atone by leading religious and cultural reform with "enlarged Zeal" ("The Hymne," 42). Given the reference in her ode to Bishop Ken, these lines might be construed as a plea to halt the ongoing persecution of nonjurors. Finch ends by evoking her rural exile, a "contemn'd Retreat obscure and low / As Grotts from whence the Winds disperse" ("The Hymne," 66–67).

The image resembles other references to her circumstances, sometimes viewed idyllically as a remnant of paradise, as in "The Petition for an Absolute Retreat," but more often as in "To the Honorable the Lady Worsley at Long-Leate Who had most obligingly desired my Corresponding with her by Letters." In that poem, she compares her home to a

> lonely and obscure recesse
> The shunn'd retreat of solitary peace
> Lost to the World and like Ardelia's Seat
> Fitt only for the Wretch opress'd by Fate. ("To . . . Lady Worsley," 1–4)

In "The Hymne," the "obscure recesse" is Finch's "Grott," a place associated with prophets and self-exiled saints. While dismissing her verse as "worthlesse in itself" (70), she commits her poem to future readers who, like contemporary readers of scriptural prophecy, might comprehend and obey its injunctions. Given her political situation, Finch was perhaps lucky that "The Hymne" was first printed as if dropped carelessly from the ode, in a pirated copy included by Delarivier Manley in *New Atalantis* (1709) as "*A Hymn to* Jupiter."[31] Separated from "Reflections . . . upon the late Hurrycane," the hymn appears a straightforward biblical paraphrase or, in Manley's context, a classical hymn. But the ode and hymn together, as Finch understood when sending them to Thynne for approval, are an exercise in Jacobite prophecy that, in this instance, celebrated divine vengeance as much as it mourned a natural disaster.

Besides her psalm paraphrases, Finch's paraphrases of Solomon confirm her religious politics. "The Second Chapter of the Wisdom of Solomon, Paraphrased," describes a political scenario in which "Justice, shall lay aside her uselesse scales, / And force, shall justice be, when force prevails" (51–52). Solomon's evocation of the suffering, in such a polity, of a solitary, righteous man resembles Jacobite images of James as a Christlike martyr.[32] "All is Vanity," transcribed into her folio manuscript and printed in *Miscellany Poems*, is part of a long tradition of poems inspired by the aged Solomon's reputed words. "The last chapter of Eclesiastes Paraphras'd. Inscrib'd to Mrs: Catherine Fleming" reworks a favorite portion of the book at a friend's request.[33] The former poem also incorporates aspects of Juvenal's tenth satire, the same pairing of texts that would inspire Samuel Johnson's "The Vanity of Human Wishes."[34] Combining her two sources allowed Finch to broaden the scope of Ecclesiastes to include all ancient and recent history. Her poem follows Juvenal's pattern of describing human aspirations, followed by examples of their futility. After Finch echoes her patterns in the classical and Hebrew texts, she reaches the Christian conclusion that, since all human ambitions are useless, we should instead "Project, and build on t'other side the Sky" (314). To that extent, Finch's poem justifies the observations of Barash, Kennedy, Wright, and others that Jacobite hopes depended on posthumous justice.

Another way of looking at "All is Vanity," however, is suggested by its Pindaric form. Since the publication of Abraham Cowley's odes in 1656, the Pindaric had been associated with Stuart apologists. Stella P. Revard has read Cowley's Pindarics, especially his Biblical odes, as propaganda intended to comfort Royalists and warn Commonwealth adherents.[35] Revard argues that Cowley's allegorical poems were subtle enough to escape the notice of government censors, which proved unfortunate once he sought reward for them from Charles II.[36] A similar fate may have befallen Finch's equally subtle but politically inflected ode.

"All is Vanity" follows the chronology of human life, observing the dangers at each stage. A brilliant young student may die before his potential is reached (44–79).

Another youth seems destined for martial greatness but dies in his first battle (80–124). A beautiful young woman might die the victim of her sexual adventures (125–184). The works of great writers might live, but their creators usually die before those works are rewarded (185–220). Those who eschew labor for pleasure are soon food for worms (221–275). Finch incorporates examples from Genesis such as the Tower of Babel (Genesis 11:1–9 in line 54), the Psalms (Psalm 84:6 in line 29), and the Book of Kings (1 Kings 5–6 in lines 304–312) and alludes to the Gospels of Matthew (6:30 in line 3; 6:19–20 in line 314) and Luke (16:19–31 in lines 65–66) to extend her poem's scope throughout biblical history. She refers to classical figures such as Seleucus (130–131), Antony (138–174), Cleopatra (179–184), Alexander the Great (200–203), Diodorus Siculus (246), and Sardanapalus (251) to demonstrate that the prophet's wisdom applies throughout ancient history.[37]

These allusions generalize, even universalize, the moral of Ecclesiastes. But Finch's ode, as a paraphrase, also inserts the prophet quite precisely into post-Revolution England. The second line of her poem compares life "To flying Posts that haste away," an allusion to contemporary express carriages. Alerted to the modernity of this setting, the reader is soon compared to a landowner's tenant (22), a familiar method of leasing or renting property. As Finch proceeds to develop her examples, she alludes to poorly educated heirs (40) and younger sons trained to earn their fortunes through trade (41–43), the law (44), higher learning (45–50), and the military (80–81), all career paths that Finch would have observed throughout the Kingsmill, Finch, and other privileged English families. Throughout the ode, readers are invited to apply the wisdom of Ecclesiastes to recognizably modern examples as well as to classical and biblical patterns. As the ode proceeds, allusions are sometimes specific and recent. Finch's young soldier wishes to emulate not only Alexander and Caesar (99–100) but also "Turene's Conduct and . . . Conde's heat" (101). The former, Henri de La Tour d'Auvergne, Vicomte de Turenne, marshal of France, and the latter, Louis II de Bourbon, fourth prince of Condé, duc d'Enghien, were renowned French commanders during a period of French ascendancy in the seventeenth century and, therefore, timely models of military renown.

Perhaps most telling, however, is that James II, while Duke of York, had served under both Turenne and Condé while exiled during the Interregnum. Finch pointedly omits James II and William III, both military leaders, from her list of heroes. James was certainly the chief, although unmentioned, illustration of the prophet's wisdom, as Finch would detail in her elegy following his death. His forced abdication would have occurred to all contemporaries, whether Jacobite or Williamite, as the exemplar of human triumph brought low. James also exemplified, in Finch's view, the potentially ennobling outcome of failure. Following the Battle of the Boyne, he gradually withdrew from attempts to regain his English throne. Becoming pious, James could be said to "Project and Build on t'other side the Skie" (314).

While Finch refrains from mentioning James, she almost certainly alludes to William in her ode's peroration:

Yett tell the Man of an Aspiring thought
 Of an Ambitious restlesse Mind
That can no ease noe Satisfaction find
'Till neighbring States are to subjection brought
'Till an obsequious awe his fellow Slaves are taught
 That shou'd he lead an Army to the field
 For whose still necessary use
 Th'extended Earth cou'd not enough produce
Nor Rivers to their thirst a full contentment yield
 Yett must their dark reverse of Fate
 Rowl round within that course of years. . . . (285–295)

The first readers of Finch's poem in the late seventeenth century would have recognized in the passage a reference to William III, criticized throughout his reign for involving the English in wars against the French and their allies. While William justified his efforts on behalf of the Protestant states threatened by French aggression, observers like Finch thought his relentless campaigns betrayed "an Ambitious restlesse Mind" incapable of "Satisfaction."[38] As the poem concludes, Finch's speaker warns, "Him that does some stately Building raise / A Winzor or Versailles erect" that, like the Temple at Jerusalem, his work will fall. Again, contemporaries would have discerned an allusion not only to Charles II, most recent improver of Windsor Castle, and to Louis XIV, currently rebuilding Versailles, but also to William III, engaged in extensive remodeling at Hampton Court Palace. William, she implies, would do well to observe the fate of the Stuarts before death and oblivion overtake him.

Finch's poem subtly predicts William's demise, which would have encouraged its confinement to a select readership. In 1713, however, she included "All is Vanity" in her *Miscellany Poems* after James and William were both dead, Anne was dying, and young James Francis Edward was the Jacobite contender for the throne. While the ode's fierce references to William could no longer be thought seditious by those who discerned them, the same allusions by then would have recalled a different figure. By her book's publication in 1713, John Churchill, Duke of Marlborough, had been dismissed from his command of the forces allied against France in the War of Spanish Succession. The once-invincible captain general had retired to the Continent, and the enormous palace Queen Anne had commissioned for him, in thanks for his victory at Blenheim, was still unfinished.

Churchill's fall from grace was aided by a propaganda campaign, devised by Jonathan Swift, Delariviere Manley, and others whose novels and periodicals portrayed him as power-hungry, avaricious, and treacherous. By 1713, "the Man of an Aspiring thought" seeks not merely to subject "neighbring States" (288), but will not be contented "'Till Universal Awe, enslav'd Mankind is taught" (269), suiting the Tory caricatures of Churchill as power-mad and grasping, and perhaps even as alluding to the rumor—promoted by Manley—that Marlborough had hoped to purchase a European throne.[39] Likewise, Finch's reference to "some stately Building" would, by 1713, have been applied to Blenheim. The palace's ongoing construction fascinated observers, who deplored its grandeur, achieved at the public's expense. That Finch shared this preoccupation is confirmed by her later reference to its still-unfinished state in "A Contemplation," the last poem recorded in the Wellesley manuscript (92). In "All is Vanity," Churchill has joined William as an example of vainglorious ambition. While James might linger in the poem's background as an object lesson in overcoming human aspiration, his recent successors to power exemplify the kind of ambition that ultimately collapses, "Whilst unconcern'd [their] secret Ashes lye" (320).

Sometime between 1708 and 1720, Finch composed a second poem based on Ecclesiastes, "The last chapter of Eclesiastes Paraphras'd," inscribed to her friend Catherine Fleming.[40] Finch prefaced her poem with dedicatory verses "To Flavia [Fleming], By whose perswasion, I undertook the following Paraphrase." In that poem, she pleads the difficulty not only of adapting the biblical text for modern readers but of commenting on "th'unequal'd Text" (20) that communicates more through its diction and expression than a modern poet can convey (21–24). Accordingly, "The last chapter of Eclesiastes Paraphras'd" is less free with its model than was "All is Vanity," although Finch clarifies the book's verses by reordering them. Perhaps in deference to her sacred prototype, she forms her commentary by weaving passages from other biblical texts such as the Psalms, the Gospel of Matthew, and Acts of the Apostles. Like "All is Vanity," "The last chapter of Eclesiastes Paraphras'd" declares that no human effort can achieve happiness: "By awfull Trust, and keeping his Commands / Obtain thy Bliss, at thy Creator's hands (174–175). Since Fleming was married to a Church of England clergyman who would later become bishop of Carlisle, Finch's poem does not carry the political overtones apparent in "All is Vanity." On the other hand, it echoes poems by other Tory and Jacobite writers on the same theme, some written at the same historical juncture. Finch's allusion to Matthew Prior's *Solomon*, for example, confirms the biblical book's popularity as a devotional text and also as a favorite within her circle.

Prior's editors have noted the influence of his 1718 *Solomon* on Pope's *Essay on Man* and Johnson's "The Vanity of Human Wishes."[41] The extent of this influence on Pope's *Essay* should also be considered beyond the frequent acknowledgment of his allusion to "The Spleen" in Epistle 1, where if humans had sharper senses, we might "Die of a rose in aromatic pain" (Epistle 1, line 200). Writing about the critical years between 1709 and 1713, Pat Rogers has discussed the importance of Marlborough's career, and the Tory campaign that toppled him in late 1711, not only to Pope's "Windsor-Forest" but also to later poems such as the *Essay on Man* (1733, 1744).[42] Perhaps Prior's *Solomon*, written in about 1708, was only one poem resonating in Pope's mind when he later speculated on the folly of human pride throughout his *Essay.*

It may be possible to trace Finch's influence on Pope in her speaker's reminder that God:

> . . . fitted every joy to every sense,
> Who, time and place, and just duration, sees,
> And gives by Crouded measures, or degrees,
> Yet to thy Contemplation, sets no bound,
> And bids thee look for something to be found,
> Which nature yet imperfect, cannot bear,
> In worlds remote, in a sublime sphere,
> Nor thirst for pleasures, till instated there. (176–183)

Pope's *Essay* seems to echo these lines in his reminders to "Know thy own point: This kind, this due degree / Of blindness, weakness, Heav'n bestows on thee" (Epistle 1, lines 283–284), and that "God, in the nature of each being, founds / Its proper bliss, and sets its proper bounds" (Epistle 3, lines 109–110). Pope may also be recalling Finch's poem when he advises his reader to "Hope humbly then; with trembling pinions soar; / Wait the great teacher Death, and God adore!" (Epistle 1, lines 91–92), and also when he claims the good person is "Slave to no sect . . . takes no private road, / But looks thro' Nature, up to Nature's God" (Epistle 4, lines 331–332). Pope's editors have noted that Pope composed in manuscript a revision of Epistle 4 applying his epitome of vainglory to Marlborough (155, note to lines 290–308). But whether or not Finch's paraphrase of Ecclesiastes directly influenced Pope's philosophical poem, it belongs to the cluster of contemporary writings inspired by the spectacular rise and fall of Marlborough, as well as the reigns of William and Anne, which gave rise to their opponents' speculation about human vanity. While "The last chapter of Eclesiastes Paraphras'd" may not be overtly political, it participated in a political culture that moralized powerful figures' deaths or falls as divine retribution for sin, and for sympathetic readers, for betraying the Stuart succession.

I conclude my study of Finch's prophetic persona by considering a cluster of poems, some written late in her life, and others possibly during the same years, all referring to the book of Revelation. These poems are among the last transcribed into the Wellesley manuscript, but the collection does not adhere to a chronological arrangement. Revelation was among Finch's favorite biblical books; in her early octavo manuscript, she alludes to it in poems as various as "On Affliction," "Hallelujah," "A Pastoral between Menalcus and Damon," and "On Easter Day." In each of these poems, Finch evokes John's vision of "the holy City" (Revelation 21:2), often—as in "Hallelujah"—imagining herself among the elect, singing God's praise until the end of time. Murray Pittock has described the appeal for Jacobites of literature featuring messianic delivery and renewal; Finch's attraction to Revelation therefore carries the political suggestion, especially in her earlier poems, of an anticipated Stuart restoration.[43]

When she asks God, as one of his "Chosen," to hasten Judgment Day ("Th'Elect, all languish for that day," "Hallelujah," line 26), Finch might also have been intimating her wish for James and Mary Beatrice's return. In the Wellesley volume, "An Ode Written upon Christmasse Eve in the Year 1714 upon These Words And Again They Said Alleluia" may comment obliquely on political uncertainty following George I's recent coronation. Jacobites had been disappointed by Anne's refusal to acknowledge her half brother James Francis Edward's claim to the throne. Finch's poem emphasizes the glorious welcome when

> Allelujahs rend the Heaven
> When to you a Son is given
> Long Expected low Adord. (127–129)

Her poem departs from the Gospels, importing apocalyptic imagery of the holy city and the chorus of the saved. Finch's addressee, Lady Catherine Jones, had served Mary Beatrice. Although Jones, the patron of Astell, would have been on friendly terms with George I, Finch evidently felt comfortable sharing with her this exuberant, even visionary, celebration of a divine—and, perhaps, also a human—savior.

Between 1715 and 1720, Finch may have been optimistic at times, but the poor success of repeated Jacobite efforts to regain the throne would have suggested appeals to a higher source of vindication. "Written after a violent and dangerous fit of Sicknesse in the year 1715" again imagines Finch dressed "In Christs clean Robe" (40) and singing in the heavenly choir. During the year witnessing the Jacobites' most concerted effort to reinstate James Francis Edward, Finch may have been too ill to contribute propaganda on his behalf. In this poem, she dedicates her future efforts "Lesse to divert then warmly Edefy" (64). Toward the end of her life, "A Suplication for the Joys of Heaven," subscribed as "Finisht February 6th. 1718," imagines a realm of "Celestial shade / For change of pleasure not Protection made" (3–4), where Finch might finally emerge from obscurity. In that place, Finch's soul and body will be perfected and her "low Poetick tendency be rais'd" (43) due to the tree of life's healing power (Revelation 22:2). Finch alludes to the sufferings of those like Bedford, whose "imputed faults" (68) led to imprisonment, and herself and Heneage, relegated "to penurious care / To scanty cloathing and precarious fare / To lingering solitude exhausting thoughts" (65–67) since the Revolution. As in "Hallelujah," Finch imagines herself surrounded by the heavenly choir, accepted and protected after years of virtual exile.

"An Aspiration" continues the theme, begging divine reassurance that Finch will be rewarded for her refusal "to court the times / For profits intermixt with crimes" (13–14). Finch also returned to Revelation in the second of a pair of poems paraphrasing chapters of *S. Augustines Manuel*, translated by Thomas Rogers in 1581. "The Happynesse of a Departed Soul" draws from psalms and epistles in addition to Revelation, once more evoking Finch's favorite projection of herself "Mixt with the tunefull choire" singing psalms in heaven (14).

Finally, in "A Contemplation," Finch describes herself and Heneage rewarded in

> that World of peace
> Where tears are wip'd from clouded Eyes
> And Sighs for ever cease. (19–21; see Revelation 21:4)

Finch repeats her now-familiar imagery of angels and the elect singing praises before the throne before describing how her "Coronet of Thorns"—the tiara she was entitled to wear as countess—will be placed beneath Christ's feet along with Charles I's and Christ's crowns of martyrdom. Heneage, likewise, will be vindicated. After a life "For Conscience here opprest," he "Shall there full retribution find / And none his claimes molest" (50–52). After years battling lawsuits when his aunt and nieces challenged his claim to Eastwell, and prevented from taking his seat in the House of Lords because of his refusal to swear allegiance to Anne, Heneage had suffered materially, and both he and Finch suspected continued surveillance due to their principles.

"A Contemplation" emphasizes the Finches' lack of prosperity. For example, Lady Margaret Tufton (65–76) invested in the Society for the Propagation of the Bible, while the wealth of others more powerful has been squandered ("Whilst Woolsey's Pallace lyes destroy'd / And Marlbrough's is not done," lines 91–92, referring to the ongoing construction of Blenheim Palace, commissioned in 1705). Finch declares that witnessing Lady Margaret's heavenly reward, and God's corresponding disdain for "those who have each wish possest" (63), will transport her, although she fully anticipates that in heaven "all good things that we have misst / With Int'rest shall return" to the Finches (61–62). "A Contemplation" might have been composed at any time after Heneage began defending his property rights and paying his predecessor's debts in 1713, but it was an appropriate choice to end the Wellesley manuscript for even more reasons than Wright argued. Here Finch drew together her hatred of the Whig political ascendancy and its mercantile values ("Mammon," 89) with her resentment of living under the continued suspicion of authorities and legal challenges by relatives ("Hypocrisy and feign'd pretence / To cover foul Dissigns," 53–55). She presented an almost ecstatic prediction of the Finches' ultimate reward, drawn from Revelation in precise detail due to her long familiarity with John's vision.

While her seventeenth-century predecessors prophesied in national terms, the poems of Finch's last seven years often retreated to a specific and personal vision of reward and punishment. But throughout her career she spoke through the biblical prophets, mixing politics and religion in a blend familiar to contemporaries if more subtle than the previous century's radical predictions. Although Finch believed herself unable to speak and judge boldly as a modern Deborah, she found a vehicle commensurate with her wish to express her opinions to fellow Jacobites and other sympathetic readers. If Finch retreated, as she claimed in "The Introduction," it was a strategic move. Through allusions and paraphrase, she could shadow—in the sense of obscure representation—her judgment of "The Land depraved where I was born" ("To the Revd. Mr. Bedford," 52), her Jacobite political opinions spoken through the words of the biblical prophets.

NOTES

1. Jane Spencer, "Anne Finch, Countess of Winchilsea (1661–1720): Sorrow into Song," in *Women and Poetry, 1660–1750*, ed. Sarah Prescott and David E. Shuttleton (Houndmills: Palgrave Macmillan, 2003), 60–61. Throughout this essay, I quote Finch's poems by line number as they appear in the *Cambridge Edition of the Works of Anne Finch*, 2 vols., eds. Jennifer Keith and Claudia Kairoff (Cambridge: Cambridge University Press, 2020), and *Cambridge Edition of the Works of Anne Finch*, vol. 2, ed. Jennifer Keith and Claudia Kairoff (Cambridge: Cambridge University Press, 2020–2021).

2. Spencer, "Anne Finch, Countess of Winchilsea," 61.

3. Phyllis Mack, *Visionary Women: Ecstatic Prophecy in Seventeenth-Century England* (Berkeley: University of California Press, 1992), 174.

4. I refer here to *shadow* as a verb, in a sense used by contemporaries like Dryden and Addison: "To represent by a shadow or imperfect image; to indicate obscurely or in slight outline; to symbolize, typify, prefigure" (*Oxford English Dictionary Online*, def. 7a).

5. Examples include Mack, *Visionary Women*, and Elaine Hobby, *Virtue of Necessity: English Women's Writing 1649–1688* (London: Virago Press, 1988).

6. Hilary Hinds, "Prophecy and Religious Polemic," in *The Cambridge Companion to Early Modern Women's Writing*, ed. Laura Lunger Knoppers (Cambridge: Cambridge University Press, 2009), 244.

7. John Dryden, *The Works of John Dryden*, 20 vols., gen. eds. E. N. Hooker, H. T. Swedenberg, et al. (Berkeley: University of California Press, 1956–2000), 2:21. Further quotations of Dryden will be cited from this edition.

8. Alexander Pope, *The Poems of Alexander Pope*, 16 vols., gen. ed. John Butt (1950; London: Methuen, 1964); vol. 5, *The Dunciad*, ed. James Sutherland, 320–321. Further quotations of Pope's poems will be taken from this edition and cited within the text.

9. David L. Orvis, "Biblical Poetics, Royalist Politics, and Anti-eschatological Prophecy in Philips's Poetry," in *The Noble Flame of Katherine Philips: A Poetics of Culture, Politics, and Friendship*, ed. David L. Orvis and Ryan Singh Paul (Pittsburgh: Duquesne University Press, 2015), 109.

10. Charles H. Hinnant, *The Poetry of Anne Finch: An Essay in Interpretation* (Newark: University of Delaware Press, 1994), 17.

11. Feminist readings began with Virginia Woolf, *A Room of One's Own* (1929; New York: Harvest Books, 1957), 63; for a French feminist reading, see Ruth Salvaggio, *Enlightened Absence: Neoclassical Configurations of the Feminine* (Champaign: University of Illinois Press, 1988), 126. For recent political readings, see Carol Barash, *English Women's Poetry, 1649–1714: Politics, Community, and Linguistic Authority* (Oxford: Clarendon Press, 1996), 262, 282–283; Wes Hamrick, "Trees and Politics in Anne Finch's Jacobite Poems of Retreat," *Studies in English Literature, 1500–1900* 533 (Summer 2013): 541–563; Nicolle Jordan, "'Where Power Is Absolute': Royalist Politics and the Improved Landscape in a Poem by Anne Finch, Countess of Winchilsea," *Eighteenth Century* 46 (2005): 255–275; Claudia Kairoff, "Anne Finch as Playwright: The Purposes of Manuscript and Print in Her Pro-Stuart

Plays," *Restoration* 38, no. 1 (Spring 2014): 19–40; Jennifer Keith, "Anne Finch's Aviary: or, Why She Never Wrote 'The Bird and the Arras,'" *Philological Quarterly* 88, no. 1–2 (Winter 2009): 77–102.

12. Gillian Wright, *Producing Women's Poetry, 1600–1730: Text and Paratext, Manuscript and Print* (Cambridge: Cambridge University Press, 2013), 160.

13. Barbara McGovern and Charles H. Hinnant, eds., *The Anne Finch Wellesley Manuscript Poems* (Athens: University of Georgia Press, 1998), xxx.

14. McGovern and Hinnant, 190.

15. Deborah Kennedy, "The Radiant Throne: Religion and the Poetry of Anne Finch, Countess of Winchilsea," *Women's Writing* 18, no. 3 (2011): 423–440.

16. Kennedy, 437.

17. Hinds, "Prophecy and Religious Polemic," 239.

18. I am grateful to Jennifer Keith for her insight into the prophetic aspects of this speech.

19. Hannibal Hamlin, *Psalm Culture and Early Modern English Literature* (Cambridge: Cambridge University Press, 2004), 1, 20. Throughout this essay, I use the term *paraphrase* in the contemporary sense defined by Dryden as a "Translation with Latitude" (see *Works of John Dryden*, 1:114–15).

20. Throughout this essay I quote *The Holy Bible: Quatercentenary Edition*, ed. Gordon Campbell (1611; Oxford: Oxford University Press, 2010), citing book, chapter, and verse within the text.

21. Hamlin, *Psalm Culture*, 219.

22. Hamlin, 240–241, 246.

23. Hamlin, 240–241.

24. Pat Rogers, *Pope and the Destiny of the Stuarts: History, Politics, and Mythology in the Age of Queen Anne* (Oxford: Oxford University Press, 2005), 126.

25. Hamlin, *Psalm Culture*, 251–252.

26. See Barbara McGovern, *Anne Finch and Her Poetry: A Critical Biography* (Athens: University of Georgia Press, 1992), 58–60, for the details of Heneage's arrest as well as the progress and dismissal of his case.

27. As cited in McGovern, 73.

28. Daniel Defoe, "The Storm. An Essay" (London, 1704), and *The Storm; or, A Collection of the Remarkable Casualties and Disasters, which happen'd in the Late Dreadful Tempest* (London, 1704).

29. See William Marshall, "Ken, Thomas, (1637–1711)," in *Oxford Dictionary of National Biography Online*, ed. H. C. G. Matthew and Brian Harrison (Oxford: Oxford University Press, 2004, January 2008), https://doi.org/10.1093/ref:odnb/15342.

30. Anne Finch to Thomas Thynne, first Viscount Weymouth, February 14, 1704 (Longleat Thynne Papers XVII ff. 282r–283r).

31. Delarivier Manley, *Secret memoirs and manners of several persons of quality, of both sexes, From the New Atalantis*, vol. 2 (London, 1709), 159–160.

32. Paul Monod discusses Jacobite descriptions of Charles I and James as royal martyrs in *Jacobitism and the English People, 1688–1788* (Cambridge: Cambridge University Press, 1989), 62–63.

33. A reference to Matthew Prior's *Solomon*, printed in 1718, but which Finch might have seen in manuscript, somewhat narrows the range for the date of composition of "The last chapter of Eclesiastes Paraphras'd." Prior mentions the poem in letters of 1706 and 1707, suggesting a terminus a quo for Finch's composition. See H. Bunker Wright and Monroe K. Spears, eds., *The Literary Works of Matthew Prior* (Oxford: Clarendon, 1959), 2:913. Finch might have known Prior as early as 1706 (McGovern, *Anne Finch and Her Poetry*, 110).

34. Finch could have read Juvenal's tenth satire in *The Satires of Decimus Junius Juvenal translated into English by Mr. Dryden and several other eminent hands* (London, 1693).

35. Stella P. Revard, *Politics, Poetics, and the Pindaric Ode: 1450–1700* (Tempe: Arizona Center for Medieval and Renaissance Studies, 2009), 142–152.

36. Revard, 148.

37. Finch most likely found most of her classical anecdotes in *Plutarch's Lives*, 5 vols., trans. John Dryden et al. (London: Jacob Tonson, 1683–1686), with the exception of *Diodorus Siculus*, trans. H. C. (London, 1653), the life of the Assyrian ruler.

38. On William's English critics and his difficulties securing parliamentary support for his wars against Louis IX, see Tony Claydon, "William III and II, (1650–1702)," in *Oxford Dictionary of National Biography Online*, https://doi.org/10.1093/ref:odnb/29450.

39. Manley speculates about the ambition of Count Fortunatus, her fictional version of Marlborough, in *The New Atalantis*, ed. Ros Ballaster (1709; repr., London: Penguin, 1992), 1:17; see also 272n52.

40. For Catherine Fleming, see William Gibson, "Fleming, Sir George, (1667–1747)," in *Oxford Dictionary of National Biography Online*, https://doi.org/10.1093/ref:odnb/9698. Catherine Jefferson married Sir George Fleming in 1708, providing the terminus a quo for the composition of Finch's poem.

41. See Wright and Spears, *Literary Works of Matthew Prior*, 2:913.

42. Pat Rogers, *Pope and the Destiny of the Stuarts: History, Politics, and Mythology in the Age of Queen Anne* (Oxford: Oxford University Press, 2005), 220.

43. Murray G. H. Pittock, *Jacobitism* (New York: St. Martin's Press, 1998), 68.

CHAPTER 8

"That Unnatural Mixture"

NOSTALGIA AND ANXIETY IN LATE RESTORATION TRAGICOMEDY

Cynthia J. Lowenthal

Early modern Europe saw a transformed economy that redefined people's relationships with each other, with their environment, and with other nations. The changes altered their sense of control, their reasons for hope, and even their understanding about what was "real." One of the best examinations of this transformation can be found in Ian Baucom's powerful and insightful *Specters of the Atlantic*. Investigating the murderous incident on the slaving ship *Zong* (when 133 slaves were thrown overboard to die) and the subsequent insurance claims lodged against the lives of the slaves, Baucom argues that a "speculative revolution" took place during the eighteenth century,[1] one that highlighted competing theories of knowledge, "a struggle between an empirical and a contractual, an evidentiary and a credible epistemology."

The tragic events of the *Zong* encode all "the central epistemological drama of the long eighteenth century": "the drama—emerging from the social rivalry of the old landed and the new moneyed classes—in which, as mobile property displaced 'real' property, and the imaginary value of stocks, bonds, bills-of-exchange, and insured property of all kinds increasingly trumped the 'real' value of land, bullion, and other tangibles, the concepts of what was knowable, credible, valuable, and real were themselves transformed."[2] The novel, as Baucom continues, was the essential partner in this epistemological revolution, teaching its readers "how to negotiate and make intelligible this new order of things; how to decode the arrangements of this suddenly more complex, shifting, social system; how to read the newly crucial trade in promise, speculations and desire; how to interpret the credibility and the creditworthiness of the 'new social persons' with whom society's deindividualized individuals were increasingly called on to transact public life. It produced a discourse devoted, above all, to training society's members to credit the existence of the abstract, imaginary, speculative values and things that had come to dominate social life."[3] Undoubtedly, the novel played an essential role in teaching early modern readers to navigate the uncharted waters of this new epistemology. But I remain skeptical that any theory about the intersections among political economy, literature, culture, and history can be altogether complete in the absence of a look at that place where the "abstract, imaginary, speculative" was always, if only temporarily, embodied; that place where the transactional and performative were always artificial and true—the theatre.

In this essay, I concentrate on four liminal figures in John Dryden's *Don Sebastian* (1690) and Aphra Behn's *Widow Ranter* (1690) in the context of these epistemic changes. I locate this investigation in a single theatrical and very Restoration-era form—tragicomedy—as acted during a single year, 1689, after the crisis over James II's declaration of his Catholicism and challenges to succession had been averted, when William and Mary had just taken the throne, after the Glorious Revolution had indeed been bloodless, and as England was on the cusp of the greatest financial revolution in its history (roughly demarcated between 1690 and 1740). *Don Sebastian* and *The Widow Ranter* were each written by an aging playwright at the end of his or her career (Behn's play was posthumously produced). These two playwrights, lifelong supporters of Tory politics and specifically supporters of the Stuarts, both suffered for their politics and their political connections. Both turned to forms other than the theatre for writing late in their careers—criticism and popular fiction—and so both were writing for money again: Dryden because he had lost the laureateship and his position as king's historiographer as a result of his politics and his own final conversion to Catholicism, and Behn because she was a woman without other reliable means of support.

I examine these two plays together for other more important thematic reasons: both writers turn to history for the subjects of their dramas, both place their dramas in non-English settings, and both comment on the current state of England's imperial or proto-imperial adventure, its conquests and encounters, and its settlements and colonial enterprises. Most tellingly, both plays feature cross-cultural encounters—Muslims with the Portuguese and Spanish, and American Indians with British colonists—in the kinds of encounters that would come increasingly to shape the new epistemology. Nabil Matar labels the years when such encounters occurred as the time between the Age of Discovery (roughly 1492 and the Elizabethan Age) and the Great Migration (roughly the Caroline period). Claiming that students of the Renaissance have long ignored the fact that Britons encountered Muslims at the same time they encountered American Indians, he writes of these "concurrent encounter[s]":

> Only three years after the Turkey Company had been established in 1581, Sir Walter Raleigh's first project for settlement in Roanoke, Virginia, was launched

> (in 1584), and in 1585, two years before the second Roanoke project was undertaken, the Barbary Company was formed to strengthen England's trade with Morocco, which had existed since the 1550s. The ventures to North American and to North Africa and the Levant occurred so close together in time that, throughout the period under study, the English were in a triangular geographical relationship. They lived and traded among the Turks and Moors while simultaneously or subsequently trading with the American Indians and living in their lands.[4]

While Dryden chooses to represent past European consequences of encounters between Muslims and Europeans, Behn opts to rehearse a more recent New World uprising. Yet out of these different elements, both aging playwrights craft a group of anachronistic characters in their upper plots, drawn from their admiration for the old heroic virtues, even as they understand those values to be bankrupt in the nonheroic present. The classical, controlled bodies of the heroes are placed in contrast to another group of low, vulgar, rabble-rousing, grotesque bodies in their "under" plots—self-interested persons driven by money and not beliefs, sometimes even transported to faraway countries against their will for someone else's benefit.

In both cases, the upper plots and the lower plots, as traditionally defined, also contain liminal figures who cross those generic boundaries—characters who deflect or incorporate the new economic elements of speculation and circulation, the imaginary and the contingent, and who carry the burden of the playwrights' fears and anxieties about the breaking down of boundaries generally as well as some tentative optimism about the new economic and imperialist ventures that will dominate British life for decades to come. Each of these figures has "gone native," if in different ways; as a result, the playwrights engage their audiences in questions of incest and miscegenation, renegades and rebels, gender inversions and fluid identities, and new economic men and women to determine to what degree these boundary crossings serve as threat or liberation.

Nostalgia: European and Native American Royalty

Tragicomedy is a form ready-made to allow an audience to hold multiple, potentially contradictory generic and perhaps even ideological forms in their heads simultaneously—the condition of life during these epistemological changes. Whether those forms are constantly warring, working in parallel, providing complementary comments, or serving as deeply mutually embedded structures, the allegorical force of the form possesses an elasticity that allows playwrights to craft comments on complex and still unsolved contemporary political subjects by setting them elsewhere or in another time. And Restoration audiences were undeniably interested in and responded to tragicomedy. Nancy Klein

Maguire goes so far as to say, "Tragicomedy lies at the center of Restoration consciousness."[5] She deftly captures the spirit of the form that attracted seventeenth-century playwrights: "Tragedy and comedy separate life into orderly structures; they have restraining borders; they are arranged. In contrast, the mood of tragicomedy is open; the playwright does not attempt to order life into neat segments. Life and tragicomedy happen."[6] Derek Hughes writes that "split-plot tragicomedy went out of fashion after 1671,"[7] a fact that makes it all the stranger that both Behn and Dryden returned to the form in the late 1680s. They chose to present an old-fashioned tragicomedy in front of a sophisticated 1689 audience there to appreciate and respond emotionally to the ephemeral actions before them but simultaneously smart enough to read the force of contemporary political and economic allegory as it unfolds onstage.

In *Don Sebastian*, Dryden chooses a story about a king of Portugal who supposedly died in battle about a hundred years earlier, in 1578, but whose body was never recovered. There were numerous Renaissance treatments of the myth, which subsequently generated a series of romances, many of which Dryden had access to and could have used as his sources. *Don Sebastian*, produced by the United Company sometime in late 1689, featured the comedian Cave Underhill in the part of the Mufti; Thomas Betterton took on the even juicier role of Dorax, while Mrs. Barry played Almeyda, the African princess. Contemporary reviewers say it garnered applause, and Dryden earned a whopping 120 guineas for his third day. The play remained popular through the mid-eighteenth century and was performed at least twenty-one times in the first half of the eighteenth century.

This popularity is all the more fascinating considering that *Don Sebastian* is a thoroughly nostalgic play. The characters in the upper plot speak in an unrhymed verse that would have been completely at home on a 1660s stage. In an upper plot that looks only backward, Don Sebastian is the tragic Portuguese hero held captive by the vicious Moors, who presents himself in the old mode of conquest—he is brave, energetic, gentlemanly, fit to rule—and his prowess on the battlefield is figured in a body count: if one wishes to find the Portuguese leader, one should look for the tallest mound of corpses—"a Mountain of the Slain"—and down below one will find Sebastian, "With his face up to Heav'n, in the red Monument, / Which his true Sword has digg'd."[8] As Geraldo U. de Sousa puts it, "Dryden gives Sebastian a double identity as an idealized monarch and victim of a failed dream. On the one hand, Sebastian embodies chivalric ideals; on the other, he embarks on a misguided, disastrous latter-day Crusade against the forces of Islam."[9]

Yet when we first see him presented to the Moroccan emperor, Sebastian is standing hidden behind other captives. He then steps forward and speaks in that high-toned allegorical language of old—a true nobleman. However, the language seems spent, worn out, a stirring but bankrupt linguistic exercise:

> Fate was not mine,
> Nor am I Fate's: Now I have pleas'd my longing,
> And trod the ground which I beheld from far,
> I beg no pity for this mouldring Clay:
> For if you give it burial there it takes
> Possession of your Earth:
> If burnt and scatter'd in the air: the Winds
> That strow my dust, diffuse my royalty,
> And spread me o'er your Clime: for where one Atome
> Of mine shall light; know there *Sebastian* Reigns. (12)

Almeyda, the Barbary queen, also taken captive and herself a prisoner, is as haughty and preemptory as Dryden's Cleopatra or Octavia. The object of Moorish lust, she is always, even from the opening moments, identified with Africa, and when she first appears onstage, among the captives and singled out for scrutiny, she is dismissive of the Moorish leader and her captives:

> Hear me; I will be heard:
> I am no Slave; the noblest blood of *Affric*
> Runs in my Veins; a purer stream than thine;
> For, though deriv'd from the same Source, thy Current
> Is puddl'd, and defil'd with Tyranny. (14)

Later, when the emperor indicates that he intends to take her for his wife, she refuses outright, by claiming that her Christian faith prohibits any marriage, but also by insisting that, at its deepest biological core, a union between them would only serve "To people *Affric* with new Monsters, / Which that unnatural mixture must produce? (34). Their differences are so extreme, as she understands them, that she defines each of them as a different species. The "unnatural mixture" of this essay's title is thus not only a comment on the generic instability of the tragicomic form but also a phrase used in defining and in resistance to the crossing of impermissible boundaries: in this case, Almeyda's definition of *miscegenation.* Nabil Matar has argued that precisely because the Europeans could not colonize the Moors, they instead demonized them: "Turks were tyrannical and deceiving; Moors were hypersexual and emotionally uncontrolled, vengeful, and hyper-religious."[10] Almeyda's "new Monsters" both participate in and confirm this demonizing strategy of containment.

What neither Almeyda nor the emperor, nor the hero realizes, at this moment, is the genuine biological and cultural injunction that she and Don Sebastian are about to break: they are about to commit an act of unintended incest. In the final scenes, Almeyda is revealed to be an "unnatural mixture"—the illegitimate child of the Christian Portuguese King and the Muslim Queen of the Moors, born from a secret and illegal (and, by contemporary standards, immoral) liaison when the African royal family was in exile in Portugal. Once Almeyda learns that she and Don Sebastian have consummated an incestuous marriage, she swoons, and Don Sebastian draws his sword to take his own life—ultimately restrained by his friends from doing so. The play, which has highlighted and insisted on the dangers of difference, ends with emphasis on the lovers' likeness and similarity:

> SEB: Nay then there's Incest in our very Souls,
> For we were form'd too like.
> ALM: Too like indeed,
> And yet not for each other.
> . . .
> SEB: Alas, I know not by what name to call thee!
> Sister and Wife are the two dearest Names,
> And I wou'd call thee both; and both are Sin. (128, 129)

In this final act, the two tragic elements in the play, the "unnatural mixtures" of miscegenation and incest, form a double comingling of realms meant to remain separate in their difference. The endings for everyone in the upper plot are disquieting and unsatisfying: Don Sebastian will travel away to an isolated cave where he will live in a separate cell and "enjoy Devotion"; Almeyda will travel to an island off the Azores where she will live with the abbess in Tercera. Brother and sister, husband and wife, part forever in the very last moments of the play, which are actually quite a moving demonstration of the grief and guilt that arise from the "unnatural mixture" of elements "form'd too like."

The heroic plot of *The Widow Ranter* similarly involves an imaginative rewriting of a real historical incident, but a more recent one, the only popular uprising in colonial American: the 1676 revolt led by Nathaniel Bacon in the Jamestown colony against a corrupt, do-nothing governor, Sir William Berkeley. A plantation owner himself, Bacon had argued that the government had done too little, in his estimation, to address the problem of Indian incursions, so he responded by mustering his own small army, without approval from the governor, to attack local tribes. The popular uprising, bloody but short-lived, was without permanent effects, and Bacon died (probably of illness) a few months later.

Unlike the Portuguese heroic figures in *Don Sebastian*, the purely heroic characters in Behn's play are not Europeans but the admirable Native Americans. Their monarchs are introduced at the beginning of the second act in a highly elaborate setting, "A Pavillion," according to the directions, and a crowded set. The stage directions read, "Discovers the Indian King and Queen sitting in State, with Guards of Indians, Men and Women attending: To them Bacon richly dress'd, attended [by other officers]; he bows to the King and Queen, who rise to receive him."[11] A truce has been called, and the warring parties are meeting in the hopes of finding an end to hostilities. The King and Queen greet Bacon with great dignity, and the King says, "I am sorry, Sir, we meet upon these Terms, we who so often have embrac'd as Friends," while the Queen confesses in an aside, "The more I gaze upon this *English* Stranger, the more Confusion struggles in my Soul: Oft I have heard of Love, and oft this Gallant Man . . . has told a thousand Tales of dying Maids; and ever when he spoke, my panting Heart, with a prophetick Fear in Sighs reply'd, I shall fall a Victim to his Eyes" (127, 128).

In the end, she does indeed fall victim—not to his eyes but to his sword. Unlike the endings for Almeyda and Don Sebastian, who exit the stage alive but journey toward a final exile, both the Indian King and Indian Queen die by Bacon's hand. They die at separate moments, and they die without the dignity one would expect from their status. The King dies not defending his people but while fighting out of jealousy: he meets Bacon on the battlefield, exclaiming, "Your Blushes do betray your Passion for her" (163), and he lunges into the violence. At the moment of his death he says, "[I am] like one—that's hovering between Heaven and Earth; I'm—mounting—somewhere—upwards—but giddy with my flight—I know not where . . . commend me to [the Queen]—I know you'll—visit—your fair Captive, Sir, and tell her–oh–but Death prevents the rest" (164). Bacon, stumbling around the battlefield in search of the Queen, mistakenly kills her because she is stumbling around the battlefield cross-dressed as an Indian warrior, with "Bow in hand and Quiver at her back," according to the stage directions. In her last words, she thanks him for saving her from dishonor: "The noblest Office of a gallant Friend, thou'st sav'd my Honour, and hast given me Death" (179).

The language the Indian characters speak is always transcendently regal, noble, and heroic. Unlike Dryden's Indigenous inhabitants, stereotypical aggressive and rapacious Muslims, Behn's Indians always read as admirable, if doomed. And for all its violence, the upper plot of *The Widow Ranter* lacks the passion and energy that one finds in *Don Sebastian*, even if those passions are guilt and despair. The emotions seem as formulaic and scripted as the language the Indians speak, generated according to generic imperatives rather than emotional intensity.

Thus, both playwrights fashion emblematic heroes for their upper plots, characters at home in the late sixteenth century and early seventeenth century, resurrected but not sustainable in late seventeenth-century imperial contexts. "By the time he wrote the elegiac Don Sebastian, a mournful tribute to Portugal's quixotic Crusader, Dryden had abandoned the possibility that the English might pursue overseas empire as a project of civilization and conversion rather than trade and settlement," writes Bridget Orr; Don Sebastian is "a despairing vision of the failure of the project of universal monarchy conceived of as Christian greatness."[12] Similarly, Behn's Indians, indistinguishable linguistically and rhetorically from Don Sebastian himself, present a despairing vision of the lack of power of the old heroic in a New World. Nor can *Don Sebastian* and *The Widow Ranter* be removed from *contemporary* English imperial impulses—colonization not for God but for profit—and a reaction to the epistemological changes that necessitates. The English might still hold on to their appreciation for old systems of inheritance and possession, with marriage being the avenue to perpetuate property and inheritances. But both of these plays forbid such unions—as incest or adultery or miscegenation. There is no reproduction, no lineage, no genealogy to be generated through "unnatural mixtures" in the new economic system. These figures remain frozen in their emblematic status. There is no resurrecting or enlivening an emblem.

The Rabble

At the opposite extreme, and serving as a counterbalance to the disciplined, classical, heroic bodies of the nostalgic tragic protagonists, are the less nuanced, more grotesque, thoroughly material, unruly bodies of the Rabble, or "mobile," as they are sometimes called (the source of our word *mob*). The collection of lower-class Moors on the edges of the upper action in *Don Sebastian* are primarily self-interested people vulnerable to the sway of men of ambition. First, they respond to the slave-trading Mustapha's bid for power. He urges them to defy the Mufti and their rightful government by revolting. The Rabble respond with "our business is only to rise upon command, and plunder" (84). Moments later, they rally around the Mufti himself, who argues that "your Emperour is a Tyrant . . . he has play'd the Turk with you; and is taking your Religion away." To this they respond, "We find that in our decay of Trade; I have seen for these hundred years, that Religion and Trade always go together" (85), and the scene vacillates between shouts of support for "Mustapha" and "Mufti."

Since colonial Virginia is the setting for *The Widow Ranter*, its settlers, not its Indigenous people, are Behn's rowdy subjects, and they are very much "Rabble" in their own right. Few of the earliest settlers had enough investment capital to purchase plantations in Virginia. As Matar notes, the rest, the majority, were poor and destitute: "Many of the 'emigrants' to Virginia and other American colonies in the Jacobean and Caroline periods—and well into the eighteenth century—were spirited men, women, and children, zealous youths, helpless vagrants, and numberless orphans who were abducted or who, under the influence of drink or fanciful rhetoric, were made to sign agreements for transportation and then locked up to await shipping."[13] One early seventeenth-century goal of the English in the colonies was to get in, make money, and get out. Advertising campaigns had to be waged to get people to make the perilous journey, especially after the publication of hair-raising reports about natural disasters from returning travelers. As Matar puts it, "In America there were swamps and marshlands, mosquitoes and typhoid-contaminated water, and, most terrifyingly, hurricanes the like of which do not exist in the Mediterranean."[14] Matar cites the example of Sir Thomas Gates's account of the ill-fated, 1609 voyage to Jamestown in the *Sea Venture*, in which he describes such hurricanes in this way: "Windes and Seas were as mad, as fury and rage could make them; for mine owne part, I had bin in some stormes before, as well upon the coast of Barbary and Algeere, in the Levant. . . . Yet all that I have ever suffered gathered together, might not hold comparison with this [hurricane]."[15] Like renegade captives in North Africa, many early seventeenth-century immigrants to America did not necessarily choose to immigrate. These forms of indentured servitude, while never the equivalent of institutionalized American slavery, presented an audience with characters possessed of limited autonomy and scarcer resources.

This new settlement also presents surprisingly easy possibilities for social mobility, for the exploitation of a new system no longer anchored in status and birth, which will elevate immigrants unsuited to controlling the future of the colonies into positions of authority. As described by *The Widow Ranter*'s Friendly, Virginia is characterized in economic terms both by what it lacks and in the ways it rewards those willing to exploit the system: "This Country wants nothing but to be peopled with a well-born Race, to make it one of the best Colonies in the World. But for want of a Governour we are ruled by a Council, some of whom have been perhaps transported Criminals, who have acquired great Estates, and now become your Honour and Right Worshipful, and possess all Places of Authority" (112).

In both plays, then, the lower plots are sites for comedy that feature undisciplined and unregulated low-status characters whose self-interest and need simply to survive override any generous impulses they might experience. More important, in their vulgarity and excessive emotionality, they serve as important contrasts to the elegant, controlled, heroic—and doomed—characters penned by Tory playwrights in the tragic upper plots.

Anxiety: Boundary-Breaching Renegades and Commodities

The most illuminating characters in both plays, however, are the liminal figures who cross the borders between the separate realms of the classical and the grotesque, beings who are *of* but not *from* the region. In the upper plots, moving between the worlds of the declamatory discourses of worn-out notions of empire and nobility and the worlds of unruly, ungovernable mobs are figures at the margins who have often "gone native" and refashioned themselves in sometimes threatening and sometimes liberating ways: they are the Renegades. In some cases, they have turned their backs on the old heroic and bankrupt colonial gestures of their former worlds, even as they still long for residual energetic heroism, knowing full well its insufficiencies. In other cases, they serve to represent, in the lower plots, the figure of the new economic man and woman: smart, exploitative, determined, quick to change, they take part in a system they can also use. More important, they are willing to self-fashion new identities—

including transgressing established gender differences—to build success on new economic opportunities.

The first such liminal figure is Dorax, from the upper plot of *Don Sebastian*, a character who travels between the European and Muslim worlds and who becomes a kind of fulcrum that holds both past and present, civilized and primitive, anchored and mobile in tension. Once Don Sebastian's loyal soldier, but feeling betrayed by the monarch years before, he has turned his back on his Portuguese heritage, renounced his birth name, Alonzo, and joined forces with the Moorish enemy. Historical records indicate that European soldiers did indeed serve Muslim leaders, sailing as pirates from North African shores. Others were captives, taken by pirates to North Africa not as mercenaries or traders but as prisoners to be sold in the slave markets. In an account published in 1670 but describing events in 1648 and later, Mr. T.S. tells the story of his enslavement after a battle at sea. He was taken to Algiers, where he was forced into the army, and confirms (in what could be pure nationalist fantasy) what many of his readers suspected—that the many English soldiers who had converted to Islam actually constituted the main strength of the Algerian army. T.S. himself writes, "The Infantry was made up of Renegado-Christians, whereof there are such number in that place, that they bear all the sway and command both by Sea and Land."[16] Between 1577 and 1704, there were twenty-two accounts written by Englishmen about captivity among the Muslims; if the captive returned to England and tried to reassimilate, "the community could only wonder whether he had apostatized and been physically marked by Islam. And short of stripping him naked to see whether he had been circumcised or not, which communities and sea captains sometimes did, there was no definite answer."[17] Thus the Renegade, even once returned home, remained an object of suspicion and distrust.

Dryden's audience would have been familiar with the figure of the Renegade, and Dryden intends Dorax to serve not as an example of disloyalty and betrayal but as a principled but headstrong and misguided rebel to his king. Like Anthony in *All for Love*, Dorax is initially described by some as noble and soldierly, while others celebrate his excellencies, calling him a "gallant Renegade," whose rusty exterior "Contains the shining Treasure of a Soul, / Resolv'd and brave" (2). From such descriptions, an audience is prepared for robust manliness and courage. His first words onstage, however, suggest otherwise. In act 1, being welcomed by the duplicitous Benducar, Dorax turns a greeting into a series of homophobic jibes. First, Dorax fails to salute Benducar with an appropriate title. "Well, Benducar!" he says. Benducar then calls him out for the insult, "Bare Benducar!" In response, Dorax doubles down: "Though wouldst have Titles, take 'em then, Chief Minister, / First Hangman of the State." When Benducar answers civilly that he prefers the title "Favourite," Dorax immediately shifts the term into the sexual arena: "What's that, his Minion? / Thou are too old to be a Catamite!" (3)—an image even more specifically secured in these next lines:

Now prithee tell me, and abate thy pride,
Is not *Benducar* Bare, a better Name
In a Friend's mouth, than all those gawdy Titles,
Which I disdain to give the Man I love? (3)

Sodomy was often linked with Islam in English discourses on the Levant, and it is perhaps Dorax's means of demonstrating that he has not been tainted by sodomy in Morocco that he invokes such references—but that possibility is undermined by the fact that he uses such language more often than anyone else in the play.

Dorax's penchant for sexual slander becomes even more disturbing when the conversation turns to the fates of Don Sebastian (Dorax's old friend and monarch) and Almeyda, now both captives of a Muslim tyrant. Benducar wonders what became of them both in the battle:

'Tis of as much import as *Affrick's* worth
To know what came of him, and of *Almeyda*
The Sister of the Vanquish'd *Mahumet,*
Whose fatal Beauty to her Brother drew
The Lands third part, as *Lucifer* did Heav'ns. (5)

To this question of her whereabouts and the memory of her beauty, Dorax responds with a vulgar, obscene, and astonishing pornographic image—one of the most brutal I know of in all of Restoration drama. Dorax imagines Almeyda in the moment of her death: "I hope she dy'd in her own Female calling, / Choak'd up with Man, and gorg'd with Circumcision" (5). This image of a violent, indeed deadly, sexual encounter is spoken by a character whom audiences are asked to admire. Dryden positions him as a man on the appropriate side of dangerous political decisions, and we are to admire Dorax when he refuses treasonous alliances with the Mufti and Benducar, owning that in his earlier years he had "rebelled but not betrayed" his king. In act 4, he has a final fateful meeting with Don Sebastian that forces him to "return" to his European identity: Don Sebastian, who never once recognized his old soldier while dressed in his Moorish garments, pushes Dorax into going offstage and returning dressed in his European clothing. The stage directions make much of Dorax's trading his turban for a peruke. Don Sebastian finally recognizes him, and they reconcile their old differences. In the final moments of the play, it is Dorax who prevents Don Sebastian from killing himself upon learning of the incest, solidifying his role as loyal European follower.

Even though Dryden assigns him some admirable traits, Dorax is hugely problematic: he has "gone native" in fundamental ways. He is, like his Muslim companions, hot-tempered and mercurial. He launches verbal assaults at women and walks the world hurling homophobic gibes at his comrades. He is the unsettled embodiment of one anxiety-provoking European response to expanding imperial impulses: even "good" Europeans can turn renegade, shift loyalties, and abandon their "real" identity, with results that disturb as deeply as these. If Sebastian and Almeyda demonstrate that like cannot come to like, Dorax is just a different dead end: his story indicates that difference cannot be sustained either. After circulating, he may return to the service of his long beloved Don Sebastian, but it is anything but a satisfying reunion: he may be able to keep Don Sebastian from suicide and secure him a place in the hermit's cave, but in the end Dorax is the figure who straddles the emblematic and the real—still an object of suspicion—without any real efficacy and, more important, without belonging to any particular culture or place.

Dorax's counterpart in Behn's drama is Nathaniel Bacon. Moving between worlds of the settlers and the Indigenous inhabitants, Bacon has gone equally native in his pursuit of the love of the Indian Queen. Behn's treatment of Bacon also hearkens back to the old heroics of the 1660s: Bacon is vainglorious and declamatory, throwing himself, Almanzor-like, headlong into the violent breach, for personal pride and for love. However, the question of inheritance is different in *The Widow Ranter*: whereas aristocratic lineage, specifically reproduction, is prohibited as a result of incest in *Don Sebastian*, the question of ownership and its transmission has a decidedly New World cast in this play. The Indian King is generous if chastising of Bacon's actions when he civilly accuses the rebel of usurpation and the abuse of hospitality: "For your part, Sir, you've been so noble, that I repent the fatal Difference that makes us meet in Arms. Yet though I am young, I'm sensible of Injuries; and oft have heard my Grandsire say, That we were Monarchs once of all this spacious World, till you, an unknown People, landing here, distress's and ruin'd by destructive storms, abusing all our charitable Hospitality, usurp'd our Right, and made your Friends your Slaves" (127). To this Bacon simply invokes European laws of inheritance. "I will not justify the Ingratitude of my Forefather," he says, "but I find here my Inheritance, I am resolve'd still to maintain it so, and by my Sword which first cut out my Portion, defend each Inch of Land, with my last drop of blood" (127). In Bacon's mind, New World "possession" is labeled Old World "inheritance," and ownership is transferred: it required nothing more than a sword. Nor does Bacon die in battle, heroically felled in a bloody fray. Instead, he stands on the battlefield and drinks poison after he stabbed and killed the Indian Queen, having failed to recognize her, cross-dressed as a warrior during the battle.

If Dryden's play is a thoroughly nostalgic one, especially in terms of its upper plot, Behn's play is different: it skirts the edges of the absurd in her figure of the Renegade. Indeed, although an audience might chuckle a bit at Almanzor's overblown rhetoric, it would also be aware that the character encodes the 1660s optimism so many of his countrymen felt in the restoration of Charles II. But by 1689, when Bacon declaims his greatness, an audience hears only anachronistic posturing—a young ambitious planter displaying characteristics not his own, an appropriator not only of others' lands but of his betters' rhetoric. Janet Todd's reading of Bacon's role is insightful: "Bacon is seemingly in the wrong play at the wrong time. . . . Unhappily for him [his death] is laughably at odds with the rest of the play in which he has been condemned to act by his knowing author."[18] Todd sees his absurdity as stemming from a failed "masculine heroism" that cannot be sustained in this context, but I think gender is less the force driving his near absurdity than is history—his is an identity drawn from an allegorical past and, by 1689, lacks any genealogical claim to heroic rhetoric and action. Bacon's behavior is mere gesture; his discourse, empty and bankrupt; he dies thousands of miles away from home trying to transport his Old World economics into the New. Behn's upper plot is thus tinged less with Dryden's regret and sadness and more with (intended or unintended) ridicule for the pretenses of greatness in a British settlement, a land formed for something less heroic, a world filled with radical self-interest and in a vacuum of governance.

The two liminal characters in the lower plots are the ones who best reveal the anxieties and the possibilities to be found in the new economics: in this world people are commodities; mobility is power, gender is merely a construct, and the ability to change identities with circumstances is essential. In *Don Sebastian*, when the emperor summons Mustapha, captain of the Rabble and a slave trader, to bring forth the captives, singled out for sale is Antonio. The scene is filled with humiliation and pain: when told to bend down on all four, Antonio says, "Thou wilt not make a Horse of me," and suffers the whip for his insolence (17). He is made to lie down, he is bridled, led by a rope, and made to "amble, trot, and gallop." Stripped, so that the buyer can see he is healthy, Mustapha says, "He's the best piece of Man's flesh in the Market" (18), an enslaved, bestial, sexual toy.

Captive, without agency, subject to ridicule and physical punishment, he is every Englishman's nightmare of slavery. Adam Beach has argued that Dryden is as interested in the ways that male slaves "are subject to the same forces of sexual degradation" as women:

> As the scene turns from the high to the low plot, Dryden creates a slave market that becomes a theater within a theater where male slaves are forced, as Dryden's stage direction indicates, to "*do Tricks*" in an attempt to entertain prospective buyers as well as show off their physical abilities . . . the slaves become puppets in the world of the market, a place where their full reduction from people to socially dead tools is enacted. . . . In this setting, verbal resistance to the slave master, however forceful, has no possibility of overcoming or even delaying the master's desires. Rather, the marketplace as well as the violence enacted within it swiftly leaves the slave a stark choice: obedience or torture, rape, and death.[19]

Antonio's fate changes a bit when he winds up in the house of the Mufti, given to the Mufti's wife for her "use": indeed, he becomes a new man—that is, a man "in a fair Lady's Service" (39), for he plays the flute, carries her umbrella, and tends to her desires (perhaps even the carnal ones, for he must also endure potential sexual assault from the Mufti's wife). Surrounded by women, he seems the perfect feminized man, the Portuguese eunuch in the harem—until presented with possibilities for enrichment and escape in the figure of the Mufti's daughter Morayma. Then he becomes a masculine, sexual man again: rapacious and desirous of wealth and social mobility, even if that requires actual theft, not just imperialist acquisition.

At this point, the plot turns to the familiar elements of sex intrigue comedy, even action coming close to slapstick: Antonio outwits an oppressive father, seizing Morayma's jewels in a casket and, in the end, wins some degree of autonomy for himself and his Moorish beloved—through the vehicle of half her father's money. He does not inherit his wealth in any Old World way. He steals it, in the form of what Morayma herself conflates as a single item of value: "my jewells and my Mayden-head" (112). As a slave, Antonio moves within the world of Moorish men, uncomfortably and always in danger; within the world of Moorish women, he is equally uncomfortable and in danger—because in both spaces he is an object of potential sexual assault. But at the conclusion of the play, he is "rewarded" for his persistence, his willingness to shed an old identity, and his dedication to achieving increased wealth and greater personal safety. As Beach puts it, "Antonio is able to use his sexual charm and ability to cater to the desires of others in order to better his own situation. And, since Antonio ultimately wins out at the end, the play suggests that men who are used to accommodating female desires and willing to play the subordinate role may, in fact, be better positioned than other types of men to maneuver after experiencing defeat and slavery."[20]

Equally radical is the liminal character in the lower plot of *The Widow Ranter*: the widow herself—a woman who emerged from a form of "slavery" to become rich and in control of her own destiny. Friendly describes her primarily in economic terms: "A Woman bought from the ship by old Colonel Ranter; she served him half a Year, and then he marry'd her, and dying in a Year more, left her worth fifty thousand Pounds Sterling, besides Plate and Jewels: She's a great Gallant, but assuming the humour of the Country Gentry, her Extravagancy is very pleasant, she retains something of her primitive Quality still, but is good-nature'd and generous" (112). The eponymous Widow Ranter smokes, drinks, swears, lives hard, and loves hard, too. As was the case with a feminized Antonio, the same act of gender reversal allows for the widow's masculine virtues to serve her, including her donning of the uniform of a fighting man to join her beloved in battle, the most masculine attire any woman could wear. But in her first appearance onstage, she forthrightly positions herself as both a commodity and an "infidel" in an exchange worth going over at some length: she may not, like Antonio, be called the "best piece of Man flesh in the Market," but she comes close. When Christante wonders whether Ranter will "lay out" all her money in the service of Darling, Bacon's "mad Lieutenant," the widow replies that she will surely "lend it the Rogue on good Security." When Christante then asks, "What's that, to be bound Body for Body," the widow answers, "Rather that he should love no body's Body besides my own; but my fortune is too good to trust the Rogue, my Money makes me an Infidel" (123). And a few moments later, to young Hazard's claim that he is not fortune-hunting in Virginia, she shoots back, "Gad, then you're a Fool, Sir; but come, my service to you; we rich Widows are the best Commodity this Country affords, I'll tell thee that" (124–125). As a straightforwardly mercantile element in the circulating economy of Virginia, she has no illusions about her beauty or her charms or anything other than the purchasing power that her bank account affords her, an infidel in love.

So the new economic man in this play turns out to be a woman. Laura Brown has argued that the female figure of Lady Credit takes one of two forms in the eighteenth century. Lady Credit can be the prototype for the sentimental heroine in later eighteenth-century works: "Excessively sensible and intensely desirable, she enters the canon of the novel with Richardson's fiction . . . she represents a major cultural investment of identification." But Brown also acknowledges that Credit prepares the way for another sort of heroine, as well—"the misogynist, burlesque, or problematic female figure who represents the contemporary cultural engagement with consumption, commodification, and capitalism"—which in her reading of that female figure with the greatest "ungovernable energies" is Pope's Dulness.[21] The widow falls decidedly within this latter category: she possesses her own ungovernable energies, is autonomous in directing her financial affairs, and unabashedly wishes to share her wealth with the man of her choice. As paraphrased by Baucom, J.G.A. Pocock, too, has argued that Credit invented a "new image of social personality," a new social person "no longer 'anchored in the land' but attached instead to a series of negotiable promises, calculations, and speculations; a person no longer readable through reference to a table of inherited status but only as legible as the entire complex system itself."[22] The widow, like Credit, is only legible in the fluid and unanchored cultural and economic system of colonial Virginia.

The boundary-breaching characters in both of these dramas have left their homes to circulate—some with intentions to conquer in the old heroic mode, like the Portuguese in *Don Sebastian*, and some with intentions to exploit a new economic system that ignores old barriers to social and financial upward mobility, like the English in Virginia. In each play, the upper characters—no matter where they are placed geographically—embrace the old epistemology: inheritance can be managed through transparent genealogies, and the transfer of possessions best occurs not through force but through the bodies of women, as was "natural" in the Old World system. Both Dryden and Behn create characters in this realm, but neither can perform the necessary reproductive and genealogical functions—they are worn out, anachronistic, relics of a past age who provoke, at best, a nostalgia for days gone by or, at worst, unintended laughter in their misplacement in this new system. That they lie dead or cloistered at the close of each play is the signal of their inefficacy.

Antonio and the Widow Ranter, the Portuguese eunuch and Lady Credit of Virginia, are "successful" characters insofar as they gather and control their resources within the new system. That it requires a new fluidity of identity, a willingness to circulate, the ability to endure forms of slavery, servitude, and even threatened sexual violence reinforces their readiness for the new system. Unlike Bacon, who could not see through the Indian Queen's assumption of a temporary identity on the battlefield, Colonel Daring recognizes at once the widow in masquerade. More important, that is the way he wants to keep her: "Give me thy Hand, Widow, I am thine—and so entirely, I will never—be drunk out of thy Company; prithee, let's in and bind the Bargain . . . while thy Breeches are on—for I never lik'd thee half so well in Petticoats" (171). They form the perfect new economic partnership.

So, these two Tory playwrights in two late tragicomic plays do indeed find a way to interrogate the large-scale epistemic changes they have at hand, even as they lament the chaos and change that will inevitably accompany them. And they do so through the familiar tropes of cross-cultural encounters in a genuinely imperial seventeenth-century context that incorporates within it the alterations that the new economy, based on trade and speculation and circulating bills, had on individual and collective life in England. Dryden might find some residue of a seductive power of the old heroics, but even he paints a scene where such old notions of conquest are obviously played out. That both playwrights are distrustful of the chaos and lack of clarity that the new economies provoke is also clear, but when the nearly enslaved feminized Portuguese captive and the wealthy, masculine, lower-class Widow emerge as the most successful contemporary new economic characters, this puts fear and, at least in Behn's case, a little bit of excitement into the hearts of two giants of the late Restoration theatre.

NOTES

1. Ian Baucom, *Specters of the Atlantic: Finance Capital, Slavery, and the Philosophy of History* (Durham, NC: Duke University Press, 2005), 32.

2. Baucom, 16.

3. Baucom, 67.

4. Nabil Matar, *Turks, Moors, and Englishmen in the Age of Discovery* (New York: Columbia University Press, 1999), ix–x.

5. Nancy Klein Maguire, "Tragicomedy," in *The Cambridge Companion to English Restoration Theatre*, ed. Deborah Payne Fisk (Cambridge: Cambridge University Press, 2000), 96.

6. Maguire, 91.

7. Derek Hughes, "Heroic Drama and Tragicomedy," in *A Companion to Restoration Drama*, ed. Susan J. Owen (Oxford: Blackwell, 2001), 206.

8. John Dryden, *Don Sebastian, King of Portugal: A Tragedy Acted at the Theatre Royal* (London: Printed for Jo. Hindmarsh, at the Golden Ball in Cornhil, 1690), 5. Edition available on Google Books at https://www.google.com/books/edition/Don_Sebastian_King_of_Portugal/gY_RVkq5qwkC?hl=%20es&gbpv=0. Hereafter cited parenthetically by page number.

9. Geraldo U. de Sousa, "Portugal, North Africa, and Dryden's Don Sebastian." *Clio* 37, no. 3 (Summer 2008): 340.

10. Matar, *Turks, Moors, and Englishmen*, 13.

11. Aphra Behn, *The Widow Ranter: Or, the History of Bacon in Virginia* in *The Plays, Histories, and Novels of the Ingenious Mrs. Aphra Behn. With Life and Memoires. Complete in Six Volumes*, vol. 4 (London: John Pearson, 1871), 127. Edition available on Google Books at https://www.google.com/books/edition/The_plays_histories_and_novels_of_mrs_Ap/DKINAAAAQAAJ?hl=es&gbpv=0. Hereafter cited parenthetically by page number.

12. Bridget Orr, *Empire on the English Stage: 1660–1714* (Cambridge: Cambridge University Press, 2001), 137, 166.

13. Matar, *Turks, Moors, and Englishmen*, 91.

14. Matar, 88.

15. Matar, 88–89. For Sir Thomas Gates, see Samuel Purchas, *Purchas his pilgrimes. part 4 In fiue bookes. The first, contayning the voyages and peregrinations made by ancient kings, patriarkes, apostles, philosophers, and others, to and thorow the remoter parts of the knowne world: enquiries also of languages and religions, especially of the moderne diuersified professions of Christianitie. The second, a description of all the circum-nauigations of the globe. The third, nauigations and voyages of English-men, alongst the coasts of Africa . . . The fourth, English voyages beyond the East Indies, to the ilands of Iapan, China, Cauchinchina, the Philippinæ with others . . . The fifth, nauigations, voyages, traffiques, discoueries, of the English nation in the easterne parts of the world . . . The first part* (London: Printed by William Stansby for Henrie Fetherstone, and are to be sold at his shop in Pauls Church-yard at the signe of the Rose, 1625), accessed July 15, 2021, http://name.umdl.umich.edu/a71306.0001.001.

16. Matar, *Turks, Moors, and Englishmen*, 77.

17. Matar, 71–72.

18. Janet Todd, "A Spectacular Death: History and Story in *The Widow Ranter*," in *Aphra Behn*, ed. Janet Todd (New York: St. Martin's Press, 1999), 75, 77.

19. Adam Beach, "Literary Form and the Representation of Slavery in Dryden's *Don Sebastian*," *Studies in Eighteenth-Century Culture* 44 (2015): 96, 108.

20. Beach, 111.

21. Laura Brown, *Fables of Modernity: Literature and Culture in the English Eighteenth Century* (Ithaca, NY: Cornell University Press, 2001), 130.

22. Brown, 66; J.G.A. Pocock, *Virtue, Commerce, and History: Essays on Political Thought and History, Chiefly in the Eighteenth Century* (Cambridge: Cambridge University Press, 1985), 111.

CHAPTER 9

Speculum Mundi

CARICATURE AND THE STAGE

Heather McPherson

> *[The caricaturist] . . . is aware that he is expected to draw with great correctness, which having attained, he flies to his pencil, and thence to etching; and thus he gives a spirit in every touch of the needle that could not be effected were he compelled to proceed with caution. By these means, his labours resemble the first conceptions of the great masters, in the rough sketches of their most celebrated performances, and which they invariably degenerate from by endeavouring to amend them.*
>
> —*J. P. Malcolm,* An Historical Sketch of the Art of Caricaturing with Graphic Illustrations

This essay examines the common preoccupations that link caricature and the stage, focusing in particular on their refractive function as a *speculum mundi* (literally, mirror of the world) through the lens of Annibel Jenkins's collection of caricatures and theatrical prints. From Shakespeare on, the English stage has been characterized as a microcosm or mirror of the world.[1] The traditional motto "Veluti in Speculum" (even as in a mirror), placed over the proscenium of eighteenth-century stages including those of Drury Lane and the Haymarket, reinforced the notion of the stage as a mirror reflecting contemporary life.[2] As print production expanded and diversified after the midcentury, caricature emerged as a multifaceted visual and verbal discourse that helped shape public opinion on matters from current events to cultural politics and aesthetic hierarchies.[3] Caricature's function as a refractive satirical lens is underscored by a folio of caricatures in the British Museum representing men as pigeons, which is bound with an engraved frontispiece of a jester pointing to a mirror inscribed "Speculum Veluti."[4] This essay contextualizes Jenkins's caricatures both historically and in relation to her research and performance studies. It shows how they can be "read" on multiple levels, individually and dialogically, and especially as a *speculum mundi*, paralleling the stage.

In the 1780s, caricature assumed new levels of cultural and iconographic complexity, becoming a trenchant, ideologically engaged visual idiom that, like the theatre, catered to a heterogeneous urban public.[5] In his appreciation of the art of caricature quoted in this chapter's epigraph, J. P. Malcolm underscores its spontaneity, expressive lines, and performative dimension, comparing caricatures to preliminary sketches by the great masters. The reign of George III (1760–1820), which has been referred to as the "age of caricature," was also the age of the actor. Leading performers such as David Garrick, Sarah Siddons, and John Philip Kemble elevated the status of acting and attained unprecedented cultural preeminence.[6] Beginning with Garrick, theatrical stars became high-profile public personalities and cultural commodities who were painted by the leading artists, widely chronicled in the press, and targeted by caricaturists. As we shall see, the stage figures both literally and metaphorically in eighteenth-century satirical prints in which political events like the William Hastings trial are restaged as theatrical spectacles.

This essay also examines the popular appeal and broader cultural significance of caricatures as a multivalent, dialogic genre; the rationale for collecting them; and how they were marketed, consumed, and displayed. In particular, it takes a closer look at how caricatures mirror and engage with performance histories and cultural politics, enriching and complicating our understanding of the eighteenth-century stage. Even though we do not know the size of their print runs, the sheer number and diversity of satirical prints produced in the late eighteenth to early nineteenth centuries demonstrate their widespread appeal across a broad socioeconomic demographic from the lower and middle orders to the aristocracy, and testify to the rapidly expanding market for prints.[7] Malcolm, caricature's first historiographer, confirmed their ubiquity and socioeconomic and cultural significance, citing the number of persons employed in producing them and the number of shops selling them as "proof of the importance the Publick has attached to them."[8] Between 1771 and 1832, upwards of 20,000 satirical prints were produced in Great Britain.[9] The diversification of the print trade and of the range of print subjects and prices, from crude penny prints to James Gillray's high-end, artistically sophisticated plates, is a further indication of the expanding market for caricatures and their widespread popular appeal.[10]

Exhibiting and Marketing Caricatures

Displayed in print shop windows to attract and amuse passersby, caricatures were a vibrant element of London's burgeoning urban topography and exhibition culture, where art and entertainment increasingly converged.[11] They were also exhibited in customized display spaces, like William Holland's Oxford Street emporium, known as the Museum of Graphic Genius, which, like the Royal Academy, charged one-shilling admission. The dense array of caricatures covering the walls and the mix of fashionable and disreputable spectators in depictions of print shops, such as Holland's or Hannah Humphrey's, mirror and parody representations of the Royal Academy exhibitions at Somerset House. In contemporary advertisements, the rival publishers Holland and Samuel W. Fores each claimed to possess the largest and most complete displays of caricatures to be seen anywhere.[12] Caricature portfolios could also be rented for the evening for private viewing, making them accessible to a wider audience.

Buyers could purchase caricatures individually, serially, or bound in volumes. They were advertised in the press and marketed globally through print publishers' catalogs and exported to continental Europe and the United States, further extending their reach. Holland's catalogs from the 1780s and 1790s provide invaluable documentation about marketing strategies and pricing. By the 1790s, most satirical prints were being issued as hand-colored impressions ranging in price from a shilling to one pound.[13] Holland's 1794 catalog clearly targeted collectors, advertising "old and scarce caricatures" and complete collections of works by artists such as Hogarth, Rowlandson, and Bunbury. Fores's and Humphrey's records indicate that large numbers of prints were purchased by mail, making them widely accessible even in rural areas. Purchasers of caricatures could display them on walls like drawings or paintings or store them in portfolios for ready viewing. Collectors often systematically arranged them in albums. Horace Walpole's extensive collection of 280 etchings and drawings by Bunbury is mounted in two large folio volumes that he stored with other rare books at Strawberry Hill.[14] What is particularly fascinating is the degree to which collectors interacted with and personalized their caricatures with annotations, most often identifying the principal figures.

The Caricature Room at Calke Abbey (figure 9.1) is a unique variant of the print room, once common in country houses of the gentry and middle classes.[15] Located in a modest room on the ground floor used as a private drawing room, it consists of some 150 caricatures by such leading printmakers as Gillray, Rowlandson, and Cruikshank.[16] The room was begun in the late 1790s or early 1800s while Sir Henry Harpur the reclusive seventh baronet was remodeling Calke Abbey, with caricatures added through the 1820s.[17] In the late 1980s, the National Trust restored the room to its original appearance. The caricatures were remounted in their original positions, the walls were repainted in green, and the flocked border was re-created using new materials.[18]

Varying in size and format, the prints were pasted directly on the walls. Although randomly arranged, most have painted frames, echoing the mode of display used at the Royal Academy and in print shop exhibitions. However, the

Figure 9.1 Caricature Room, Calke Abbey, early nineteenth century.

Caricature Room at Calke Abbey is more haphazard and less symmetrically laid out than other surviving period print rooms such as those at Castletown in County Kildare, or Stratfield Saye, perhaps reflecting the disruptive, anti-hierarchical nature of caricatures.

Although the expanding production and market for caricatures can be documented, the paucity of contemporary references makes it far harder to gauge their cultural significance—how they were appreciated, discussed, and displayed in the eighteenth century and what motivated people to collect them.[19] What we do know is that caricatures were collected across a broad socioeconomic spectrum from the royal family and aristocratic connoisseurs, like Walpole, to politicians, like Charles James Fox, to actors and fellow artists. Ranging widely in quality, pictorial sophistication, and price, caricatures were niche-marketed and no doubt appreciated for a variety of reasons. Much of their appeal hinged upon their topical subject matter, lively graphic style, and satirical punch, making them forerunners of modern-day comic strips and graphic novels. The rise of graphic satire was also intimately linked to the fiercely contested political landscape, becoming a powerful means for shaping and contesting partisan politics and national identity, especially from the 1780s on. Another less widely recognized factor that contributed to caricatures' widespread appeal was their ability to mirror and mock contemporary society and mores much as social comedies did on the stage.

Collecting Caricatures

Horace Walpole, a leading connoisseur and omnivorous collector, amassed hundreds of caricatures that he mounted in albums, reflecting his interest in contemporary politics as well as fashion and the theatre.[20] Even though he collected caricatures, discussed them in letters, and sent them to friends, Walpole also disparaged them, as did many eighteenth-century commentators.[21] The extensively annotated, extra-illustrated copy of his *Description of Strawberry Hill* (1784) at the Lewis Walpole Library includes numerous caricature sketches by his brother Edward and others, including copies after George Townshend, and a series of caricatures by Anne Seymour Damer, attesting to the taste for drawing amateur caricatures as a form of social interchange and amusement, paralleling the taste for amateur theatricals.[22] Sir Robert Peel's comprehensive collection of more than 3,300 political caricatures, broadsides, and portraits, dating from 1642 to 1830 and housed at the Pierpont Morgan Library, focuses on political satire. Organized chronologically and thematically, the prints are mounted in twelve large volumes. A noted connoisseur, Peel created a portrait gallery where he displayed portraits of politicians of every stripe, complementing their caricatural representations.[23] The manuscript *Notebook of Lord Eldon*, in which he comments on the first thirty-eight caricatures in James Sayers's personal album, offers a fascinating window into the impact and historical significance of political caricatures, underscoring their lasting value in evoking the contested politics of the period.[24]

In an era in which wit reigned supreme, it is not surprising that the victims of defamatory caricatures were amused as well as infuriated by them and not infrequently collected them. That was true of John Philip Kemble, particularly pilloried during the savage O.P. (Old Price) Riots, who collected caricatures and enjoyed showing them to friends.[25] The Prince of Wales, later George IV, one of the most frequently caricatured figures of the era, owned some 10,000 satirical prints. His extensive collection, including many royal subjects, was sold en bloc to the Library of Congress in 1920.[26] He owned numerous satires (some of which he paid to suppress) that are not in the British Museum. The prince formed his collection over an extended period, purchasing new prints as they appeared. In 1803 he opened an account with Hannah Humphrey, the exclusive purveyor of Gillray's prints.

Annibel's Caricatures

Like any serious collector, Annibel Jenkins lived with her collection. Caricatures were displayed throughout the house she shared with her sister Virginia Peacock; Virginia's husband, George; and their son, Robert. Her collection included at least thirty-six caricatures and half a dozen or more theatrical prints and portraits.[27]

With the exception of Gillray, she owned prints by the leading caricaturists of the Georgian era: William Hogarth, Charles Bunbury, Thomas Rowlandson, James Sayers, and Isaac Cruikshank, and such lesser-known figures as Robert Dighton, Charles Williams, William Elmes, and Samuel De Wilde. I suspect most of her caricatures were purchased from dealers on her research trips to London.[28] Since her research focused on the theatre, especially Elizabeth Inchbald, she was naturally drawn to prints dealing with the stage and cultural politics and topical subjects such as fashion and ballooning. Like many eighteenth-century Londoners, Inchbald frequented print shops, where she saw friends and purchased caricatures.[29] Annibel's taste in prints, like everything else, was impeccable, wide-ranging, and historically informed.[30] In analyzing her collection, I have come to realize that the individual prints also constitute a sort of mini-history of the development of caricature as a distinctive artistic genre from Hogarth's groundbreaking satirical prints in the early 1720s to Rowlandson's phenomenally popular Dr. Syntax illustrations and the rise of populist publishers like Thomas Tegg and illustrated journals like *The Scourge* in the late 1790s to early 1800s. While researching her collection at the Walpole Library, I made a number of discoveries (discussed later) that highlight the multivalent dialogic nature of caricature; the confluence of the Hogarth revival and the expansion of caricature production; and innovative marketing strategies such as reissuing prints in multiple editions, often with variants, and experimenting with formats.

Although I was not able to document the collection in situ, I have reconstituted it virtually. Most of the caricatures hung in Annibel's study except the Hogarths, which were displayed on the ground floor.[31] Visitors entering the front hall were greeted by the *Analysis of Beauty*, plate 2. Other Hogarth prints adorned the living room walls, notably *The Times*, plate 1, and *A Country Inn Yard at the Time of an Election*, displayed as pendants. Although they have the same dimensions, these two prints are not true pendants: *The Country Inn Yard* was published in 1747, *The Times* in 1762. Initially, I thought they were paired because *The Times*, plate 2, was suppressed by Hogarth and only published posthumously in 1790 by John Boydell. On further investigation, I discovered that they are reimpressions, printed on a single plate from Thomas Cook's *Hogarth Restored* (1806).[32] Cook's ambitious reissue of the complete graphic oeuvre testifies to the ongoing Hogarth revival and blurring of the concepts of original and copy in reproductive printmaking.[33] Cook's subscription notice emphasized the rarity and high cost of Hogarths and hence the need to provide a correct high-quality edition of all his prints to restore his fame.[34] Annibel owned a second combination print composed of three Hogarth designs printed on a single plate: *The Laughing Audience*, originally published as a subscription ticket for *A Rake's Progress* in 1733; *The Oratorio of Judith*, issued as a subscription ticket for *A Midnight Modern Conversation Piece* in 1732; and *The South Sea Scheme*, published circa 1721, an early allegorical print (figure 9.2). While the first two are similar

Figure 9.2 William Hogarth, combination print *The Laughing Audience*, *The Oratorio of Judith*, and *The South Sea Scheme*, 1800. Lewis Walpole Library, Farmington, Yale University.

in format and focus on comical responses of audiences and performers, *The South Sea Scheme* is anomalous. I suspect its rarity and dimensions dictated its inclusion. Cook's innovative combination plates may also be linked to the growing interest in displaying prints.

Annibel owned two other Hogarths, *Garrick as Richard III* (discussed later) and *The Bruiser* (1763).[35] In response to Churchill's stinging "Epistle to William Hogarth" mocking the artist's decline and age, Hogarth reworked his *Self-Portrait with his Pug* (1748–1749), transforming it into a vicious personal attack on Churchill, a telling demonstration of how satirical prints functioned dialogically, commenting on topical events and referencing other prints. Besides demonstrating her interest in Hogarth as a pioneering printmaker enamored of the stage, Annibel's Hogarths document his continuing popularity in the early nineteenth century and Cook's ambitious reissuing of his plates, making them available to a wider public.

The caricatures displayed in Annibel's study were elegantly framed in the eighteenth-century manner, often with colored mattes and borders, covering the walls in a dense, multilevel hang. That her collection was a direct corollary and offshoot of her research is further confirmed by the fact that a dozen of her prints appeared as illustrations in her Inchbald biography. Appropriately, Hogarth's *Garrick as Richard III* (1746) and the theatrical subjects that related most closely to Annibel's scholarship were displayed in her study, surrounding her when she was working. Like the Caricature Room at Calke Abbey, the study functioned as a private retreat, an intimate salon for receiving friends, and, I would argue, a *speculum mundi*. Adding to the dialogic and visual spectacle, the dense hang and close proximity of the prints to one another created thematic groupings and pictorial dialogues between them.[36] Among the prints on display was Bunbury's *A Long Minuet* (discussed later), which she referred to as "the first comic strip."

Theatrical Caricatures

In satirical prints the stage figures on multiple levels both literally and metaphorically, from personal caricatures of individual performers to depictions of theatre interiors and actual performances to the restaging of political events as theatrical spectacle. The decline of taste and philistine managers, notably Richard Brinsley Sheridan, are recurring themes that underscore the theatre's central role in shaping and contesting national identity as public personalities, actors, like politicians, were seized upon by caricaturists. Ranging from high art to popular prints, visual images and the burgeoning press fostered the development of modern media-based celebrity culture.

Personal caricatures, which mocked and denigrated the subject, were the flip side of the celebrity cult. The two Dighton prints in the collection are representative examples. *Derby and Joan* (1795), a gentle satire on the long, platonic

Figure 9.3 Robert Dighton, *Derby and Joan*, 1795, British Museum, London.

relationship between the comedian Elizabeth Farren and the Earl of Derby, pictures the couple companionably seated in a stage box, holding opera glasses, an earl's coronet suspended above their heads (figure 9.3).[37] A self-referential playbill for Farquhar's *Constant Couple* reiterates the theme. Elegantly coiffed and holding an immense muff, Farren is scarcely caricatured, but the doll-like Derby sports a ridiculous queue. *Derby and Joan* illustrates how caricature mirrored and mocked contemporary celebrities and social mores. Derby's infatuation with Farren was frequently caricatured in the 1780s and 1790s. The *Derby Diligence* (1781), which Annibel also owned, depicts Lord Derby on horseback following Farren's coach.[38] They are commonly referred to as "Derby and Joan" in other more scurrilous satires. In 1797, the "constant couple" finally married after the death of Derby's wife.

In *Hamlet in Scotland* (1794), Dighton portrays Stephen Kemble as a gargantuan, lumbering Hamlet whose wide-legged stance and exaggerated gestures satirize the histrionics of the stage. The caption, "A large manager in a Great Character," references his role as manager of the Edinburgh theatre, slyly playing on the conflation of greatness and obesity and "character" and "caricature."

Hanging from his wide blue sash is the elephant of the Danish order. This volatile mix of topicality, bodily distortion, and searing wit is what made caricature such a devastating weapon of ridicule. Caricature's modus operandi of mirroring and grossly distorting humanity is reinforced by the lines from *Hamlet* inscribed below. Stephen's ungainly Hamlet is mercilessly contrasted with John Philip Kemble's distinguished portrayal. Stephen was better known for his Falstaff, becoming so stout no padding was required. Dighton reprised the obesity theme and elephant analogy in *A Great Personage* (1797), which characterizes the colossally fat Duke of Wurtemberg as a royal elephant, implicitly invoking the corpulent Prince of Wales and underscoring the dialogic nature of caricature.[39]

On occasion printmakers represented performances and audiences, as Rowlandson did in *Dr. Syntax at Covent Garden Theatre* (1817).[40] The pedantic schoolmaster Dr. Syntax, seated at the back of the pit, misses the performance—Falstaff posturing with his sword and shield toward a soldier and a prostrate man—because his attention is focused on tangential elements. Although Rowlandson depicted Covent Garden quite accurately, it is viewed through the distorted lens of Dr. Syntax, questioning and deconstructing the aesthetics and illusionism of the stage. At the other end of the spectrum, Hogarth's *Garrick as Richard III*, engraved by Hogarth and Grignion (1746; figure 9.4) focuses on Garrick's ground-

Figure 9.4 William Hogarth, *Garrick as Richard III*, 1746, British Museum, London.

breaking performance. Blurring the distinction between actor and role, it is a heroic individualized portrait rather than a caricature, in which Hogarth endeavors to translate Garrick's charismatic performance in pictorial terms, creating a hybrid genre midway between portraiture and history painting. *Garrick as Richard III*, which launched the vogue for theatrical portraiture, was widely reproduced throughout the nineteenth century. Although better known for his modern moral subjects, Hogarth invented the theatrical portrait, making this print a noteworthy exemplar of the heightened public profile and commodification of the actor. Garrick was recognized as having revolutionized the stage, much as Hogarth was immortalized as the founding father of English art.

The amateur caricaturist Henry Bunbury, whom Walpole called a "second Hogarth" and avidly collected, figures prominently in Annibel's collection.[41] Inchbald knew the Bunburys, and Sir Charles, Henry's older brother, was an intimate friend. Jenkins argues that caricatures like the *St. James's Macaroni* (1772) influenced Inchbald's conception of the fashionable beau Cyrus in *I'll Tell You What*, underscoring the close connections between caricature and the stage.[42] Bunbury was devoted to the theatre and involved with amateur theatricals as Inchbald herself was.[43] One of Annibel's prized possessions was a reduced version of Bunbury's most famous print, *A Long Minuet as Danced at Bath* (1787), a seven-foot strip design printed on four plates representing ten couples in different stages of the minuet.

Lawrence's pastel portrait of Bunbury (ca. 1788), engraved in 1789, pictures him working on the *Long Minuet*. Annibel's undated impression depicts the first ten figures arranged in two parallel registers, which necessitated breaking up the third couple and interrupting the continuous narrative flow (figure 9.5).[44] Bunbury brilliantly captures the awkwardness, anxiety, and effort of each couple as they attempt to gracefully perform the minuet. The original strip print included Latin texts referencing Horace's odes, which are omitted in the reduced versions. At the British Museum, there is an unmounted fan leaf (ca. 1790–1811), copied from Bunbury's drawing but augmented with close-ups, illustrating its popularity and adaptation to different formats.[45] *A Long Minuet*, which made Bunbury famous, inaugurated the strip print, giving caricaturists the opportunity to design more dynamic prints with narrative sequences.[46] It is also a witty sequel to Hogarth's multivalent commentary on aesthetics as embodied in dance in *Analysis of Beauty*, plate 2, and a summation of earlier prints, like those after John Collett, exploiting the comic possibilities of trying to teach grown gentlemen and ladies to dance.[47]

Bunbury's *A Tour to Foreign Parts* (1778) exists in multiple states, including a reduced hand-colored version by Rowlandson with modifications, attesting to its continuing popularity. Satirizing both the grand tour and the foibles of the French, it depicts a fashionable young English gentleman, accompanied by his bear leader, confronting an obsequious French innkeeper in enormous sabots.

Figure 9.5 Henry Bunbury, *A Long Minuet as Danced at Bath*, 1787, British Museum, London.

The undated, hand-colored impression in reverse that Annibel owned, probably from the early nineteenth century, does not exactly coincide with any of the versions, dated 1778, 1799, and 1807, respectively, at the Walpole. It is another instance of the reissuing of prints in different formats often with variants.[48] Annibel owned two other early Bunburys: *I Will Pay No More Debts of Her Contracting*, a lively confrontation staged like a theatrical set piece, and *The Judgment of Paris*, which also exists in multiple versions. Annibel's hand-colored impression, like the Walpole version, appears to be a later reissue.[49] There are significant variants in the different versions, including reversing the position of the principal figures and the rustic cottage, documenting how Bunbury reimagined the design like a movable stage set.

Perhaps the most daunting challenge was identifying mystery prints, like the untitled satire, attributed to Bunbury, published June 4, 1800, by R. Ackermann. On examining the image, I suspected it might be by Rowlandson rather than Bunbury, but the only documentary evidence was the publication information. Fortunately, I was working at the Walpole, which catalogs prints by date of publication. There was just one print with that date, *Pictures of Prejudice*, attributed to Rowlandson (figure 9.6), which I promptly requested.[50] It was a much larger print with two registers and dialogue above, like a modern-day comic strip. When I juxtaposed the digital printout, which appeared to be cropped, with *Pictures of Prejudice*, I realized Annibel's print was the lower left quarter of the

Figure 9.6 Thomas Rowlandson, *Pictures of Prejudice*, 1800, Lewis Walpole Library, Farmington, Yale University.

plate—the part that dealt with antitheatrical prejudice. Better yet, the phrase "I'll tell you what," the title of Inchbald's 1784 play and Jenkins's biography, appeared in the print. That Annibel owned the theatrical portion specifically referencing Inchbald was mind-boggling.

Altogether, Annibel owned six prints by Rowlandson. Enamored of the stage and acting and a friend of the comic actor Jack Bannister, Rowlandson frequently represented theatrical subjects and audiences.[51] Even subjects that were not explicitly theatrical, like *An Essay on the Sublime & Beautiful* and *The Maiden Speech*, were infused with theatricality. Consisting of two designs etched on the same plate, the print was published in 1785 and reissued by Fores in 1792.[52] *An Essay on the Sublime & Beautiful* resonates on many levels, embodying the historiography of caricature by referencing and parodying Burke's famous treatise and Hogarth's *Sleeping Congregation* (1736), notably in the depiction of the congregation. The radical preacher is a ragged cobbler, whose crazed oratory and violent gestures are neither sublime nor beautiful. Sayers's print of the same title, published on April 6, 1785, possibly a catalyst, represents Burke, dramatically posed on the shoulders of Powys and Sawbridge in the House of Commons. The equally theatrical *Maiden Speech* depicts a new member awkwardly addressing the bored and contemptuous House of Commons. As a longtime educator, Annibel doubtless appreciated Rowlandson's unsparing exposé of the challenges of public speaking.

A Theatrical Candidate (1797) likewise exploits the convergence of politics and the stage encapsulated by Sheridan. The Opposition leader and famously impecunious manager at Drury Lane is depicted interviewing a ragged, aspiring actor. The title mockingly conflates political candidacy with bad acting. Referencing *Hamlet*, act 3, scene 2, "Oh, there be Players . . . ," the caricature is a hilarious spoof on actors, cataloging their faults, including Mrs. Inchbald's stutter.[53] The would-be theatrical candidate's singularity is that he possesses all the defects combined. Annibel owned several other prints attacking Sheridan, who was widely caricatured from the 1780s on in his double capacity as theatrical manager and Opposition politician.

Besides *Dr. Syntax at Covent Garden* (discussed earlier), there were two other Dr. Syntax prints, displayed as a pair. Although I quickly identified the top one, *Dr. Syntax Present at a Coffee-house Quarrel at Bath*, as an illustration from *The Second Tour of Dr. Syntax in Search of Consolation*, plate 44, the other unsigned print, *Dr. Syntax at the Exhibition*, was more perplexing. Although it depicted Dr. Syntax, it was not from any of the Three Tours. Moreover, the subject and more garish coloring did not quite jibe with the other illustrations. Through surfing the internet and viewing the extraordinary Rowlandson holdings at the Yale Center for British Art, I eventually discovered that it was an illustration from *The Tour of Dr. Syntax through London or the Pleasures and Miseries of the Metropolis*, an anonymous knockoff, published by J. Johnston in 1820. The illustrations are not by Rowlandson, but their authorship remains uncertain.[54] The print depicts Dr. Syntax and his buxom wife viewing pictures at the Royal Academy, and the accompanying text refers to actual paintings on view, grounding it in modern actuality and highlighting the role of caricature as a refractive mirror.

Although I do not have space to discuss all the caricatures, in concluding I would like to highlight some of the common themes and dialogic relationships linking them and the representativeness and significance of Annibel's collection. Since it focused on theatrical caricatures, it is striking that it included three satires by James Sayers, primarily known as a political caricaturist. Sayers turned to the theatre in the 1780s, depicting topical subjects such as *Werter* (17860, a wicked satire on sentimental tragedy in which the main characters are diagrammed and the pictures on the back wall depict scenes from the play, blurring the distinction between pictures and performance. She also owned *A Peep Behind the Curtain at Drury Lane* (1789) and *The Manager and His Dog* (1803), both of which portray Sheridan as a trickster and master manipulator of the stage from cynically attempting to placate the patriotic audience during the Regency crisis to debasing the stage by introducing performing animals, with Carlo the Dog shown literally holding Sheridan's head above water.[55] Sayers's expressively

Figure 9.7 Charles Williams, *Dramatic Action Illustrated, or Hamlet's Advice to Players*, 1811, British Museum, London.

etched caricatures reiterate the links between politics and the stage and caricature's mirroring function.

An overarching theme to which I have already alluded is bad acting. Annibel owned two prints satirizing William Coates's misguided attempts at acting. A stage-mad, wealthy West Indian who termed himself an "Amateur of Fashion," Coates appeared as Lothario in Rowe's *Fair Penitent* in an unforgettable costume, featuring a jeweled hat with enormous ostrich plumes, and a tunic tied with a wide sash that made him the laughingstock of London and generated caricatures, including William Elmes's *The Gay Lothario: The Great and Celebrated Amateur of Fashion* (1813), which pictures Coates falling awkwardly to the ground to general merriment, and Charles Williams's *Dramatic Action Illustrated, or Hamlet's Advice to Players*, originally published in 1811 (figure 9.7).[56] *Dramatic Action Illustrated*, with its reference to Hamlet, is a wicked parody of formulaic gestures that attempt to convey literal meanings. Divided into two registers with six compartments, the print depicts Coates in six different attitudes. To portray Coates as equally ridiculous offstage, Williams satirized Coates's extravagant curricle shaped like a chamber pot in *The Game Chicken* (1812).[57] Since he was known as "Cock-a-doodle doo Coates," the carriage and harness are covered with crowing cocks, and the cock on his head resembles a bizarre theatrical costume. It dialogues with Williams's *The Regent's Hack* (1812), in which Sheridan,

Figure 9.8 George Cruikshank, *Quadrupeds, or, the Managers Last Kick*, 1811, British Museum, London.

in political rather than theatrical guise, is portrayed as the "hack" catering to the regent's whims. Williams is one of the many highly talented caricaturists competing in a crowded field, who never attained the name recognition enjoyed by Gillray, Cruikshank, and Rowlandson.

Despite the proliferation of caricatures, their position within the artistic hierarchy was tenuous at best, and controversial prints were often published anonymously. Samuel De Wilde, primarily known for his theatrical portraits, designed a few caricatures such as *A Drop Scene for D.L.T.*, published in *The Satirist* on May 1, 1808, to illustrate "The Board of Management."[58] A satire on Drury Lane's management, the print was published under the pseudonym Thumaso Scrutiny, Esq. It is linked to other prints, like *The Manager and His Dog*, which satirize the introduction of performing animals and attack the decadence of the stage. It is also emblematic of the increasingly complex iconography of the caricatures published in journals like *The Satirist* and *The Scourge* in the early 1800s, accompanied by lengthy descriptions. The prints adopt a horizontal friezelike format, dictated by the format of the publications in which they appeared, which also points forward to the format of motion pictures in the predigital era and modern-day comic strips. My final example is Cruikshank's uproarious *Quadrupeds; Or, The Managers Last Kick*, published in *The Scourge* (1811; figure 9.8), which Annibel and I both owned.[59] The wild melee of tailors, some mounted on asses, encapsulates the raucous wit and transgressive tendencies that caricatures and the stage shared.

NOTES

Research for this chapter was generously supported by an ASECS/LWL Fellowship from the Lewis Walpole Library (hereafter referred to as LWL) in July 2014. I wish to thank the Walpole staff, especially Susan Walker, head of public services, for their assistance; Lisa

Thornell and the print room staff at the Yale Center for British Art; Martha Bowden for sharing her recollections of Annibel's collection; and Robert Peacock and Hardy and Halpern, Inc., for providing the inventory and digital images.

1. John Swan, *Speculum Mundi. Or a glasse representing the face of the world* . . . (Cambridge: Thomas Buck and Roger Daniel, 1635). The term was frequently used in religious or moralizing contexts.

2. The motto appears in caricatures, including depictions of amateur theatricals, such as *The Way to Keep Him as Perform'd at the Richmond Theatre*, 1787, *BM* 7215, and in political satires like Thomas Rowlandson's *Veluti in Speculum*, 1788, *BM* 9675, or James Sayers's *The Last Scene of the Managers Farce*, 1795, *BM* 8647. I am greatly indebted to M. Dorothy George, *British Museum Catalogue of Political and Personal Satires*, vols. 5–11 (London: British Museum, 1935–1942), hereafter abbreviated as *BM*.

3. On the print trade, see Tim Clayton, *The English Print, 1688–1802* (New Haven, CT: Yale University Press, 1997); and Diana Donald, *The Age of Caricature: Satirical Prints in the Reign of George III* (New Haven, CT: Yale University Press, 1996), 1–11. Following Donald, I am employing caricature in the general sense of graphic satire rather than limiting it to personal caricature, which would narrow the field and eliminate popular types such as John Bull.

4. This unique caricature folio, ca. 1766–1776, bound in eighteenth-century wrappers with manuscript identifications, includes a quotation by John Gay. British Museum, 2010.7081, 1501–1504, not in *BM* catalog.

5. How truly "popular" caricatures were is subject to debate. See Sheila O'Connell, *The Popular Print in England 1550–1850* (London: British Museum, 1999), 9–14. Although O'Connell maintains that caricatures were too costly to qualify as popular prints, V. A. Gatrell and Diana Donald have argued convincingly for the breadth and diversity of the audience for popular prints and their widespread intelligibility (with which I concur).

6. See Donald, *Age of Caricature*, 1–9; Shearer West, *The Image of the Actor: Verbal and Visual Representation in the Age of Garrick and Kemble* (New York: St. Martin's Press, 1991).

7. See Donald, *Age of Caricature*, 2–5; Simon Turner, "William Holland's Satirical Print Catalogues, 1788–1794," *Print Quarterly* 116, no. 2 (1999): 127–138. The Darlys, the first caricature specialists, paved the way for the dominant West End print publishers Hannah Humphrey, William Holland, and Samuel Fores. Thomas Tegg in Cheapside catered to the lower end of the market, reissuing and pirating earlier plates.

8. J. P. Malcolm, *An Historical Sketch of the Art of Caricaturing with Graphic Illustrations* (London: Printed for Longman, Hurst, Orme, and Brown, 1813), iii. He also notes the degrees of perfection achieved in the art of caricaturing and its utility as a means for the correction of vice and improper conduct, the same arguments defenders of the stage advanced to counter the antitheatrical discourse.

9. See Vic Gatrell, *City of Laughter: Sex and Satire in Eighteenth-Century London* (New York: Walker, 2007), 230–257. There are 10,000 satirical prints in the British Museum (1760–1820) and thousands more at the Library of Congress and the Lewis Walpole Library. In addition, popular prints were often reissued.

10. See Mark Hallett, "James Gillray and the Language of Graphic Satire," introduction to *James Gillray: The Art of Caricature* by Richard T. Godfrey (London: Tate Publishing, 2001), 25, who notes that Gillray's hand-colored prints were marketed as luxury works of graphic art to elite monied collectors. From 1793, Gillray's prints were marketed exclusively by Hannah Humphrey.

11. See Rosie Dias, *Exhibiting Englishness: John Boydell's Shakespeare Gallery and the Formation of a National Aesthetic* (New Haven, CT: Yale University Press, 2013).

12. Donald, *Age of Caricature*, 4. Fores also advertised his "Grand Caricatura Exhibition" as offering "an entire Caricature History, political and domestic, of past and present times."

13. Turner, "William Holland's Satirical Print Catalogues," 132–133.

14. Few such original albums remain intact. Walpole's Bunbury albums, which are arranged chronologically with manuscript annotations, are at the Lewis Walpole Library. On July 13, 1776, Walpole wrote Lady Ossory that he was pasting Bunbury's prints in a volume. He continued to add later prints.

15. See Donald, *Age of Caricature*, 23; Stephen Calloway, "Engraving Schemes," *Country Life* 185 (April 1991): 102–105; Mark Purcell and Nicola Thwaite, *The Libraries at Calke Abbey* (London: National Trust, 2013), 29. More than forty eighteenth-century and early nineteenth-century print rooms are documented, but Calke Abbey's is the only one featuring satirical prints. Calloway links print rooms, which became popular in the 1750s, to decoupage. The Calke library owns Hudibras the Younger's *Sultan Sham and his Seven Wives* (London, 1820), an attack on George IV with a satirical frontispiece by John Lewis Marks (which remained in the volume).

16. It is near the garden entrance. The ground floor consists primarily of domestic offices. The elegant formal drawing room where paintings are displayed is directly above, suggesting a sort of aesthetic hierarchy.

17. Howard Colvin et al., *Calke Abbey* (London: National Trust, 1990), 46. It is not known exactly when the room was created or by whom. Sir Henry's son George took an interest in caricatures and worked on the room in 1825. There is an undated letter from a friend of his that tantalizingly mentions bringing caricatures.

18. See Howard Colvin, "Calke Abbey, Derbyshire," *Country Life* 183 (April 1989): 142–143. The printed borders came from the famous print publisher Rudolph Ackermann (1764–1834), proprietor of the Repository of Arts, no. 101 The Strand.

19. Donald, *Age of Caricature*, 22–23. Henry Angelo is one of the few contemporaries to write about eighteenth-century caricaturists.

20. The LWL collection has 10,000 caricatures and satirical prints, including many from Walpole's collection, notably the Bunbury albums and his unparalleled Hogarth holdings. Walpole also owned a portfolio of 135 satirical prints, the majority political, which are in the New York Public Library. His portfolio of Gillrays was sold separately; the number of prints listed in the sales catalogs is inconsistent. Walpole's album is not intact, but his manuscript annotations indicate the prints were arranged by subject beginning with political prints from the 1780s and concluding with fashion and dress. Most of the annotations identify the figures, but Walpole occasionally added explanatory comments. The album included caricatures by Gillray, Rowlandson, Sayers, and Darly.

21. Donald, *Age of Caricature*, 22–23. See, for example, Walpole's letter of November 24, 1760, to Montagu, in *Yale Edition of Horace Walpole's Correspondence*, ed. W. S. Lewis, vol. 9 (hereafter referred to as Yale Walpole; New Haven, CT: Yale University Press, 1970), 326.

22. See *A Description of the Villa of Horace Walpole at Strawberry-Hill, near Twickenham, . . .* (Strawberry-Hill: Printed by Thomas Kirgate, 1784), LWL 49 2523 49 33641 49 2619.4, https://babel.hathitrust.org/cgi/pt?id=gri.ark:/13960/t3fx8v531&view=1up&seq=1&skin=2021. The Bunbury albums and the collection of Hogarth's works are listed in the 1842 sale catalog, but there is no mention of the other caricatures.

23. See Richard Gaunt, *Sir Robert Peel: The Life and Legacy* (London: I. B. Tauris, 2010), 11.

24. See the *Notebook of Lord Eldon*, LWL Mss, Vol. 202. Lord Eldon, a lawyer, member of the House of Commons, and later lord chancellor, was given Sayers's album containing his own copies of his caricatures by his sister. Eldon also assesses Sayers's influence in forming public support for William Pitt's government.

25. Percy Fitzgerald, *The Kembles*, 2 vols. (London: Tinsley Brothers, 1871), 2:87–88.

26. The Hogarths and Rowlandsons were retained at Windsor. See Richard T. Godfrey, *English Caricature 1620 to the Present* (London: Victoria and Albert Museum, 1984), 8.

27. Since I was not able to study the collection in situ, I have relied on the inventory furnished by Hardy & Halpern, Inc., Appraisers, which lists thirty-eight prints, thirty-

five caricatures, and engraved portraits of Mrs. Inchbald, Thomas Otway, and Mr. Harley as Caleb. Additional theatrical prints and caricatures, which she owned, are reproduced in *I'll Tell You What: The Life of Elizabeth Inchbald* (Lexington: University Press of Kentucky, 2003), including *Mrs. Siddons as Isabella* by De Wilde (1792); *Mrs. Inchbald in Rowe's Lady Jane Gray* (1791); and Bunbury's *St. James's Macaroni* (1772), *The Derby Diligence* (1781), and a portrait of Bunbury.

28. Many of the prints, including the Hogarths, were likely purchased from The Print Room, which was located around the corner from the British Museum. Some of her later purchases were probably made online.

29. Jenkins, *I'll Tell You What*, 385. Jenkins further argues that the plot of *Art and Nature* is a simple progression of anticipated events resembling the structure of Hogarth's series in which almost every episode could be "read" as a print.

30. Annibel and I owned two of the same prints: Cruikshank's *Quadrupeds; Or, The Managers Last Kick* (1811), and a print of *Sarah Siddons as Isabella* (1792), after Samuel De Wilde. We shared an interest in Siddons, a close friend of Inchbald's, and I have written about several caricatures Annibel owned.

31. In reconstructing where the prints were displayed, I have relied on Martha Bowden's recollections and my own and the inventory numbers.

32. See *Hogarth Restored. The whole works of the celebrated William Hogarth, as originally published; with a supplement, consisting of such of his prints as were not published in a collected form. Now re-engraved by Thomas Cook* (London: Printed for J. Stockdale by T. Davidson, 1806). The double impression, plate 64, p. 66, is dated December 1, 1800. The plates, issued by subscription, were engraved between 1795 and 1803. Although I cannot prove it, I suspect the combination plates were commercially dictated—a convenient way to group smaller prints and fill the large folio format. They may also be linked to the dictates of display. Rowlandson designed similar pairings etched on the same plate from the 1780s on. Annibel's print is the first combination print Cook published.

33. See Walter Benjamin, "The Work of Art in the Age of Mechanical Reproduction," in *Illuminations*, ed. Hannah Arendt (New York: Schocken Books, 1968), 216–241.

34. Thomas Cook, *Hogarth Restored. Proposals for the Engraving, Printing, and Publishing by Subscription, A Complete Edition of the Works of that much Admired Artist William Hogarth* (London, n.d.), n.p.

35. There are multiple states. Annibel's impression is a later state with a framed picture placed in front of the palette. In reworking the plate, Hogarth substituted Churchill's portrait as a bear with a pot of beer and soiled clerical bands and depicted the dog pissing on Churchill's "Epistle." See Ronald Paulson, *Hogarth's Graphic Works Third Edition Revised* (London: The Print Room, 1989), no. 215, 183–185.

36. This type of dynamic engagement occurred at the Royal Academy exhibitions, especially with portraits. See Mark Hallett, "Reading the Walls: Pictorial Dialogue at the British Royal Academy," *Eighteenth-Century Studies* 37, no. 4 (2004): 581–604.

37. See *BM* 8727. Admired for her elegance, Farren moved in the upper social circles.

38. Though not inventoried, it is illustrated in *I'll Tell You What* below *Derby and Joan*. In a letter of December 29, 1781, to Lord Carlisle, Hare noted Derby's public pursuit of Farren, adding: "The Caricatura has had the good effect of mending his seat on horseback which is totally changed and consequently improved." See *BM* 5901.

39. Not in *BM*; see LWL 797.05.25.01. When Wurtemberg reached London, he was described as shorter and even more corpulent than the Prince of Wales. Dighton was primarily known for his full-length portraits, which included depictions of Kemble and Siddons in *Pizarro* (1799).

40. Published as an illustration to *The Tour of Doctor Syntax in Search of the Picturesque* (1812), with verses by William Combe, plate 28, Annibel's print, dated February 1, 1817, is a reissue. The history of the Dr. Syntax illustrations is complicated; there are numerous

editions and the prints were also issued separately by Ackermann. See also Pugin and Rowlandson's large topographical depiction of *Covent Garden Theatre* in *Microcosm of London*, 3 vols. (London: R. Ackermann's Repository of Arts, 1808–1810), 1: facing p. 212, with an oratorio being performed.

41. In 1787, Walpole, referring to *A Long Minuet*, wrote to Lady Ossory: "You may be sure I have [it], as I get everything I can of Mr. Bunbury's." He annotated his copy, noting, "Tyson was Master of Ceremonies at Bath." Walpole to Lady Ossory, September 6, 1787, Yale Walpole, XXXIII, 572.

42. Jenkins, *I'll Tell You What*, 176. The *St. James's Macaroni*, *BM* 4712, is one of a series of macaronis Bunbury drew in the 1770s. Although it is not listed in the inventory, Annibel owned it.

43. Annibel also owned an oval bust-length portrait of Bunbury after Lawrence (1812), which depicts him against a neutral background. Bunbury created tickets of admission for the Theatre at Wynnstay in 1786. See *BM* 7068, 7069.

44. It is cataloged as *BM* 7229A. There is a pendant print depicting the second half of the original print in the Walpole Library. Although Bunbury is listed as the author, no printmaker is indicated. The original strip print was engraved by W. Dickinson in 1787.

45. See BM 1891.0713.639. The full strip print was reissued by Fores in 1794 on four separate sheets.

46. Bunbury exploited the strip print design in *The Propagation of a Lie*, 1787, *BM* 7230, a hilarious satire on different reactions to rumors of the prince's marriage to Mrs. Fitzherbert, and *Lumps of Pudding*, 1811, *BM* 11834, representing couples vigorously performing a country dance, which was published posthumously.

47. See *BM* 4250, 4251, and 4252 (after Dodd); John Riely, *Henry William Bunbury, 1750–1811* (Sudbury: Gainsborough House, 1988), 2–8. However, these companion prints, which are linked to dancing manuals and the desire of the middle class to master dancing, differ in their focus on individual instruction from a dancing master. In 1787, Bunbury also published *An Academy for Grown Horsemen*, satirizing equestrian misadventures.

48. See *BM* 4732. The 1807 version reworked by Rowlandson is much smaller, and there are numerous changes. See Joseph Grego, *Rowlandson: The Caricaturist*, 2 vols. (London: Chatto and Windus, 1880), 2:78–79, titled *Englishman at Paris.*

49. See *BM* 4752, 4920. According to Tim Clayton, *BM* 4920 is the original version, published in 1771, with verses. Annibel's copy most closely resembles the Walpole's hand-colored version, Bunbury 772.07.04.02+, dated ca. 1815, based on the watermark. The Walpole also owns a smaller etching dated 1766 in which the composition is much more cluttered and reversed, with many different details. In this instance, it appears to be Bunbury himself who significantly reworked the image in later impressions.

50. Susan Walker's assistance was invaluable in identifying the print, LWL 800.06.04.02++, not in the *BM*. In the original the registers are marked off with lines so the two parts could have been separated and displayed separately or presumably joined as a long frieze like Bunbury's strip prints. The fact that the coat of the figure on the far right is slightly cropped in Annibel's print indicates that the section was cut out from the print.

51. See Patricia Phagan, ed., *Thomas Rowlandson: Pleasure and Pursuits in Georgian England* (London: Giles, 2011), 145–146, 156–157. As in his depictions of the art world, he frequently mixed high and low.

52. See *BM* 6863, 6864, cataloged as if two separate prints. Annibel's reissue, dated March 7, 1786, is not mentioned in the catalog entry.

53. See *BM* 9086. There are references to the Chancery and unpaid salaries.

54. See Jerold J. Savory, *Thomas Rowlandson's Doctor Syntax Drawings* (London: Cugnus Arts, 1997), 105–106. Both Isaac and Robert Cruikshank have been proposed as possible authors. One of the most successful Syntax imitations, it attests to the extraordinary popularity of the doctor, who was also reproduced in porcelain.

55. See *BM* 7484 and 10172.

56. See *BM* 11170 and 11769. Annibel's print, which is dated May 3, 1813, appears to be a reissue.

57. See *BM* 11768. It was originally published in 1811 and republished with variants in 1812. Annibel owned the more elaborate 1812 version that was reworked.

58. See *BM* 11079.

59. See *BM* 11762.

CHAPTER 10

"Hazardous Purchasing Almost Anything"

THE INTRIGUING RELATIONSHIP OF THE WARTONS, SUBSCRIPTION LISTS, AND THE EIGHTEENTH-CENTURY BOOK TRADE

Hugh Reid

Thomas Warton—now known as "the elder" to distinguish him from his younger, more prominent son also named Thomas—died on September 10, 1745, aged fifty-eight, in Basingstoke, Hampshire, where he was the vicar. He had had a varied and distinguished, although minor, career. A fellow of Magdalen College, Oxford, he became professor of poetry and served two terms in that capacity. Warton also had a number of modest literary connections. He was a friend of Elijah Fenton and Edward Young and had been introduced to Alexander Pope, to whom he gave his copy of *Gorboduc* (1561). He had also gained some celebrity—some might term it notoriety—at Oxford and elsewhere by giving a pro-Jacobite speech in the University Church of St. Mary's on May 29, 1719. At the time of Warton's death, his eldest son, Joseph, who was twenty-three and serving as vicar at Chobham in Surrey, became the family's sole support. Joseph's mother was still alive; his sister, Jenny, twenty-one, was disabled; and his younger brother, Thomas, was a student at Trinity College, Oxford. Oxford was expensive, and even though Thomas had been awarded the Tylney Exhibition worth twenty pounds a year, he was finding it financially difficult, and continuing there might have proved impossible without his late father's financial support.[1]

On October 29, 1745, just over six weeks after their father's death, Joseph Warton, the future critic of Pope, wrote to his brother Thomas, the future poet laureate and historian of English poetry:

> I have now another scheme to communicate to you, of which I desire you not to speak till I have further consider'd it. Since you left Basingstoke I have found a great many poems of my Father's, much better than any we read together. These I am strongly advised to publish by subscription, by Sir Stukely Shuckburgh, Dr. Jackson, and other friends. There are sufficient to make a six shilling octavo volume, and they imagine, as my Father's acquaintance was large, it would be easy to raise two or three hundred pounds; a very solid argument in our present situation. It would more than pay all my Father's debts. Let me know your thoughts upon this subject; but do not yet tell Hampton, or Smythe, who would at first condemn us, without knowing the prudential reasons which induce us to do it.[2]

As was the custom, a proposal was printed and published on February 27, 1746:

> Proposals for Printing by Subscription Poems on Several Occasions by the Rev. Mr. Thomas Warton B.D. Late Vicar of Basingstoke in Hampshire and sometime Professor of Poetry in the University of Oxford. Conditions
>
> 1. That the book shall be printed in large octavo, on good letter and paper.
> 2. That the price to the subscribers (whose names shall be printed) shall be six shillings; three to be paid at the time of subscribing, and three at the delivery of the book, which shall be put to the press immediately.
>
> Subscriptions are taken by Mr. Dodsley in Pall-mall, Mr. Parker and Mr. Fletcher in the Turl at Oxford, Mr. Micklewright at Reading, and Mr. Dawson at Basingstoke.[3]

Attached to the bottom of the proposal, again as was common, was a blank receipt to be torn off and given to the subscriber.

Joseph and Thomas, later thought of as something of literary pioneers—Joseph for his *Essay on Pope* (1756), which was the first reevaluation of the poet and placed Pope not as the foremost of poets but rather at the head of the second group of poets, and Thomas for his innovative *History of English Poetry* (vol. 1, 1774; vol. 2, 1778; vol. 3, 1781) and the part he played in the sonnet revival—were not here being all that revolutionary in turning to subscription publishing in an attempt to raise needed money. Earlier in the century, Pope had published his edition of Homer by subscription and had successfully shown how this approach could be used to publish with significant financial gain. Many would try to emulate him. Essentially, subscription publishing avoided risk. Those, like the Wartons, who wished to publish something approached a bookseller, who would arrange printing, but only after a sufficient number of subscribers were found to cover costs. It was an arrangement that suited everyone involved. Before 1701, there had been fewer than 100 books published by subscription. By 1801, estimates place the number between 2,000 and 3,000. Approximately 40 books were published by subscription in the first decade of the eighteenth century, and 91 in the second decade. For various reasons, including the successes of Pope and others, the number jumped significantly to approximately 270 in the 1720s. The average for each decade for the rest of the century was 250. While this is a large number of books (there are estimates that the subscribers' lists contain more than one million names), it forms a relatively small percentage of books published in the eighteenth century. And these were usually more expensive or appealed to individual or specialized groups.[4]

This growth in subscription publishing was motivated by a number of factors. After 1695, copyright was no longer held in perpetuity, and booksellers began to reissue well-known works whose copyright had expired. This occasioned little or no risk, while there was often some significant financial peril in publishing new books. Publishing by subscription effectively eliminated that possibility. The money for all the costs of printing and other expenses was collected, and effectively guaranteed, beforehand. Subscription publishing was, therefore, beneficial for both the writer, however major or minor (and this is important), and the bookseller.[5]

There were, however, some inconveniences. Most authors did not relish finding subscribers, and sometimes people trying to get subscriptions gained a reputation for trickery, for as many as half the books promised for publishing by subscription never materialized. Famously, Samuel Johnson spoke of one Thomas Cooke, who had lived for twenty years taking subscriptions and promising a translation of Plautus that never appeared. As this was not uncommon, an air of cynicism grew around many who were trying to raise subscriptions, especially if those raising the subscription, or the person for whom it was being raised, were unknown. But there were always some notable successes, which encouraged the practice of publishing in this way. Elizabeth Carter made more than £1,000 from the 1,200 subscribers to her *All the Works of Epictetus* (1758), enough to allow her financial freedom for life.

The subscription for Thomas Warton the elder's *Poems* proved successful as well. There were 332 subscribers, for a total of 432 copies. Notable among the subscribers were the poet Edward Young, author of *Night Thoughts* (1742–1745); the printer William Bowyer; General Oglethorpe, who founded a colony in Georgia; and William Blackstone, author of the *Commentaries of the Laws of England* (1765–1770). While Thomas Warton the elder's *Poems* (1748) was the first venture into subscription publishing for the Warton family,[6] it was not the first time that members of the family purchased books in this manner. Indeed, Thomas Warton the elder began what became something of a family tradition, one that lasted the whole century, culminating with the publication by subscription of his grandson's poems. Early in the century, when it was not yet so common, Thomas Warton the elder had purchased a number of works that were published by subscription, and these prove of interest.

The Business of Subscriptions

Understanding the nature of subscription publishing in the eighteenth century may involve arcane and convoluted study, but it may be made somewhat clearer by examining how one family was involved with the practice throughout the century. While the Wartons might not be typical, they do provide various examples of involvement with subscription publishing that deserve examination. We cannot know for certain exactly how many books the Warton family subscribed, but likely it was around fifty, which is not an insubstantial number for one family. We cannot know the number precisely because sometimes the name Warton is listed without any identifying signifier, no Dr. Warton, Headmaster or Rev. Warton of Trinity College, poet laureate. And sometimes the name is spelled as "Wharton." But while we cannot be entirely definitive, we can confidently determine the number we know for certain and make an educated guess at some others (e.g., "Warton, Wykeham, Hants." Joseph retired to Wykeham in Hampshire in 1793 and lived there until his death in 1800). He, perhaps not surprisingly, subscribed to *The Works of Addison*, edited by Thomas Tickell (1721). This work occasioned much controversy. Tickell was reputed to have earned £1,350 for the four quarto volumes, after which there was a dispute with Jacob Tonson over the copyright. And a year later, Steele, thinking he had been maligned by Tickell, published Addison's 1716 play *The Drummer*, which was not included in the Tickell edition. In a prefatory epistle, Steele wrote that Addison had written the Homer translation that Tickell had claimed as his own.[7]

In addition to two Latin texts, he also subscribed to *The Last Judgement of Men and Angels. A poem*, by Thomas Newcomb (1723). This Miltonic epic in twelve books had, curiously, Newcomb's own portrait as its frontispiece, somewhat unusual for the time, although the practice of using the author's portrait as such would grow over the century. Later, in Basingstoke, where he became vicar, Warton subscribed to *The Destruction of Troy*, translated from the Greek by James Merrick in 1739. Merrick somewhat exemplifies the frequently complex relationships that were involved with subscription publishing. Merrick had matriculated at Trinity College, Oxford on April 14, 1736, and graduated with a bachelor of arts in 1739, the same year he published *The Destruction of Troy* (to which Joseph Warton, while a student at Oriel College, Oxford, also subscribed). The work was an undergraduate production to be sure, but his abilities must have been noticed, for he was made a probationer fellow of Trinity College in May 1744 and a fellow there a year later. It was as a fellow of Trinity College, Oxford, that he got to know Thomas Warton the younger, who had matriculated there. So even here, relatively early in the century, we may see how intertwined some of these subscription endeavors were.

Thomas Warton the elder had earlier subscribed to *The Aeneid of Virgil* by Joseph Trapp (1718), in another example of the interwoven nature of authors and subscribers. Trapp's son, also named Joseph Trapp, sent his own son to Trinity in 1766, where Thomas Warton the younger had become a fellow. There is also a further connection with Joseph Warton. Trapp's poem on Virgil's tomb is commended by Joseph in his *Essay on Pope*.[8] So we see in Thomas Warton the elder's subscriptions a pattern that would be repeated and enlarged by his sons,[9] a pattern of buying by subscription books of interest and books by acquaintances as a form of patronage. This nature of some of the books acquired through subscription continued to be, at times, somewhat predictable and illustrative of this type of publishing, while at other times it moved into the curious and inexplicable.

After their father's book, the brothers continued to be involved with subscription publishing not by publishing but by subscribing. We know for sure that Joseph subscribed to at least twenty different books, while brother Thomas subscribed to twenty-three. Many of these subscriptions are easily understandable, for the Wartons were scholars and teachers. Joseph was, for much of his life, headmaster of Winchester College, as well as the first major critic of Pope. Thomas never left Trinity College, Oxford. After matriculating there in 1744, and later graduating, he became a fellow of the college where he would live for the rest of his life.[10]

Examples of what might be considered professional subscriptions are Joseph's subscriptions to Beresford's translation of *The Aeneid* (1794) and *The Four Gospels Harmoniz'd and reduced into one* by Arthur Hele (1750), subscribed to while Joseph was a vicar at Winslade in Hampshire and also subscribed to by brother Thomas. Others in this category include, as mentioned earlier, *The Destruction of Troy*, translated from the Greek by James Merrick (1739) while he was still an undergraduate, and *Twenty Sermons* (1772) by William Fletcher and James Beattie's 1770 book with the fantastically long title, *Essays. On the nature and immutability of truth, in opposition to Sophistry and Scepticism. On poetry and Music, as they affect the Mind. On Laughter, and Ludicrous Composition. On the Utility of Classical Learning.* Beattie, a rather well-known essayist, had collected many of his essays for this volume and seemed to want to get the titles of many into the title of the work itself. *The Works of Lucian from the Greek* (1780) by Thomas Francklin was also subscribed to by Thomas. Joseph subscribed, also, to Francklin's *The Tragedies of Sophocles* in 1759. And there were others of such ilk as well as collections of sermons, such as *A Sermon preached in the Cathedral Church Winchester* (1769) by Alured Clarke and *Sermons preached in the Abbey Church at Bath by a late dignified Clergyman, John Chapman* (1790). As these subscriptions were typical, subscribing to these works is unsurprising and provides few interesting insights into subscription publishing.

Personal Subscriptions

But there is also another side to Joseph's subscriptions. He subscribed to some works by friends and acquaintances. This was, of course, common during the century, but some of these subscriptions, upon further examination, seem a bit unusual. *Poems on several occasions*, by William Vernon (1758), provides an example. The title page of the volume identifies Vernon as a "Private soldier in the Buffs" (at this time the Third [Kent] Regiment of Foot, later the Royal East Kent Regiment), and this subscription shows another side of Warton's personality. What little is known about Vernon comes from some letters of Robert Dodsley, wherein Vernon is described as coming from poor parents with a rudimentary education (his Horatian poems all come from translations), and after an apprenticeship to a buckle maker, he enlisted in the Buffs. From the poems, it is clear he was stationed on the Isle of Wight and visited Winchester often.[11] We do not know how this unlikely friendship developed, but in Winchester he met and became friends with the Warton brothers, who, it appears, encouraged him in his poetic endeavors. The poems are "inscrib'd to the Honourable Roger Townsend, Captain of the Grenadiers in the Buffs." And in the advertisement, Vernon states: "The many obligations I am under to a very valuable friend of mine at Winchester (The Rev. Mr. ______)," most certainly a reference to Joseph Warton. The brothers must also have helped in obtaining subscriptions as many of the nearly 200 subscribers, who include Joseph and Thomas Warton, were students of Winchester College. The Wartons seem here, clearly, to be encouraging someone in his poetic endeavors, someone who is neither a student nor a relative nor a long-standing friend.

Joseph's subscription to *Poems* (1762) by Robert Lloyd offers another unusual example. After an early career trying to make his way in the London literary world (Lloyd had worked with Coleman in the theatre and had become editor of the poetry section of *The Library, or Moral and Critical Magazine*) and having engaged in a number of literary disputes, he decided to enlarge his literary reputation (and make some much-needed money) by publishing his poems. He worked very hard on getting the "right" subscribers.[12] Besides the Wartons, the list includes Reynolds, Sheridan, Sterne, Johnson, Garrick, and Hogarth, as well as two bishops, numerous fellows of Oxford and Cambridge colleges, and fifty peers. Fortunately for Lloyd, the volume proved a financial success, but perhaps more important, the impressive list of subscribers helped enhance his reputation as a literary man. Lloyd's *Poems* affords a clear example of how the subscription lists themselves were beginning to function as more than the mere identification of the names of those who purchased the book.

Warton also subscribed to a curious volume that would seem, on the surface, to hold no interest for him, nor did the author have any personal connection to him. John Nott was a physician who traveled widely and learned Persian while acting as a ship's surgeon on an East India Company ship on its way to China. Nowhere else does Warton display any interest in things oriental, but he did subscribe to Nott's *Select Odes, from the Persian poet Hafaez, translated into English Verse* (1787). Warton subscribed, many years apart, to two works by Glocester (also known as "Gloster") Ridley, the first being *The Life of Dr. Michael Ridley sometime bishop of London* (1763), Ridley being a descendant of Bishop Ridley. Then, eighteen years later, he subscribed to *Melampus, A Poem in Four Books, with notes: by the late Gloster* [*sic*] *Ridley* (1781). What occasioned this book is a further example of the need to raise money. Ridley had had the living of Weston, and once Ridley died, the living was given to James Woodforde, the diarist. Apparently, the rectory had been left in a somewhat dilapidated state, and Woodforde sought to gain the money for its repair from Ridley's widow. She eventually paid him £115 12s 4d, money that was raised by the publication of *Melampus*.

Another set of subscriptions reveals an additional, and to some extent unanticipated, aspect of Warton's character: He subscribed to the works of many female authors. John Brewer estimates that male literacy rates rose from 50 percent in 1714 to 60 percent in 1750, and while female literacy rates were lower, not surprisingly, he estimates that the rate rose from 25 percent in 1714 to 40 percent in 1750.[13] The number of female subscribers of books also climbed steadily throughout the century. For Pope's Homer, where the percentage of female subscribers was slightly higher than average for the time, 8 percent of subscribers to the *Iliad* were women, and for the *Odyssey* this grew to 13 percent. This can be compared to Thomas Warton's *Poems*, which had 332 subscribers of whom 97 were women, or just over 29 percent, a rise in female subscribers that was typical as the century progressed.

It might be claiming a bit too much to say Warton was an early feminist, but his subscriptions to books by female authors certainly show a willingness to encourage poetic talent wherever he saw it (as he did in the case of William Vernon), whether male or female. *Poems on several occasions* (1785) by Ann Yearsley, a *milkwoman of Bristol* with a prefatory letter by Hannah More (addressed to Elizabeth Montagu), provides a good illustration. Yearsley (née Cromartie) was born near Bristol and brought up by her mother to be a milk woman as she was, but, remarkably, she also taught her daughter how to read and write. In 1774, she married John Yearsley, with whom she had seven children, five boys and two girls. By the end of 1784, the family was destitute, and they were aided by a number of local people, including Hannah More. More worked tirelessly to arrange for Yearsley's poems to be published by subscription, and her work resulted in more than a thousand subscribers, many of whom had important literary and social connections, including Horace Walpole, Joshua Reynolds, Frances Burney, and many peers and churchmen.

Not long after the publication, More and Yearsley fell out over the profits from the book, which More had placed in a trust so that Yearsley's husband would not have access to it. After some time and discord, More relented and closed the trust and helped Yearsley publish two more editions of the work. However, in 1786 there came a final break with More. Yearsley, with help from many local people, including Augustus Hervey, the fourth Earl of Bristol, published a second volume of her poems. The subscription list is much shorter and consists mostly of those in and around Bristol, the literary and social connections of Hannah More dropping off. Warton did not subscribe for the second volume. It appears Yearsley gave up selling milk as her literary success grew and she opened a circulating library in the catalog of which for 1793 is listed Thomas Warton's *Poems on Various Subjects*.

Another volume of interest was *Poems on various subjects* by Miss Cave (now Mrs. W.) (1785). Thomas, and Joseph's wife, also subscribed to this volume. The volume to which the Wartons subscribed was the second edition of the *Poems*, the first one listing the author only as Miss Cave. Jane Cave married Thomas Winscom on May 18, 1783, and thereafter added the parenthetical "(now Mrs. W.)" in each edition. There were several more editions, each adding only the names of new subscribers. In the first edition, the dedication takes the form of a poem "To the Subscribers"; in it, she speaks of her admiration for, but not her attempts to imitate, Anna Seward, Anne Steele, and Hannah More.

Joseph also subscribed to *Elegiac Sonnets*, by Charlotte Smith (1789), to which Thomas also subscribed. Joseph and his wife subscribed to the rather unremarked, and unremarkable, *The Sorrows of Werter* (1788) by Amelia Pickering, as well as to *A Poetical Translation of the Song of Solomon* (1781) by Ann Francis. This significant number of works by women to which Joseph subscribed indicates at least a willingness to accept women as authors, even if publishing by subscription was their only way into print. He must have encouraged such subscriptions in his family, as well. Joseph's second wife subscribed to *Miscellanies in Verse* by Eliza Garrard (1799) and, curiously, in 1788 she subscribed (so Joseph's name did not appear perhaps?) to *A sermon preached in the cathedral church of St. Paul* by Henry Whitfield.

Thomas also subscribed to the "usual suspects" on literature and religion. And he, too, was interested in helping young poets, but these were generally ones whom he had taught. Among them was Henry Headley, who had been admitted to Trinity College, Oxford, on January 14, 1782. Here he met William Lisle Bowles and others, a group of young poets who were to become known as part of the "school of Warton." Warton himself was instrumental in the sonnet revival, and many of these young men had an influence far beyond their current reputations. Wordsworth's use of the sonnet can be traced back to Warton, and Wordsworth acknowledged the influence that Bowles had on his own work. Early on, Warton had asked John Nichols to insert a poem by Headley in his anthology "the production of an ingenious young friend." Headley's volume, *Select Beauties of Ancient English Poetry* (1787) counted among its subscribers

Thomas, who had vigorously encouraged its publication. It was a success, but unfortunately, Headley, who had always been of rather delicate health, became consumptive and died the following year. His poems, however, published by subscription with Warton's encouragement, continued to have an influence on poetic taste.

There were other, less well-known works to which Warton subscribed, such as *Poems on Several Occasions* (1774) by John Bennet, a journeyman shoemaker (Warton subscribed for four books), and *Poems of Several Occasions* (1761) by Myles Cooper, at the time chaplain of the Queen's College, Oxford. Cooper later emigrated to America and became something of an American loyalist. Other subscriptions of this nature include *Miscellaneous Poems, To which is added a farce, called What will the World Say?* (1787) by William Gillum, and *Immortality reveal'd. A Poem in four epistles . . . To a friend* (1745) by Thomas Cooke. Some of the other less well-known works to which Warton subscribed are, nevertheless, understandable. *Collectanea curiosa; or, miscellaneous tracts, relating to the history and antiquities of England and Ireland, the Universities of Oxford and Cambridge* by John Gutch had 750 subscribers, but it was chiefly of interest to those in Oxford or Cambridge and caused something of a controversy by including some anti-Jacobite material and presenting an argument limiting fellowships to twenty years in length. Similarly, William Tasker's *Select Odes of Pindar and Horace translated*, published in 1780, has long remained unnoticed. While this work is something that would be of obvious interest to Warton, Tasker has remained more in modern memory for the description of him in Boswell when Tasker submitted his poems to Johnson to judge: "The bard was a lank, bony figure, with short black hair; he was writhing himself in agitation while Johnson read, and, showing his teeth in a grin of earnestness, exclaimed in broken sentences and in a keen, sharp tone, 'Is that poetry, sir—is it Pindar?'"[14]

The Wartons and Johnson were friends, and so it is no surprise to see Warton subscribing to John Hoole's 1763 translation of Tasso's *Gerusalemme liberate, Jerusalem delivered; an heroic poem*. The work had originally been printed only for his friends in 1761, but with Johnson's encouragement, he published this volume by subscription in 1763. It was favorably received, and a number of later authors credited Hoole with introducing them to Tasso. Even as a young fellow of Trinity in 1750, Warton subscribed to some more unusual works. Like his brother, these were often by women. *Miscellanies in prose and verse* by Mary Jones was a hugely successful subscription enterprise with more than 1,400 subscribers. Many of these poems were reprinted in other works, and she became known to Johnson, who, according to Boswell, called her "the Chantress." Boswell asked Warton for his recollections of her (Jones lived all her life in Oxford), and he described her as "a most sensible, agreeable and amiable woman."[15]

In 1751, Warton subscribed to *Amelia or The Distress'd wife: a history founded on real circumstances. By a private gentlewoman*. The author was Elizabeth Justice (née Surby), and this semi-autobiographical novel was published, as with many mentioned earlier, in an attempt to raise money. It tells the story of a young woman who marries at sixteen to a man seven years her senior and relates the financial difficulties encountered when the man is shown to be more interested in his books than in his family. Amelia, after the breakdown of the marriage, receives a settlement of twenty-five pounds per annum, which is not nearly sufficient to pay off her debts and so, of necessity, she becomes a governess. Justice had done the same and had traveled to Russia as part of her new profession. Oddly, and perplexingly, Edmund Curll published, without Justice's knowledge or approval, four of her letters to a friend in the fifth volume of Pope's *Literary Correspondence* (1737). The reason for this unethical (but, then, Curll was never really considered ethical) action may have been because she had earlier published, by subscription, *A Voyage to Russia* (1739) which sold 600 copies with 281 subscribers. But the money raised from *A Voyage to Russia* was still inadequate, hence the publication of *Amelia* (1751), which proved more successful. Sadly, it provided only short relief to Justice, for she died the following year.

Perhaps the most curious of Thomas's subscriptions was to the novel *The Life of Miss Fanny Brown, a Clergyman's daughter: with a history . . . of Mrs. Julep, an Apothecary's wife. . . . to which are added a description of the . . . Monuments in Westminster Abbey* (1760) by John Piper, whose dedication and preface ramble on interminably, which perhaps should not surprise when he connects the lives of these two women with a description of monuments in Westminster Abbey. As with *Amelia*, this, too, is a semiautobiographical novel. John Piper was really John Alcock, an organist and choirmaster at Litchfield. The *Oxford Dictionary of National Biography* describes Alcock as "a pedantic (and somewhat irascible) perfectionist,"[16] so it is no wonder this novel describes in some detail the problems, social and political, as he saw them, of those involved with church music. In yet another example of art imitating life, these problems proved personal the next year (1761), when the choir petitioned the dean to remove Alcock from his position of choirmaster. They did not succeed, but, ironically, the petition allowed Alcock to rid himself of a number of the duties that he did not enjoy.

As they grew older, Joseph's wife began to subscribe to some books. She, too, subscribed to Chapman's *Sermons*, as had her husband, and to Henry Whitfield's *A sermon preached in the cathedral church of St. Paul, London: on Thursday June 7, 1798. Being the time of the yearly meeting of the children.* She also subscribed to poems by women, again as had her husband, in 1788 *The Sorrows of Werter*, a poem by Amelia Pickering, and in 1799 *Miscellanies in verse and prose* by Eliza Garrard, of Bath. Joseph Warton's sons, as well, subscribed to a number of books, but we should note that near the end of Joseph's life in 1794, the family, that is, Joseph (Thomas had died in 1790), his wife, his sister, and daughter, all subscribed to *Poems, original and translated* by John Warton, at the time a schoolmaster in Blandford. John, Joseph's youngest son, had had what David

Fairer called a "chequered" career at Trinity College, where he had matriculated in 1773 as his Uncle Thomas's student. It was the second and final effort at subscription publishing for the Warton family and one that, unlike his grandfather's venture into subscription publishing, did little, in the long run, to help him with his finances. John Warton was prosecuted for debt in 1815 and was forced to abandon his family.[17]

Subscription publishing would largely die out in the nineteenth century, but it had an important, although at times confusing and complicated, place in the eighteenth-century book trade. The Wartons' involvement seems to exemplify much of the nature of this important, if somewhat transient, development in the history of the book. Their subscriptions characterize much of the nature of subscription publishing, and they cover and illustrate the eclectic area of reasons for subscribing. Moreover, through them, we see that subscription publishing was not limited to better-known authors of the time, such as Pope. Their subscriptions illustrate how the practice of subscription publishing encouraged the development of minor authors or authors who would otherwise have gone unpublished. We also note that some books purchased this way were not subscribed to solely out of interest in the material of the book itself, thus making us rethink some analyses of sale catalogs.[18] Paul Korshin calls the subscription publishing method a form of democratization.[19] Seeing the Wartons' subscriptions enables us to understand more clearly how this short-lived publishing trend operated and what it meant to one small segment of the book-procuring public.

So, we began our look at the Warton family's involvement in subscription publishing with a subscription for Thomas Warton the elder as a way of making money, and the family's involvement concluded at the end of the century with a subscription list for the grandson as a means for making money. The Wartons subscribed for all the conventional and predictable reasons, but they also subscribed, at times, for reasons not so common. However whimsical it may be, I like to think there is sometimes another, very human, reason for subscribing to a book, one that is not professional or a form of patronage or friendship. On August 16, 1746, Hannah Glasse published, by subscription, *The Art of Cookery made plain and easy. By a lady.* There is a Mr. Warton, with no *h*, on the subscription list. Joseph Warton at the time of publication, or, rather, at the time the subscriptions were gathered, was a single, young curate. In the second edition in 1747, a Mr. Wharton, with an *h*, is listed. Joseph Warton married Mary Daman on September 21, 1747, and the third edition of this popular cookery book was published in 1748. On the subscription list for it are a Mr. Wharton and, for the first time, a Mrs. Wharton, both with an *h*" I like to think that the critic of Pope, and friend of Johnson, subscribed as a single man to something as unliterary, but very practical, as a cookbook.

NOTES

1. From a letter from Robert Dodsley to Thomas Warton the younger about printing Warton's *The Pleasures of Melancholy* "for so very few Poems sell, that it is very hazardous purchasing almost anything," as quoted in *The Correspondence of Thomas Warton*, ed. David Fairer (Athens: University of Georgia Press, 1995), 16.

2. Fairer, *Correspondence of Thomas Warton*, 14–15, cites John Wooll, *Biographical Memoirs of the late Rev. Joseph Warton* (London, 1806), 214–215, and accepts Wooll's misdating of the letter. The correct date (October 29, 1745) is used in this chapter. See Hugh Reid, "The Re-dating of an Important Joseph Warton Letter," *Notes and Queries* 62, no. 2 (June 1, 2015): 301–302.

3. Thomas Warton, *Proposals for printing by subscription, Poems on several occasions. By the Rev. Mr. Thomas Warton,* . . . [London]: n.p., [1746]. Eighteenth-Century Collections Online (accessed November 29, 2021).

4. Hugh Reid, *The Nature and Uses of Eighteenth-Century Book Subscription Lists* (Lewiston, ME: Edwin Mellen, 2010), 15.

5. I am using the term *bookseller* in the eighteenth-century sense as one who arranged for copyright and the printing of a book. He may also have sold it in a shop. In short, he was what we would today refer to as a publisher. A publisher in the eighteenth century was what we would call a distributor of books.

6. This volume would gain in significance as time passed. Many saw in it indicators of a changing poetic taste and considered Thomas Warton the elder something of a transitional figure between the poetic aesthetic of the early part of the century and all that came later, beginning with Gray and ending with Wordsworth. However, work by David Fairer and Christina le Prevost on the manuscripts in the Bodleian has proved that the poems that seemed the most forward-reaching were, in fact, written or heavily edited by the sons, Joseph and Thomas, as a way of "improving" the poems of their father. See David Fairer, "The Poems of Thomas Warton the Elder," *Review of English Studies* 26 (1975): 287, 395–406; and Christina le Prevost, "More Unacknowledged Verse by Joseph Warton," *Review of English Studies* 37 (August 1986): 317–347, https://www.jstor.org/stable/516548.

7. For a complete discussion, see James Sambrook, "Tickell, Thomas (1685–1740)," in *Oxford Dictionary of National Biography*, ed. H.C.G. Matthew and Brian Harrison (Oxford: Oxford University Press, 2004).

8. ". . . in which are as much lively and original imagery, strong painting, and manly sentiments of freedom, as I have ever read in our language. It is a Copy of Verses written at Virgil's Tomb, and printed in Dodsley's *Miscellanies*." Joseph Warton, *An Essay on the Writings and Genius of Pope* (London: Printed for M. Cooper, at the Globe in Pater-Noster Row, 1756), 267.

9. He also subscribed to *An Exposition on the Thirty Nine Articles* (1725) by John Veneer.

10. He died of a stroke in the Senior Common Room in 1790 and was buried in the college chapel.

11. One poem is entitled "From the camp on the Isle of Wight, September, 1757." And a poem that was published in the *Gentleman's Magazine* on August 9, 1759, is even more specific: "Written in a copy of Dr. Young's Night Thoughts at Winton College, December 1757." See James E. Tierney, *The Correspondence of Robert Dodsley* (Cambridge: Cambridge University Press, 1988), 357n5.

12. It was not uncommon to claim that certain well-known people were subscribing to a work as a way of encouraging others to subscribe. Swift found himself on a number of subscription lists for books of which he had never heard.

13. John Brewer, *The Pleasures of the Imagination: English Culture in the Eighteenth Century* (New York: Farrar, Straus and Giroux, 1997), 167–174.

14. W. P. Courtney, "Tasker, William (1740–1800), poet and antiquary" in *Oxford Dictionary of National Biography.*

15. James Boswell, *The Life of Samuel Johnson, LL.D.* (London: Printed for H. Baldwin & Son, For Charles Dilly, in the Poultry, 1799), 215n2.

16. H. Diack Johnstone, "Alcock, John (1715–1806)," in *Oxford Dictionary of National Biography*.

17. Fairer, *Correspondence of Thomas Warton*, 715–716.

18. Examining sale catalogs can tell us much about the owner of the books, but an analysis must note what books were bought by subscription and whether such books were bought as a form of patronage or general interest. Merely owning a book does not guarantee that it was read or that the owner was in the least interested in it.

19. "The subscription method democratized literary patronage, and made it possible for a community of wealthy people to contribute to the support of many authors. The sense of obligation which pervades and often exacerbates the traditional patron-client relationship is usually diminished or wholly absent in the author-subscriber relationship," notes Paul Korshin in "Types of Eighteenth-Century Literary Patronage," *Eighteenth Century Studies* 7 (Summer 1974): 464.

CHAPTER 11

After the Great War

THE RESTORATION AND EIGHTEENTH CENTURY ON THE LONDON STAGE, 1919–1929

John A. Vance

No London theatre season could have been more joyously anticipated than that which commenced in the fall of 1918. Even though London theatres had remained active during the Great War—with memorable productions featuring the best actors of their time—few could completely escape the horrific effects of the war, in which more than 650,000 British troops were killed and another 2.4 million were wounded or missing in action. For many, the unsettling feelings of escape and guilt at enjoying an evening at the theatre had their effect, especially as patrons poured out on the street after a performance and thought about the horrors taking place across the English Channel—not to mention those brought closer to home by the Zeppelin bombing runs on London, with the Lyceum Theatre being hit on the evening of October 13, 1915. Even though the conflict was not officially over as the 1918–1919 theatre season got underway, Germany's major spring offensive of 1918 had failed, so that by August 8 the Allies—now reinforced by troops and matériel from the United States—launched the Hundred Days Offensive,[1] which over the next three months pushed the German army out of France and led shortly afterward to the armistice on November 11.

London audiences would soon be introduced and reintroduced to returning war veterans such as Charles Laughton, Basil Rathbone, Ronald Coleman, Cedric Hardwicke, Claude Rains, Nigel Bruce, Leo G. Carroll, Ernest Thesiger, Herbert Marshall, Leslie Howard, Stanley Holloway, John Laurie, and Nicholas Hannen—all now adding to the popular male depicters active during the war years, including Herbert Beerbohm Tree, Philip Merivale, Fred Terry, Henry Ainley, Henry B. Irving (son of the great Henry Irving), Arthur Bourchier, George Alexander, Ben Greet, William Stack, and Russell Thorndike. Among the popular and talented actresses during the war years were Marie Lohr, Julia

Nielson, Phyllis Neilson Terry, Irene Vanbrugh, Constance Collier, Lilian Braithwaite, Florence Saunders, Mary Sumner, and Sybil Thorndike.

In spite of the psychological effects of the Great War, with the devastating loss of family members and friends, the war years were still notable ones on the London stage. In addition to contemporary plays and revivals of more recent British and continental works, including Brandon Thomas's *Charley's Aunt*, Henrik Ibsen's *A Doll's House*, Augusta Gregory's *The Gaol Gate*, J. M. Barrie's *Peter Pan*, and John Millington Synge's *Playboy of the Western World*, there were a plethora of productions continuing and adding to a more than two-century tradition of staging Shakespeare. During the war, *The Tempest*, *As You Like It*, *Henry V*, *Julius Caesar*, *Macbeth*, *A Midsummer Night's Dream*, *Romeo and Juliet*, *The Taming of the Shrew*, and *Twelfth Night* had at least four runs each,[2] with the two most popular of Shakespeare's plays being *The Merchant of Venice* with eight runs and *Hamlet* with seven. From 1919 to 1929, Shakespearean productions shifted into an even higher gear, with all thirty-seven recognized plays having at least one London run. Twenty-four of the plays received four runs, with the most frequently staged being *Othello* and *Macbeth* with ten each; *The Taming of the Shrew* with eleven; *Romeo and Juliet*, *Twelfth Night*, and *A Midsummer Night's Dream* with twelve, and *The Merchant of Venice* with fourteen. *Hamlet* was now the most popular with twenty-three runs from 1919 to 1929.[3]

Revivals

Audiences also enjoyed late Victorian and Edwardian revivals during the first decade following the end of the Great War. Both *Charley's Aunt* and Barrie's *Peter Pan* continued as favorites with nine and ten London runs, respectively, in the 1920s. Continental playwrights remained favorites of London audiences, who saw Ibsen's *A Doll's House* and *Hedda Gabler* and Chekhov's *Uncle Vanya* over the course of nine runs. Even the 1901 version of the morality play *Everyman* had a revival of nine runs during these years.[4] Another very popular Edwardian revival was "Charles Marlowe's" (Harriet Joy's) *When Knights Were Bold*, which had ten runs during the 1920s. Joy's comedy was brought to film in 1916 and 1929 (both silent versions), and with sound in 1936. But the king of the late Victorian and Edwardian (and early Georgian) revivals in the 1920s was George Bernard Shaw, with forty-one London runs of eight of his plays: *Candida*, *Mrs. Warren's Profession*, *Arms and the Man*, *Major Barbara*, *Pygmalion*, *Man and Superman*, *Dark Lady of the Sonnets*, and *You Can Never Tell*.[5]

But what of the period plays literary history has come to rank second behind those of Shakespeare—the memorable comedies and tragedies written from 1660 to 1800? As I have noted previously,[6] the period from the last decade of the nineteenth century through the Great War found no "ancient" British playwright more popular, with the exception of Shakespeare, than Richard Brinsley Sheridan, particularly his *School for Scandal* (1777), which was the most frequently staged non-Shakespearean revival of the age. Yet the other accepted stage favorites and masterpieces of the Restoration and eighteenth century remained unseen at London theatres—with the exception of a single offering of Hannah Cowley's *Belle's Stratagem* (1780) in 1913 and two performances of Congreve's *Double Dealer* (1694) in 1916. *St. Patrick's Day; or the Scheming Lieutenant* (1788) and *The Critic* (1781)—four performances of each play in 1917—were no doubt offered owing to theatregoers' fondness for Sheridan.[7] And they came to see Goldsmith's *She Stoops to Conquer* (1773), which had four runs during the war years (in 1915, 1916, and 1918) for a total of twenty-nine performances featuring the likes of such stage favorites as Estelle Stead, William Stack, Arthur Fayne, and the highly popular Sybil Thorndike. As for *The Rivals* (1775), the war years featured nine performances from November 1915 through March 1916 and four more in September 1916, with Ben Greet, Sybil Thorndike, William Stack, and Florence Saunders assaying the roles of Bob Acres, Lydia Languish, Jack Absolute, and Julia Melville, respectively. *School for Scandal* was played on twenty-three occasions at Covent Garden and the Old Vic from 1915 to 1918 with splendid casts composed of the notable Herbert Beerbohm Tree, Henry Ainley, Fred Terry, Irene Vanbrugh, William Stack, Sybil Thorndike, Estelle Steed, Ben Greet, Russell Thorndike, and Florence Saunders performing the major parts.

Even though the war years gave short shrift to the famous plays of the Restoration and other favorites of the eighteenth century, there were revivals of more recent plays about the theatrical and historical figures from 1660 to 1800. Staged between February 27 and April 3, 1915, was Paul Kester's play *Sweet Nell of Old Drury Lane* (1900), a favored offering that starred Fred Terry as Charles II and Julia Neilson as Nell. F. Frankfort Moore's *Kitty Clive*, staged initially in London in 1895, was also revived in 1915. And in that year were the ninety-eight performances of Louis Parker's *Mavourneen*,[8] "A Comedy in Three Acts," which debuted at His Majesty's Theatre on October 23 and ran until January 29, 1916. Set in the court of Charles II, the play featured the king, Samuel Pepys, Lady Castlemaine, and the members of the famous Cabal. But the most popular of the plays about the stage personalities from the years 1660 to 1800 was T. W. Robertson's *David Garrick*, which made its initial London appearance in 1864 and was briefly revived in January 1918.[9] Garrick's friend Samuel Johnson was the subject of Leo Trevor's frequently staged 1896 play, which had thirty-two performances starring the celebrated Arthur Bourchier at His Majesty's Theatre in February and March 1916. But perhaps the most intriguing depiction of the figures from the eighteenth century was the single matinee performance of *The Pageant of Drury Lane Theatre* on September 27, 1918, during the middle of the Hundred Days Offensive, a day after the Allies broke through the Hindenburg Line and a day before Hindenburg and Ludendorff recommended an armistice. *The Pageant* was constructed as a series of episodes and scenes, featuring Charles II, Samuel

Pepys, dramatist and theatre manager Thomas Killigrew, Samuel Johnson, James Boswell, David Garrick, Oliver Goldsmith, and Joshua Reynolds and actresses Susannah Cibber, Peg Woffington, and Hannah Pritchard.[10]

Biographical and Historical Productions

One may surmise that these plays and *The Pageant* stimulated a desire to become acquainted with the forgotten stage works of the Restoration and eighteenth century. With a war about to end, theatregoers realized that escape into the theatre had been and would continue to be an antidote to painful and depressing realities uneffaced by the armistice on November 11, 1918. Why not see if other, earlier British plays might contribute to the amusement theatregoers sought, even if these works had not been staged for decades or even for more than two centuries? A citizenry proud of achievements and sacrifice on the battlefield would naturally look back on its nation's history—literary and theatrical, as well as military and political. After all, England's dispatching of Spain's Armada in 1588 sowed the Elizabethan theatre world with considerable pride in the past, which bore fruit in the history plays of Shakespeare and others.

Following the Great War, audiences continued to enjoy plays about the famous historical and literary personalities from the years 1660 to 1800.[11] Nell Gwynne trod the boards again in the eponymous play, which had twelve stagings at the Regent with Lettie Paxton in the title role, Gerard Neville as Charles II, and Dorothy Dewhurst as Lady Castlemaine.[12] Louis Parker's *Our Nell*, which played at the Gaiety Theatre for 140 performances from April to August 1924, included dancing and music by Ivor Novello and Harold Fraser-Simson, with José Collins in the lead.[13] Finally, Nell also appeared in *Mr. Pepys* at the Everyman Theatre in February and March 1926 and later at the Royalty from March to mid-April 1926. With Frederick Renalow as Pepys, this production featured as Nell the thirty-four-year-old Isabel Jeans, who at the time was a successful actress (and the divorced wife of Claude Rains).[14]

Louis Parker, author of *Our Nell*, also gave the stage *Mr. Garrick*, which ran for twenty-six performances at the Court Theatre in early fall of 1922. Gerald Lawrence played Garrick, with Roy Byford as Johnson, Herman de Lange as Boswell, Richard Anderson as Oliver Goldsmith, and George Mallet as Joshua Reynolds. Lawrence had already depicted Garrick in the silent film adaptation of T. W. Robertson's *David Garrick*, released in November 1912, with other British film versions of the play appearing in 1913 (two films that year) and in 1922, with Charles Wyndham, Seymour Hicks, and Milton Rosmer, respectively, in the title role.[15] Also in 1922 (and for one performance in 1920) appeared a musical based on Robertson's play, which had seven performances at the Queen's Theatre in March. The straight stage version of Robertson's *David Garrick* returned at the end of the decade with twelve performances in July 1929,[16] with Bernard Lee listed as the Garrick of this run.[17]

The immediate postwar period was especially significant in its reintroductions of hitherto little considered or completely ignored Restoration and eighteenth-century drama. The increasing quality of Shakespearean revivals must have also stimulated the curiosity of audiences, actors, and producers to experience more of the stage era that followed the Elizabethan and Jacobean periods. And one might also argue that the blooming of the period's scholarship complemented the new stage revivals of these plays. More specifically, editions, essays, notes, and book-length critical studies by the likes of John Palmer, Bonamy Dobrée, B. J. Pendlebury, K. M. Lynch, H.T.E. Perry, and A. H. Thorndike from 1913 to 1929 testify to the critical attention the Restoration plays were beginning to receive.[18]

The Return of the Augustan Stage

Following the war, the London stage gave its audience at least a taste of the more famous Restoration playwrights. John Dryden's *All for Love* (1678) ran for two performances at London's Shaftesbury Theatre in March 1922 and starred the great Edith Evans as Cleopatra, a role she would reprise in Shakespeare's version of the story three years later. Dryden's comedy *Marriage à la Mode* (1673) ran for two performances at the Lyric Hammersmith on February 8 and 9, 1920, the same number of performances given five years later to Buckingham's satire at Dryden's expense, *The Rehearsal* (1672), which appeared on July 5 and 6, 1925. Likewise, Thomas Otway's two major tragedies were also served as theatrical appetizers with their two-performance runs. The Lyric presented *Venice Preserved* (1682) on November 28 and 30, 1920, and *The Orphan* (1680) on May 10 and 11, 1925. Most memorably, a young John Gielgud appeared as Castalio in *The Orphan*—the part first performed by the great Thomas Betterton in 1680.[19] Performing the roles Betterton's costar Elizabeth Barry had made famous, Monimia in *The Orphan* and Belvidera in *Venice Preserved*, were Ray Litvin and Cathleen Nesbitt.[20] In the secondary role of Aquilina in *Venice* was Edith Evans, who in 1920 was about to make her mark as one of the most accomplished actresses on the London stage, with Shakespeare's Cleopatra, Mistress Page, *Midsummer*'s Helena, Rosalind, Katherine the Shrew, Beatrice, and both Portias soon added to her triumphs—all at the Old Vic.

Of the three major comic playwrights of the Restoration, the London stage in the 1920s unfortunately ignored George Etherege and his *Man of Mode* (1676) but did offer a sampling of the controversial William Wycherley, whose work through the eighteenth and nineteenth centuries was considered "indecent," "obscene," "profligate," and "heartless."[21] After short scenes from *The Gentleman Dancing Master* were presented on June 27, 1922, the full play made its modern London debut at the Regent on December 20, 1925. For this one performance the part of Hippolita, the play's young and devious heroine, was taken by Vera Lennox, who had already appeared in two George and Ira Gershwin musicals at London's Winter Garden Theatre. Wycherley's notorious *Country Wife* (1675), which had been sanitized by Garrick as *The Country Girl* in 1766,[22] also had its modern London debut at the Regent on February 17 and 18, 1924, with Isabel Jeans, now thirty-three, acting the role of Margery Pinchwife. Wycherley's other acclaimed comedy, *The Plain Dealer* (1676), had one staging on November 15, 1925, at the "New Scala Theatre,"[23] starring Leah Bateman as Fidelia and Verna Lennox as Eliza.

If these plays served as appetizers, there is no question that the main course of Restoration comedies was the work of William Congreve. His first comedy, *The Old Bachelor* (1693), ran for two performances at the Regent in June 1924, with Leo G. Carroll as the capricious Vainlove's man, Setter.[24] But the major Restoration event of the 1920s was the staging of Congreve's masterpiece, *The Way of the World* (1700), which had its initial run of 158 performances at the Lyric Hammersmith from February 7 to June 28, 1924. Nigel Playfair's casting of Edith Evans as Millament was a stroke of theatrical genius.[25] Critics simply adored her in the role, with one reviewer noting that this was a part "in which she definitely 'arrives'": "She has the art and the wit that transfigure the woman and give us the great lady, the coquette, the rogue, and the lover all in one."[26]

Three years later, Evans reprised the role for ninety-six more performances, this time at Wyndham's from mid-November 1927 to early February 1928. The Lady Wishfort of this run was Ruth Maitland, and taking the part of Betty was the up-and-coming Peggy Ashcroft.[27] As for Edith Evans and her turn as Millament, James Agate observed, "Let me not mince matters. Miss Edith Evans is the most accomplished of living and practising English actresses." And Gielgud would later comment that it was as Millament that Evans "took the town by storm. It was a unique and exquisite performance. She purred and challenged, mocked and melted. . . . Her words flowed on, phrasing and diction balanced in perfect cadences, as she smiled and pouted in delivering her delicious sallies."[28] Few productions ever did as much for the appreciation of an age in which a play initially appeared.

Other than the three major plays of Goldsmith and Sheridan, drama of the eighteenth century was represented after the Great War initially by a single staging of Farquhar's *The Beaux Stratagem* (1707) in 1919. But from January 20 to May 28, 1927, the play was reprised for 143 performances. Surely, the popularity of this run was in large part due to Edith Evans being cast as Mrs. Sullen. One can imagine the broad smiles as Evans launched into her character's memorable monologue: "Country pleasure! Racks and torments! Dost thou think, child, that my limbs were made for leaping of ditches and clambering over stiles?" One may also feel certain that not since Nan Oldfield played the part in the 1707 premiere was the role more effectively performed.

With the postwar years' continued delight in musical entertainment—from opera to the lighter fare—it may be of little surprise that John Gay's *The Beggar's Opera* (1728) caught fire with audiences of the 1920s. The ballad opera appeared throughout the decade from its initial three-year tenure (June 1920 to December 23, 1923) of an incredible 1,463 performances to other runs in 1925, 1926, 1928, and 1929. Nigel Playfair was responsible for producing this highly successful revival at the Lyric Hammersmith—with Johann Pepusch's music rearranged and supplemented by the noted operatic baritone and composer Frederic Austin.[29] The production played in Paris, Canada, Australia, and America and spawned the staging of Gay's sequel *Polly* (1729), again with Austin (and Clifford Bax) revising the music, at the Kingsway and Savoy Theatres for 324 performances beginning on December 30, 1922. One commentator credited as "One of the Audience" noted, "One of the astonishing episodes of the modern theatre in London is the success of 'The Beggar's Opera.'"[30]

As for the most popular English tragedy of the early eighteenth century, Lillo's *The London Merchant* (1731) represents perhaps the most creative revival of the period's plays. Nigel Playfair once more allowed his imagination free rein—this time by having the homespun impresario Vincent Crummles and other characters from *Nicholas Nickleby* perform Lillo's tragedy—now set in Dickens's own time—in the stage drama *When Crummles Played* (1927). With Miriam Lewes as Millwood, Hermione Baddeley as Maria, and Ernest Thesiger as George Barnwell, Playfair's unique construct played for 115 performances at the Lyric from February 6 to October 9, 1927, and made its New York debut the following autumn at the Garrick Theatre, with forty performances from October 1 to December 1, 1928.[31]

As for later eighteenth-century plays, George Colman and David Garrick's *The Clandestine Marriage* (1766) ran for six performances in late November and early December 1928, twenty-five years after its revival at the Haymarket in March 1903. Given Sheridan's status as the most successful eighteenth-century playwright in early twentieth-century revivals, one would expect productions of his two lesser plays. His two-act farce *St. Patrick's Day; or, the Scheming Lieutenant* had a solid, twelve-performance run at the Old Vic from March 28 to April 18, 1927, with Duncan Yarrow as Lieutenant O'Connor.[32] More successful that year was Sheridan's *The Critic*, initially presented at Playfair's Lyric Hammersmith from October 24 to November 17, 1928, before being transferred to the Court Theatre from November 19 to December 29, 1928—for a total of seventy-seven performances.

Moving to the comic and sparkling literary triumvirate of the 1770s, Goldsmith's masterpiece *She Stoops to Conquer* had its first postwar London production at the Old Vic in December 1919. For these eleven performances, Sybil Thorndike's brother, the fine Shakespearean actor Russell Thorndike, took the role of Tony Lumpkin, after having played Young Marlow eighteen months earlier. Depicting Kate Hardcastle was the charming Florence Saunders, who was promoted from the role of Constance Neville, which she had performed in 1916. Two years later, between December 22, 1921, and February 4, 1922, the Court Theatre staged *Stoops* fifty-nine times with H. O. Nicholson, Margaret Yarde, and Ena Grossmith as the Hardcastles—Richard, Dorothy, and Kate.[33] During this run at the Court Theatre, the rival Old Vic mounted the show for seven performances during the holiday season (December 26, 1921, to January 3, 1922) with Florence Buckton, fresh off her success as Beatrice in *Much Ado about Nothing*, as Kate. Richard Hardcastle was assigned to the diminutive D. Hay Petrie—the Old Vic's favorite Puck and other Shakespearean clowns.[34]

Three years later, the Old Vic brought the play back for eight more performances during the holiday season—from December 26, 1924, to January 16, 1925—with a cast that featured the respected Shakespearean actor and director Andrew Leigh as Tony Lumpkin, John Garside as Hardcastle, stage favorite Ion Swinley as Young Marlow, and Marie Ney as Kate.[35] Garside reprised his role as Hardcastle in the Old Vic's next run of fourteen *Stoops* performances in January and February 1926. But the major addition to this production was the new Kate Hardcastle—the incomparable Edith Evans, then just a few days shy of her thirty-eighth birthday. She already had sixteen years' stage experience by this time, having first appeared as Viola in *Twelfth Night* in 1910, and was exactly two years removed from her rise to stardom with Millament. *Stoops* wrapped up its appearance on the London stage in the 1920s with a healthy seventy-eight-performance run at the Lyric from August 16 to October 20, 1928. The wee Scot D. Hay Petrie now had another opportunity to play Hardcastle, with Marie Ney moving over from the Old Vic to reprise her Kate.

Sheridan Revived

Staged but fourteen times from 1910 to 1916, Sheridan's *The Rivals* earned its rightful place as the second member of the comic triumvirate in the 1920s. The Old Vic offered thirteen performances from March 8 to April 30, 1920, featuring the admired Russell Thorndike as Bob Acres and the up-and-coming Florence Saunders as Lydia Languish.[36] Also in the cast were Frederick Keen as Sir Anthony Absolute and Catherine Willard as Mrs. Malaprop. Four years later, the Old Vic brought back Sheridan's comedy for nine performances in March 1924, with the now established star Florence Saunders reprising her Lydia. This time, the part of Sir Anthony was taken by Wilfred Walter, who began his career at the Old Vic as a stage decorator.[37] Ethel Harper assayed Mrs. Malaprop, along with Old Vic regulars Kingsley Baker as Sir Lucius O'Trigger, Claude Ricks as Bob, Jane Bacon as Julia Melville, and as Jack Absolute, Ion Swinley, by now a noted Shakespearean performer—particularly for his Hamlet.

The Rivals' major run during the decade (and clear evidence that the play had earned its place in the "big three") occurred not at the Old Vic but at the Lyric Hammersmith in March, April, and May 1925. Headlining the ninety-three performances were Norman V. Norman as Sir Anthony and Dorothy Green as Mrs. Malaprop, both experienced Shakespearean actors.[38] Douglas Burbidge appeared as Jack Absolute, and the aforementioned Isabel Jeans as Lydia.[39] Other notables in this exceptional ensemble were the Lyric's head man Nigel Playfair as Bob Acres (sharing the role with Miles Maleson) and the sometimes playwright and later aviatrix Beatrix Thomson as Julia.[40] Rounding out the cast was thirty-five-year-old Claude Rains as Faulkland. Discovered by Herbert Beerbohm Tree, Rains later guided Gielgud and Olivier at the Royal Academy of Dramatic Art. After Rains moved to Broadway in 1927, his impressive and distinctive voice would earn him his first major film role, as the title character in *The Invisible Man* (1933), which would lead to a sterling film career, including Academy Award nominations (as Supporting Actor) in *Mr. Smith Goes to Washington*, *Notorious*, *Mr. Skeffington*, and as Louis Renault in *Casablanca*. What makes his appearance in *The Rivals* rather bizarre is the fact that he shared the stage with his current wife, Beatrix Thomson, and his two *former* wives, Isabel Jeans and Marie Hemingway.

The decade's final run of *The Rivals* was at the Old Vic in March and April 1929—fourteen performances with lesser-tier actors. The busy Shakespearean Eric Adeney took on Sir Anthony Absolute, with William Babbage as Jack Absolute, Andrew Leigh as Bob Acres, and later film and television actor Torin Thatcher as Faulkland. Fresh from her turns as Mistress Page, Gertrude, Viola, and Lady Macbeth, Esmé Church acted Mrs. Malaprop and Iris Baker, Lydia Languish in this production. Although this run pales in comparison with the one at the Lyric four years earlier, it did enough to demonstrate that *The Rivals* had finally earned its place among the most favored eighteenth-century plays on the current London stage. Yet, without question, the decade's healthy number of *Rivals* performances were also encouraged and enhanced by the continued popularity of Sheridan's other brilliant comedy, *School for Scandal*.

The first postwar staging of *Scandal* ran for sixty-three performances at the Court Theatre from March 17 to May 24, 1919. Previously a Toby Belch, Polonius, and Autolycus, Arthur Whitby undertook the role of Sir Peter Teazle, with Herbert Waring (aged sixty-one), a highly praised Torvald Helmer in *A Doll's House* and Malvolio in *Twelfth Night*, as Joseph Surface and a rather young (twenty-seven) Leah Bateman as Lady Sneerwell.[41] A year later, the Old Vic presented *Scandal* for fifteen performances in two separate runs, October 25 to November 6, 1920, and then from January 10 to 15, 1921. Frederick Harker, also appearing that season in *Julius Caesar*, *A Midsummer Night's Dream*, and *Twelfth Night* (as Malvolio), essayed the role of Sir Peter, with Cyril Sworder as Charles Surface, and the reliable and American-born Ernest Milton as Joseph Surface.

The Old Vic's popular trio of Ethel Harper, Florence Saunders, and Mary Sumner took the roles of Mrs. Candour, Lady Sneerwell, and Lady Teazle, respectively. Both Saunders and Sumner had appeared in the Old Vic's 1916–1917 production of *Scandal*, with the then twenty-six-year-old Saunders in the same role of Lady Sneerwell and Sumner in the secondary part of Maria. The highly acclaimed Sybil Thorndike was the Lady Teazle on that occasion.

The Old Vic brought the play back for a ten-performance run over the holidays, December 1923 through January 1924. Florence Saunders reprised her Lady Sneerwell, and Ethel Harper, her Mrs. Candour. However, on this occasion and fresh from her appearance as Julia Melville in *The Rivals*, Jane Bacon took the role of Lady Teazle. The Sir Peter Teazle for these performances was Reyner Barton, with George Hayes as Joseph Surface, and—as Charles Surface—Ion Swinley, who had depicted Jack Absolute earlier in the year. John Gielgud reminisced that Swinley, whom Gielgud had understudied, was a "most enchanting man," and Sydney Carroll thought Swinley was the "finest speaker of Shakespeare" of his time.[42]

The London Hippodrome offered a single matinee performance of *Scandal* on November 8, 1927, with Angela Baddeley as Lady Teazle and as Charles Surface, Nicholas "Beau" Hannen, who would later appear in Olivier's *Henry V* (1944) and *Richard III* (1955). Playing Sir Peter Teazle was the splendid Cedric Hardwicke. Making his first stage appearance at the Lyric in 1912, Hardwicke cut his teeth on Shakespearean roles, moving on to become the leading Shavian actor of his day.[43] Complementing his impressive stage work was a notable film (and later television) career, including important roles in *Nell Gwynn* (1934), *Peg of Old Drury Lane* (1935), *Stanley and Livingstone* (1939), Hitchcock's *Suspicion* (1941), and Olivier's *Richard III* (1955).

Some five months later, the Old Vic brought the play back for another fourteen performances from March 26 to April 20, 1928, with several new cast members such as two future film actresses, Barbara Everest (*Scrooge* in 1935 and *Jane Eyre* in 1943) as Lady Sneerwell, and Elizabeth Allan (*David Copperfield* and *A Tale of Two Cities* in 1935) as Maria. John Garside, who had already depicted Sir Richard Hardcastle, was cast as Sir Peter, and making her debut as Lady Teazle was twenty-three-year-old Jean Forbes-Robertson, daughter of the famous Johnston Forbes-Robertson. Jean had come into her own in 1926 and 1927 playing Juliet and Barrie's Peter Pan—a role she reprised annually until 1935. She would go on in the next several years to earn accolades for her Cordelia, Viola, Titania, Hedda Gabler, and the male parts of Oberon and Puck.[44]

The final staging of *Scandal* in the 1920s was at the Kingsway Theatre from November 28, 1929, to March 8, 1930. These 121 performances featured a four-act version of the comedy, which starred Angela Baddeley once again as Lady Teazle, twenty-eight-year-old Grizelda Hervey as Lady Sneerwell, and Frank

Cellier as Sir Peter. Cellier was an accomplished Shakespearean actor—with Hamlet, Touchstone, Kent, and most notably Shylock, Macbeth, and Toby Belch to his credit. The cast also included Henry Hewitt as Charles Surface, a role he reprised in the first sound film of the play (now lost) in 1930. (The then little known Rex Harrison had a bit part in the film.) The Joseph Surface in this staging also reprised his role in the 1930 film—Ian Fleming. This Ian Fleming—not the spy novelist—was an experienced stage actor who would go on to appear in films and television and is best remembered for having played Dr. Watson in four Sherlock Holmes films of the 1930s, with Arthur Wontner as Holmes.

These 121 performances of *School for Scandal* brought the total presented on the London stage following the Great War to 224, as compared with 129 for *The Rivals* and 112 for *She Stoops to Conquer. Scandal* still ruled, but by 1930 London audiences had maintained and broadened their appreciation of Sheridan's other brilliant comedy and Goldsmith's theatrical triumph. In addition, the startling successes of *The Beggar's Opera*, *The Beaux Stratagem*, and *The Way of the World*, and the reintroduction of Wycherley's, Dryden's, Otway's, Lillo's, and Colman and Garrick's comedies and tragedies—plus the renewal of stage works about Nell Gwynn, Samuel Pepys, and David Garrick—make clear that the immediate years after the end of the First World War were both an exciting and a highly significant period for the plays and famous figures from the Restoration and eighteenth century. The trauma of war and the destruction on the Continent of landscape, farms, houses, schools, factories, and livestock as well as the massive loss of human life (close to 1 million military personnel and civilians throughout the United Kingdom) surely prompted a desire to draw more from the well of earlier British stage comedy. A sense of artistic continuation—a stronger link to the theatrical past—was vital during such devastating times, when much was questioned and a dreadful future was feared and anticipated. The plays of the 1660–1800 period staged immediately following the war years provided one link to the past but also made clear that this laughter was not and never would be effaced by the tragedy of the Great War.

In addition, the struggle for women's suffrage resulting in the Representation of the People Acts of 1918 and 1928, which finally gave the vote to all women over age twenty-one, surely added to the appeal of the sparkling, sexually charismatic and liberated, witty, resourceful, competitive, dominant, and successful Restoration and eighteenth-century women who competed on more than equal terms with their male counterparts and looked forward to and likely encouraged the popular film genre of "screwball comedies" in the next two decades. Without question, London audiences in the aftermath of the Great War went to see these productions and came away realizing and further appreciating that their country's rich and enjoyable theatrical heritage clearly extended beyond the works of William Shakespeare.

NOTES

Annibel Jenkins was the one who encouraged me to explore theatre history, noting that I would likely come up with many "interesting bits" of information about theatres and actors that "ought to be shared." This essay is the result of her advice and encouragement.

1. Following the Allied victory at the Battle of Château-Thierry in mid-July, the Hundred Days Offensive consisted of a series of individual battles, such as Amiens, and the Second Battle of the Somme.

2. Still underappreciated, though not ignored, in the 1914–1918 period were *Richard III*, *Much Ado about Nothing*, and *Othello* with three runs each, and *King Lear* with two.

3. Dates and cast lists for all plays come from J. P. Wearing's multivolume *A Calendar of Plays and Players* (Metuchen, NJ: Scarecrow Press, 1976, 1981, 1982, 1984). Of the theatrical overviews of the period, one might begin with Clive Barker and Maggie Barbara Gale, eds., *British Theatre between the Wars, 1919–1939* (Cambridge: Cambridge University Press, 2000).

4. In 1920, Lilian Baylis, producer and manager of the Old Vic, revived the 1901 version of *Everyman*, which had previously been produced and directed by the actor and stage impresario Ben Greet. Greet broke tradition and cast women in the title role. Edith Wynne Mathison, Constance Crawley, and Sybil Thorndike played the character in the initial runs, which also toured Britain and North America.

5. Not including the first nine 1920s runs of Shaw's most recent piece *Back to Methuselah*, first staged in New York (1922).

6. John Vance, "The Rule of *Scandal*: Sheridan in the Age of Wilde and Shaw," in *Richard Brinsley Sheridan: The Impresario in Political and Cultural Context*, ed. Jack E. DeRochi and Daniel J. Ennis (Lewisburg, PA: Bucknell University Press, 2013), 123–143.

7. The performances of *The Critic* were also enhanced by a cast that featured Ben Greet, Sybil Thorndike, and Florence Saunders.

8. "Mavourneen" is Irish for "Little Darling."

9. The play depicts the young Garrick in 1742 falling hard for a lovely audience member, whom he finally and ironically meets after agreeing to take part in a scheme to put an end to a wealthy man's daughter's infatuation for him. That daughter is, of course, the lovely audience member he has been seeking. Robertson published a prose version of the story in 1865, although it had first been brought out in serial form the previous year.

10. For more on these plays, see Vance, "The Rule of *Scandal*," 125–127.

11. They also saw two plays adapted from eighteenth-century fiction. *Robinson Crusoe*, with music, ran for twenty-four performances at the Garrick Theatre in December 1927 and January 1928, and the stage version of *The Vicar of Wakefield* had four performances at the Aldwych Theatre in April 1921. Primrose was played by Norman Forbes and Sophia by Viola Tree, the eldest daughter of the great Herbert Beerbohm Tree. Forbes (Forbes-Robertson) was the younger brother of the more famous Johnston Forbes-Robertson, colleague of Henry Irving and one of the best Hamlets ever on the London stage. Viola Tree depicted Shakespeare's Viola, Ophelia, Helena, Ariel, and Perdita. Right before her death, she played the social reporter Perfide in the 1938 film version of *Pygmalion*—the role of Henry Higgins first being played by her father in the play's 1914 premiere.

12. Neville was a stage Dracula in 1927 and 1928, and Dewhurst went on to perform in the 1950s film and ITV productions of *Hedda Gabler* and *Arsenic and Old Lace*.

13. An earlier version, titled *Our Peg*, was given in Manchester at the end of 1919. In New York, José Collins sang with Al Jolson and appeared in the *Ziegfeld Follies* in 1912 and 1913. She was Nell in *Our Peg* and continued to appear onstage, in musical revues, and in several films.

14. Jeans had a career that lasted for more than fifty years. She appeared in three Hitchcock films—*Downhill* (1927), *Easy Virtue* (1928), and *Suspicion* (1941)—and in the musical

Gigi in 1958. From her midfifties to her midseventies, she had roles on the London stage in plays by Wilde, Chekhov, Noël Coward, and T. S. Eliot, and in William Congreve's the *Double Dealer* in 1959. One of her last film performances was as Dame Agnes Grand in *The Magic Christian* (1969), starring Peter Sellers, John Cleese, Christopher Lee, Richard Attenborough, and Ringo Starr.

15. There were also two American films in 1914 and 1915. Of the film Garricks, the most famous is Sir Charles Wyndham, who made his stage debut in 1862, appearing with Ellen Terry. After sailing to America, where he became a Civil War surgeon, Wyndham returned to England and made his reputation as an actor (and later theatre manager), with Sheridan's Charles Surface in *School for Scandal* being one of his most popular roles in addition to his stage Garrick. Wyndham was seventy-six when he appeared in the film.

16. Other early twentieth-century dramas written about Garrick include those by H. M. Holles (1901), Alex MacLean (1910), and Max Pemberton (1913). See Daniel Meyer-Dinkgräfe, *Biographical Plays about Famous Artists* (Newcastle: Cambridge Scholars Press, 2005), 98.

17. The name should ring a bell with James Bond fans. Lee attended the Royal Academy of Dramatic Art and made his West End debut in 1928, remaining primarily a stage actor through the 1930s. His active film career is, of course, best known for his portrayal of "M" in the first eleven Bond movies, beginning with *Dr. No* in 1962 and concluding with *Moonraker* in 1979. He died in 1981. Biographical entries do not mention this performance as Garrick, but Wearing's *A Calendar of Plays and Players* notes the twenty-one-year-old actor playing the part.

18. John Palmer, *The Comedy of Manners* (London: G. Bell and Sons, 1913); Bonamy Dobrée, *Restoration Comedy* (Oxford: Clarendon Press, 1924) and *Restoration Tragedy* (Oxford: Clarendon Press, 1929); B. J. Pendlebury, *Dryden's Heroic Plays: A Study of Origins* (London: Selwyn and Blount, 1923); K. M. Lynch, *The Social Mode of Restoration Comedy* (New York: Macmillan, 1926); H.T.E. Perry, *Comic Spirit in Restoration Drama* (New Haven, CT: Yale University Press, 1925); and A. H. Thorndike, *English Comedy* (New York: Macmillan, 1929).

19. Gielgud made his professional debut in 1921 at the age of seventeen. He went on in 1924–1925 to perform such London theatre roles as Romeo in Shakespeare's play and Trofimov, Konstantin, and Tusenbach in Chekhov's *Cherry Orchard*, *The Seagull*, and *Three Sisters*.

20. Rachel (Ray) Litvin was a favorite at the Old Vic during the war years and immediately afterward. Her career suffered a fatal blow after a serious illness left her deaf. She was the mother of Lady Natasha Spender—concert pianist, socialite, and wife of poet Stephen Spender.

21. Most memorably by Jeremy Collier and Thomas Babington Macaulay in *A Short View of the Immorality and Profaneness of the English Stage* (1698) and "Comic Dramatists of the Restoration," *Edinburgh Review* 72 (1841): 490–528.

22. Garrick's "Advertisement" is worth quoting: "Tho' near half of [*The Country Girl*] is new written, the Alterer claims no Merit, but his Endeavour to clear one of our most celebrated Comedies from Immorality and Obscenity. He thought himself bound to preserve as much of the Original, as could be presented to an Audience of these Times without Offence. . . . There seems indeed an absolute Necessity for reforming many Plays of our most eminent Writers: For no kind of Wit ought to be received as an Excuse for Immorality, nay it becomes still more dangerous in proportion as it is more witty."

23. Before its demolition after a fire in 1969, the Scala served as the site of the concert footage at the end of the Beatles' *A Hard Day's Night*, filmed in 1964.

24. Carroll left for the United States after this production and had an extensive film career, although to many he is best known for his television work in *Topper* (1953–1956)

and *The Man from U.N.C.L.E.* (1964–1968). Among his film credits are roles in six important Hitchcock films: *Rebecca, Suspicion, Spellbound, The Paradine Case, Strangers on a Train*, and *North by Northwest* (1940 to 1959).

25. In 1904, Playfair had starred in the Mermaid Society's London production of *The Way of the World* and would go on to produce a controversial yet revolutionary staging of *As You Like It* at the Lyric in 1920, as well as to encourage and oversee the BBC's radio transmissions of Shakespeare beginning in 1923. In 1918, Playfair purchased the lease of the Lyric Hammersmith when it was in a state of dilapidation and quickly converted it into one of London's busiest and most imaginative theatres.

26. "Congreve at Hammersmith," *Manchester Guardian*, February 8, 1924, 12. Also in this production was Elsa Lanchester as the maid Peggy. Lanchester began on the London stage in 1922 before embarking on an active movie career of more than fifty films, several of which costarred her husband, Charles Laughton. To many she is best known for a role in which she had no lines: the Bride of Frankenstein (although she also played Mary Shelley in the film) in the 1935 James Whale movie by the same name.

27. As a Shakespearean actress, she would go on in the 1930s to play Juliet opposite Laurence Olivier's and John Gielgud's Romeos and opposite Gielgud in *Much Ado about Nothing* and *King Lear*. She would also star in *Antony and Cleopatra, The Taming of the Shrew*, and *Cymbeline*; in 1937, she appeared with Greer Garson in a thirty-minute excerpt from *Twelfth Night*, the first recognized depiction of Shakespeare on television.

28. James Agate, *The Contemporary Theatre, 1924* (London: Chapman and Hall, 1925), 83; John Gielgud, John Miller, and John Powell, eds., *An Actor and His Time* (London: Sidgwick and Jackson, 1979), 72.

29. In 1920, Austin made his final operatic bow as Count Almaviva in Mozart's *Marriage of Figaro*, but he did sing Peachum in the run of *The Beggar's Opera*. Also in the cast were the Irish tenor Frederick Ranalow as Macheath and Sylvia Nellis as Polly.

30. "The Theatre: Polly of the Present," *International Interpreter: The International News Weekly* 1, no. 46 (February 17, 1923): 1457–1458.

31. Regarding Miriam Lewes, one reviewer in 1908 claimed that the actress "had an emotional sensibility out of the ordinary"; twenty years later, another wrote that, as Alice in Strindberg's *Dance of Death*, Lewes reminded him of the incomparable Stella Campbell at her prime: "It took me some time to rally from this shock of reminiscence." *The Athenaeum* February 29, 1908, 268; *The Spectator* January 28, 1928, 11. Hermione Baddeley (Maria) became a highly successful character actress onstage, in film, and later on television, receiving an Academy Award nomination for Best Supporting Actress in 1959 for her role in *Room at the Top*. This role, lasting less than two and half minutes, was the shortest ever to receive an Academy Award nomination. Ernest Thesiger (George Barnwell) inspired G. B. Shaw to write for him the part of the Dauphin in *Saint Joan* (London premiere in March 1924). Striking up a friendship with the director James Whale led to Thesiger's being cast as Dr. Septimus Pretorius, the mentor of "Baron" Frankenstein, in *The Bride of Frankenstein* (1935). He went on to appear in film and onstage with John Gielgud, Alec Guinness, Vivian Leigh, Ralph Richardson, and, as Jacques, with Katherine Hepburn in the longest-running Broadway production of *As You Like It*.

32. Yarrow had his coming out during the 1925–1926 season at the Old Vic, in which he appeared in a number of Shakespearean productions with Edith Evans, Margaret Rutherford, and the highly respected Baliol Holloway.

33. Margaret Yarde made a specialty of the overbearing and argumentative domestic, landlady, and wife. In 1923, she played Mistress Ford in the short silent film *Falstaff the Tavern Knight*.

34. Petrie's extensive film career included character roles in *The Private Life of Henry the Eighth* with Charles Laughton and Merle Oberon (1933); in *Pickwick Papers* with John Mills and Alec Guinness (1946); and in two films on 1660–1800 period actresses: *Nell Gwynn*

(1934) with Anna Neagle and Cedric Hardwicke and *Peg* [Woffington] *of Drury Lane* (1935) also with Neagle and Hardwicke.

35. Marie Ney also appeared as the Spirit of Christmas Past in the 1935 film *Scrooge*. The previously mentioned Margaret Yarde played Scrooge's laundress in the film.

36. Born in Valparaiso, Chile, Saunders met an untimely end at age thirty-five in January 1926.

37. Decorated in the Great War, Walter went on to play major Shakespearean comic and tragic parts as Falstaff, Bottom, Marc Antony, and Othello.

38. Dorothy Green's Mistress Ford was matched with Edith Evans's Mistress Page in the Lyric's 1923–1924 production of *The Merry Wives of Windsor*. Norman V. Norman worked with seventeen-year-old Laurence Olivier in *Hamlet* at St Christopher School, Letchworth, in April 1925 and with him in *Henry VIII* at the end of that year at the soon-to-be demolished Empire Theatre. Two years earlier, on October 18, 1923, Norman took the role of Macbeth for a radio broadcast of selected scenes, which also included the talents of nineteen-year-old John Gielgud.

39. Jeans shared the role during the long run with the lovey and aristocratic-looking Griselda Hervey. Later in her career, Jeans performed in the Old Vic's revival of Congreve's *The Double Dealer* (1959) and appeared in other plays that season with Judi Dench. Jeans also acted in three of Wilde's best: *Lady Windermere's Fan* (1945 and 1966), *A Woman of No Importance* (1953), and *The Importance of Being Earnest* (1968), in which she took her turn as Lady Bracknell, a role Edith Evans had earlier made her own onstage from 1939 to 1947, in film (1952), and on television (1960).

40. Thomson was the first actress to earn her pilot's license, which she received at the end of December 1929.

41. Five years earlier, the American Kenean Buel directed a filmed version of *Scandal*. Another would appear in 1923 under the direction of Bertram Phillips and starring Frank Stanmore as Sir Peter Teazle and the rather striking Queenie Thomas as Lady Teazle. The most famous member of the cast, however, was Basil Rathbone as Joseph Surface. Of his prolific work on-screen, Rathbone was perhaps the most memorable Sherlock Holmes—fourteen films from 1939 to 1946—with Nigel Bruce as Watson. His stage career included Romeo, Ferdinand, and Cassius—as well as Tybalt in the 1936 Leslie Howard and Norma Shearer film of *Romeo and Juliet*, for which he was nominated for an Academy Award.

42. Gielgud, *An Actor and His Time* (London: Sidgwick and Jackson, 1979), 24–25.

43. These included leading roles in *Pygmalion*, *Caesar and Cleopatra*, *Candida*, and *Major Barbara*. One oft-repeated anecdote had Shaw wittily (or not) noting that Hardwicke was "my fifth favorite actor, the first four being the Marx Brothers."

44. St. John Ervine claimed "never [to have] witnessed anything so beautiful" as her Juliet. See "At the Play," *The Observer*, December 19, 1926, 13.

CHAPTER 12

One of Thomas Bray's Apostles of Literacy

THOMAS BACON

Calhoun Winton

Literacy is a difficult concept to discuss: hazy in its origins, with respect both to society and to an individual—but almost universally held to be important. Just when did American society become literate? Name the year or decade. Precisely when in our lives did you or I cease to be illiterate? Cite the day, month, and year. To both questions the answer is, of course, no one knows. And yet the answers are accepted as being, without dispute, important. If a society is pronounced to be largely illiterate, we shake our heads in dismay. If a fourteen-year-old is judged similarly, we say he or she must receive literacy education.

In recent years, considerable scholarship in English has emphasized the role of religion and religious education in the spread of literacy. Harry Gamble, for example, in his groundbreaking work on the early Christian world, *Books and Readers in the Early Church*, has judged that "in the early period, just as later on, it appears that those who exercised leadership usually possessed the skills of literacy."[1] Leadership was thus equated with literacy. Perhaps the association has some value in reducing the enormous conundrum of literacy to size, as it were. Recently, for example, Fred Witzig has shown that a school was, improbably, established in colonial South Carolina in the 1740s by prominent Anglicans there. The school taught reading and writing, successfully, to slaves for a number of years, in defiance of an act passed by the General Assembly specifically forbidding slave education. The General Assembly feared literacy among slaves as potentially leading to rebellion.[2] They may have been correct in their fears, as will be seen. Literacy can lead to leadership.

Books, the vade mecum of literacy, were coming into colonial America from various sources by the 1740s, and the most important source was London. Acting there since the 1690s on behalf of the Anglican Church, but perhaps more significantly on behalf of education, had been the Reverend Thomas Bray, a true believer in the efficacy of the written word. Through the societies he imagined and brought to life around 1700, the Society for the Propagation of the Gospel in Foreign Parts and the Society for Promoting Christian Knowledge (SPCK), Bray sent both men to teach and books to be taught in, among many other places, the American colonies. The activities were continued by these organizations and by Dr. Bray's Associates, an organization established after his death to continue his work. Nothing, Bray once wrote, "can so directly tend to encourage Good Men . . . to venture themselves in the Labours of the Gospel abroad, as good Books; and nothing can so immediately tend to render 'em Good and useful when they are there, as the same."[3] (It is interesting, and perhaps symbolically important, that Samuel Johnson and Benjamin Franklin, bookmen to the core, met at a meeting of the Associates in 1761.)

The work of the ministers Bray sent out and of the churches they led has been viewed from various perspectives. These ministers have been, for example, portrayed in recent years as agents of emerging British imperialism, sent abroad to influence in favorable ways the political aims of that imperialism.[4] But Bray himself was cautious about partisan involvement, although he recognized it was often unavoidable and could even be helpful, and the present essay will emphasize bibliographic rather than political activities. The subject of the essay, one of Bray's "Good Men" named Thomas Bacon, came from an interesting background involving books, in the broader sense, on the British side of the Atlantic. Bacon used the skills and knowledge he had acquired on the other side to considerable effect in the new colony of Maryland.

Bacon as Minister

Bacon's origins are still being investigated.[5] He seems to have grown up in Cumberland, but when he enters this account in the 1740s, he is a bookseller in Dublin and also the proprietor of a coffeehouse on Essex Street there. Dublin coffeehouses, like those in London, were first established in the mid-seventeenth century. Maire Kennedy has demonstrated that, by the 1740s, they had become, as they were elsewhere in Europe, social centers—for men only. Several in Dublin had also, and importantly for present purposes, become hubs for printing and bookselling. For example, Defoe's friend and colleague John Dunton had held book auctions at Dick's coffeehouse on Skinner Row as early as the 1690s. Dunton described the establishment and its proprietor, Richard Pue, in *The Dublin Scuffle* (1699). Pue, "a witty and ingenious man . . . has a peculiar knack at bantering, and will make rhymes to any thing." A wordsmith, a linguistic bartender, was serving coffee.[6] Bacon's establishment, which he acquired when he married the widow who owned it, was strategically located: near the Custom

House and Essex Quay on the Liffey. Coastal and oceangoing ships tied up at Essex Quay. Across Essex Street from his coffeehouse was the Smock Alley Theatre, Dublin's first commercial stage, founded in 1662. In this arena, Bacon was associated every day with the world of commerce and trade, and that of entertainment, and with the people who made those worlds work: sea captains and stage managers; customs inspectors and customers; and actors, political and dramatic. All his long life, Thomas Bacon showed marked aptitude in getting along with the people he met, an aptitude no doubt refined when he brewed his coffee and sold his books on Essex Street. It was an aptitude he would need in Maryland.

Dublin was not a backwater, though many Londoners then and since have consigned it to that category. For example, in March 1742, Handel's *Messiah* received its world premiere in Dublin, with the composer conducting and Thomas Bacon in the audience listening. As he reported on April 17 in the *Dublin Mercury*, which he owned and edited, "Words are wanting to express the most exquisite Delight it afforded to the admiring crowded Audience, the sublime, the grand, and the tender, adapted to the most elevated, majestic, and moving Words."[7] At some point, perhaps during this period, Bacon learned to play the violin well, and to compose music. Music would be a solace, later, and an aid to his endeavors. In the serious, or non-entertainment category, Bacon was not idle. He wrote and published *A Compleat System of the Revenue of Ireland* (1737). He was fully capable, as he was to demonstrate in Maryland, of publishing long, complex works. By the summer of 1742, he had for a while edited and published the official government newspaper, the *Dublin Gazette*, like his fellow Dubliner Richard Steele, who had published the similar *London Gazette* at the beginning of his own career in letters. Bacon was selling books and pamphlets, writing, editing, and publishing. Then everything changed.

Was it a matter, as has usually been assumed, of his business suffering and his consequently turning to formal religion? Or was it perhaps the other way around, that he became interested in formal religion, and his business took second place? Who is to know? At any rate, a gene for business did run in the Bacon family blood: his brother Anthony later made, as one says in the twenty-first century and allowing for inflation, billions in London. By the next summer, of 1743, Thomas Bacon, with publishing behind him, was on the Isle of Man, studying theology with the Right Reverend Thomas Wilson, bishop of Sodor and Man. The instructor and his subject matter are of particular significance because Wilson, in his tiny diocese, was a zealous recruiter of clergy for overseas service and, in his capacity as a leader of the SPCK in London, exercised his influence in matters of printing and publishing. For example, on March 12, 1744/45, Wilson chaired the general meeting of the SPCK at which John Oliver was named the society's printer. Oliver would later publish many of Bacon's sermons for circulation by the society.[8]

Bacon's brother Anthony, who had taken his bachelor's degree at Trinity College, Dublin, in 1739, was by 1744 already fostering his economic aptitude as a merchant in Maryland, with success.[9] One guesses that Thomas sought assignment in that colony because his brother was there. At any rate, ordained as a priest by Bishop Wilson in March 1745, Bacon sailed for his new position that summer, accompanied by his wife and his son John, known as Jacky. His post was as curate of St. Peter's, Talbot County; the family was to live in Oxford, Maryland, which was in every respect a true backwater, an isolated hamlet on the eastern shore. Gazing across the silent Chesapeake Bay, Bacon must sometimes have asked himself what he had done.

But Thomas Bacon was not one for idle meditation. In the summer of his arrival, the Tuesday Club of Annapolis had its initial meeting at the home of Dr. Alexander Hamilton, its founder, an ambitious Scot physician who was determined to induce some intellectual ferment in the sleepy, provincial capital. At its twenty-fifth meeting in September of that year, 1745, the club's minutes reveal that "the Reverend Mr. Thomas Bacon, Being Invited to the Society, entertained them agreeably with Instrumental music on the violin"—Handel, perhaps?—"and was by the Society admitted an Honorary member."[10] Honorary, because he came from across the bay, and membership in the beginning years was for Annapolitans. Six years later, Bacon engineered creation of an affiliate on his side of the water "under the name of the worshipful Eastern Shore Triumvirate."

No doubt the musical activities of the club were pleasant for Bacon, but one guesses that he sought membership so as to become acquainted with some of the intellectual leadership of the colony. Elaine Breslaw has pointed out in her edition of the club records that the people who attended meetings, as members and guests, in its eleven-year existence "came from all corners of the British Empire and represented a variety of social classes."[11] Significantly, members of both the proprietary Court and anti-proprietary Country political parties met amiably at the club. Jonas Green, bookseller and current publisher of the *Maryland Gazette*, was a regular, specializing in comic verse. The club's membership variety was the reason, I would argue, that Bacon sought and maintained affiliation with the organization. He required advice and support from different sources to achieve his primary objective: increasing education in a province that, he saw, sorely needed it. Music was good, but education was essential.

Contacts—valuable contacts—in Annapolis, and work to do at home. Quite soon, to the consternation of some of his parishioners, he addressed the education of slaves. He argued that slaves should be introduced to Christianity, which involved either reading the sacred texts or having the texts read to them, just as had been the case in the early Christian communities of the Mediterranean. In a sermon directed to the slaves and, of course, over their heads to their masters and to the general public, Bacon referred his listeners to the Epistle to the Ephesians, which was aimed at similar congregations of slave and master. Bacon took an ingenious, even audacious tack: since every person, slave or free over the age of sixteen, paid a poll tax with his or her labor, he argued that every person was entitled to instruction. Each slave "pays as much as the Master he belongs to, and, consequently [has] an equal Right to Instruction with their Owners."[12] One can almost hear murmurs from some of the congregation: "Now the Parson has gone too far!" But Bacon was determined. He attempted to explain this process to the slaves, he wrote, "as Opportunity offers, at the Funerals several of which I had attended, and to such small Congregations as their Marriages have brought together, as well as at my own House, on Sunday, and other Evenings, when those in the Neighbourhood come in." But, he noted, all the families, slave and free, were too scattered in rural Maryland for easy association: what was needed was a school, or schools, for the area.

Bacon as Educator

Bacon was by no means alone in his desire to form schools in the Chesapeake area. Antonio Bly has recently documented that, in 1723, a group of Virginia slaves wrote the bishop of London (who supervised the Anglican Church in North America), asking him to put their children "to Scool and Larnd to Reed through the Bybell." A number of priests, with the bishop's encouragement, complied.[13] Anglican priests who came out under the auspices of Dr. Bray were encouraged and expected to educate, not least because Bray often sent parochial libraries with them, modest library collections designed to be read by the parishioners and used in parish schools. Some of these libraries are in the possession of the parishes to this day. But Bacon appears to be among the first to educate in Maryland, or at least so he believed. In a sermon delivered at St. Peter's on October 14, 1750, he referred to a general meeting held there the previous month at which trustees were elected and funds gathered for a charity working school "for the Maintenance and Education of Orphans, Poor Children, and Negro Slaves." This, he says, would be "the first Attempt of the Kind in this Province." He tells the parishioners of similar charity schools in Britain and reminds them of their blessings: "We are indeed, my Brethren, by God's Blessing, in Possession of a very plenteous Land—We ought therefore to shew our Thankfulness."[14]

He was drawing, however, not solely on the parishioners of St. Peter's but on prominent Marylanders from elsewhere, as well. John Goldsborough and Matthew Tilghman were trustees of the enterprise, men bearing distinguished surnames still well known in Annapolis and vicinity. Dr. Andrew Hamilton, he of the Tuesday Club, ponied up two pieces of eight—the Spanish silver coin, or peso, that was standard currency along the American coast. Bacon was also advertising the school in his friend Jonas Greene's *Maryland Gazette*. He likewise announced his plans and sought contributions from Virginians in Williamsburg's *Virginia Gazette* in July 1751 and, by October, was able to report in the paper that payments were arriving. By May 1755, the building was complete, a schoolmaster hired, and classes began. Over the years, financial problems developed, and this school may have been one of the two Bacon was authorized to oversee in 1760 by Dr. Bray's Associates. It would thereby come directly under the Associates' care. Bacon stood well with the proprietor and his family, Lord Baltimore and the Calverts, and with the proprietary political party. He was named domestic chaplain to the proprietor in 1754, perhaps through Bishop Wilson's influence. But Bacon, then and always, was his own man. He was to demonstrate this in the edition of the laws of Maryland, a large project he determined to undertake sometime in the early 1750s.

In a real sense, the project was an act of literacy: writing and printing the laws that existed for most Marylanders only in the abstract—except when they violated one. Laws in colonial America were a continuing problem. Did they consist of the laws of Great Britain? Some British laws applied or were assumed to apply to the colonies: that forbidding premeditated murder, for example. But other British laws did not: the laws of copyright did not apply, as colonists such as Jonas Green were learning. Or was it the laws passed by the assemblies of the several colonies, excluding of course those so-called private laws passed at the specific request of petitioners? Even this seemingly simple definition had complications. In Maryland, some laws were held to be passed by the General Assembly under pressure, for the benefit of the proprietor and his interests rather than the interests of the citizenry as a whole.[15] So the anti-proprietary partisans held, and when Bacon proposed to publish all the extant laws, these partisans were able to prevent the General Assembly from supporting financially the enterprise. Either print the laws we like, they argued, or do not print at all. Bacon believed that his collection should be comprehensive and was not deterred by the Assembly's inaction: he began raising funds for the private printing of the laws with, as will be seen, spectacular results.

Meanwhile, Bacon was conducting the spiritual life of his parish, supervising the local school, and making music with his friend Henry Callister—pronounced "Collister," we are told by an early history of Talbot County. Callister, a transplanted Manxman, was a resident of Talbot County.[16] Presumably Bishop Wilson had sent word of Bacon's arrival, for Callister had met Bacon soon after he got there and judged him, in a letter to a friend back home, to be "a very agreeable companion, and a sober and learned man." Three years later, Callister wrote his brother Ewan on the Isle of Man that Bacon was held "in great esteem with every man from the Governor to the Parish Clerk.... I have sent you enclosed a couple of his minuets, which are excellent."[17] This had been tobacco country, and clergy salaries, among others, were still denominated in pounds of tobacco. Here and elsewhere in the colony, different crops had been entering the financial equation; in the 1750s, wheat was supplanting tobacco as the principal export in Talbot County. But in those years, Bacon had more urgent, personal concerns than surveying crop production. Maryland and the other colonies were to be engaged in the largest war ever seen to that time on the North American continent, and Bacon was involved very personally. What in Europe is called the Seven Years' War came to be known in North America as the French and Indian War. Tensions in the colonies were bubbling toward confrontation in the early 1750s. Young George Washington, not yet twenty-one, was named an adjutant of the colonial militia in Virginia on the death of his brother Lawrence, who had held the post. It bore the titular rank of major when he took the oath in February 1753. He was already a qualified and practicing surveyor.

From the global perspective, the approaching conflicts, which would spread around the world, were part of the struggle among Spain, France, and Britain for control of territories each desired. From the English colonists' point of view in 1754, the threat appeared to come from French Canada, which was reaching toward the areas beyond the Appalachian Mountains that the colonists regarded as theirs, and which Washington had recently been surveying. The French had American Indian allies of considerable military skill, and good troops of their own.[18] The colonies began raising volunteers to augment whatever British troops became available, and one of the early volunteers, like George Washington, was John ("Jacky") Bacon. By September 1754, he was in Annapolis, an officer on duty, and attended there a session of the Tuesday Club on the September 24, as "Champion of the Eastern Shore Triumvirate." The champion—the title, of course, refers to the traditional sovereign's representative in war—was reprimanded, the minutes tell us, because he did not "rise and make obeisance to the Chair.—Mr. Bacon excused himself for this behavior, alleging that he had been on guard all night, and watching the Guard house, with the recruits, and was not really able to Support himself long on his legs. His honor was pleased to excuse him."[19]

That week, young Bacon marched away from Annapolis with his company, almost certainly under orders to join Colonel Washington, who had received his own orders on September 15 to proceed to the northwest, in the direction of the French headquarters at Fort Duquesne, now Pittsburgh. Washington had already won his first combat victory out there in the wilderness, and suffered his first combat defeat earlier in the year. It is of some historical interest that, a quarter century later, Maryland troops would be following Washington again, as he led the Maryland Line to their rendezvous with history at Brooklyn Heights.

Jacky Bacon would not be among them, although he was about Washington's age. Washington, this time, returned to Williamsburg and the next year would be serving in Braddock's disastrous campaign and defeat. Later, in the winter of 1754–1755, at some disputed barricade near Fort Cumberland (what is now Cumberland, Maryland), Jacky was killed and scalped. (Braddock himself would offer the large sum of five pounds sterling to any of his troops who brought back an enemy scalp.) In one of those ironies with which life abounds, a shipload of

Acadians, some of those French Canadians whom Jacky had died fighting, were swept ashore in rural Maryland, on their way to exile in, one supposes, Louisiana. Thomas Bacon showed them kindness that, according to Lawrence Wroth writing in Maryland in 1922, is "remembered to the present day."[20]

Bacon as Editor

Jacky's death appears, if anything, to have galvanized his father into continued action on printing the laws of the colony. In some respects, the undertaking seems to have been a kind of attempted compensation, a turning away from his feelings no matter what. He wrote Callister in March 1757: "I would not write to you on such a scrap of Paper, if I had plenty as formerly; but the Man without Money or Credit must do as he can. Musick is departed & gone into another World from me. The Laws are my only Employment and Amusement, yet they are a dry sort of stuff and sometimes apt to stick in the Throat."[21] Lawrence Wroth, bibliographer of Maryland and later director of the John Carter Brown Library, has judged Bacon's work in these terms: it "formed the most elaborate and laborious piece of editorial work until that time undertaken in America. A painstaking, scholarly fellow, he copied his versions of the laws whenever possible from the originals in the office of the Provincial Secretary, and with the most painful labor he rescued the titles of many laws not otherwise recorded from the manuscript House journals."[22]

Having been rebuffed, as we have seen, by the General Assembly, Governor Sharpe undertook to finance the printing by subscription. Lord Baltimore gave one hundred pounds sterling, and Governor Sharpe led off the Maryland contributors with one hundred pounds local currency—presumably making the point that this was a local, not a London-ordered, operation. Many distinguished colonists followed with fifty pounds currency: Stephen Bordley, Thomas Johnson, and both Charles Carroll of Carrollton and Charles Carroll of Annapolis. These are all of the group referred to by Trevor Burnard as "Creole" gentlemen: native-born rich men who had made their money on this side of the water.[23]

This, as well as being a legal landmark, was a beautiful piece of bookmaking: a massive folio, with generous margins. One can imagine Bacon, eminently qualified as he was to work on folio production, looking over the shoulder of Jonas Green, a skilled author of light verse and also a master printer who did the actual manufacturing. An enclosed sheet of highly detailed errata may have been Bacon's very last contribution to the book, as if to say, we are going to get this one right. They did: Wroth writes of its "quiet splendor, a mellow and harmonious blending of paper and types which was not surpassed in any book printed in colonial America."[24]

Bacon's book, in a sense, had a life longer than one would expect of a collection of colonial laws, not ending a decade later with the American Revolution.

As Jeffrey K. Sawyer has written, delegates to Maryland's constitutional convention in 1776 adopted Article 3 of their Declaration of Rights, which "strongly affirmed a general principle of legal continuity with the colonial past using explicit language to define the criteria for the continuing authority of the common law (with a particular emphasis on trial by jury) and British statutes." On the drafting committee of Article 3 were both Charles Carrolls and Mathew Tilghman, Bacon's old friend, three of the Creole gentlemen who had contributed cash to printing Bacon's *Laws of Maryland* and received the massive volume.[25]

Posthumous Influence

By then, Bacon himself was no longer alive to enjoy the continuing usefulness of his contribution to legal literacy. From his arrival in 1745 until his death in 1768, Bacon had worked hard at his chosen vocation. All these years, Thomas Bacon was, of course, principally engaged in conducting the life of a parish: baptisms, marriages, funerals, worship services, day-to-day advice, help, and prayer. The evidence indicates that he excelled at his profession: in late 1758 or 1759, Bacon was appointed to the rectorship of All Saints Parish, Frederick, a large congregation in one of the most rapidly developing areas of the colony. Bacon participated in that development: for example, he worked at opening the Potomac River for navigation from the Great Falls, at what is now Georgetown, to Fort Cumberland (where Jacky had met his end). He looked after the parish school, as he had that of St. Peter's. In May 1768 he was elected to membership in the American Philosophical Society, Benjamin Franklin's creation.[26] A few days later, Bacon died. One hopes that news of the election reached him before his death. In June, the *Maryland Gazette* wrote of him: "His humane, benevolent Disposition and amiable Deportment, gained him the Love and Esteem of all his Parishioners. He was likewise an affectionate Husband, a tender Parent, a kind Master, and a most agreeable Companion; which renders his Death not only a loss to his Acquaintances, but to Society in general."[27]

A fine human being but what, one must ask, does this have to do with literacy? Perhaps more than appears on first reflection. The schools he founded and supervised, along with the other schools in the region, were having an effect at all levels of society with the spread of literacy. Lawyers, of course, had to know how to read and write. But these skills were useful for others as well: artisans, tradesmen, and farmers could keep their own records and also discern their place in those laws that Bacon collected. Edmund Burke, who knew the colonists well, having served as colonial agent for New York, pointed out in his great speech in March 1775 this last activity: all "who read, and most do read, endeavour to obtain some smattering in" the law.[28]

But, one might object, these are generalizations. If most did read, perhaps they learned to do so in the old country and passed the custom along to their children.

Literacy, as noted earlier, is difficult to discuss in specific cases. Take, as an example, a boy born into slavery about 1818 in Talbot County, Maryland, the very county to which Bacon had first come and where he started the first school. This boy, Frederick Augustus Washington Bailey, never had access to a school and did not know how to read when he was sent to Baltimore as the property of a white couple there. The mistress taught him the alphabet and was encouraging him to read until her husband directed that she stop. But as the boy later wrote:

> The first step had been taken. Mistress, in teaching me the alphabet had given me the *inch*, and no precaution could prevent me from taking the *ell*. . . . The plan which I adopted, and the one by which I was most successful, was that of making friends of all the little white boys whom I met in the street. As many of these as I could, I converted into teachers. With their kindly aid . . . I finally succeeded in learning to read. When I was sent to errands, I always took my book with me.[29]

The boy grew up and later escaped across the Mason-Dixon Line to freedom. Changing his name to Frederick Douglass, he, of course, became one of the leaders of the abolitionist movement, famous for his speeches but especially for his writings. His *Narrative of the Life of Frederick Douglass* (1845) may be the finest slave autobiography ever published. Here is a man who, in his own person, exemplified the juxtaposition of literacy and leadership. Those South Carolina and Virginia slaveholders had been correct in their fears. Here was a slave who learned to read, rebelled, freed himself, and spent the rest of his life assisting others to freedom and self-realization. But literacy, as I have written previously, is difficult to discuss. Anna, Douglass's devoted wife for forty-four years and the mother of his children, never learned to read or write.

NOTES

1. Harry Y. Gamble, *Books and Readers in the Early Church: A History of Early Christian Texts* (New Haven, CT: Yale University Press, 1995), 9.

2. Fred Witzig, "Beyond Expectation: How Charles Town's 'Pious and Well-Disposed Christians' Changed Their Minds about Slave Education during the Great Awakening," *South Carolina Historical Magazine* 114 (October 2013): 286–315.

3. Scholarship on Bray is voluminous. The standard biography is H. P. Thompson, *Thomas Bray* (London: Society for Promoting Christian Knowledge, 1954). For a recent overview, see Leonard Cowie, "Bray, Thomas (bap. 1658, d. 1730)," in *Oxford Dictionary of National Biography*, ed. H.C.G. Matthew and Brian Harrison (Oxford: Oxford University Press, 2004), accessed July 16, 2021, https://doi.org/10.1093/ref:odnb/3296. The Bray quotation comes from an unnumbered page in the prefatory letter to his *Bibliotecha Parochialis: or, A scheme of such theological heads both general and particular, as are more peculiarly requisite to be well studied by every pastor of a parish* (London: Printed for Robert Clavel, and are to be sold by John North, bookseller in Dublin, 1697), available at *EEBO*, http://name.umdl.umich.edu/B08553.0001.001.

4. See, e.g., James B. Bell, *The Imperial Origins of the King's Church in Early America, 1607–1783* (New York: Palgrave Macmillan, 2004).

5. The fullest treatment is still that of J. A. Leo Lemay in *Men of Letters in Colonial Maryland* (Knoxville: University of Tennessee Press, 1972), 313–342, 382–387. Recent information on Bacon in Dublin is in M[ary] Pollard, *A Dictionary of the Dublin Book Trade, 1550–1800* (Cambridge: Cambridge University Press for the Bibliographical Society, 2000), s.v. Bacon, Thomas.

6. Dunton as quoted in Maire Kennedy, "Dublin's Coffee Houses of the Eighteenth Century," *Dublin Historical Record* 63 (Spring 2010): 29–38.

7. As quoted in Lemay, *Men of Letters*, 316.

8. SPCK Ms. A1: Minutes of General Meeting, 20 (1743–1746), Minutes of 12 March 1744/45, Cambridge University Library.

9. For information about Anthony's later career, see L. B. Namier, "Anthony Bacon, M.P., an Eighteenth-Century Merchant," *Journal of Economic and Business History* 2 (1929–1930): 20–70.

10. Elaine G. Breslaw, ed., *Records of the Tuesday Club of Annapolis 1745–56* (Urbana: University of Illinois Press, 1988), 19.

11. Breslaw, xiii.

12. *Two Sermons, Preached to a Congregation of Black Slaves, at the Parish Church of S.P., in the Province of Maryland, by an American Pastor* (London: John Oliver [for the SPCK], 1749).

13. Antonio T. Bly, "'Reed through the Bybell': Slave Education in Early Virginia," *Book History* 16 (2013): 5.

14. *A Sermon Preached at the Parish Church of St. Peters, Talbot County, Maryland, on Sunday, the 14th of October* . . . (London: John Oliver [for the SPCK], 1751), 19, 21.

15. For a recent, lucid discussion of these problems, see Jeffrey K. Sawyer, "The Rhetoric and Reality of English Law in Colonial Maryland–Part II, 1689–1732," *Maryland Historical Magazine* 109 (Spring 2014): 81–95.

16. Oswald Tilghman, *History of Talbot County Maryland 1661–1861* (Easton: n.p., 1915), 1:83.

17. Tilghman, 1:276, 279.

18. Information on Washington and the campaigns of 1754–1755 derived from Douglas Southall Freeman, *George Washington; A Biography*, vols. 1 and 2, *Young Washington* (New York: Scribner's, 1948).

19. Breslaw, *Records of the Tuesday Club*, 493.

20. Lawrence C. Wroth, *A History of Printing in Colonial Maryland, 1686–1776* (Baltimore: Typothetae of Baltimore, 1922), 96.

21. As quoted in Wroth, 99.

22. Wroth, 105.

23. Trevor Burnard, *Creole Gentlemen: The Maryland Elite 1691–1776* (New York: Routledge, 2002).

24. Wroth, *History of Printing*, 110.

25. Jeffrey K. Sawyer, "English Law and American Democracy in the Revolutionary Republic: Maryland, 1776–1822," *Maryland Historical Magazine* 108 (Fall 2013): 261, 264.

26. Records of the Society, quoted in Lemay, *Men of Letters*, 342.

27. Issue of June 9, 1768, quoted in Wroth, *History of Printing*, 9

28. *Speech of Edmund Burke, Esq., On Moving His Resolutions for Conciliation with the Colonies, March 22nd 1775*, in *Edmund Burke: Pre-Revolutionary Writings*, ed. Ian Harris (Cambridge: Cambridge University Press, 1993), 225.

29. David W. Blight, ed., *Narrative of the Life of Frederick Douglass*, 2nd ed. (Boston: Bedford/St. Martin's Press, 2003), 66–67.

CHAPTER 13

The World of *The World*

Annibel Jenkins

Editors' note: A study of an eighteenth-century London newspaper called *The World* was Annibel Jenkins's last scholarly project. She called it her "biography of a newspaper." A portion of that project was delivered as a plenary address at the annual meeting of the Southeastern American Society for Eighteenth-Century Studies (SEASECS) in Athens, Georgia, in 2006. Both editors of this volume were present at that address. A manuscript draft of that project was kindly provided to the editors of this volume by Jenkins's nephew, Robert Peacock.

Annibel was an active scholar well into her eighties. Her last presentation, at the thirty-fourth SEASECS meeting in Auburn in 2008, was entitled "Kotzebüe, Two Playwrights and a Novelist: Inchbald, Plumptre, and Austen." Thereafter, Jenkins's declining health made it difficult for her to participate in subsequent conferences, but she continued to work on *The World* in her retirement. The full manuscript grew to over 80,000 and more than 350 pages. Much of the text, however, consists of notes, quotations unframed by context, and fragmented ideas. It would require a heavy editorial hand—indeed, a coauthor—to shape the full manuscript for publication. We have confined ourselves here to reconstructing and publishing the portion of the manuscript Jenkins chose to share with her colleagues at SEASECS 2006.

As received by the editors of this volume, the manuscript did not include any scholarly apparatus. The following text has been edited for clarity, and bibliographic and explanatory notes have been inserted as appropriate (all notes are the responsibility of the editors). In terms of the prose, we have employed a light hand; the direct address, the asides, and colloquial style capture Dr. Jenkins's voice. The author added an enormous amount of source material to the comments as delivered in 2006, as she was evidently in the process of expanding her SEASECS address into a larger work for publication. The editors have attempted to reconstruct Jenkins's comments as given in 2006. As such, we have excised interpolated material, much of which consisted of quotations and notes—the sources of which are unclear—and reordered the remaining paragraphs in the service of readability and strength of organization.

I would like to justify my selecting such an immense topic as *The World* by saying that I think discussions of poetry, of the theatre, of novels, and of social backgrounds in our scholarship are based on our world—*not* the world of the eighteenth century. Such an approach I find not to be acceptable. "The world" of the title of this study is *The World*, a newspaper published in London from 1787 to 1790; as a newspaper, it offers an invaluable source for at least some precise reality. That is, for three years in its pages, the life of London and its inhabitants was presented in great detail. And here, the facts the newspaper gives are supported by details and precise dates whereas, far too often, it seems to me, the examination of evidence—as for example on the subject of the theatres—covers too wide a span. Of more importance to us are the reports of Parliament, the reports of commerce, the reports of society, and those of the royal family, since these give us an understanding of the events that were actually happening in the years 1787–1790. Again, this precise dating gives us the details of an exact time that would be missing in a longer account. Since all of these reasons seem enough to examine at least one newspaper, I would like to prove my case by examining *The World*.

Perhaps it would seem a somewhat odd exercise to present a biography of a newspaper, especially one from the late eighteenth century, to readers in the twenty-first. We know, of course, there were no modern conveniences such as automobiles or paved roads—indeed, there were hardly any passable roads other than the post roads. Town houses were small and crowded or large and required servants; there was no plumbing, refrigeration, or electricity, and there were no telephones and no television. While we know these circumstances, we sometimes forget about them when we read about the great events—the War for American Independence or the French Revolution, for instance. But there were people, there were books—novels, poetry, plays; there was entertainment—music, theatre, sports, balls, receptions, masquerades; and there were sermons, speeches in Parliament, and pamphlets on every subject imaginable. Altogether, there was a world to engage our interest for its living at the moment, for the readers to follow the happenings from day to day and from year to year.

For the readers as it appeared every day, *The World* had information and commentary for forming opinions, providing information of events, and of people. For us, the opinions and information on people and events give us both an understanding of a time still a part of our past and an opportunity to meet people, participate in events, and become at least briefly a citizen in London in 1787. I think the people in *The World* include a great many who were very important then but who have not been introduced to us, since in our research we usually are introduced to those who have been remembered for their associations in our world. The people reported in *The World* were those who, living in 1787–1789, fashioned the events of the French Revolution, of the reigns of George IV and William IV, and of the nineteenth century.

The world of *The World* began one day in the fall of 1786 at the British Library, a lending library on the Strand that not only was much frequented by booklovers but also was a place to see and be seen, to talk of the theatre and politics as well as books. It was also famous for the nude figure of Apollo just outside. Perhaps famous is not the word, according to *The Times*:

IN ancient times when modesty prevailed
The female eye was not by vice assail'd:
A thought improper soon received a check,
Nor did Indecent words our phrases deck.
The Scene's now changed—immodesty's caress'
And that which shows least shame is liked the best.
E'en Music's GOD stark naked's made to stand
And have all modest females in the Strand.
May some kind artist, whom no vice bewitches
Give J. Bell's Pol a decent pair of breeches.[1]

The proprietor of the library was John Bell, a well-known London publisher, bookseller, and journalist who for years had been selling books in the Strand at the corner of Exeter exchange and, in 1769, at the British Library. At one time he had been a member of the group that published the *Morning Post or Cheap Daily Advertiser.* In 1773, he began publishing the acting editions of Shakespeare's plays in *Bell's British Theatre*, the editions coming out from 1773 until 1778, and in 1776, he began to publish *Poets of Great Britain*.

In June, Captain Edward Topham, being, Bell said, "casually at my house," learned of Bell's plan to begin a new journal. A plan was agreed upon to make Bell and Topham partners in the new undertaking.[2] Topham was the son of Francis Topham, judge of the Prerogative Court of York. Edward Topham was from an old and distinguished family in Yorkshire. His father died at fifty-eight, losing his son some agreements that would have promised him a career. It seems that one of these agreements was made with the Dean of York, who, finding that he did not wish to engage in a pamphlet war with the elder Topham, turned to Laurence Sterne, then a poor curate in the Chapter of York. The pamphlet Sterne produced was called *The Watchcoat*; afterward, Francis Topham wittily declared that he was responsible for Sterne's literary career.[3]

After being at Eton, Edward Topham went to Cambridge, but upon his father's death he left the university and went on the grand tour on the Continent. Returning to England, he toured Scotland, publishing an account of his travels there in *Letters from Edinburgh*—his first publication.[4] The next year, he went to London, secured a commission in the Horse Guards, and began to join enthusiastically in the life of London. He published a pamphlet against Burke's American policy and began to frequent the green rooms of Drury Lane, Covent Garden, and the Haymarket, where he soon became known to all the "smart set." Topham was as eccentric as anyone in London and his "set," his dress and his equipage as distinctive as any in London.

Before his venture with *The World*, Edward Topham had acquired an estate in Suffolk, where he was an active magistrate. He also promoted the new agricultural improvements. According to his friend Frederick Reynolds, "[Topham] drove a curricle, (constructed to a plan of his own) with four black horses splendidly caparisoned, and followed by two grooms in conspicuous liveries." His dress, Reynolds said, "consisted of a short scarlet coat, with large cut steel buttons; a very short white waistcoat, top-boots, and leather breeches so very short that half the day and one whole hand were entirely employed in raising them *en derriere* to avoid any awkward declension, *en avant*."[5]

Miles Peter Andrews was very close to Topham, and his part in *The World* was considerable. Andrews was quite wealthy, his fortune acquired by his contracts with the government for gunpowder. He, like everyone else, indulged in writing poetry for the papers. Many of the poems and prologues printed and reprinted in *The World* are his. Andrews and Topham appeared everywhere together. Indeed, it was reported "that they met every morning to form plans for distinguishing themselves by witty dialogues and mutual bon mots in the evening."[6] Andrews wrote a great many prologues and epilogues, especially for two of the most celebrated comics—Lewis and Mrs. Mattocks, who by their using them made him famous and quoted. Andrews, like Topham, was singular in his dress, appearing in public places, such as in the pleasure garden, Ranelagh, with sword and bag. He was quite outspoken and once was so directly critical at a private theatrical that he and Topham, who was with him, were not invited to stay for the party afterward.

As the chief editor for *The World*, Topham chose Charles Este, who had been educated for the church. Although for a while Este devoted himself to his calling, he was also enamored with the stage and became intimate with several of the leading actors of the time. He began to write for *The Public Advertiser*. According to one commentator, "His learning and extensive reading enabled him to supply an abundance of illustrative quotations, classical and modern. There was always point, humor, and judgment in his theatrical decisions."[7]

Another close friend of Topham's was Robert Merry, who was in Italy when *The World* began. Something of a poet, he was to become an important contributor of poetry to the paper. He signed his poems with his poetry name, Della Crusca. Another slightly younger friend, Fredrick Reynolds, a playwright, completed the circle—that is, the men in the circle. Elizabeth Inchbald was a close friend of Topham and Mary Wells, and, if we may take her pocketbook diaries as a record, Inchbald, too, helped with the paragraphs while, in turn, *The World* praised her plays. These friends who contributed to the paper all knew each other, all talked together, and all appeared in the paper in one way or another. They were all interested in the theatres, the social events, and the political events that were reported daily, especially because they knew personally many of the people reported about in the political, literary, social, and entertainment world—that is, the world within *The World*.

The first issue of *The World* came out in January 1787; it was immediately very successful. The full title, *The World and Fashionable Advertiser*, was followed by the date and, on the far right, the price, threepence. Each issue consisted of four pages, with four columns on a page. Some features were repeated in every issue; the playbills for the theatres and the opera were always included, along with a report of the plays as they were presented. *The World* knew all the theatre people, and information and gossip about them was included in every issue. James Boaden, in his *Memoirs of Kemble*, found "the chief features of [*The World*] were a more marked reflexion of literary and fashionable existence, than had been displayed by other papers of the day. With an intimate knowledge of both its conductors, I can safely say that much was to be expected from their powers of mind, more from their experience of actual life. They assumed a style utterly unknown in English literature. It seemed always to hint rather than discuss, and to lighten rather than shine. They were at all times entertaining and often instructive."[8] I believe anyone reading *The World* will agree, and indeed this "more marked reflexion of literary and fashionable existence" is one of the most important features of the paper.

When *The World* was proposed, Topham was living with Mary "Becky" Wells and their two daughters. From the beginning, there were those who maintained that Topham used the paper to promote Wells's career on the stage. Any real examination of the situation, however, makes very clear that this was not the case, that, in fact, from the beginning she was an important part of the paper's organization. It was Wells who did the "paragraphs," and she helped handle the business on a day-to-day basis while Topham remained in the country attending to his estate. Wells (née Davies) was born in Birmingham in 1762; her father, Thomas Davies, was a woodcarver and gilder who had been commissioned by Garrick to make a box from the celebrated mulberry tree at Stratford. Upon the death of Wells's father when she was six, her mother opened a tavern. Richard Yates, the manager of the Birmingham theatre, appears to have met young Mary at the tavern and encouraged her to become an actress. At first, she had such severe stage fright that it was doubtful she would succeed, but she had a nice voice and gradually became more at ease. At Birmingham, Mary Wells (billed as Miss Davies) played the Duke of York in *Richard III*. At Gloucester, she played Juliet to the Romeo of an actor named Ezra Wells. They were married at St. Chad's in

Shrewsbury. Hardly had the ceremony been completed when Ezra Wells ran away with one of the bridesmaids. In the years afterward, Mary continued to use the Wells name. In the summer of 1781, Mary Wells came to London to act at the Haymarket.

Wells, called Becky or Cowslip from her part in John O'Keeffe's play *The Agreeable Surprise*, had been in a production of *The Beggar's Opera* when the men and the women played reverse roles—Wells had been Macheath, and her friend Elizabeth Inchbald played Grub. Topham had seen the production and was immediately attracted to Wells. Topham's farce *The Fool*, in which Wells played a part, also brought her to the author's attention. Topham began their association by asking Wells to come to rehearse the prologue at his place.[9] By all accounts Wells was beautiful and was celebrated for her clever imitations of various stage figures. Topham, who could never tolerate dull people, frequently entertained where she was a part of the witty conversation.

Both as entertainment and as business, the theatres were reported in every issue of *The World*. There were announcements of the programs, with listings of the players. The program would also have announced the mainpiece, the afterpiece, the prelude, the epilogue, and the music and dance to be a part of the entertainment for the evening. No doubt, as in our world of "stars," some readers would follow their favorite performers. And since the theatres operated in repertory, no doubt familiar plays would attract good audiences. As for the playwrights, those who understood the way the audience required certain patterns were the ones who were successful, becoming professionals and thereby making money. One such playwright was Elizabeth Inchbald, who, as a friend of Mrs. Wells—Cowslip—helped with the copy and no doubt giving views of the theatres, since both she and Wells were still acting. Both of them knew the actors and actresses and the management of the theatres, and they were familiar with the gossip that went on as well as the facts and opinions to which the public had access. Moreover, Topham, Reynolds, Anderson, and Merry all had written for the stage; it is not surprising that information, gossip, opinions, and stage business filled the paper.

While, as mentioned earlier, it is not true that Topham started *The World* to promote Wells's career, it is true that *The World* was filled with news—views—about the theatres. In 1787, Garrick was no longer the leading figure in the theatre, for he had died in 1779; I am always surprised at how frequently the discussion of the eighteenth-century theatre stops with Garrick's death. Sheridan had followed Garrick in conducting Drury Lane, but in 1788 Sheridan persuaded John Philip Kemble to take over the management at Drury Lane, since Sheridan's role in Parliament meant he no longer had the time or the interest to conduct the theatre. The reports of the theatres in *The World* are given day by day with current information and opinion. The daily report of the performances made a record not only of the plays and actors but also of the audience reactions, the stage sets, the costumes, and the people in the audience. *The World* reported the events at the theatres quite aside from the action on the stage. Frequently those who attended were identified, especially when the play was one the king "commanded." *The World* also reported about the financial situations of the theatres, the salaries of the players, and the financial success or lack of success of new plays in such a way that players and proprietors had few secrets. The details of these reports as they were presented make a record of audiences, performers, and plays in a contemporary setting not to be realized in later histories.

One of the subjects in 1787–1788 was John Palmer's attempt to establish a new theatre. Palmer was one of the leading players at Drury Lane, said to be the highest-paid member of the company, but he was not satisfied; he wanted his own company to direct and also wanted to make even more money. He thought he had a way to evade the Licensing Act by establishing a theatre in the West End. By 1785, he thought he had permission, and on December 26, 1785, the cornerstone of his new building was laid. But the building itself could not be completed for lack of some £2,000 and various problems about the construction. From the beginning, *The World* argued on his behalf. Palmer called his playhouse the Royalty. He completed the building, hired a cast, and announced the first performance. The other three proprietors of the patent theatres objected vehemently, threatening to take him and the players to court after the first performance. These proprietors—Thomas Harris, Covent Garden; Thomas Linley, Drury Lane; and George Colman, the Haymarket—were unwilling to give up or share their government monopoly. The opening of the Royalty, on June 20, 1787, was filled with people come to see Shakespeare's *As You Like It*.[10]

In spite of Palmer's efforts, those of his friends, and the support of *The World*, Palmer was not allowed to produce plays; instead, for more than a year he presented a variety of acts that *The World* reported and promoted. One fellow named Hall, "Carpenter and Scene Shifter to Covent-Garden Theatre," was accused by *The World* of being an informer for Covent Garden; Hall apparently attended performances at the Royalty and reported back to Harris: "You confessed, that a manager, as he calls himself, employed you, and you had not yet received any reward; two shillings only being given you to pay for a seat among men of more honesty than common informers, yourself excepted. . . . I take it for granted, that your illustrious Employer gave you privately the cue, as to the person against whom you were to inform."[11] The playbills for these performances appeared along with the others until the spring of 1788, when Palmer, evidently in debt for his building, gave up. For those of us interested in theatre history, *The World*'s support of the Royalty and the whole problem of monopoly are of great interest.

One of the special pleasures of reading the daily news for *The World*'s readers—and for us—are the reports of what was playing at Drury Lane or Covent Garden or when there would be a balloon ascent or what opera was to be played at the King's Theatre: "Last Thursday Mr. Blanchard made his twenty-second ascension with great success. This skilful aerial navigator took his departure from the citadel, and descended in the province of Lexembourg, in a meadow near Neaux, seven leagues from hence. A great concourse of people were present at this experiment. The day before yesterday Mr. Blanchard returned to this city, and appeared at the comedy in the evening, when he was highly congratulated by the audience."[12] This report reminded readers no doubt of the other times Blanchard had ascended and, for patrons of the theatre, reminded them of Inchbald's *The Mogul Tale*, a play about a balloon and what might happen, since the balloon could not be precisely given direction but simply went wherever the winds blew it. Her play was presented at the Haymarket in the summer of 1784 before any balloon ascension in London. By 1787 and the time of *The World*, such ascensions had become a regular part of summer entertainment both in England and in France.

The plays presented during the years of *The World* had more than entertainment value; most of them had political comments to make that would have been recognized by the newspaper's readers. For example, Inchbald's play *Such Things Are*, presented on February 10, 1787, at the beginning of the Hastings trial, suggested to the audience people and situations that were current; the setting, the characters, and the events all reflect the immediate discussions in the newspapers and in Parliament, and actual important contemporaries. Haswell, the chief character, is based on John Howard, the prison reformer who was known all over the world and at this time was in England. The setting, while not directly in India, is in Sumatra, and the mention of the Dutch envoy as a place for social gatherings reminded the audience that the Dutch had been rivals of the English since the sixteenth century in seeking to control commerce on the high seas. In 1787, the English were far behind in trading for tea and porcelain, as they were far behind in discovering the method for making porcelain. In fact, one of the accomplishments of Hastings's time in India was the regulation of trading to favor the government.

Three of the characters in the play illustrate another situation of the current interest in Hasting and India. Sir Luke had gone to make his fortune, and his wife had gone to find a husband. Throughout the play their relationship is a parody of such a situation. The situation of women who went to India to seek a husband was quite a familiar one to Inchbald's audience. In fact, she herself once considered doing so. Another of the characters, Twineall, appears to seek a fortune, a reminder to the audience of the hundreds of young men who had gone to India to do so and, being successful, returned to England to become wealthy country gentlemen and—by their own estimation at least—establish belonging in the gentry. Inchbald's play is only one of many plays, both new and old, that comment on the political and social world documented in the pages of *The World*. Sheridan, now one of the most prominent of those conducting the Hastings trial, had used his plays to make comments about current affairs, and while during the years of *The World* he did not write any new ones, his *School for Scandal* and *The Duenna* were among the most frequently performed plays in England between 1776 and 1800.

While society and entertainment were very important features of *The World*, the reports from Parliament and the various views the paper entertained made it an important voice in political circles. This is especially interesting because the paper reported the first arguments in the Hasting' trial. In fact, the beginning of the Hastings trial was recounted in the weeks and months of 1787 along with the essays and paper's views about Hastings, Sheridan, Burke, Pitt, and those who favored Hastings and those who did not. Along with reporting the actual events, *The World* was full of opinions not only of the events in the daily sessions but of the speakers. One report was followed by a declaration of *The World*'s policy: "We hope—and at the close of this Cause for the Season, we hold it right so to hope—that in giving this Trial, we have given it without Prejudice or Predilection. For with us, Politics are compatible with Manners: Where there are Talents, who should be warped by Party? This Paper shall be free; and with no attachment, but to Excellence: no preference but for Truth, shall Praise, single and sincere, wherever PRAISE is Due."[13] The policy of *The World* clearly placed it in the center between the Tories and the Whigs, and as time went by and events changed, it is significant to remember that the politics of the French and their monarchy would change dramatically. The year 1789, the last in which *The World* was published, was the beginning of the French Revolution—indeed, July 14 saw the destruction of the Bastille. With the drama of the French Revolution, *The World* changed: Bell began a new paper of his own; Topham joined the other newspapers controlled by the establishment and eventually accepted a subsidy from the government. The change in the newspapers was an important political matter, and for Pitt and the government to regulate the whole newspaper industry was a difficult task.

NOTES

1. "Poetry," *The* [London] *Times*, January 1, 1789, 3. This same passage is cited in Daniel Robinson's *The Poetry of Mary Robinson: Form and Fame* (New York: Palgrave Macmillan, 2011), 37. Jenkins would not have been aware of Robinson's volume, given that this portion of her manuscript was read aloud at SEASECS in 2006.

2. Stanley Morison, *John Bell, 1745–1831: A Memoir* (Cambridge: Cambridge University Press, 1930), 7.

3. Topham's witticism is recorded in Frederick Reynolds, *The Life and Times of Frederick Reynolds*, vol. 1 (London: Colburn, 1826), 107. It is unclear if Jenkins is citing the London edition or the Philadelphia edition (Carey and Lee, 1826).

4. Edward Topham, *Letters from Edinburgh Written in the Years 1774 and 1775 Containing Some Observations on the Diversions, Customs, Manners, and Laws, of the Scotch Nation, During a Six Months Residence in Edinburgh* (London: J. Dodsley, 1776).

5. Frederick Reynolds, *The Life and Times of Frederick Reynolds*, vol. 2 (London: H. Colburn, 1827), 39.

6. John Taylor, *Records of My Life: In Two Volumes*, vol. 2. (London: Edward Bull, 1832), 296.

7. Taylor, 1:290.

8. James Boaden, *Memoirs of the life of John Philip Kemble* (Philadelphia: Robert H. Small, 1825), 216.

9. Readers will have to trust the memories of the editors when we assure you that Jenkins delivered this line with an arched brow.

10. A cogent accounting of this controversy appears in Jane Moody's *Illegitimate Theatre in London, 1770–1840* (London: Cambridge University Press, 2007). It does not appear Jenkins was aware of this source.

11. Hall is listed as Covent Garden's boxkeeper in Charles Beecher Hogan, *The London Stage, 1660–1800: A Calendar of Plays, Entertainments & Afterpieces Together with Casts, Box-receipts and Contemporary Comment*, Part 5 (Carbondale, Ill: Southern Illinois University Press, 1968). There appears to be some confusion about Hall's role. If he were acting as boxkeeper for Covent Garden during the Royalty controversy, he would have been occupied with collecting admission and not free to spy on the rival playhouse. It is possible that Hall delegated his boxkeeper duties to another Covent Garden employee so as to be free for skullduggery. John Ansell is also listed as a boxkeeper for Covent Garden at that time. See Philip H. Highfill Jr., Kalman A. Burnim, and Edward A. Langhans, *A Biographical Dictionary of Actors, Actresses, Musicians, Dancers, Managers, and Other Stage Personnel in London, 1660–1800* (Carbondale: Southern Illinois University Press, 1973); "To One Hall, Carpenter and Scene Shifter to Covent-Garden Theatre," *The World and Fashionable Advertiser*, December 31, 1787, 3.

12. "Foreign News," *The World and Fashionable Advertiser*, January 16, 1787.

13. "Westminster-Hall," *The World and Fashionable Advertiser*, June 14, 1788.

Afterword

DR. JENKINS AND MRS. INCHBALD

Paula R. Backscheider

Annibel Jenkins (figure A.1) devoted her life to Mrs. Elizabeth Inchbald, one of the most important dramatists of the last twenty years of the eighteenth century, and to friends, family, students, colleagues, scholarly societies, and a little collecting. As all of us do when we write a book, Dr. Jenkins lived with Mrs. Inchbald, and she shared their mutual lives with her friends. Inchbald would suddenly become a vivid presence and sit down with Annibel and me, and the meetings never grew old or repetitive. The details of Inchbald's life, the endless hunts for evidence, and the strategies for writing a clear, gripping biography seamlessly flowed, animating these conversations. After much experimentation and indecision, I decided to replicate their presences as "Annibel" and her "Mrs. Inchbald," as Annibel always called her.

Mrs. Inchbald is an exceptionally difficult biographical and critical subject. She lived a long time, knew everyone, and wrote in a variety of genres and excelled in each. Her novel *A Simple Story* (1791) is frequently taught in today's classrooms, and she had nineteen plays produced on the London stages between 1784 and 1805. Fourteen of them ran ten or more nights in their first seasons, and six ran twenty or more. *The Midnight Hour* (1787), which did not open until May 22, played ten nights in its first season and thirty-six the next. When her *I'll Tell You What* (1785) was paired in its first season with her afterpiece *Mogul Tale* (1784), and she played Selima, the audience gave her standing ovations. Six of her plays were performed in the 1788–1789 season, and during the week of March 16, 1790, three of her plays were performed at Covent Garden. Only a few other dramatists of the eighteenth century had as much success.

Inchbald wrote her memoirs, and they might have provided important information about her and a number of very important, influential people. Why, for

Figure A.1. Annibel Jenkins. Photo courtesy of Robert Peacock.

instance, did she really refuse to marry John Philip Kemble, the greatest tragic actor and theatre manager of his time? What did she and William Godwin, the novelist and most famous radical political philosopher of his time, do in their long meetings? After Thomas Harris's attempted sexual assault, how did she continue working with him so productively? That memoir almost assuredly would not have been of the tell-all kind. Inchbald was exceptionally discreet and, somehow, in the midst of the small London theatre world in a time of numerous gossip periodicals and with friendships like these, she managed to maintain an impeccable reputation. On the advice of her confessor, she destroyed the memoir. Deprived of that source and facing a scattered and incomplete set of Inchbald's pocketbooks, Annibel was undaunted and, in fact, was armed with some unusual strengths that began with her work as Richmond P. Bond's graduate research assistant at the University of North Carolina at Chapel Hill. Anyone who has browsed his book *The Tatler: The Making of a Literary Journal* (1971) can imagine what a capacious introduction she received to the life and culture of the early eighteenth century. The annotations to the text range through every imaginable subject—economics, politics, philosophy, science, fashion, literature, gender. In a time before databases and a much more comprehensive *Oxford Dictionary of National Biography*, Bond's team identified almost unimaginably obscure people. And *The Tatler* was much concerned with playwrights, the theatre, and their participation in the life of British people. So valuable was Dr. Jenkins's work to him that Bond magisterially refused to grant her degree until she spent an additional year as his research assistant.

Annibel received her PhD in 1965, and Bond's book was published by Harvard University Press in 1971. Her dissertation was a study of *The Post-Angel*, one of the first monthly magazine-style periodicals. It was written by one of the most influential figures in the history of eighteenth-century periodicals, John Dunton, the eccentric but innovative man who had started the *Athenian Mercury* (1691–1697). The dissertation carefully re-creates *The Post-Angel*'s contexts and its readership. This attention, somewhat unusual in literary analysis at that time, was characteristic of Annibel's work throughout her career. Before moving to Georgia Tech, she taught at Blue Mountain College (where she had received her BA), Mississippi College, and then Wake Forest when it was still a college rather than a university. Her essay "Dunton's *Post-Angel*, 1701–1702" was published in the Festschrift for Bond, *The Dress of Words* (1978), and her Twayne series study of Nicholas Rowe appeared the previous year.[1]

Year after year, Annibel presented stimulating and deeply learned papers at the American Society for Eighteenth-Century Studies. Her authority as a Restoration drama specialist became universally acknowledged, and she was a pioneering scholar of women's place in the history of the theatre. She was a leader in writing about topics then little studied, presenting on regional theatres in the late 1980s, and she joined some of the best theatre scholars of her generation in delving into the difficult subject of dramatic spectacles. She never neglected women and shared in a 1983 conference presentation an engraving of Inchbald as Jane Gray from her impressive collection of theatrical prints; this print is reproduced with the illustrations in Annibel's biography of Inchbald, *I'll Tell You What.*[2] Gradually, conference audiences were treated to carefully focused papers from her work on her Inchbald biography. Some were specifically about Inchbald, but she also focused on practical matters, such as in her 1993 presentation on the challenges of writing plays. By proposing and leading such seminars, she encouraged other scholars to undertake these kinds of research. In fact, Annibel brought many people into the study of topics that engaged her mind. I remember vividly meeting her at the first meeting of the Southeastern American Society for Eighteenth-Century Studies (SEASECS), which I attended in 1973. She and Shirley Kenny surrounded me and celebrated my own first paper on eighteenth-century drama. The list of other theatre specialists she mentored might stretch to triple figures.

Annibel was a founding member SEASECS, and so well was this society formed that, when I started the Northeastern American Society for Eighteenth-Century Studies, I copied the former's constitution nearly verbatim. She continued to recruit and welcome members to SEASECS, and to encourage universities to host it, and her final conference attendance was at the SEASECS conference at Auburn University in 2008. The society now gives a prize in her honor, the Annibel Jenkins Prize in Performance and Theater Studies. Almost until her death at age ninety-five, she worked on a book on *The World*, a major periodical, and her last plenary at SEASECS, included in this collection, gave a report on this book and was typical of her approach to periodicals, the theatre, and their contexts: "The World of *The World*" (2006).

Annibel's *I'll Tell You What: The Life of Elizabeth Inchbald* was published in 2003, by which time the American Society for Eighteenth-Century Studies was already awarding the biennial Annibel Jenkins Biography Prize. Of Inchbald, she wrote astutely: "In the last two decades of the eighteenth century and the first of the nineteenth, Elizabeth Simpson Inchbald was at the center of the world of the theatre and the world of publishing. She was also one of the leading social figures in the intellectual group that made up the writers and artists in London" (3). Remarkably, the Inchbalds lived and traveled with Sarah Siddons and her brother John Philip Kemble, and Jenkins shows both women oppressed by domestic chores, especially doing the laundry. One of her gifts here was re-creating Inchbald's mundane daily life, her laborious work as a playwright and minor actress in a company, and the heights of her success and justified pride. At intervals, Jenkins gives us sketches of the experiences of other theatrical people, including Thomas Holcroft, which allow us to see both how typical and how remarkable Inchbald was. Their worlds are fully created here, and the woman who took care of her extended family, worried about daily expenses, and recorded mending her clothes is as present as the uncommonly beautiful and intelligent actress and hostess.

For my edition of Inchbald's plays,[3] I selected a 1794 drawing of her in profile by George Dance, which shows how beautiful she remained into old age; Annibel gave us two remarkable portraits in her biography of Inchbald. The cover illustration is the lovely, brooding engraving by J. G. Wooding from a portrait by J. Russell, which appeared in the *European Magazine* (ca. 1788); reproduced in full with the illustrations at the center of the book, its delicate coloring ideally complements Inchbald's graceful figure and hand and her carefully styled, curly hair. The interior set of pictures includes several of Inchbald playing various parts and concludes with an engraving from a fashionable, informal portrait of her painted by her friend Thomas Lawrence (ca. 1796). Among this collection of illustrations is a satiric print of her writing in her bedroom on a cheap table. Her cat is urinating on *Pastorals*, and it appears Inchbald has been studying Richard Brinsley Sheridan's "The Art of Puffing" from *The Critic* (1781) and Defoe's *Moll Flanders* (1722), then considered improper reading. On her table are equally inappropriate authors, including John Wilmot, Earl of Rochester, and William Congreve, whose plays had been controversial since Jeremy Collier's attack on the profanity and obscenity of the stage. The caption emphasizes the phrase "I'll Tell You What."[4]

One of the greatest achievements of the biography is the portrayal of Inchbald's determination. At no point was her life easy, and from her amazing acceptance into the Covent Garden theatre company, through her finally getting a series of hit plays accepted, to her writing "Remarks" for 125 plays published as *The British Theatre* (1806–1808)—a task she undertook to compensate for the thousand pounds she had been offered for her memoirs—her persevering, hard work repeatedly impressed her contemporaries and all who study her life and work. Jenkins provides one of the most detailed accounts of an actress's initial training and maneuverings to appear onstage, with sexual invitations and even assaults appearing as just part of the milieu. The picture Jenkins gives us of just how important the relationships among different theatre people were, how collaborative and also how competitive they could be, and how Inchbald's talent and charm mingled with their self-interest anticipates current directions in performance history studies.[5] Inchbald's relationships with a series of the most respected and successful publishers of plays, novels, and general literature are explicated, and her "Remarks," written at the solicitation of her then-current publisher, Longman, Hurst, Rees, and Orme, are milestones in the history of theatrical criticism. The "Remarks" manage to treat the published plays as acting pieces as well as texts embedded in the times in which they were written yet influenced by changing audience taste.

The biography is named after Inchbald's first mainpiece, which was named by George Colman, who had helped her make it stageworthy. At that time, the phrase was an ejaculation, not the announcement of an imminent explication. It answered someone who had asked for what should be left unspoken even as the asking exposed "an indescribable something," the definition Major Cypress gives in the play and that Jenkins uses to capture Inchbald's singularity. Colman's phrase centers *I'll Tell You What* around Harriet, whose sexuality draws Cypress into a compromising position and leads to her divorce; Inchbald's focus is the second Lady Euston, whom Jenkins characterizes as the first "Inchbald woman," one who is "clever and forthright, sure of herself and her virtue" (171).[6] Whereas Harriet and Cypress are subject to their sexual desires, Lady Euston is one of the first of Inchbald's women to be firmly in control of herself and able to awe the men around her into behaving virtuously.[7] Lady Euston notes, "The man who wou'd endeavor to wrong a virtuous wife shou'd be held too despicable for the resentment of the husband, and only worthy the debasement inflicted by our sex" (178).[8] Cypress insists that no one is to blame, that his being in the closet "was entirely owing to 'I'll Tell You What.'"[9]

By giving the play that title and having Cypress make a fool of himself through telling the story of his discovery in the closet with the phrase, Colman focused on the comedy and the sexual innuendo, whereas Inchbald's play had more serious themes. Jenkins taps into the mysteries of Inchbald's life with the title and suggests how enigmatic Inchbald's public persona finally was. Even as Jenkins gives a vivid picture of what Inchbald did, she draws out what a complex personality Inchbald was and how skilled her performances were. She maintained absolute respectability while often being alone in the company of some of the sexiest and some of the most radical men in London. When playwrights were being arrested and London was on the verge of bread riots and social uprisings, she wrote a play in which the line "Provisions are so scarce" was repeated.[10] Anecdotes of her correcting actors performing parts in her plays and of occasional acerbic comments are of a piece with her acute and honest assessments of plays in *The British Theatre*. Jenkins does not shy away from Inchbald's complexities even as she keeps the woman for whom the theatre was the center of her life before us—Inchbald was "an indescribable something" and the mold of the "Inchbald woman."

There are many myths about the relationship between authors and their subjects, and after studying this topic, I am deeply skeptical of that relationship, and especially of those who find strong affinities between author and subject. I also believe that authors who identify with the person whose life and motives they are describing are particularly vulnerable to making errors. Even with these reservations, however—and I am certainly not saying that Annibel identified with Inchbald—I have always been struck by some admirable similarities between them. Both Annibel and Elizabeth were "fascinating, independent" women, the description Jenkins gives of Inchbald (3). Neither lived in a time that took for granted women professors or playwrights. Carolyn Heilbrun alerted us to being aware of women who creatively and purposely avoided marriage "consciously or not"; certainly Inchbald did.[11] The first example of such avoidance, after the death of her husband, occurred with Dicky Suett (84); perhaps Annibel practiced such avoidance as well.

Both left enduringly important published work and evinced behavior we identify with lasting role models. Quietly aware of their strengths, Annibel authoritatively corrected interpretations of Inchbald that were swinging too far in one direction, as she did when Inchbald was coming to be seen as narrowly moral. Inchbald once wrote to Tate Wilkinson as she negotiated a place in his company, "Dress me as bad as you please, I am sure to look better than any other person" (119). On the other hand, Inchbald covered her mirrors so she would not be distracted while she wrote; once she emerged like a mole, blinked, and observed, "How old I looked!" At the same time, both Inchbald and Annibel were charming, stimulating, generous friends with wide social circles. Both had convivial sides and enjoyed beautiful things. Loving their independence, loving their professions, and well aware of what their time expected of women, they preserved their freedom, continued to entertain friends as they pleased, and spoke directly and sometimes bluntly. Both were quite serious about their work and capable of becoming deeply immersed in it. They set high standards, did not allow their gender to compromise these standards, and unapologetically felt free to talk about their work at length, at a high level, and with enthusiasm.

NOTES

1. Annibel Jenkins, "Dunton's *Post-Angel*: Messenger of Remarkable Providences," in *The Dress of Words: Essays on Restoration and Eighteenth Century Literature in Honor of Richmond P. Bond*, ed. Robert B. White Jr. (Lawrence: University of Kansas Libraries, 1978), 151–166.

2. Annibel Jenkins, *I'll Tell You What: The Life of Elizabeth Inchbald* (Lexington: University Press of Kentucky, 2003). The illustrations appear *hors-texte* between pages 312 and 313. Hereafter, all references to this work are cited parenthetically.

3. Paula R. Backscheider, ed., *The Plays of Elizabeth Inchbald*, 2 vols. (New York: Garland, 1980).

4. Frances Burney defends Congreve's *Love for Love* in *Evelina*; I discuss this episode in Backscheider, "Shadowing Theatrical Change," in Michael Cordner and Peter Holland, eds., *Players, Playwrights, Playhouses: Investigating Performance, 1660–1800* (Houndmills: Palgrave Macmillan, 2007), 82–84.

5. Cf., Robert W. Jones, "Competition and Community: Mary Tickell and the Management of Sheridan's Drury Lane," *Theatre Survey* 54, no. 2 (2013): 187–206.

6. This is one of the many original literary-critical contributions that Annibel's biography makes.

7. My reading of this play has been influenced by that of Misty Anderson, a contributor to this volume, in *Female Playwrights and Eighteenth-Century Comedy* (New York: Palgrave, 2002), 176–183, and draws upon ideas in my "Retrieving Inchbald," in *Oxford Companion to the Georgian Theatre, 1737–1832*, ed. Julia Swindells and David Francis Taylor (Oxford: Oxford University Press, 2014), 601–618.

8. Elizabeth Inchbald, *I'll Tell You What. A Comedy in Five Acts, as it is performed at the Theatre Royal, Haymarket. By Mrs. Inchbald* (London: Printed for G. G. J. and J. Robinson, Pater-Noster Row, 1786), 51; hereafter cited parenthetically. Also cited in Jenkins's biography *I'll Tell You What*, 178.

9. Inchbald, *I'll Tell You What*, 16–18. Also cited in Jenkins, *I'll Tell You What*, 173.

10. Elizabeth Inchbald, *Every One Has His Own Fault: A Comedy in Five Acts, as it is performed at the Theatre Royal, Covent-Garden* (London: Printed for G. G. J. and J. Robinson, Pater-Noster Row, 1793). First performed in 1793.

11. Carolyn Heilbrun, *Writing a Woman's Life* (New York: Norton, 1988), 28.

Her Worded World

A TRIBUTE TO ANNIBEL JENKINS

Don Russ

She told me she had run across
her patterns for some of their mother's clothes.
We were having our dessert and coffee
in the living room. I paused.

She sewed for them all, she said—
even made her sister's wedding clothes. It all
came back, she said, unfolding like leaves
of paper memory in her hands:

some little measure of a mother
and of the presence there of all their pasts,
still living. And now, today, as friends
of this tireless maker,

we pray these lines, these pages,
measure out and shape our memories of her—
our inspiration—which we give back
to a worded world she loved.

Notes on Contributors

Misty G. Anderson is the James R. Cox Professor and professor of English at the University of Tennessee, where she also holds courtesy appointments in the Departments of Theatre and Religious Studies. She is the author of *Imaging Methodism* and *Female Playwrights and Eighteenth-Century Comedy* and is the coeditor, with Daniel O'Quinn and Kristina Straub, of *The Routledge Anthology of Restoration and Eighteenth Century Performance* and *The Routledge Anthology of Restoration and Eighteenth Century Drama*. She is a former editor of the journal *Restoration* and author of multiple articles on drama, performance, gender, and religion on the Restoration and eighteenth-century stage. She is currently working on a book-length manuscript titled "God on Stage."

Paula R. Backscheider, Philpott-Stevens Eminent Scholar, Auburn University, is the author of several books, including *Daniel Defoe: His Life* (winner of the British Council Prize), *Spectacular Politics*, *Reflections on Biography*, and *Eighteenth-Century Women Poets and Their Poetry: Inventing Agency, Inventing Genre* (winner of the Modern Language Association Lowell Prize). She has published articles in *MLA*, *Theatre Journal*, *ELH*, and many other journals. A former president of the American Society for Eighteenth-Century Studies, she has held a Guggenheim Fellowship and is one of the few American members of the Institute for Advanced Studies, University of Edinburgh. Her latest book is *Wartime Women: Intimate Conscripts on the British Stage, 1660–1810*.

Martha F. Bowden, professor emerita of English, Kennesaw State University, is a literary historian who has written about women's writing, Laurence Sterne's texts in the context of the Church of England, and historical fiction. Her book publications include an edition of three of Mary Davys's novels, *The Reform'd Coquet*, *Familiar Letters Betwixt a Gentleman and a Lady*, and *The Accomplish'd*

Rake; *Yorick's Congregation: The Eighteenth-Century Church of England in the Time of Laurence Sterne*; and *Descendants of Waverley: Romancing History in Contemporary Historical Fiction*. Her current project argues that women writers of the eighteenth century combined the structures of the fable with other literary forms, including the novel, satire, and plays, to create the fabular hybrid. These forms allowed them to claim by stealth the moral authority normally restricted to the male writers who compiled and created the many fable collections published in the period.

MITA CHOUDHURY is professor of English at Purdue University Northwest. Her publications include *Interculturalism and Resistance in the London Theater, 1660–1800: Identity, Performance, Empire*; *Monstrous Dreams of Reason: Body, Self, and Other in the Enlightenment*, coedited with Laura J. Rosenthal; and *Nation-Space in Enlightenment Britain: An Archaeology of Empire*. Among her recent publications are "Circulation: Emergent Modalities of Intercultural Performance," in *A Cultural History of Theatre in the Age of Enlightenment*, vol. 4, ed. Mechele Leon; and "Mapping Cosmopolitanism and the Global Space at Home," in *World-Making and Other Worlds: Restoration to Romantic*, a special issue of *1650–1850: Ideas, Aesthetics, and Inquiries in the Early Modern Era*, ed. Betty Joseph and Elizabeth Sauer. She is currently working on a book-length project tentatively titled "Deep Mapping Imperial Collections of the Enlightenment."

ROBERT M. CRAIG is professor emeritus, Georgia Tech, where he taught architectural history for nearly four decades. Craig was a founding member and served as president and longtime treasurer of the Southeast Chapter, Society of Architectural Historians; he also served as president of two interdisciplinary societies, the Nineteenth Century Studies Association and the Southeastern Society for Eighteenth-Century Studies. He served for fourteen years on the board of directors of the Society of Architectural Historians, and for ten years as its national secretary. He was also editor of the Southeastern College Art Conference's *SECAC Review*, now *Art Inquiries*, and was architecture editor of the five-volume *Grove Encyclopedia of American Art*. Craig has published nine books, including award-winning monographs on twentieth-century American architects, institutional histories, and a book of memoirs of Vietnam veterans.

DANIEL J. ENNIS is provost and vice president for academic affairs at Coastal Carolina University in Conway, South Carolina, where he has been a member of the Department of English since 1999. The author of *Enter the Press Gang: Naval Impressment in Eighteenth-Century British Literature* and coeditor of the essay collections *Prologues, Epilogues, Curtain-Raisers and Afterpieces: The Rest of the Eighteenth-Century London Stage* (with Judith Bailey Slagle) and *Richard Brinsley Sheridan: The Impresario in Political and Cultural Context* (with Jack

DeRochi), he has published on John Dryden, Aphra Behn, and Christopher Smart.

W. B. GERARD taught literature and creative writing as professor of English at Auburn University at Montgomery until his untimely death in August 2020. He authored *Laurence Sterne and the Visual Imagination* and was editor of *Divine Rhetoric: Essays on the Sermons of Laurence Sterne.* The coeditor of volume 9 of the Florida Edition of the Works of Laurence Sterne, *The Miscellaneous Writings,* he coedited two additional essay collections. He was also the coeditor of the semiannual journal *The Scriblerian and the Kit-Cats,* and general editor of *THAT Literary Review.*

RANDA GRAVES, who died in September 2021, was associate professor emerita in the English Department at the University of Alabama at Birmingham. The first woman to serve as president of her university's faculty senate, she also served as director of graduate studies in English and established interdisciplinary freshman courses in critical thinking, composition courses for international students, and online courses in sophomore literature. She published articles and reviews on Laurence Sterne, Henry Fielding, Samuel Richardson, Patrick Delany, and Jane Austen.

E. JOE JOHNSON is professor of French at Clayton State University. A past president of the Southeastern American Society for Eighteenth-Century Studies, he is currently serving as the general editor of the society's annual journal, *XVIII New Perspectives on the Eighteenth Century.* The author of *Once There Were Two True Friends, or Idealized Male Friendship in French Narrative from the Middle Ages through the Enlightenment,* and editor of four volumes, he has also published numerous translations of French comic books and graphic novels. In addition, he has published an annotated co-translation of Camille Lebrun's 1845 novel *Friendship and Devotion, or Three Months in Louisiana.*

CLAUDIA THOMAS KAIROFF is professor of English at Wake Forest University, where she has taught eighteenth-century British literature since 1986. In addition to numerous articles and book chapters on Pope, Finch, Johnson, and Seward, she is the author of *Alexander Pope and His Eighteenth-Century Women Readers* and *Anna Seward and the End of the Eighteenth Century.* With Catherine Ingrassia, she coedited *"More Solid Learning": New Perspectives on Pope's* Dunciad. With Jennifer Keith, she edited *The Cambridge Edition of the Works of Anne Finch, Countess of Winchilsea.* She is working on a monograph entitled "'I May Rise To Morrow': Religion, Politics and Gender in the Poems of Anne Finch."

CYNTHIA J. LOWENTHAL is professor emerita of English and former dean of the School of Humanities and Social Sciences at the College of Charleston.

Her research focuses on Restoration theatre and women's writing during the long eighteenth century. She has received grant support from the Clark Library and the Newberry Library and has published articles in various journals, including *The Eighteenth Century: Theory and Interpretation* and *Eighteenth-Century Life*. Her books include *Lady Mary Wortley Montagu and the Eighteenth-Century Familiar Letter* and *Performing Identities on the Restoration Stage*.

HEATHER MCPHERSON is professor of art history at the University of Alabama at Birmingham. Her research focuses on portraiture, caricature and cultural politics, and the intersection of the visual and performing arts. She is the author of *Art and Celebrity in the Age of Reynolds and Siddons* and *The Modern Portrait in Nineteenth-Century France* and has published widely on French and British art in essay collections and in journals such as *Eighteenth-Century Studies, Studies in Eighteenth-Century Culture, The Eighteenth-Century: Theory and Interpretation*, and the *Gazette des Beaux-Arts*. She is a past president of the American Society of Eighteenth-Century Studies.

HUGH REID, adjunct research professor in the Department of English at Carleton University, is the author of *The Nature and Uses of Eighteenth-Century Book Subscription Lists* and numerous articles on Johnson, Reynolds, Hogarth, Grainger, the eighteenth-century book trade, and most notably the Wartons, including their entries in the *Oxford Dictionary of National Biography*. His current research interest is in the paratext of eighteenth-century book publishing.

DON RUSS, professor emeritus of English, Kennesaw State University, has published and continues to publish widely in the field of his first literary interest, poetry. He has authored two chapbooks, a volume of poetry (*Dream Driving*), and "Up toward Light: Resurrection, Transfiguration, Metamorphosis, and Evolution in David Bottoms' *Armored Hearts*," a paper delivered at the South Central Modern Language Association, published in *Southern Quarterly*, and eventually listed in Georgia Humanities' web-based *New Georgia Encyclopedia* as recommended reading for the study of the former poet laureate.

JOHN A. VANCE is professor emeritus of English at the University of Georgia. His research reflects his interest in Restoration and eighteenth-century literature and drama. His books include *Joseph and Thomas Warton*, *Joseph and Thomas Warton: An Annotated Bibliography*, *Samuel Johnson and the Sense of History*, and *William Wycherley and the Comedy of Fear*. He is also the editor of *Boswell's "Life of Johnson": New Questions, New Answers* and (with Donald Greene) *Johnsonian Studies, 1970–1985*. He has also published essays on Milton, Pepys, Cibber, Dryden, Swift, Johnson, Boswell, the Wartons, Garrick, and Sheridan. He is now an author of fiction, with fifteen published novels to his credit.

Calhoun Winton, a scholar of eighteenth-century British theatre and a founding member of the American Society for Eighteenth-Century Studies, is professor emeritus of English at the University of Maryland and past president of the East-Central Society for Eighteenth-Century Studies. He is the author of the monographs *Captain Steele: The Early Career of Richard Steele*, *Sir Richard Steele, M.P.: The Later Career*, and *John Gay and the London Theatre*; he also edited *The Plays of Aaron Hill* and Richard Steele's *Tender Husband.*

Index